Study Guide F...

Gwendolyn E. Nyden
Oakton Community College

Mark Thomas
York University

Sociology

A Down-to-Earth Approach

Second Canadian Edition

James M. Henslin

Dan Glenday

Ann Duffy

Norene Pupo

Toronto

ISBN 0-205-33614-0

Acquisitions Editor: Jessica Mosher
Developmental Editor: Marta Tomins
Production Editor: Joe Zingrone
Production Coordinator: Wendy Moran

1 2 3 4 5   04 03 02 01

Printed and bound in Canada.

TABLE OF CONTENTS

INTRODUCTION

Welcome to Sociology! You are about to embark on a fascinating journey in which you will discover all sorts of new and interesting information about yourself and the world around you. This study guide has been prepared to accompany the textbook *Sociology: A Down-to-Earth Approach*, 2nd Canadian Edition, by James M. Henslin, Daniel Glenday, Ann Duffy, and Norene Pupo.

The study guide includes the following:

- A **Chapter Summary** that summarizes the main ideas found in the chapter.
- A set of **Learning Objectives** that provides statements concerning the main ideas of the chapter. If you want to check your responses, refer back to the page numbers listed with each question.
- A **Chapter Outline** that provides a point-by-point overview of the theories and substantive topics of the chapter.
- A listing of **Key Terms to Define** that contains all of the sociological concepts that are introduced within the chapter.
- A listing of **Key People** that includes some of the major sociologists whose work is discussed within the chapter. In some cases, these are early sociologists who contributed theoretical understanding and research insights to the discipline; in other cases, they are contemporary sociologists who are doing research and developing theory on the subject.
- A **Self-Test** that provides you with an opportunity to see how much of the information you have retained. Each self-test includes multiple choice, true-false, fill-in, and matching questions.
- A section entitled **Down-to-Earth Sociology** that asks questions about the material you have read so that you can relate it to your own life and the world with which you are familiar. Remember there is not necessarily a right or wrong answer for these; rather, they are designed to get your opinion, based on your understanding of the facts you have read.
- An **Answer Key** that provides answers for all of the questions in the self-test. Check your answers against this; if you got the question wrong, refer back to the pages in the textbook and read those again.

The study guide is intended to be used together with the text to maximize your mastery of the material. Here are some suggestions for making the best use of the resources in both the text and the study guide:

- Before reading each chapter, **refer to the Chapter Summary and Learning Objectives** that are found in the Study Guide. The Summary will provide you with a capsule statement of what the chapter is about, and the Learning Objectives will tell you how you should be focusing your attention. Then read the textbook.
- Rather than plunging headlong into the chapter, **take a few minutes and orient yourself**. Start with the chapter title. This tells you what broad area of sociology will be discussed. Keep the title in mind as you read through the chapter and try to create a mental picture of how the various parts of the chapter fit together within this broad area.
- **Approach each chapter one section at a time.** Use the section headings to pose questions that you can ask yourself when you finish reading the section. As you finish a section, go back to the Learning Objectives in the Study Guide and try to answer the statement(s) that apply. If you can provide an answer, then proceed to the next section; if you can't, go back to the textbook and review the section you've just read.
- **Remember to read the boxed texts;** these pertain to the material in the body of the textbook and are included to give you insights into Canadian society as well as societies around the world. They are designed to bring sociology alive for you.

Once you feel you have achieved some familiarity with the material, go back to the study guide and follow these steps:

- **Check the list of Key Terms to Define.** Try and define each word and think of an example. Then check the definitions that are provided within each chapter of the Study Guide to see if you are correct. If you need help thinking of an example, refer back to the textbook chapter.
- **Check the list of Key People.** See how many you know and whether or not you can identify their contribution to sociology. If you can't, go back to the textbook and locate them within the chapter. (A quick way to do this is to refer to the Index at the back of the textbook, and then go directly to the page listed.)
- **Take the Self-Test.** Mark those questions that you got wrong, and go back to the text to find the correct answer. Then a few days later try them again to see if you've now mastered the material. Use the self-test to review the material just before a test.

We hope you have found the preceding tips useful. If you begin to incorporate some of them into your regular study routines, attend class regularly, take good notes on material covered in class, read each chapter (ideally before the material is presented in class and then review the chapter as you are going over the material in class), and use the resources in the Study Guide, you should finish the semester with good grades and a better understanding not only of the discipline of sociology, but of yourself and your social world. We hope that you will enjoy your adventure and find that this subject opens new vistas of understanding to you. Good luck!

Gwen Nyden, Ph.D.   Mark Thomas
Oakton Community College   York University
Des Plaines, Illinois   Toronto, Ontario

CHAPTER 1

THE SOCIOLOGICAL PERSPECTIVE

☞ **CHAPTER SUMMARY**

- Sociology offers a perspective—a view of the world—which stresses that people's social experiences underlie their behavior.
- Sociology is the scientific study of society and human behavior and, as such, is one of the social sciences, which study human behavior, in contrast to the natural sciences, which focus on nature.
- Although it is difficult to state precisely when it began, sociology emerged during the upheavals of the Industrial Revolution. Early sociologists such as Auguste Comte, Karl Marx, Emile Durkheim, and Max Weber focused on how the sweeping social changes brought about by the Industrial Revolution affected human behavior.
- Sociologists agree on the ideal of objectivity, but disagree concerning the proper purposes and uses of sociology. Some believe its purpose should be only to advance understanding of human behavior; others, that its goal should be to reform harmful social arrangements.
- Weber believed that sociologists must try to see the world from another's perspective in order to understand their behavior (*Verstehen*); Durkheim stressed the importance of uncovering the objective social conditions that influence behavior (social facts).
- In the early years of sociology, only a few wealthy women received an advanced education. Harriet Martineau was an Englishwoman who wrote about social life in Great Britain and the United States and published a book entitled *Society in America*.
- In North America, departments of sociology began to be established at the end of the nineteenth century. In the early years, the contributions of women and minorities were largely ignored.
- A theory is a general statement about how sets of facts are related to one another. Because no one theory encompasses all of reality, sociologists use five primary theoretical frameworks: (1) symbolic interactionism, concentrating on the meanings that underlie people's lives, usually focuses on the micro level; (2) functional analysis, stressing that society is made up of various parts which, when working properly, contribute to the stability of society, focuses on the macro level; (3) conflict theory, emphasizing social inequalities and seeing the basis of social life as a competitive struggle to gain control over scarce resources, also focuses on the macro level; (4) feminist theories, which examine the social, historical, and cultural aspects of gender and gender relations, focusing on both the micro and macro levels; and (5) postmodernism, emphasizing the complex patterns of social and cultural difference in contemporary societies, focusing on the micro level.
- Pure sociology is research whose only purpose is to make discoveries, while applied sociology is the application of sociology to solve social problems in a variety of settings from the workplace to the family.

☞ **LEARNING OBJECTIVES**

As you read Chapter 1, use these learning objectives to organize your notes. After completing your reading, briefly state an answer to each of the objectives, and review the text pages in parentheses.

1. Explain the sociological perspective and discuss the contribution that it makes to our understanding of human behavior, including the growing global context of our lives. (4-5)
2. Define sociology and compare it with the other social sciences. (5-6)

3. Discuss how and why sociology emerged as a science in the middle of the nineteenth century in Europe. (8)
4. Explain each of the following sociologists' contributions to the development of sociology: Auguste Comte, Karl Marx, Emile Durkheim, and Max Weber. (9-12)
5. State the key issues in the debate about the proper role of values in sociology. (12)
6. Explain what Max Weber meant by *Verstehen* and Emile Durkheim by social facts and how these two can fit together. (13)
7. Explain the absence of women in the early years of sociology. (13)
8. Trace the development of sociology in Canada and the United States from its origins in the late 19th century to its present-day perspectives. (14-16)
9. Identify the contributions that each of the following made to the development of sociology in North America: Leon Gérin, Carl Dawson, Harold Innis, Dorothy Smith, Margrit Eichler, Albion Small, Jane Addams, W.E.B. Du Bois, Talcott Parsons, Robert Merton, C. Wright Mills. (14-16)
10. Explain the chief differences in five major theoretical perspectives: symbolic interactionism, functional analysis, conflict theory, feminist theories, and postmodernism. (17-20)
11. Compare micro-level and macro-level analysis and state which level of analysis is utilized by each of the major theoretical perspectives. (20-21)
12. Describe the three phases of sociology and note the differences in pure, applied, and clinical sociology. (21-22)

☞ CHAPTER OUTLINE

I. **The Sociological Perspective**
    A. This perspective is important because it provides a different way of looking at familiar worlds. It allows us to gain a new vision of social life.
    B. This perspective stresses the broader social context of behavior by looking at individuals' social location—employment, income, education, gender, age, and race—and by considering external influences—people's experiences—which are internalized and become part of a person's thinking and motivations. We are able to see the links between what people do and the social settings that shape their behavior.
    C. This perspective enables us to analyze and understand both the forces that contribute to the emergence and growth of the global village and our unique experiences in our own smaller corners of this village.

II. **Sociology and the Other Sciences**
    A. Sociology is defined as "the scientific study of society and human behavior."
        1. Science is the systematic methods used to obtain knowledge and the knowledge obtained by those methods.
        2. Science can be divided into the natural sciences and the social sciences.
    B. The natural sciences attempt to comprehend, explain, and predict events in our natural environment.
    C. Social sciences attempt to objectively study the social world. Like the natural sciences, the social sciences are divided into specialized fields based on their subject matter.
        1. Political science focuses on politics or government.
        2. Economics analyzes the production, distribution, and allocation of the material goods and services of a society.
        3. Anthropology attempts to understand culture (a people's total way of life) by focusing primarily on preliterate people.
        4. Psychology concentrates on processes that occur within the individual.

5. Sociology is similar to the other social sciences in some ways but it is distinct because it looks at all social institutions, focuses on industrialized societies, and looks at external factors which influence people.

III. **The Development of Sociology**
A. Sociology developed in the middle of the 19th century when European social observers began to use scientific methods to test their ideas. Three factors led to its development:
   1. the social upheaval in Europe as a result of the Industrial Revolution and the political revolutions in America and France;
   2. the development of imperialism—as the Europeans conquered other nations, they came in contact with different cultures and began to ask why cultures varied; and
   3. the success of the natural sciences, which created a desire to apply scientific methods in order to find answers for the questions being raised about the social world as well.
B. Auguste Comte coined the term "sociology" and suggested the use of positivism—applying the scientific approach to the social world—but he did not utilize this approach himself.
C. Karl Marx, founder of the conflict perspective, believed that class conflict—the struggle between the proletariat and the bourgeoisie—was the key to human history.
D. Emile Durkheim played an important role in the development of sociology.
   1. One of his primary goals was to get sociology recognized as a separate academic discipline.
   2. He was interested in understanding the social factors that influence individual behavior; he studied suicide rates among different groups and concluded that social integration, the degree to which people are tied to their social group, was a key social factor in suicide.
   3. Durkheim's third concern was that social research be practical; sociologists should not only diagnose the causes of social problems but should also develop solutions for them.
E. Max Weber defined religion as a central force in social change (i.e., Protestantism encourages greater economic development and was the central factor in the rise of capitalism in some countries).

IV. **The Role of Values in Social Research**
A. Max Weber advocated that sociological research should be value free—personal values or biases should not influence social research—and objective—totally neutral.
   1. Sociologists agree that objectivity is a proper goal but acknowledge that no one can escape values entirely.
   2. Replication—repeating a study to see if the same results are found—is one means to avoid the distortions that values can cause.
B. The proper purposes and uses of sociology are argued among sociologists.
   1. Some take the position that the proper role of sociology is to advance understanding of social life, while others believe that it is the responsibility of sociologists to explore harmful social arrangements of society.
   2. Some feel that the knowledge gained by social research belongs to the scientific community and the world, to be used by anyone for any purpose, while others feel that the knowledge should be used to reform society.

V.   *Verstehen* and Social Facts

    A.   Weber argued that sociologists should use *Verstehen* ("to grasp by insight") in order to see beyond the social facts to the meanings that people attach to their own behavior.

    B.   Durkheim believed that social facts, patterns of behavior that characterize a social group, reflect some underlying condition of society and should be used to interpret other social facts.

    C.   Social facts and *Verstehen* fit together because they reinforce each other; sociologists use *Verstehen* in order to interpret social facts.

VI.   Sexism in Early Sociology

    A.   In the early years of sociology, the field was dominated by men because rigidly defined social roles and the realities of economic life prevented most women from pursuing an education.

        1.   Women were supposed to devote themselves to the four K's—*Kirche, Kuchen, Kinder, und Kleider* (church, cooking, children, and clothes).

        2.   At the same time, a few women from wealthy families managed to get an education; a few even studied sociology although the sexism in the universities stopped them from earning advanced degrees, becoming professors, or having their research recognized.

    B.   Harriet Martineau studied social life in both Great Britain and the United States, publishing *Society in America* decades before Durkheim and Weber were even born. While her original research has been largely ignored by the discipline, she is known for her translations of Comte's ideas into English.

VII.   Sociology in Canada and the United States

    A.   Sociology in Canada was influenced by both the British and American traditions. The first program in sociology in Canada was at McGill University (1922).

        1.   American sociologists at the University of Chicago influenced the development of sociology at McGill, under the direction of Carl Dawson.

        2.   The other predominant approach to the development of sociology in Canada was the British tradition, which influenced sociology at the University of Toronto.

        3.   At the University of Toronto, Harold Innis and Samuel Clark studied the economic history of Canada and illustrated the ways in which Canada developed as a distinct economy and society.

        4.   Contemporary feminist scholars such as Margrit Eichler and Dorothy Smith are widely recognized for their work in nonsexist research methods and studies of feminist theory.

    B.   The first departments of sociology in the U.S. were at the University of Kansas (1889) and the University of Chicago (1892);

        1.   Albion Small, founder of the Department of Sociology at the University of Chicago, also established the *American Journal of Sociology*.

        2.   Other early sociologists from the University of Chicago were Robert E. Park, Ernest Burgess, and George Herbert Mead.

    C.   The situation of women in North America was similar to that of European women and their contributions to sociology met a similar fate. Denied a role in the universities, many turned to social activism, working with the poor and regarded as social workers.

        1.   Jane Addams is an example; she founded Hull House, a settlement house for the poor, and worked to bridge the gap between the powerful and the powerless.

        2.   She invited sociologists from nearby University of Chicago to visit.

        3.   She is the only sociologist to have won the Nobel Peace Prize, being awarded this in 1931.

D. African American professionals also faced problems.
  1. W.E.B. Du Bois was the first African American to earn a Ph.D. from Harvard. He conducted extensive research on race relations in the U.S., publishing a book a year on this subject between 1896 and 1914.
  2. Despite his accomplishments he encountered prejudice and discrimination in his professional and personal life, helping to found the National Association for the Advancement of Colored People (NAACP).
  3. Until recently, his contributions to sociology were overlooked.

E. Many early North American sociologists combined the role of sociologist with that of social reformer. For example, University of Chicago sociologists Park and Burgess studied many urban problems and offered suggestions on how to alleviate them.

F. In the 1940s, as sociologists became more concerned with establishing sociology as an academic discipline, the emphasis shifted from social reform to social theory.
  1. Talcott Parsons developed abstract models of society to show how the parts of society harmoniously work together.
  2. Countering this development was C. Wright Mills, who urged sociologists to get back to social reform.
  3. Robert K. Merton stressed the development of middle-range theories—explanations of human behavior that go beyond the particular observation or research but avoid sweeping generalizations that attempt to explain everything.

G. Sociology in North America today is not dominated by any one theoretical orientation or single concern.
  1. Social activism remains an option.
  2. Sociologists are employed in teaching, the government, the private sector in management and planning positions, and in a number of other fields.

VIII. Theoretical Perspectives in Sociology

A. Theory is a general statement about how some parts of the world fit together and how they work; it is an explanation of how two or more facts are related to one another. Sociologists use five different theoretical perspectives to understand social behavior.

B. Symbolic interactionism views symbols, things to which we attach meaning, as the basis of social life.
  1. Through the use of symbols people are able to define relationships to others, to coordinate actions with others, making social life possible, and to develop a sense of themselves.
  2. A symbolic interactionist studying divorce would focus on the changing meaning of marriage, family, and work and how they have contributed to the increase in the rate of divorce in our society.

C. The central idea of functional analysis is that society is a whole unit, made up of interrelated parts that work together.
  1. To understand society, we must look at both structure, how the parts of society fit together to make up the whole, and function, how each part contributes to society.
  2. Robert Merton used the term function to refer to the beneficial consequences of people's actions to keep society stable and dysfunction to refer to consequences that undermine stability. Functions can be either manifest (actions that are intended) or latent (unintended consequences).
  3. In trying to explain divorce, a functionalist would look at how industrialization and urbanization both contributed to the changing function of marriage and the family.

D.   According to conflict theory, society is viewed as composed of groups competing for scarce resources.
1.   Karl Marx focused on struggles between the bourgeoisie, the small group of capitalists who own the means of production, and the proletariat, the masses of workers exploited by the capitalists.
2.   Contemporary conflict theorists have expanded this perspective to include conflict in all relations of power and authority.
3.   Divorce is seen as the outcome of the shifting balance of power within a family; as women have gained power and try to address inequalities in their relationships, men resist.

E.   Feminist theories study the social, historical, and cultural aspects of gender and gender relations.
1.   Marxist–Feminist theories relate gender inequalities in society to economic inequities, specifically the property relations of capitalism.
2.   Liberal Feminists claim that legal restraints and customs are at the root of the subservience of women in society.
3.   Non-Marxist Feminist theories focus on the ways in which women are oppressed by patriarchy, a system of power, dominance, hierarchy, and competition.

F.   Postmodernism emphasizes the complex patterns of social and cultural difference in contemporary societies.
1.   Postmodernism views present-day society as a cultural collage where people can live in their own cultural and social spaces.
2.   Jean Baudrillard studies the ways in which symbols have become detached, or autonomous, from the real world.

G.   The perspectives differ in their level of analysis. Functionalists and conflict theorists provide macro-level analysis because they examine the large-scale patterns of society. Symbolic interactionists carry out micro-level analysis because they focus on the small-scale patterns of social life.

H.   Each perspective provides a different and often sharply contrasting picture of the world. However, sociologists often use all five perspectives because no one theory or level of analysis encompasses all of reality.

IX.   **Applied and Clinical Sociology**
A.   Sociologists Paul Lazarsfeld and Jeffrey Reitz divide sociology into three phases.
1.   In the first phase the primary concern of sociologists was making the world a better place.
2.   During the second phase sociologists sought to establish sociology as a respected field of knowledge.
3.   In the third (current) phase there has been an attempt to merge sociological knowledge and practical work.

B.   Applied sociology is the attempt to blend sociological knowledge and practical results. It refers to the use of sociology to solve problems. Applied sociologists recommend practical changes to solve problems.

C.   Clinical sociologists become directly involved in bringing about social change through work in various social settings.

D.   In the future, it is likely that applied sociology will grow, as more departments of sociology offer courses, specialties, and even internships in applied sociology.

☞ KEY TERMS

After reading the chapter, review the definitions for each of the key terms listed below.

anomie: Durkheim's term for a condition of society in which people become detached, cut loose from the norms that usually guide their behavior

applied sociology: the use of sociology to solve social problems—from the micro level of family relationships to the macro level of crime and pollution

authority: power that people consider legitimate

bourgeoisie: Karl Marx's term for capitalists; those who own the means to produce wealth

class conflict: Marx's term for the struggle between the proletariat and the bourgeoisie

clinical sociology: the direct involvement of sociologists in bringing about social change

conflict theory: a theoretical framework in which society is viewed as composed of groups competing for scarce resources

feminist theories: theories that examine the social, historical, and cultural aspects of gender and gender relations from Marxist, Liberal, and Non-Marxist perspective

functional analysis: a theoretical framework in which society is viewed as composed of various parts, each with a function that, when fulfilled, contributes to society's equilibrium; also known as functionalism and structural functionalism

macro-level analysis: an examination of large-scale patterns of society

micro-level analysis: an examination of small-scale patterns of society

middle-range theories: explanations of human behavior that go beyond a particular observation or research but avoid sweeping generalizations that attempt to account for everything

natural sciences: the intellectual and academic disciplines designed to comprehend, explain, and predict events in our natural environment

nonverbal interaction: communication without words through gestures, space, silence, and so on

objectivity: total neutrality

positivism: the application of the scientific approach to the social world

postmodernism: a theoretical perspective that emphasizes the complex patterns of social and cultural difference in contemporary societies

proletariat: Marx's term for the exploited class, the mass of workers who do not own the means of production

pure or basic sociology: sociological research whose only purpose is to make discoveries about life in human groups, not to make changes in those groups

replication: repeating a study in order to check the findings of a previous study

science: the application of systematic methods to obtain knowledge and the knowledge obtained by those methods

scientific method: the use of objective, systematic observations to test theories

social facts: Durkheim's term for the patterns of behavior that characterize a social group

social integration: the degree to which people feel a part of social groups

social interaction: what people do when they are in one another's presence

social location: the group memberships that people have because of their location in history and society

social sciences: the intellectual and academic disciplines designed to understand the social world objectively by means of controlled and repeated observations

society: a term used by sociologists to refer to a group of people who share a culture and a territory

sociological perspective: an approach to understanding human behavior by placing it within its broader social context

sociology: the scientific study of society and human behavior

subjective meanings: the meanings that people give to their own behavior

symbolic interaction: a theoretical perspective in which society is viewed as composed of symbols that people use to establish meaning, develop their views of the world, and communicate with one another

theory: a general statement about how some parts of the world fit together and how they work; an explanation of how two or more facts are related to one another

value free: the view that a sociologist's personal values or biases should not influence social research

values: ideas about what is good or worthwhile in life; attitudes about the way the world ought to be

Verstehen: a German word used by Weber that is perhaps best understood as "to have insight into someone's situation"

☞ KEY PEOPLE

The following are key people in the development of sociology.

Jane Addams: Addams was the founder of Hull House—a settlement house in the immigrant community of Chicago. She invited sociologists from nearby University of Chicago to visit. In 1931 she was a winner of the Nobel Peace Prize.

Jean Baudrillard: Baudrillard is a postmodern theorist who argues that symbols have become autonomous from the real world in contemporary society.

Auguste Comte: Comte is often credited with being the founder of sociology, because he was the first to suggest that the scientific method be applied to the study of the social world.

Lewis Coser: Coser pointed out that conflict is likely to develop among people in close relationships because they are connected by a network of responsibilities, power and rewards.

Ralf Dahrendorf: Dahrendorf's work is associated with the conflict perspective; he suggested that conflict is inherent in all relations that have authority.

Carl Dawson: Dawson led the development of Canada's first sociology program at McGill University. Dawson used the University of Chicago sociology program to develop sociology at McGill.

W.E.B. Du Bois: Du Bois was the first African American to earn a doctorate at Harvard University. For most of his career he taught sociology at Atlanta University. He was concerned about social injustice, wrote about race relations, and was one of the founders of the National Association for the Advancement of Colored People.

Emile Durkheim: Durkheim was responsible for getting sociology recognized as a separate discipline. He was interested in studying how individual behavior is shaped by social forces and in finding remedies for social ills. He stressed that sociologists should use social facts—patterns of behavior that reflect some underlying condition of society.

Harold Innis: Innis was the head of the Department of Political Economy at the University of Toronto, where there was no independent department of sociology until the 1960s. Innis created the model of economic development known as the staples theory of international trade to explain Canada's economic history.

Paul Lazarsfeld: Along with **Jeffrey Reitz**, Lazarsfeld divided the development of sociology into three stages: (1) an initial period in which sociologists were engaged in social reform; (2) a period in which sociologists worked to have sociology established as a respected field of knowledge; and (3) the contemporary period in which sociologists are trying to merge sociological knowledge with practical work.

Harriet Martineau: An Englishwoman who studied British and U.S. social life and published *Society in America* decades before either Durkheim or Weber was born.

Karl Marx: Marx believed that social development grew out of conflict between social classes; under capitalism, this conflict was between the *bourgeoisie*—those who own the means to produce wealth—and the *proletariat*—the mass of workers. His work is associated with the conflict perspective.

George Herbert Mead: Mead was one of the founders of symbolic interactionism, a major theoretical perspective in sociology.

Robert Merton: Merton encouraged the development of middle-range theories—explanations that tie together research findings but avoid sweeping generalizations that try to account for everything. Merton contributed the terms *manifest and latent functions* and *dysfunctions* to the functionalist perspective.

C. Wright Mills: Mills suggested that external influences—or a person's experiences—become part of his or her thinking and motivations and explain social behavior.

Talcott Parsons: Parsons' work dominated sociology in the 1940s-1950s. He developed abstract models of how the parts of society harmoniously work together.

Albion Small: Small was the founder of the sociology department at the University of Chicago and the *American Journal of Sociology*.

Dorothy Smith: Smith is a Canadian feminist sociologist who is best known for her studies of feminist theory, in particular her work on the sociology of the "everyday world" of people's lives.

Max Weber: Weber's most important contribution to sociology was his study of the relationship between the emergence of the Protestant belief system and the rise of capitalism. He believed that sociologists should not allow their personal values to affect their social research; objectivity should become the hallmark of sociology. He argued that sociologists should use *Verstehen*—those subjective meanings that people give to their behavior.

☞ SELF-TEST

After completing this self-test, check your answers against the Answer Key at the back of this Study Guide and against the text on the page(s) indicated in parentheses.

MULTIPLE CHOICE QUESTIONS

1. An approach to understanding human behavior by placing it within its broader social context is known as: (4)
    a. social location.
    b. the sociological perspective.
    c. common sense.
    d. generalization.

2. Using systematic methods to study and explain the social and natural worlds is the intent of: (5)
    a. arm-ch air philosophers.
    b. scientists.
    c. methodologists.
    d. religious leaders.

3. Sociology is the scientific study of: (5)
    a. the production and distribution of the material goods and services of a society.
    b. preliterate cultures.
    c. society and human behavior.
    d. mental processes that occur within the individual.

4.   The application of the scientific approach to the social world is known as: (9)
     a.   ethnomethodology.
     b.   sociobiology.
     c.   natural science.
     d.   positivism.

5.   Interested in the twin problems of social order and social change, this individual was responsible for giving the name "sociology" to this emerging social science. (9)
     a.   Auguste Comte
     b.   Herbert Spencer
     c.   Emile Durkheim
     d.   Max Weber

6.   According to Karl Marx, capitalists, who own the means of production, exploit the: (9)
     a.   bourgeoisie.
     b.   proletariat.
     c.   masses.
     d.   peasants.

7.   According to Emile Durkheim, suicide rates can be explained by: (10)
     a.   social factors.
     b.   common sense.
     c.   the oppression of the proletariat by the bourgeoisie.
     d.   the survival of the fittest.

8.   Max Weber's research on the rise of capitalism identified _____ as the key. (11)
     a.   ownership of property
     b.   political reforms
     c.   religious beliefs
     d.   slavery

9.   Replication: (12)
     a.   helps researchers overcome distortions that values can cause.
     b.   makes it possible to see how results compare when a study is repeated.
     c.   involves the repetition of a study by other researchers.
     d.   All of the above.

10. Social facts and *Verstehen*: (13)
     a.   have no relationship to each other.
     b.   have been disproved.
     c.   go hand-in-hand.
     d.   were both concepts developed by Durkheim.

11. In the 19th century, it was unlikely that women would study sociology because: (13)
     a.   they were more interested in fields of study like English and foreign languages.
     b.   sex roles were rigidly defined and it was not considered appropriate or necessary for women to get an education.
     c.   they had no training in scientific methods.
     d.   they were not interested in social inquiry or social reform.

12. Which of the following North American sociologists wrote extensively on race relations, experienced prejudice and discrimination personally and professionally, and helped to found the NAACP? (16)
    a. C. Wright Mills
    b. Talcott Parsons
    c. W.E.B. Du Bois
    d. Jane Addams

13. The theoretical perspective which views society as composed of symbols that we use to establish meaning, develop our views of the world, and communicate with one another is: (17)
    a. functionalism.
    b. symbolic interactionism.
    c. dramaturgical theory.
    d. conflict theory.

14. The _____ perspective focuses on the symbolic meaning attached to social relationships to understand the social world. (17)
    a. conflict
    b. functional
    c. symbolic interaction
    d. exchange

15. According to Robert Merton, an action intended to help maintain a system's equilibrium is a: (18)
    a. manifest function.
    b. latent function.
    c. dysfunction.
    d. latent dysfunction.

16. Conflict theory was first asserted by: (18)
    a. Karl Marx.
    b. Emile Durkheim.
    c. Ralf Dahrendorf.
    d. Auguste Comte.

17. Contemporary conflict theorists such as Dahrendorf attribute conflict in society to: (19)
    a. the changing meanings associated with social equality.
    b. relations of authority in all layers of society.
    c. social changes that have weakened the family unit.
    d. the increasing division of labor associated with postindustrial capitalism.

18. Feminist theories that attribute gender inequality to legal restrains and customs in a society are: (19)
    a. Non-Marxist.
    b. Marxist.
    c. Liberal.
    d. Positivist.

19. Postmodernism emphasizes the following characteristic of contemporary societies: (20)
    a. that they are structured by inequalities based on gender
    b. that they are characterized by cultural and sexual diversity
    c. that they are divided into interrelated parts that all work together
    d. that they are based on the principles of reason and science

20. All of the following are true regarding the symbolic interactionist perspective, *except*: (21)
    a. this perspective tends to focus on macro-level analysis.
    b. this perspective tends to focus on micro-level analysis.
    c. this perspective looks at social interaction.
    d. this perspective focuses on communications—both talk and nonverbal interactions.

21. In studying the homeless, functionalists would focus on: (21)
    a. what the homeless say and what they do.
    b. how changes in parts of the society are related to homelessness.
    c. the micro-level inequalities in society.
    d. the macro-level inequalities in society.

22. According to your text, which theoretical perspective is best for studying human behavior? (21)
    a. the functionalist perspective.
    b. the symbolic interactionist perspective.
    c. the conflict perspective.
    d. A combination of all of the above.

23. Research which makes discoveries about life human groups rather than make changes in those groups is: (21)
    a. pure or basic sociology.
    b. applied sociology.
    c. clinical sociology.
    d. None of the above.

24. Sociologists who research social problems for government commissions or agencies are: (21)
    a. politically correct.
    b. basic sociologists.
    c. applied sociologists.
    d. pure sociologists.

25. According to the text, in recent years sociologists have once again emphasized: (21)
    a. pure research.
    b. clinical sociology.
    c. applied sociology.
    d. grantsmanship.

TRUE-FALSE QUESTIONS

T F   1. The sociological perspective helps us to understand that people's social experiences underlie what they feel and what they do. (4)

T F   2. Social location is where people are located in history and society. (4)

T F   3. Sociologists believe that internal mechanisms are very important in explaining an individual's thinking and motivations. (4)

T F   4.   Political scientists study the ways in which people govern themselves. (5)

T F   5.   Anthropology focuses on preliterate peoples. (5-6)

T F   6.   Sociology has few similarities to other social sciences. (6)

T F   7.   Historically, the success of the natural sciences led to the search for answers to the social world as well. (8)

T F   8.   Karl Marx thought that a classless society eventually would exist. (9-10)

T F   9.   According to Durkheim, social integration is the degree to which people feel that they are a part of a social group. (10)

T F   10.   The ideas of Max Weber and Karl Marx are almost identical. (11)

T F   11.   According to Weber, subjective meanings are important in understanding human behavior. (13)

T F   12.   To Durkheim, social facts are patterns of behavior that characterize a social group. (13)

T F   13.   Harriet Martineau was widely recognized for her pioneering studies of social life in Great Britain and the United States. (13)

T F   14.   There are five major theoretical perspectives within the discipline of sociology. (17)

T F   15.   Symbolic interactionists primarily analyze how our definitions of ourselves and others underlie our behaviors. (17)

T F   16.   According to functionalists, the family has lost all of its traditional purposes. (17-18)

T F   17.   All conflict theorists focus on conflict between the bourgeoisie and the proletariat. (19)

T F   18.   The three feminist theories – Marxist-Feminist, Liberal Feminist, and Non-Marxist Feminist - have no common elements. (19)

T F   19.   Postmodernism emphasizes the cultural homogeneity of contemporary societies. (20)

T F   20.   Currently, most sociologists do not feel that sociology should be used to solve social problems. (21)

FILL-IN QUESTIONS

1.   People's group memberships because of their location in history and society are known as _____. (4)

2.   The _____ are the intellectual and academic disciplines designed to comprehend, explain, and predict the events in our natural environment. On the other hand, the _____ examine human relationships. (5)

3.   The use of objective systematic observation to test theories is _____. (8)

4.   _____ was Karl Marx's term for the struggle between the proletariat and the bourgeoisie. (9)

5.   Durkheim used the term _____ to refer to the degree to which people feel a part of social groups. (10)

6.   _____ is the view that a sociologist's personal values or biases should not influence social research, while _____ is total neutrality. (12)

7.   The meanings that people attach to their own behavior is called _____. (13)

8.   Durkheim used the term _____ to refer to patterns of behavior that characterize a social group. (13)

9.   A _____ is a general statement about how some parts of the world fit together and how they work. (17)

10.   The theoretical perspective in which society is viewed as composed of symbols that people use to establish meaning, develop their views of the world, and communicate with one another is _____. (17)

11.   _____ analysis is a theoretical framework in which society is viewed as composed of various parts, each with a function that contributes to society's equilibrium. (17)

12.   Power that people consider legitimate is known as _____. (19)

13. _____ stresses that the exploitation of women includes their objectification into roles that serve men's interests. (19)

14. _____ analysis examines large-scale patterns of society, while _____ analysis examines small-scale patterns of society. (21)

15. _____ sociology makes discoveries about life in human groups, not to make changes in those groups; _____ sociology is the use of sociology to solve problems. (21)

MATCH THESE SOCIAL SCIENTISTS WITH THEIR CONTRIBUTIONS

__1. Auguste Comte
__2. Karl Marx
__3. C. Wright Mills
__4. Emile Durkheim
__5. Harriet Martineau
__6. Robert Merton
__7. W.E.B. Du Bois
__8. Max Weber

a. *was an early African American sociologist*
b. *proposed the use of positivism*
c. *stressed social facts*
d. *believed religion was a central force in social change*
e. *believed the key to human history was class struggle*
f. *encouraged the use of the sociological perspective*
g. *published* Society in America *and translated Comte's work into English*
h. *stressed the need for middle-range theories*

ESSAY QUESTIONS

1. Explain what the sociological perspective encompasses and then, using that perspective, discuss the forces that shaped the discipline of sociology.

2. The textbook notes that *Verstehen* and social facts go hand in hand; explain how this is so. Assume that you have been asked to carry out research to find out more about why growing numbers of women and children are homeless and what particular problems they face. Discuss how you could you use both *Verstehen* and social facts in your study.

3. Explain each of the theoretical perspectives that is used in sociology and describe how a sociologist affiliated with one or another of the perspectives might undertake a study of gangs. Discuss how all five can be used in research.

"DOWN-TO-EARTH SOCIOLOGY"

1. Were you surprised to learn that all of the common sense notions in the quiz on page 7 were not true? Can you think of other common sense ideas that may or may not be true?

2. In the debate over the purposes and uses of sociological research, what is your position? Do you think sociologists should only advance our understanding of social life or is it their responsibility to explore harmful social arrangements and try to alleviate human suffering?

3. Reflecting on the introduction to sociological perspectives that was presented in this chapter, does your view on social life fit most closely with the symbolic interactionist, functionalist, conflict, feminist, or postmodern perspective? Why?

CHAPTER 2

WHAT DO SOCIOLOGISTS DO?

☞ CHAPTER SUMMARY

- Sociologists conduct research about almost every area of human behavior. The choice of research topics depends on the sociologist's interests, the availability of subjects, the appropriateness of methods, and ethical considerations.
- Sociological research is needed because common sense is highly limited and its insights are often incorrect.
- Sociologists use seven research methods for gathering data: surveys, participant observations, qualitative interviews, secondary analysis, documents, unobtrusive measures, and experiments. The choice of a research method depends on the research questions to be answered, the researcher's access to potential subjects, the resources available, the researcher's training, and ethical considerations.
- Eight basic steps are included in scientific research: (1) selecting a topic, (2) defining the problem, (3) reviewing the literature, (4) formulating a hypothesis, (5) choosing a research method, (6) collecting the data, (7) analyzing the results, and (8) sharing the results.
- Ethics are of concern to sociologists, who are committed to openness, honesty, truth, and protecting subjects.
- Research and theory must work together because without theory research is of little value, and if theory is unconnected to research it is unlikely to represent the way life really is. Real-life situations often force sociologists to conduct research in less than ideal circumstances, but even research conducted in an imperfect world stimulates the sociological theorizing by which sociology combines data and theory.

☞ LEARNING OBJECTIVES

As you read Chapter 2, use these learning objectives to organize your notes. After completing your reading, briefly state an answer to each of the objectives, and review the text pages in parentheses.

1. Explain why common sense is an inadequate source of knowledge behavior. (29)
2. List and describe each of the seven research methods, noting the major advantages and disadvantages of each. (29-34)
3. Enumerate the four primary factors involved in a researcher's choice of method. (34-35)
4. Differentiate between quantitative techniques and qualitative techniques. (35)
5. Identify the eight steps in a research model. (35-40)
   Describe how sociologists go about selecting a topic for their research. (35, 38)
6. Define the following terms: hypothesis, operational definition, validity, reliability, and replication. Explain the role each plays in the research process. (38-40)
7. Describe the major ethical issues involved in sociological research; demonstrate these issues by using the Brajuha, Scarce, and Humphreys research as examples. (40-41)
8. Discuss how research and theory work together. Note reasons why most research must be conducted under less than ideal circumstances. (41-42)

☞ CHAPTER OUTLINE

I.   What Is a Valid Sociological Topic?

A.   Sociologists research just about every area of human behavior.

B.   Sociologists study social interaction; no human behavior is ineligible for research, whether it is routine or unusual, respectable or reprehensible.

II.   Common Sense and the Need for Sociological Research

A.   Common sense cannot be relied on as a source of knowledge because it is highly limited and its insights often are incorrect.

B.   To move beyond common sense and understand what is really going on, it is necessary to do sociological research.

III.   Seven Research Methods

A.   Surveys involve collecting data by having people answer a series of questions.

1.   The first step is to determine a population, the target group to be studied, and selecting a sample, individuals from within the target population who are intended to represent the population to be studied.

2.   In a random sample everyone in the target population has the same chance of being included in the study.

3.   The respondents (people who respond to a survey) must be allowed to express their own ideas so that the findings will not be biased.

4.   The questionnaires can be administered either by asking respondents to complete the survey themselves (self-administered questionnaires) or by directly questioning respondents (interviews).

5.   In designing a questionnaire, the researcher must consider the effects that interviewers have on respondents that lead to biased answers (interview bias), and whether to make the questions structured (closed-ended questions in which the answers are provided) or unstructured (open-ended questions which people answer in their own words).

6.   It is important to establish rapport—a feeling of trust between researchers and subjects.

B.   In participant observation, the researcher participates in a research setting while observing what is happening in that setting.

1.   Personal characteristics of the researcher—such as gender, age, race, personality, and even height and weight—are very important in this type of research.

2.   Generalizability—the extent to which the findings from one group (or sample) can be generalized or applied to other groups (or populations)—is a problem in participant observation studies.

C.   A qualitative interview, or structured conversation, is used to gather in-depth information from one or more participants. The interviewer is a participant in this conversation, but records it on tape and asks most of the questions.

1.   Qualitative interviews are used to obtain detailed, descriptive information, and can be used, in conjunction with other methods, to construct sociological explanations.

2.   Feminist researchers have attempted to develop a distinctive feminist methodology that uses qualitative interviews to allow women to "tell their own stories."

D.   Secondary analysis—analysis of data already collected by other researchers—is used when resources are limited and/or existing data are an excellent source of information. However, because the researcher did not directly carry out the research, he or she can not be sure that the data were systematically gathered, accurately recorded, and biases avoided.

E. Documents—written sources—may be obtained from many sources, including books, newspapers, police reports, and records kept by various organizations.

F. Unobtrusive measures is the process of observing social behavior of people who do not know they are being studied.

G. Experiments are especially useful to determine causal relationships.
   1. Experiments involve independent (factors that cause a change in something) and dependent variables (factors that are changed).
   2. Experiments require an experimental group—the group of subjects exposed to the independent variable—and a control group—the group of subjects not exposed to the independent variable.
   3. Experiments are seldom used in sociology because sociologists are interested in broad features of society or social behavior, or in the actual workings of some group in a natural setting, neither of which lends itself well to an experiment.

H. Deciding which method to use involves four primary factors:
   1. resources; the researcher must match the method to both time and money available.
   2. access to subjects; the sample may be physically inaccessible to the researcher, thereby influencing the choice of methods.
   3. purpose of the research; the researcher will choose the method that will be most suitable for obtaining answers to the questions posed.
   4. the researcher's background or training; those trained in use of quantitative research methods (emphasis is placed on precise measurement, the use of statistics and numbers) are likely to choose surveys, while those trained in use of qualitative research methods (emphasis is placed on describing and interpreting people's behaviour) lean toward participant observation.

IV. A Research Model

A. Selecting a topic is guided by sociological curiosity, interest in a particular topic, research funding from governmental or private source, and pressing social issues.

B. Defining the problem involves specifying exactly what the researcher wants to learn about the topic.

C. Reviewing the literature uncovers existing knowledge about the problem, helps to narrow down the problem, and provides ideas about what questions to ask.

D. Formulating a hypothesis involves stating the expected relationship between variables, based on a theory. Hypotheses need operational definitions—precise ways to measure the variables.

E. Choosing a research method is influenced by the research topic.

F. Collecting the data involves concerns over validity, the extent to which operational definitions measure what was intended, and reliability, the extent to which data produce consistent results. Inadequate operational definitions and sampling hurt reliability.

G. Analyzing the results involves the use of either qualitative or quantitative techniques to analyze data. Computers have become powerful tools in data analysis because they reduce large amounts of data to basic patterns, take the drudgery out of analyzing data, allow the researcher to use a variety of statistical tests, and give the researcher more time to interpret the results.

H. Sharing the results by writing a report and publishing the results makes the findings available for replication.

V.   **Ethics in Sociological Research**
    A.   Ethics are of fundamental concern to sociologists when it comes to doing research.
    B.   Ethical considerations include being open, honest, and truthful, not harming the subject in the course of conducting the research, protecting the anonymity of the research subjects, and researchers not misrepresenting themselves to the research subjects.
    C.   The Brajuha and Scarce research demonstrates the lengths sociologists will go to in order to protect the anonymity of research subjects, while the Humphreys research illustrates questionable research ethics.

VI.   **How Research and Theory Work Together**
    A.   Sociologists combine research and theory in different ways. Theory is used to interpret data (i.e., functionalism, symbolic interaction, conflict theory, feminist theories, and postmodernism provide frameworks for interpreting research findings) and to generate research. Research helps to generate theory.
    B.   Social researchers must operate under less than ideal circumstances because of real-life situations. Researchers must often settle for something that falls short of the ideal.
        1.   Sociology needs more imaginative, and sometimes daring, research conducted in an imperfect world under less than ideal conditions.
        2.   Research takes people beyond common sense and allows them to penetrate surface realities so they can better understand social life.

☞ KEY TERMS

After studying the chapter, review the definition for each of the following terms.

closed-ended questions: questions followed by a list of possible answers to be selected by the respondent

control group: the group of subjects not exposed to the independent variable in the study

dependent variable: a factor that is changed by an independent variable

documents: in its narrow sense, written sources that provide data; in its extended sense, archival material of any sort, including photographs, movies and so on

experiment: the use of control groups and experimental groups and dependent and independent variables to test causation

experimental group: the group of subjects exposed to the independent variable in a study

feminist methodology: an approach to sociological research that attempts to avoid sexist value judgements when investigating social phenomena; generally relies upon qualitative interviews to allow women to "tell their own stories"

generalizability: the extent to which the findings from one group (or sample) can be generalized or applied to other groups (or populations)

hypothesis: a statement of the expected relationship between variables according to predictions from a theory

independent variable: a factor that causes a change in another variable, called the dependent variable

interview: direct questioning of respondents

interviewer bias: effects that interviewers have on respondents that lead to biased answers

operational definition: the way in which a variable in a hypothesis is measured

participant observation (or fieldwork): research in which the researcher *participates* in a research setting while *observing* what is happening in that setting

population: the target group to be studied

qualitative interview: a research method used to gather in-depth information from one or more participants through a structured conversation that is tape recorded

qualitative research method: research in which the emphasis is placed on observing, describing and interpreting people's behavior

quantitative research method: research in which the emphasis is placed on precise measurement, the use of statistics and numbers

questionnaires: a list of questions to be asked

random sample: a sample in which everyone in the target population has the same chance of being included in the study

rapport: a feeling of trust between researchers and subjects

reliability: the extent to which data produce consistent results

replication: repeating a study in order to test its findings

research method (or research design): one of seven procedures sociologists use to collect data: surveys, participant observation, qualitative interviews, secondary analysis, documents, unobtrusive measures, and experiments

respondents: people who respond to a survey, either in interviews or in self-administered questionnaires

sample: the individuals intended to represent the population to be studied

secondary analysis: the analysis of data already collected by other researchers

self-administered questionnaire: questionnaires filled out by respondents

structured interviews: interviews that use closed-ended questions

survey: the collection of data by having people answer a series of questions

unobtrusive measures: the various ways of observing people who do not know they are being studied

validity: the extent to which an operational definition measures what was intended

variable: a factor or concept thought to be significant for human behavior, which varies from one case to another

☞ KEY PEOPLE

Review the major theoretical contributions or findings of these people.

Mario Brajuha: During an investigation into a restaurant fire, officials subpoenaed notes taken by this sociologist in connection with his participant observation research on restaurant work. He was threatened with jail.

Laud Humphreys: This sociologist carried out doctoral research on homosexual activity, but ran into problems when he misrepresented himself to his research subjects. Although he earned his doctorate degree, he was fired from his position because of his questionable ethics.

Elton Mayo: Mayo is famous for his research at the Western Electric Company Hawthorne plant during the 1920s. He found that workers' productivity changed in directions that had not been originally hypothesized. He concluded that workers adjusted their productivity because they knew they were being observed. This phenomenon came to be known as the *Hawthorne effect*.

C. Wright Mills: Mills argued that research without theory is of little value, simply a collection of unrelated "facts," and theory that is unconnected to research is abstract and empty, unlikely to represent the way life really is.

Rik Scarce: Scarce was a graduate student doing research on animal rights groups when there was a break-in and vandalism in one of his university's research labs. He become famous because he refused to turn over research information that he had collected to authorities investigating the crime. He was imprisoned for 159 days on contempt charges.

Diana Scully and Joseph Marolla: These two sociologists interviewed convicted rapists in prison and found that rapists are not sick or overwhelmed by uncontrollable urges, but rather men who have learned to view rape as appropriate in various circumstances.

☞ SELF-TEST

After completing this self-test, check your answers against the Answer Key at the back of this Study Guide and against the text on page(s) indicated in parentheses.

MULTIPLE CHOICE QUESTIONS

1.   A researcher interested in doing a macro-level study would choose _____ as a topic. (28)
     a.   waiting in public places
     b.   race relations
     c.   interactions between people on street corners
     d.   meat packers at work

2.   Sociologists believe that research is necessary because: (28)
     a.   common sense ideas may or may not be true.
     b.   they want to move beyond guesswork.
     c.   researchers want to know what really is going on.
     d.   All of the above.

3.   Which of the following is *not* a method for gathering data? (29-30)
     a.   ethnomethodology.
     b.   surveys.
     c.   unobtrusive measures.
     d.   secondary analysis.

4.   A sample is defined as: (30)
     a.   a selection from the larger population.
     b.   a partial representation of the target group.
     c.   the individuals intended to represent the population to be studied.
     d.   specific subgroups of the population in which everyone in the subgroup has an equal chance of being included in the study.

5.   Which method of sampling ensures that each member of the population has the same chance of being included in a research project? (30)
     a.   target sampling
     b.   self-administered questionnaire sampling
     c.   random sampling
     d.   random sub-sampling

6.   You have been hired to do a survey of a community's views on a proposed anti-crime program. With only a small budget, you need to contact at least 70 percent of the residents living in the affected areas within the next month. Which method are you most likely to choose? (30)
     a.   participant observation
     b.   self-administered questionnaires
     c.   interviews
     d.   structured interviews

7. The advantage of structured interviews is that: (30)
    a. a larger number of people can be sampled at a relatively low cost.
    b. they are faster to administer and make it easier for answers to be coded.
    c. they make it possible to test hypotheses about cause and effect relationships.
    d. None of the above.

8. Problems which must be dealt with in conducting participant observation include: (31-32)
    a. the researcher's personal characteristics.
    b. developing rapport with respondents.
    c. generalizability.
    d. All of the above.

9. Why might a researcher "load the dice" in designing a research project? (31)
    a. The researcher doesn't know any better.
    b. The researcher may have a vested interest in the outcome of the research.
    c. The researcher doesn't have much time or money and wants to guarantee that the desired results are obtained.
    d. All of the above

10. Qualitative interviews are a useful method for collecting: (32-33)
    a. extremely important descriptive information.
    b. data that are generalizable to a larger population.
    c. data that have been previously analyzed by other researchers.
    d. information from a large number of people at low cost.

11. The analysis of data already collected by other researchers is referred to as: (33)
    a. surveying the literature.
    b. use of documents.
    c. secondary analysis.
    d. replication.

12. Sources such as newspapers, diaries, bank records, police reports, household accounts and immigration files are all considered: (33)
    a. unreliable data sources.
    b. documents that provide useful information for investigating social life.
    c. useful for doing quantitative research, but not necessarily valid when doing qualitative analysis.
    d. of limited validity because it would be difficult to replicate the study.

13. To study patterns of alcohol consumption in different neighborhoods, you decide to go through the recycling bins and count the beer cans, wine and liquor bottles. You would be using: (34)
    a. participant observation.
    b. experimental methods.
    c. unobtrusive methods.
    d. qualitative methods.

14. Which method will a researcher use if he/she is interested in determining causal relationships? (34)
    a.   an experiment
    b.   survey research
    c.   participant observation
    d.   None of the above

15. In an experiment, the group not exposed to the independent variable in the study is: (34)
    a.   the guinea pig group.
    b.   the control group.
    c.   the experimental group.
    d.   the maintenance group.

16. _____ steps are involved in scientific research. (35)
    a.   Four
    b.   Six
    c.   Eight
    d.   Ten

17. The change in behavior that occurs when subjects know they are being studied is: (35)
    a.   the Hawthorne effect.
    b.   the Humphreys effect.
    c.   the unobtrusive effect.
    d.   the obtrusive effect.

18. Surveys are more likely to be used by researchers trained in: (35)
    a.   social psychology.
    b.   ethnomethodology.
    c.   quantitative research methods.
    d.   qualitative research methods.

19. Marketing researchers use: (36)
    a.   a combination of quantitative and qualitative methods.
    b.   quantitative methods.
    c.   secondary analysis.
    d.   participant observation.

20. Which of the following is *not* one of the reasons why researchers review the literature? (38)
    a.   To help them to narrow down the problem by pinpointing particular areas to examine.
    b.   To get ideas about how to do their own research.
    c.   To find out whether or not the topic is controversial.
    d.   To determine whether or not the problem has been answered already.

21. A relationship between or among variables is predicted: (38)
    a.   by a hypothesis.
    b.   by use of operational definitions.
    c.   when the researcher selects the topic to be studied.
    d.   when the researcher is analyzing the results.

22. Reliability refers to: (38)
    a. the extent to which operational definitions measure what they are intended to measure.
    b. the extent to which data produce consistent results from one study to the next.
    c. the integrity of the researcher.
    d. the ways in which the variables in a hypothesis are measured.

23. In analyzing data gathered by participant observation, a researcher is likely to choose: (38)
    a. computer analysis.
    b. quantitative analysis.
    c. qualitative analysis.
    d. statistical analysis.

24. Replication: (40)
    a. is the extent to which operational definitions measure what was intended.
    b. is the examination of a source to identify its themes.
    c. is the repetition of research by others in order to test its findings.
    d. is copying the work of some other researcher.

25. Research ethics require: (40)
    a. openness.
    b. that a researcher not falsify results or plagiarize someone else's work.
    c. that research subjects should not be harmed by the research.
    d. All of the above.

TRUE-FALSE QUESTIONS

T F   1.   Date rape is an acceptable topic for sociological research. (28)
T F   2.   Research generally confirms common sense. (29)
T F   3.   One of the first steps in conducting survey research is to determine a population. (30)
T F   4.   In survey research, it is undesirable for respondents to express their own ideas. (30)
T F   5.   The wording of questionnaires can affect research results. (30)
T F   6.   Structured interviews always use closed-ended questions. (30)
T F   7.   The researcher's personal characteristics are extremely important in participant observation. (31-32)
T F   8.   Feminist methodologists attempt to replicate the objective, scientific method in their research. (33)
T F   9.   Secondary analysis and use of documents mean the same thing in terms of research methods. (33)
T F   10. The purpose of an experiment is to identify causal relationships. (34)
T F   11. It is always unethical to observe social behavior in people when they do not know they are being studied. (34)
T F   12. In an experiment, the experimental group is not exposed to the independent variable in the study. (34)
T F   13. Quantitative research methods emphasize precise measurement, the use of statistics and numbers. (35)
T F   14. After selecting a topic, the next step in the research model is defining the problem. (38)
T F   15. An operational definition refers to the precise ways in which researchers measure their variables. (38)
T F   16. In general, researchers give higher priority to reliability than validity. (38)

T F   17. Reliability is the extent to which data produce consistent results. (38)
T F   18. Computers are valuable to research sociologists because they can store a great deal of information very efficiently. (39)
T F   19. Sharing the results is the final step in the research model. (39)
T F   20. The research by Scully and Marolla demonstrates that research must be done under ideal conditions in order for the findings to be valid. (42)

FILL-IN QUESTIONS

1. The seven research methods are: (1) _____, (2) _____, (3)_____, (4) _____, (5) _____, (6)_____, (7) _____. (29-30)
2. A(n) _____ allows a large number of people to be sampled at a relatively low cost. (30)
3. Closed-ended questions are used in _____. (30)
4. _____ is a feeling of trust between researchers and subjects. (30)
5. _____ is a form of research where the researcher spends a great deal of time with the people he or she is studying. (31)
6. Generalizability is one of the major problems in _____. (32)
7. Sociologists rarely use _____ , as they do not reveal broader social relationships or the workings of social groups. (34)
8. To conduct an experiment, the researcher has two groups: (1) _____ and (2)_____. (34)
9. Research in which the emphasis is placed on precise measurement, the use of statistics and numbers is _____. (35)
10. Research in which the emphasis is placed on describing and interpreting people's behavior is _____. (35)
11. A factor or concept thought to be significant for human behavior, which varies from one case to another, is a(n) _____. (38)
12. Hypotheses need _____, which are precise ways to measure variables. (38)
13. _____ is the extent to which data produce consistent results. (38)
14. Research _____ require openness, honesty, and truth. (40)
15. Research and _____ are interdependent, and sociologists combine them in their work. (41-42)

MATCH THESE CONCEPTS WITH THEIR DEFINITIONS

__1. Hawthorne effect   a. *the observations of people who are unaware of being watched*
__2. population   b. *behavior change due to subject's awareness of being studied*
__3. sample   c. *the intervierwer effect on respondents that leads to biased answers*
__4. interview bias   d. *a factor that is changed by an independent variable*
__5. secondary analysis   e. *written sources*
__6. documents   f. *the target group to be studied*
__7. independent variable   g. *the analysis of data already collected by other researchers*
__8. dependent variable   h. *the individuals intended to represent the population to be studied*
__9. unobtrusive measures   i. *a factor that causes a change in another variable*

ESSAY QUESTIONS

1. Choose a topic and explain how you would go through the different steps in the research model.
2. Discuss some of the things that can go wrong in the process of doing research and provide suggestions on how to overcome such problems.
3. Explain why ethical guidelines are necessary in social science research.

"DOWN-TO-EARTH SOCIOLOGY"

1. If you were to pursue a career in sociology what research topics would you find interesting? What methods would you use?
2. Can you give examples similar to those in your text where researchers have loaded the dice (p. 31) to enhance the qualities of a product or a political candidate?
3. Have you ever changed your appearance or behavior because you knew you were being observed or studied? Was your change an example of the Hawthorne effect (p. 35)?
4. After reading about how some sociologists use their training and knowledge to do marketing research (p. 36), do you see this as a legitimate area of research for them? How does it relate to the ethical concerns of the profession? the need to be objective?
5. Were you surprised by the findings on homelessness reported on pages 36-37? How did the reaction to the research reflect the political nature of the problem? Why do you think the homeless advocates were upset by the outcome of the research?
6. The author provides examples of three different research projects that involved some ethical considerations. In each of these cases, did you agree or disagree with the position taken by the researcher? How would you have reacted in the same situation?
7. Why do you think that sociologists like Scully and Marolla (p. 42) pursue certain research topics even when it requires them to work under less than ideal conditions?

CHAPTER 3

CULTURE

☞ CHAPTER SUMMARY

- Culture is universal; all human groups create a design for living that includes both material and nonmaterial culture. Ideal culture, a group's ideal norms and values, exists alongside its real culture, the actual behavior which often falls short of the cultural ideals.
- All people perceive and evaluate the world through the lens of their own culture. People are naturally ethnocentric, that is, they use their own culture as a standard against which to judge other cultures. In comparison, cultural relativism tries to understand other peoples within the framework of their own culture.
- The central component of nonmaterial culture is symbols; these include gestures, language, values, norms, sanctions, folkways and mores. Language is essential for culture because it allows us to move beyond the present, sharing with others our past experiences and our future plans. According to the Sapir-Whorf hypothesis, language not only expresses our thinking and perceptions but actually shapes them.
- All groups have values and norms and use positive and negative sanctions to show approval or disapproval of those who do or don't follow the norms.
- A subculture is a group whose values and behaviors set it apart from the general culture; a counterculture holds values that stand in opposition to the dominant culture.
- Although Canada is a pluralistic society made up of many groups, each with its own set of values, certain core values dominate. Some values cluster together to form a larger whole. Core values that contradict one another indicate areas of social tension and are likely points of social change.
- Cultural universals are values, norms or other cultural traits that are found in all cultures.
- To the extent that some animals teach their young certain behavior, animals also have culture; however, no animals have language in the sociological sense of the term.
- Cultural lag refers to a condition in which a group's nonmaterial culture lags behind its changing technology. Today the technology in travel and communication makes cultural diffusion occur more rapidly around the globe than in the past, resulting in some degree of cultural leveling, a process by which cultures become similar to one another.

☞ LEARNING OBJECTIVES

As you read Chapter 3, use these learning objectives to organize your notes. After completing your reading, briefly state an answer to each of the objectives, and review the text pages in parentheses.

1. Define culture and explain its material and nonmaterial components. (48)
2. Explain why ethnocentrism is a natural tendency and why this orientation towards your own and other cultures can lead to culture shock. (49)
3. State what cultural relativism is and discuss why it is a worthwhile goal even though it presents challenges to us. (50)
4. Discuss the components of symbolic culture. (51-55)
5. Identify the different ways in which language makes human life possible. (52-54)
6. Define the following terms: values, norms, sanctions, folkways, mores, and taboos. (54-55)
7. Compare and contrast dominant culture, subcultures, and countercultures. (55-56)

26

8. List the examples of values in Canadian society as identified by The National Magazine/Maclean's poll. (56-60)
9. Explain what is meant by value clusters and value contradictions. (60-61)
10. Discuss why core values do not change without meeting strong resistance. (61)
11. Explain the difference between "ideal" and "real" cultures. (61-62)
12. Define cultural universals and state whether, in actuality, they exist or not. (62-63)
13. Answer the question, "Do animals have culture?" (63-64)
14. State what technology is and explain its sociological significance. (64-66)
15. Define cultural lag and explain its role in relationship to cultural change. (66)
16. Discuss the link between technology, cultural diffusion, and cultural leveling. (66-67)

☞ **CHAPTER OUTLINE**

I. **What is Culture?**
  A. Culture is defined as the language, beliefs, values, norms, behaviors, and even material objects passed from one generation to the next.
    1. Material culture is things such as jewelry, art, buildings, weapons, machines, clothing, hairstyles, etc.
    2. Nonmaterial culture is a group's ways of thinking (beliefs, values, and assumptions) and common patterns of behavior (language, gestures, and other forms of interaction).
  B. Culture provides a taken-for-granted orientation to life.
    1. We assume that our own culture is normal or natural; in fact, it is not natural, but rather is learned. It penetrates our lives so deeply that it is taken for granted and provides the lens through which we evaluate things.
    2. It provides implicit instructions that tell us what we ought to do and a moral imperative that defines what we think is right and wrong.
    3. Coming into contact with a radically different culture produces "culture shock," challenging our basic assumptions.
    4. A consequence of internalizing culture is ethnocentrism, using our own culture (and assuming it to be good, right, and superior) to judge other cultures. It is functional when it creates in-group solidarity, but can be dysfunctional if it leads to harmful discrimination.
  C. Cultural relativism consists of trying to appreciate other groups' ways of life in the context in which they exist, without judging them as superior or inferior to our own.
    1. This view helps to avoid "cultural smugness."
    2. Robert Edgerton argues that those cultural practices that result in exploitation should be judged morally inferior to those that enhance people's lives.

II. **Components of Symbolic Culture**
  A. Sociologists sometimes refer to nonmaterial culture as symbolic culture.
    1. A central component of culture is the symbols—something to which people attach meaning—that people use to communicate.
    2. Symbols include gestures, language, values, norms, sanctions, folkways, and mores.
  B. Gestures, using one's body to communicate with others, are shorthand means of communication.
    1. Gestures are used by people in every culture, although the gestures and the meanings differ; confusion or offense can result because of misunderstandings over the meaning of a gesture or misuse of a gesture.

2.   There is disagreement over whether there are any universal gestures.

C.   Language consists of a system of symbols that can be put together in an infinite number of ways in order to communicate abstract thought. Each word is a symbol to which a culture attaches a particular meaning. It is important because it is the primary means of communication between people.

1.   It allows human experiences to be cumulative; each generation builds on the body of significant experiences that is passed on to it by the previous generation, thus freeing people to move beyond immediate experiences. It extends time back into the past and forward into the future, enabling us to share with others both past experiences as well as future plans. It expands connections beyond our immediate, face-to-face groups.

2.   It allows shared perspectives or understandings of the past and the future.

3.   It allows humans to exchange perspectives, i.e., ideas about events and experiences.

4.   It allows people to engage in complex, shared, goal-directed behavior.

5.   The Sapir-Whorf hypothesis states that our thinking and perception are not only expressed by language but are actually shaped by language. This is because we are taught not only words but also a particular way of thinking and perceiving. Rather than objects and events forcing themselves onto our consciousness, our very language determines our consciousness.

D.   Culture includes values, norms, and sanctions.

1.   Values are the standards by which people define good and bad, beautiful and ugly. Every group develops both values and expectations regarding the right way to reflect them.

2.   Norms are the expectations, or rules of behavior, that develop out of a group's values.

3.   Sanctions are the positive or negative reactions to the way in which people follow norms. Positive sanctions (a money reward, a prize, a smile, or even a handshake) are expressions of approval; negative sanctions (a fine, a frown, or harsh words) denote disapproval for breaking a norm.

E.   Norms vary in terms of their importance to a culture.

1.   Folkways are norms that are not strictly enforced, such as passing on the left side of the sidewalk. They may result in a person getting a dirty look.

2.   Mores are norms that are believed to be essential to core values and we insist on conformity. A person who steals, rapes, and kills has violated some of society's most important mores.

3.   Norms that one group considers to be folkways another group may view as mores. A male walking down the street with the upper half of his body uncovered may be violating a folkway; a female doing the same thing may be violating accepted mores.

4.   Taboos are norms so strongly ingrained that even the thought of them is greeted with revulsion. Eating human flesh and having sex with one's parents are examples of such behavior.

F.   Subcultures and countercultures are often found within a broader culture.

1.   Subcultures are groups whose values and related behaviors are so distinct that they set their members off from the dominant culture. Each subculture is a world within the larger world of the dominant culture, and has a distinctive way of looking at life, but remains compatible with the dominant culture.

2.   Countercultures are groups whose values set their members in opposition to the dominant culture. Countercultures are usually associated with negative behavior,

although some are not. Countercultures are often perceived as a threat by the dominant culture because they challenge the culture's values; for this reason the dominant culture will move against a particular counterculture in order to affirm its own core values.

III. Values in Canadian Society
A. Identifying core values in Canadian society is difficult because it is a pluralistic society with many different religious, racial, ethnic, and special interest groups.
1. On many social and political issues, Canadians display liberal moral values. Liberal values are even more strongly expressed in the province of Quebec.
2. Sociologist John Porter remarked that Canadians, unlike Americans, lack a unifying ideology. Canadians, however, are preoccupied with who we are as a nation.
B. Some values conflict with each other. There cannot be full expressions of democracy, equality, racism, and sexism at the same time. These are value contradictions and, as society changes, some values are challenged and undergo modification.
C. Values are not independent units; value clusters are made up of related core values that come together to form a larger whole. A cluster that is emerging within Canadian society — in response to fundamental changes in the society — is one made up of the values of leisure, self-fulfillment, physical fitness, and youngness.
D. Core values do not change without meeting strong resistance.
E. Values and their supporting beliefs may emerge in relation to our social circumstances. In recent years, Canadians have developed a genuine and long-term concern for the environment because we now recognize our dependence on our natural resources.
F. Ideal culture refers to the ideal values and norms of a people. What people actually do usually falls short of this ideal, and sociologists refer to the norms and values that people actually follow as real culture.

IV.   Cultural Universals
A. Anthropologist George Murdock concluded that all human groups have certain cultural universals: customs about courtship, cooking, marriage, funerals, games, laws, music, myths, incest taboos, and toilet training are present in all cultures.
B. Even so, the specific customs differ from one group to another: by way of example, there is no universal form of the family, no universal way of disposing of the dead, and even the methods of toilet training differ from one culture to another.

V.   Animals and Culture
A. Animal behavior is largely controlled by instincts, inherited patterns of behavior common to all members of a species. By definition, that is not culture. Sociologists ask whether or not there are any behaviors that animals learn and that they pass on to others.
1. Anthropologist Jane Goodall discovered that chimpanzees made and used a form of simple tool (a blade of grass, stripped of its leaves and licked on one end) that they would stick into a nest of termites and then pull out, enabling them to eat the termites. This conduct on the part of the chimpanzees was a form of animal culture: learned, shared behavior among animals.
2. Other scientists have learned that the mating behavior of some animals is learned, rather than pure instinct. Young gorillas raised in captivity seem to want to mate, but don't know how; watching a movie of two adult gorillas mating changes that.
B. To the extent that some animals teach their young certain behaviors, they have culture. No animals, however, have language in the sociological sense of that term, although some animals apparently do have the capacity to learn language.

VI.   Technology in the Global Village

  A.   In its simplest sense, technology can be equated with tools. In its broadest sense, technology also includes the skills or procedures necessary to make and to use those tools.

   1.   The emerging technologies of an era that make a major impact on human life are referred to as new technologies. The printing press and the computer are both examples of new technologies.

   2.   The sociological significance of technology is that it sets the framework for the nonmaterial culture, influencing the way people think and how they relate to one another.

  B.   Not all parts of culture change at the same pace; cultural lag was Ogburn's term for situations where the material culture changes first and the nonmaterial culture lags behind.

  C.   Although for most of human history cultures had little contact with one another, there has always been some contact with other groups, resulting in groups learning from one another.

   1.   This transmission of cultural characteristics is cultural diffusion; it is more likely to produce changes in material culture than the nonmaterial culture.

   2.   Cultural diffusion occurs more rapidly today, given the technology.

   3.   Travel and communication unite the world to such an extent that there almost is no "other side of the world." For example, Japan, no longer a purely Eastern culture, has adapted Western economic production, forms of dress, music, and so on. This leads to cultural leveling—cultures become similar to one another.

☞ KEY TERMS

After studying the chapter, review the definition for each of the following terms.

animal culture: learned, shared behavior among animals

counterculture: a group whose values, beliefs, and related behaviors place its members in opposition to the values of the broader culture

cultural diffusion: the spread of cultural characteristics from one group to another

cultural lag: William Ogburn's term for a situation in which nonmaterial culture lags behind changes in the material culture

cultural leveling: the process by which cultures become similar to one another, and especially by which Western industrial culture is imported and diffused into developing nations

cultural relativism: understanding a people in the framework of its own culture

cultural universal: a value, norm, or other cultural trait that is found in every group

culture: the language, beliefs, values, norms, behaviors, and even material objects that are passed from one generation to the next

culture contact: encounter between people from different cultures, or coming in contact with some parts of a different culture

culture shock: the disorientation that people experience when they come in contact with a fundamentally different culture and can no longer depend on their taken-for-granted assumptions about life

ethnocentrism: the use of one's own culture as a yardstick for judging the ways of other individuals or societies, generally leading to a negative evaluation of their values, norms, and behaviors

folkways: norms that are not strictly enforced

gestures: the ways in which people use their bodies to communicate with one another

ideal culture: the ideal values and norms of a people, the goals held out for them

language: a system of symbols that can be combined in an infinite number of ways and can represent not only objects but also abstract thought

material culture: the material objects that distinguish a group of people, such as their art, buildings, weapons, utensils, machines, hairstyles, clothing, and jewelry

mores: norms that are strictly enforced because they are thought essential to core values

negative sanction: an expression of disapproval for breaking a norm, ranging from a mild, informal reaction such as a frown to a formal prison sentence or an execution

new technology: the emerging technologies of an era that have a significant impact on social life

nonmaterial culture: a group's ways of thinking (including its beliefs, values, and other assumptions about the world) and doing (its common patterns of behavior, including language and other forms of interaction)

norms: the expectations, or rules of behavior, that develop out of values

pluralistic society: a society made up of many different groups

positive sanction: a reward given for following norms, ranging from a smile to a prize

real culture: the norms and values that people actually follow

sanctions: expressions of approval or disapproval given to people for upholding or violating norms

Sapir-Whorf hypothesis: Edward Sapir and Benjamin Whorf's theory that language itself creates ways of thinking and perceiving

social construction of technology: the view (opposed to *technological determinism*) that culture (people's values and special interests) shapes the use and development of technology

sociobiology: a framework of thought that views human behavior as the result of natural selection and considers biological characteristics to be the fundamental cause of human behavior

subculture: the values and related behaviors of a group that distinguish its members from the larger culture; a world within a world

symbol: something to which people attach meaning and then use to communicate with others

symbolic culture: another term for nonmaterial culture

taboo: a norm so strong that it brings revulsion if it is violated

technological determinism: the view that technology determines culture, that technology takes on a life of its own and forces human behavior to follow

technology: in its narrow sense, tools: its broader sense includes the skills or procedures necessary to make and use those tools

tool: an object that is created or modified for a specific purpose

value clusters: a series of interrelated values that together form a larger whole

value contradictions: values that conflict with one another; to follow the one means to come into conflict with the other

values: the standards by which people define what is desirable or undesirable, good or bad, beautiful or ugly

☞ KEY PEOPLE

Review the major theoretical contributions or findings of these people.

Reginald Bibby: Bibby studied the tendency towards Americanization in Canadian life.

Charles Darwin: Darwin studied the principles upon which natural selection occurred.

Robert Edgerton: Edgerton attacks the concept of cultural relativism, suggesting that because some cultures endanger their people's health, happiness, or survival, there should be a scale to evaluate cultures on their "quality of life."

Allen and Beatrice Gardner: These psychologists taught American Sign Language to a young female chimpanzee, who not only learned the signs but put them together in simple sentences.

Jane Goodall: Goodall studied the behavior of chimpanzees and discovered that they not only communicate using gestures, hoots, and facial expressions, but they also use tools.

Harold Innis: Innis examined the effects of technological revolutions on culture, noting the relationship between literacy and human geographic expansion.

Marshall McLuhan: An optimist about technology, McLuhan tried to understand the impact of electronic media on people's ideas, values, and way of life.

George Murdock: Murdock was an anthropologist who sought to determine cultural values, norms, or traits universally across the globe.

William Ogburn: Ogburn coined the term "cultural lag."

John Porter: Porter saw Canadians as lacking a unifying ideology; we are not brought up with a set of beliefs and values that tell us who we are and what we should strive for in order to make our lives meaningful and fulfilling.

Edward Sapir and Benjamin Whorf: These two anthropologists argued that language not only reflects thoughts and perceptions, but that it actually shapes the way a people think and perceive the world.

William Sumner: Sumner developed the concept of ethnocentrism.

Edward Wilson: Wilson is an insect specialist who claims that human behavior is also the result of natural selection.

☞ SELF-TEST

After completing this self-test, check your answers against the Answer Key at the back of this Study Guide and against the text on page(s) indicated in parentheses.

MULTIPLE CHOICE QUESTIONS

1. Which of the following would you use to describe a group's ways of thinking and doing, including language and other forms of interaction? (48)
   a. material culture
   b. nonmaterial culture
   c. ideological culture
   d. values

2. Which of the following is *not* part of material culture? (48)
   a. weapons and machines
   b. eating utensils
   c. jewelry, hairstyles, and clothing
   d. language

3. In the textbook the author describes his reaction to life in Morocco. Which of the following best describes what he was feeling? (48)
   a. cultural diffusion
   b. cultural leveling
   c. cultural relativism
   d. cultural shock

4. Which of these statements regarding culture is *not* true? (49)
   a. People generally are aware of the effects of their own culture.
   b. Culture touches almost every aspect of who and what a person is.
   c. At birth, people do not possess culture.
   d. Culture is the lens through which we perceive and evaluate what is going on around us.

5. A Canadian thinks citizens of another country are barbarians if they like to attend bullfights. Which of the following concepts best describes this reaction? (49)
    a. cultural shock
    b. cultural relativism
    c. ethnocentrism
    d. ethnomethodology

6. Which of the following statements about gestures is correct? (51-52)
    a. Gestures are studied by anthropologists but not sociologists.
    b. Gestures are universal.
    c. Gestures always facilitate communication between people.
    d. Gestures can lead to misunderstandings and embarrassment.

7. Which of the following makes it possible for human experience to be cumulative and for people to share memories? (52)
    a. language
    b. cultural universals
    c. gestures
    d. computers

8. As Inuit children learn their language they learn distinctions between types of snowfalls in a way that is not apparent to non-Inuit children. Which of the following perspectives is reflected in this example? (54)
    a. sociobiology
    b. the Davis-Moore theory
    c. the Sapir-Whorf hypothesis
    d. the Linguistic perspective

9. As you are rushing from one class to the next, you absentmindedly forget to hold the door open for the person coming through behind you. The consequence is that the person has the door slammed in his face. Which of the following cultural components has been violated as a result of your behavior? (54-55)
    a. taboos
    b. mores
    c. values
    d. folkways

10. Which of the following statements about mores is correct? (55)
    a. Mores are essential to our core values and require conformity.
    b. Mores are norms that are not strictly enforced.
    c. Mores state that a person should not try to pass you on the left side of the sidewalk.
    d. Mores are less important in contemporary societies.

11. Subcultures: (55-56)
    a. are a world within a world.
    b. have values and related behaviors that set their members apart from the dominant culture.
    c. include occupational groups.
    d. All of the above.

12. Heavy metal adherents who glorify Satanism, cruelty, and sexism would be an example of: (55-56)
    a. ethnocentrists.
    b. perverted people.
    c. a counterculture.
    d. a subculture.

13. Canadian society is made up of many different groups. Which of the following terms would a sociologist use to describe this type of society? (56)
    a. a melting pot
    b. a pluralistic society
    c. a conflicted society
    d. a counterculture

14. Which of the following statements concerning Canadian core values is *not* correct? (56-61)
    a. In general, Canadians display liberal moral values.
    b. An emerging cluster of core values includes leisure, self-fulfillment, physical fitness, and youth.
    c. They change over time.
    d. They rarely create much conflict as they change.

15. Which of the following reflects conditions under which value contradictions can occur? (59-60)
    a. A value, such as the one that stresses group superiority, comes into direct conflict with other values, such as democracy and equality.
    b. Societies have very little social change.
    c. A series of interrelated values bind together to form a larger whole.
    d. Values blind people to many social circumstances.

16. Which of the following statements about ideal culture is correct? (61)
    a. Ideal culture is a value, norm, or other cultural trait that is found in every group.
    b. Ideal culture reflects the values and norms which people in a culture attempt to hold.
    c. Ideal culture is the norms people follow when they know they are being watched.
    d. Ideal culture is not a sociological concept.

17. What is the perspective that views human behavior as the result of natural selection and considers biological characteristics to be the fundamental cause of human behavior? (62)
    a. natural science
    b. social science
    c. anthropology
    d. sociobiology

18. Which of the following is a conclusion drawn from studies of animal culture? (63-64)
    a. Animals do not have culture.
    b. We can't say if animals have culture or not if we cannot communicate with them.
    c. Animal culture exists, but researchers are still studying to learn more about it.
    d. Animals not only have culture but also have an extensive capacity for language.

19. There are computer tests that outperform physicians in diagnosing and prescribing treatment, yet most of us still visit doctors and rely on their judgment. What does this situation reflect? (66)
   a.   resistance to new technologies
   b.   cultural diffusion
   c.   the social construction of technology
   d.   cultural lag

20. Today bagels, woks, and hammocks are all a part of Canadian culture. The adoption of these objects illustrates which of the following processes or concepts? (67)
   a.   cultural leveling
   b.   nonmaterial culture
   c.   cultural diffusion
   d.   cultural universals

TRUE-FALSE QUESTIONS

T F   1.   Speech, gestures, beliefs and customs usually are taken for granted by people. (49)
T F   2.   Culture has little to do with people's ideas of right and wrong. (50)
T F   3.   No one can be entirely successful at practicing cultural relativism. (50)
T F   4.   Robert Edgerton is a strong critic of cultural relativism, arguing that cultures should be rated on the basis of their "quality of life." (50)
T F   5.   The gesture of nodding the head up and down to indicate "yes" is universal. (51-52)
T F   6.   Without language, humans could still successfully plan future events. (54)
T F   7.   Sanctions are positive or negative reactions to the ways people follow norms. (55)
T F   8.   While folkways may change across cultures, mores are universally the same. (55)
T F   9.   Motorcycle enthusiasts who emphasize personal freedom and speed, while maintaining values of success, form part of a counterculture. (56)
T F   10.   Canadians, in general, have liberal moral values. (57)
T F   11.   Only a small minority of Canadians believe the government should more actively intervene to narrow the gap between the rich and poor. (59)
T F   12.   Racism and group superiority are core values in Canadian society. (60-61)
T F   13.   John Porter remarked that Canadians, unlike Americans, are brought up with a unifying national ideology. (61)
T F   14.   Concern for the environment has always been a core value in Canadian society. (61)
T F   15.   Core values do not change without meeting strong resistance. (61)
T F   16.   Although certain activities are present in all cultures, the specific customs differ from one group to another. (62-63)
T F   17.   Most sociologists do not agree with sociobiology. (62)
T F   18.   Research by Allen and Beatrice Gardner provides evidence that animals are capable of acquiring language. (64)
T F   19.   While new technologies may affect material culture, including the way things are done in a society, they have only minimal impact on nonmaterial culture, including the way people think and what they value. (64)
T F   20.   According to William Ogburn, a group's nonmaterial culture usually changes first, with the material culture lagging behind. (66)

FILL-IN QUESTIONS

1. Objects such as art, buildings, weapons, utensils, machines, hairstyles, clothing, and jewelry, which distinguish a group of people, are known as _____; their ways of thinking and doing are _____. (48)
2. A _____ is something to which people attach meaning and then use to communicate with others. (51)
3. _____ is a system of symbols that can be combined in an infinite number of ways and can represent not only objects but also abstract thought. (52)
4. _____ are ideas of what is desirable in life. (54)
5. The expectations or rules of behavior that develop out of values are referred to as _____. (55)
6. A _____ is a norm so strongly ingrained that even the thought of its violation is greeted with revulsion. (55)
7. _____ are a series of interrelated values that together form a larger whole. (60)
8. _____ may not exist because even though there are universal human activities, there is no universally accepted way of doing any of them. (62)
9. Studies of chimpanzees indicate that they were able to make and use _____; they actually modified objects and used them for specific purposes. (63)
10. In its broader sense, _____ includes the skills or procedures necessary to make and use tools. (64)
11. Both the printing press and the computer represent _____ because they had a significant impact on society following their introduction. (64)
12. The idea that technology is the single greatest force in shaping our lives is central to the point of view called _____. (65)
13. William Ogburn used the term _____ to reflect the condition in which not all parts of a culture change at the same pace. (66)
14. The spread of cultural characteristics from one group to another is _____. (67)
15. When Western industrial culture is imported and diffused into developing nations, the process is called _____. (67)

MATCH THESE SOCIAL SCIENTISTS WITH THEIR CONTRIBUTIONS

__1. Edward Sapir and Benjamin Whorf
__2. John Porter
__3. George Murdock
__4. Jane Goodall
__5. Robert Edgerton
__6. Edward Wilson
__7. William Sumner
__8. Allen and Beatrice Gardner
__9. William Ogburn
__10. Marshall McLuhan

a. *studied animal culture*
b. *intoduced the concept of cultural lag*
c. *looked for cultural universals*
d. *taught chimps a gestural language*
e. *coined the term "global village"*
f. *stated that language shapes perceptions of reality*
g. *believed natural selection produces human behavior*
h. *criticized aspects of cultural relativism*
i. *remarked that Canadians lack a unifying ideology*
j. *developed the concept of ethnocentrism*

ESSAY QUESTIONS

1. Explain cultural relativism and discuss both the advantages and disadvantages of practicing it.
2. Consider the degree to which the real culture of Canada falls short of the ideal culture. Provide concrete examples to support your essay.
3. Evaluate what is gained and what is lost as technology advances in society.

"DOWN-TO-EARTH SOCIOLOGY"

1. What is your evaluation of the sociobiology argument (p. 62)? Do you think you were "programmed" from birth to be a certain person and to do specific things in your life? Do you think people are prisoners of their genes?

2. With which side of the technology debate would you place yourself (Global Village or Big Brother?, p. 65)? Are we able to control technology or does it control us?

CHAPTER 4

SOCIALIZATION

☞ **CHAPTER SUMMARY**

- Scientists have attempted to determine how much of people's characteristics come from heredity and how much from the social environment. Observations of feral and isolated children help to answer this question. These studies have concluded that language and intimate interaction are essential to the development of human characteristics.
- Charles H. Cooley, George H. Mead, Jean Piaget, and Sigmund Freud provide insights into the social development of human beings. The work of Cooley and Mead demonstrates that the self is created through our interactions with others. Piaget identified four stages in the development of our ability to reason: (1) sensorimotor; (2) preoperational; (3) concrete operational; and (4) formal operational. Freud defined the personality in terms of the id, ego, and superego; personality developed as the inborn desires (id) clashed with social constraints (superego).
- Socialization influences not only *how* we express our emotions, but *what* emotions we feel.
- Gender socialization is a primary means of controlling human behavior, and a society's ideals of sex-linked behaviors are reinforced by its social institutions.
- The main agents of socialization—family, religion, day care, school, peer groups, the mass media, sports, and the workplace—each contribute to the socialization of people to become full-fledged members of society.
- Resocialization is the process of learning new norms, values, attitudes and behaviors. Intense resocialization takes place in total institutions. Most resocialization is voluntary, but some is involuntary.
- Socialization, which begins at birth, continues throughout the life course; at each stage the individual must adjust to a new set of social expectations.
- The life course is not experienced by all in the same ways, however; our socialization experiences are shaped by social and historical location.

☞ **LEARNING OBJECTIVES**

As you read Chapter 4, use these learning objectives to organize your notes. After completing your reading, briefly state an answer to each of the objectives, and review the text pages in parentheses.

1. Discuss major studies of feral and isolated children, as well as studies of deprived animals, and state what they demonstrate about the importance of early contact with other humans for the social development of children. (72-74)
2. Define socialization. (74)
3. Explain and distinguish between the theories of social development by Charles H. Cooley, George H. Mead, and Jean Piaget and consider the limits of applying Piaget's work to cultures around the globe. (74-77)
4. Review Freud's theory of personality development and note what sociologists appreciate about this theory as well as their criticisms of it. (77)
5. Discuss what the example of smoking tells us about processes of socialization. (78)
6. Describe ways in which gender socialization by the family channels human behavior. (78-80)
7. Identify the ways in which cultural stereotypes of the sexes are perpetuated in the mass media and how peer groups use media images to construct ideas about gender appropriate behavior. (80-81)

8. List and describe the influence of each agent of socialization on individuals. (81-84)
9. Define the term resocialization and discuss the process of resocialization that takes places within total institutions. (85)
10. Discuss socialization through the life course by summarizing each of the stages. (85-89)
11. Explain the influence of historical and social location on processes of socialization. (89)

☞ CHAPTER OUTLINE

I. **Genes or Environment?**
    A. Feral (wild) children, supposedly abandoned or lost by their parents at a very early age and then raised by animals, act like wild animals. Most social scientists believe that the children were raised by their parents as infants but then abandoned because of mental retardation.
    B. Isolated children show what humans might be like if secluded from society at an early age. Isabelle is a case in point. Although initially believed to be retarded, a surprising thing happened when she was given intensive language training. She began to acquire language and in only two years she had reached the normal intellectual level for her age.
    C. Research on children raised in orphanages, and cases like Genie's, the 13 1/2-year-old who had been kept locked in a small room for years, demonstrate the importance of early interaction for human development.
    D. Studies of monkeys raised in isolation have reached similar results. The longer and more severe the isolation, the more difficult adjustment becomes.
    E. Babies do not "naturally" develop into human adults; although their bodies grow, human interaction is required for them to acquire the traits we consider normal for human beings.

II. **The Social Development of the Self, Mind, and Emotions**
    A. Socialization is the process by which we learn the ways of our society.
    B. Charles H. Cooley (1864-1929) concluded that human development is socially created—that our sense of self develops from interaction with others. He coined the term "looking-glass self" to describe this process.
        1. According to Cooley, this process contains three steps: (1) we imagine how we look to others; (2) we interpret others' reactions (how they evaluate us); and (3) we develop a self-concept.
        2. A favorable reflection in the "social mirror" leads to a positive self-concept, while a negative reflection leads to a negative self-concept.
        3. Even if we misjudge others' reactions, the misjudgments become part of our self-concept.
        4. This development process is an ongoing, lifelong process.
    C. George H. Mead (1863-1931) agreed with Cooley, but added that play is critical to the development of a self. In play, we learn to take the role of others: to understand and anticipate how others feel and think.
        1. Mead concluded that children are first able to take only the role of significant others (parents or siblings, for example); as the self develops, children internalize the expectations of other people, and eventually the entire group. Mead referred to the norms, values, attitudes and expectations of people "in general" as the generalized other.
        2. According to Mead. the development of the self goes through stages: (1) imitation (children initially can only mimic the gestures and words of others); (2) play (beginning at age three, children play the roles of specific people, such as a

firefighter or the Lone Ranger); and (3) games (in the first years of school, children become involved in organized team games and must learn the role of each member of the team).

3.   He distinguished the "I" from the "me" in development of the self: the "I" component is the subjective, active, spontaneous, creative part of the social self (for instance, "I shoved him"), while the "me" component is the objective part—attitudes internalized from interactions with others (for instance, "He shoved me").

D.   After years of research, Jean Piaget (1896-1980) concluded that there are four stages in the development of cognitive skills.

1.   The sensorimotor stage (0-2): Understanding is limited to direct contact with the environment (touching, listening, seeing).

2.   The preoperational stage (2-7): Children develop the ability to use symbols (especially language) which allow them to experience things without direct contact.

3.   The concrete operational stage (7-12): Reasoning abilities become much more developed. Children now can understand numbers, causation, and speed, but have difficulty with abstract concepts such as truth.

4.   The formal operational stage (12+): Children become capable of abstract thinking, and can use rules to solve abstract problems ("If X is true, why doesn't Y follow?").

E.   While it appears that the looking-glass self, role taking and the social mind are universal phenomena, there is not consensus about the universality of Piaget's four stages of cognitive development.

1.   Some adults never appear to reach the fourth stage, whether due to particular social experiences or to biology.

2.   The content of what we learn varies from one culture to another; with very different experiences and the thinking processes that revolve around these experiences, we can not assume that the developmental sequences will be the same for everyone.

F.   Sigmund Freud (1856-1939) believed that personality consists of three elements—the id, ego, and superego.

1.   The id, inherited drives for self-gratification, demands fulfillment of basic needs such as attention, safety, food, and sex.

2.   The ego balances between the needs of the id and the demands of society.

3.   The superego, the social conscience we have internalized from social groups, gives us feelings of guilt or shame when we break rules, and feelings of pride and self-satisfaction when we follow them.

4.   Sociologists object to Freud's view that inborn and unconscious motivations are the primary reasons for human behavior, for this view denies the central tenet of sociology: that social factors shape people's behaviors.

G.   Emotions are not simply the result of biology; they also depend on socialization within a particular society.

H.   Most socialization is meant to turn us into conforming members of society. We do some things and not others as a result of socialization. When we contemplate an action, we know the emotion (good or bad) that would result; thus, society sets up controls on our behavior.

III.   Socialization Into Gender

A.   By expecting different behaviors from people because they are male or female, society nudges boys and girls in separate directions from an early age, and this foundation carries over into adulthood.

B.   Parents begin the process; researchers have concluded that in our society mothers unconsciously reward their female children for being passive and dependent and their male children for being active and independent.

C. The mass media reinforce society's expectations of gender in many ways:
1. Ads perpetuate stereotypes by portraying males as dominant and rugged and females as sexy and submissive.
2. On TV, male characters outnumber females two to one and are more likely to be portrayed in higher-status positions.
3. Males are much more likely than females to play video games; we have no studies of how these games affect their players' ideas of gender.
4. Sociologist Melissa Milkie concluded that males used media images to discover who they were and what was expected of them as males.

IV. Agents of Socialization
A. Our experiences in the family have a lifelong impact on us, laying down a basic sense of self, motivation, values, and beliefs.
1. Parents—often unaware of what they are doing—send subtle messages to their children about society's expectations for them as males or females.
2. Recent feminist analysis of gender socialization is tending to emphasize the multiple differences which may occur within gender, depending upon age, race, ethnicity, social class, religion, and sexual orientation.
B. Religion plays a major role in the socialization of many Canadians, even if they are not raised in a religious family. Religion especially influences morality, but also ideas about the dress, speech, and manners that are appropriate.
C. With more mothers working for wages today, day care has become a significant agent of socialization.
1. Researchers have found that the effects of day care depend on the child's background and the quality of the care provided.
2. Overall, the research findings suggest that children from stable homes receive no clear benefit or detriment from day care, and children in poverty and from dysfunctional families benefit from it.
D. Schools serve many manifest (intended) functions for society, including teaching skills and values thought to be appropriate. Schools also have several latent (unintended) functions.
1. At school children are placed outside the direct control of friends/relatives and exposed to new values and ways of looking at the world. They learn universality, or that the same rules apply to everyone.
2. Schools also have a hidden curriculum: values not explicitly taught but inherent in school activities.
E. One of the most significant aspects of education is that it exposes children to peer groups. A peer group is a group of persons of roughly the same age who are linked by common interests. Next to the family, peer groups are the most powerful socializing force in society.
F. Sports are also powerful socializing agents; children are taught not only physical skills but also values. Researchers have examined the role of sports in gender socialization.
G. The workplace is a major agent of socialization for adults; from jobs, we learn not only skills but also matching attitudes and values. We may engage in anticipatory socialization, learning to play a role before actually entering it, and enabling us to gradually identify with the role.

V. Resocialization
A. Resocialization refers to the process of learning new norms, values, attitudes and behaviors. Resocialization in its most common form occurs each time we learn

something contrary to our previous experiences, such as going to work in a new job. It can be an intense experience, although it does not have to be.

B.   Erving Goffman coined the term total institution to refer to a place—such as boot camps, prisons, concentration camps, or some mental hospitals, religious cults, and boarding schools—in which people are cut off from the rest of society and are under almost total control of agents of the institution.

1.   A person entering the institution is greeted with a degradation ceremony through which his or her current identity is stripped away and replaced (e.g., fingerprinting, shaving the head, banning personal items, and being forced to strip and wear a uniform).

2.   Total institutions are quite effective as a result of isolating people from outside influences and information; supervising their activities; suppressing previous roles, statuses, and norms, and replacing them with new rules and values; and controlling rewards and punishments.

VI.   **Socialization Through the Life Course**

A.   Socialization occurs throughout a person's entire lifetime and can be broken up into different stages.

B.   Childhood (birth to 12): In earlier times, children were seen as miniature adults, who served an apprenticeship. To keep them in line, they were beaten and subjected to psychological torture. The current view is that children are tender and innocent, and parents should guide the physical, emotional, and social development of their children, while providing them with care, comfort, and protection.

C.   Adolescence (13-17): Economic changes resulting from the Industrial Revolution brought about material surpluses that allowed millions of teenagers to remain outside the labor force, while at the same time the demand for education increased. Biologically equipped for both work and marriage but denied both, adolescents suffer inner turmoil and develop their own standards of clothing, hairstyles, language, music, and other claims to separate identities.

D.   Young Adulthood (18-29): Adult responsibilities are postponed through extended education. During this period the self becomes more stable, and the period usually is one of high optimism.

E.   The Middle Years (30-65): This can be separated into two periods.

1.   Early Middle Years: People are surer of themselves and their goals in life than before, but severe jolts such as divorce or being fired can occur. For Canadian women, it can be a trying period due to trying to "have it all"—job, family, and everything.

2.   Later Middle Years: A different view of life—trying to evaluate the past and to come to terms with what lies ahead—emerges. Individuals may feel they are not likely to get much farther in life, while health and mortality become concerns. However, for most people it is the most comfortable period in their entire lives.

F.   Older years (66 and beyond): This can also be separated into two periods.

1.   The Early Older Years: While we live longer and there has been an improvement in general health, older people are not given the respect they previously received, having undergone social devaluation. They often are viewed as people who once knew something worthwhile, but now can only offer useless advice. They become more concerned with death—that their time is "closing in" on them.

2.   The Later Older Years: This period is marked by growing frailty and illness, and eventually death.

G.   The social significance of the life course is how it is shaped by social factors—the time period in which the person is born and lives his or her life as well as social location, the individual's social class, gender and race.

☞ **KEY TERMS**

After studying the chapter, review the definition for each of the following terms.

agents of socialization: people or groups that affect our self-concept, attitudes or orientations towards life

anticipatory socialization: because one anticipates a future role, one learns part of it now

degradation ceremony: a term coined by Harold Garfinkel to describe an attempt to remake the self by stripping away an individual's self-identity and stamping a new identity in its place

ego: Freud's term for a balancing force between the id and the demands of society

feral children: children assumed to have been raised by animals, in the wilderness isolated from other humans

gender role: the behaviors and attitudes considered appropriate because one is male or female

gender socialization: the ways in which society sets children onto different courses in life because they are male or female

generalized other: the norms, values, attitudes, and expectations of people "in general"; the child's ability to take the role of the generalized other is a significant step in the development of a self

id: Freud's term for the individual's inborn basic drives

latent function: the unintended consequences of people's actions that help to keep a social system in equilibrium

life course: the sequence of events that we experience as we journey from birth to death

looking-glass self: a term coined by Charles Horton Cooley to refer to the process by which our self develops through internalizing others' reactions to us

manifest function: the intended consequences of people's actions designed to help some part of the social system

mass media: forms of communication, such as radio, newspapers, and television, directed to huge audiences

peer group: a group of individuals roughly the same age and linked by common interests

personal identity kit: items people use to decorate their bodies

resocialization: process of learning new norms, values, attitudes, and behaviors

self: the uniquely human capacity of being able to see ourselves "from the outside"; the picture we gain of how others see us

significant other: an individual who significantly influences someone else's life

social environment: the entire human environment, including direct contact with others

social inequality: a social condition in which privileges and obligations are given to some but denied to others

socialization: the process by which people learn the characteristics of their group—the attitudes, values, and actions thought appropriate for them

superego: Freud's term for the conscience, the internalized norms and values of our social groups

taking the role of the other: putting oneself in someone else's shoes; understanding how someone else feels and thinks and thus anticipating how that person will act

total institution: a place in which people are cut off from the rest of society and are almost totally controlled by the officials who run the place

☞ KEY PEOPLE

Review the major theoretical contributions or findings of these people.

Patricia Adler, Steven Kless, and Peter Adler: These sociologists have documented how peer groups socialize children into gender-appropriate behavior.

Charles H. Cooley: Cooley studied the development of the self, coining the term "the looking-glass self."

Sigmund Freud: Freud developed a theory of personality development that took into consideration inborn drives (id), the internalized norms and values of one's society (superego), and the individual's ability to balance the two competing forces (ego).

Erving Goffman: Goffman studied the process of resocialization within total institutions.

Susan Goldberg and Michael Lewis: Two psychologists studied how parents' unconscious expectations about gender behavior are communicated to their young children.

Harry and Margaret Harlow: These psychologists studied the behavior of monkeys raised in isolation and found that the length of time they were in isolation affected their ability to overcome the effects of isolation.

Mary and James Maxwell: The Maxwells studied socialization processes in a private school.

George Herbert Mead: Mead emphasized the importance of play in the development of the self, noting that children learn to take on the role of the other and eventually learn to perceive themselves as others do.

Melissa Milkie: This sociologist studied how adolescent boys use media images to discover who they are as males.

Jean Piaget: Piaget studied the development of reasoning skills in children.

☞ SELF-TEST

After completing this self-test, check your answers against the Answer Key at the back of this Study Guide and against the text on page(s) indicated in parentheses.

MULTIPLE CHOICE QUESTIONS

1. Which of the following statements best describes feral children? (72-73)
   a. After their parents supposedly abandoned or lost them, they were raised by someone else.
   b. They supposedly were abandoned or lost by their parents and then raised by animals.
   c. They are considered by most social scientists to be very significant to our knowledge of human nature.
   d. They quickly recovered from their experiences of deprivation once they were rescued.

2. What conclusions can be drawn from the case of Isabelle? (72-73)
   a. Humans have no natural language.
   b. Isabelle was retarded.
   c. A person who has been isolated cannot progress through normal learning stages.
   d. All of the above.

3. What conclusions does the textbook suggest can be drawn from the case of Genie? (73)
   a. Mental retardation is biological.
   b. Early physical contact does little to change the intelligence levels of children.
   c. If bonding and learning to communicate with others does not occur prior to age 13, the biological window of opportunity may close.
   d. Linguistic acquisition in the teenage years is fundamental to development into adulthood.

4. What do studies of isolated rhesus monkeys demonstrate? (73-74)
    a. The monkeys were able to adjust to monkey life after a time.
    b. They instinctively knew how to enter into "monkey interaction" with other monkeys.
    c. They knew how to engage in sexual intercourse.
    d. The monkeys were not able to adjust fully to monkey life and did not know instinctively how to enter into interaction with other monkeys.

5. Which of the following statements about the looking-glass self is *incorrect*? (74)
    a. The development of self is an ongoing, lifelong process.
    b. We move beyond the looking-glass self as we mature.
    c. The process of the looking-glass self applies to old age.
    d. The self is always in process.

6. According to Mead's theory, at what stage do children pretend to take the roles of specific people? (75)
    a. imitation
    b. game
    c. play
    d. generalized other

7. To George Mead, what is the "I"? (76)
    a. It is the self as subject.
    b. It is the self as object.
    c. It is the same as the id.
    d. It represents the passive robot aspect of human behavior.

8. According to Jean Piaget, at what stage do children develop the ability to use symbols? (76)
    a. sensorimotor
    b. preoperational
    c. concrete operational
    d. formal operational

9. Researchers have suggested that these stages of cognitive development as identified by Piaget may be modified by: (77)
    a. biological factors
    b. the influence of the mass media
    c. psychoanalysis
    d. social experiences

10. What is the term Freud used to describe the balancing force between the inborn drives for self-gratification and the demands of society? (77)
    a. id
    b. superego
    c. ego
    d. libido

11.   Why have sociologists been critical of Freud's theories? (77)
    a.   Sociologists object to the view that unconscious motivations are the primary reasons for human behavior.
    b.   Freud's theories deny the critical principle of sociology: that social factors underlie people's behaviors.
    c.   Freud assumed that what is "male" is "normal."
    d.   All of the above.

12.   What is the significance of the example of smoking for our understanding of socialization? (78)
    a.   Young people around the world feel the same pressures to smoke.
    b.   It illustrates that the pressures from our social environment influence our behavior.
    c.   For the most part, smoking results in biological pressures.
    d.   Smoking tells us very little about socialization.

13.   According to this chapter, socialization is significant because: (78)
    a.   it allows us to overcome innate biological instincts.
    b.   it ensures that we abide by the rules of society.
    c.   it shapes our fundamental sense of self.
    d.   it helps us learn appropriate male and female roles.

14.   What do we call the ways in which society sets children onto different courses for life purely because they are male or female? (78)
    a.   sex socialization.
    b.   gender socialization
    c.   masculinization and feminization
    d.   brainwashing

15.   What conclusions did psychologists Susan Goldberg and Michael Lewis reach after observing mothers with their six-month-old infants in a laboratory setting? (79)
    a.   The mothers kept their male children closer to them.
    b.   They kept their male and female children about the same distance from them.
    c.   They touched and spoke more to their sons.
    d.   They unconsciously rewarded daughters for being passive and dependent.

16.   Which of the following statements reflects the findings of research by Melissa Milkie? (81)
    a.   Young males actively used media images to help them understand what was expected of them as males in our society.
    b.   Young males avoided talking about male images in television and movies because they wanted to avoid being labeled a "weenie."
    c.   Young females are passive consumers of media images, rather than active ones.
    d.   Young males were very similar to young females in how they used media images as role models for "cool" behavior.

17.   What term does Erving Goffman use to define the family? (81)
    a.   a total institution
    b.   a backstage setting
    c.   a socialization depot
    d.   a primary agent of socialization

18. What is it that participation in religious services teaches us? (82)
    a. beliefs about the hereafter
    b. ideas about dress
    c. speech and manners appropriate for formal occasions
    d. All of the above

19. Which of the following statements summarizes the research findings on the impact that day care has on preschool children? (82)
    a. Regardless of the quality, day care benefits children.
    b. Children from poor and dysfunctional families do not benefit from day care, while children from stable families do.
    c. Children from poor and dysfunctional families benefit from quality day care.
    d. It is not the quality of the day care, but the quality of home life that makes the difference.

20. What is it that teachers are doing when they use stories and examples to teach math and English grammar that contain lessons in gender inequality? (82-83)
    a. following the formal curriculum
    b. teaching the hidden curriculum
    c. fulfilling a manifest function of education
    d. satisfying a latent function of education

21. What conclusions can be drawn about peer groups and academic achievement from Adler, Kless, and Adler's research? (83)
    a. Both boys and girls avoid doing well academically.
    b. Boys want to do well academically in order to boost their standing in the peer group, but girls avoid being labeled as smart, because it will hurt their image.
    c. Both boys and girls believe that good grades will translate into greater popularity among their respective peer groups.
    d. For boys, to do well academically is to lose popularity, while for girls, getting good grades increases social standing.

22. Under which of the following conditions is resocialization likely to occur? (85)
    a. When we take a new job.
    b. If we were to join a cult.
    c. When we are sent to military boot camp.
    d. All of the above would involve resocialization.

23. Which of the following statements about total institutions is incorrect? (85)
    a. They suppress preexisting statuses, so that the inmates will learn that previous roles mean nothing and that the only thing that counts is their current role.
    b. They are not very effective in stripping away people's personal freedom.
    c. They are isolated, with barriers to keep inmates in and keep outsiders from interfering.
    d. They suppress the norms of the "outside world," replacing them with their own values, rules and interpretations.

24. What is it that historians have concluded about childhood? (86-87)
    a. It has always existed as a special time in a child's life.
    b. It was not as harsh in the past as it is today.
    c. It didn't exist in the past, as we know it; children were viewed as miniature adults.
    d. It was longer in the past, because children stayed home until they were married.

25. Which of the following best describes the "sandwich generation"? (88)
    a. women who are in the early middle years, caring for young children
    b. grandparents who find themselves saddled with the care of grandchildren while their adult children are employed in the workforce
    c. older people who are caught between the world of retirement and their impending death
    d. people in their later middle years who are caught between caring for their own children and their aging parents

TRUE-FALSE QUESTIONS

T F   1.   Without language, there can be no culture. (73)
T F   2.   Studies of feral and isolated children demonstrate that some of the characteristics that we take for granted as being "human" traits result from our basic instincts. (72-73)
T F   3.   Because monkeys and humans are so similar, it is possible to reach conclusions about human behavior from animal studies. (74)
T F   4.   George H. Mead introduced the concept of the generalized other to sociology. (75)
T F   5.   Research by Jean Piaget concluded that children undergo two stages in the development of their reasoning abilities. (76)
T F   6.   According to Freud, the ego is the balancing force between the id and the demands of society that suppress it. (77)
T F   7.   Since smoking results from a biological addiction, socialization has very little to do with it. (78)
T F   8.   Socialization is important because it shapes what we desire, who we love, and how we experience sadness. (78)
T F   9.   Because social groups do not see boys and girls as fundamentally different from one another, they do not encourage them to develop different aspirations in life. (78)
T F   10. Advertisements continue to perpetuate gender stereotypes by portraying males as dominant and rugged and females as sexy and submissive. (80)
T F   11. Researchers have found that video games have a profound impact on their players' ideas of gender. (80)
T F   12. The benefits of day care depend on the quality of the day care. (82)
T F   13. A latent function of education is to provide a broader perspective to prepare children to take a role in the world beyond the family. (82)
T F   14. Next to the family, the peer group is the most powerful socializing force in society. (83)
T F   15. Resocialization always requires learning a radically different perspective. (85)
T F   16. Total institutions are very effective in stripping away people's personal freedom. (85)
T F   17. Adolescence is a social creation in industrialized societies. (87)
T F   18. In the middle years, some Canadian women find that "having it all" may be somewhat a myth. (88)
T F   19. Industrialization brought with it a delay in the onset of old age. (89)
T F   20. Sociologists consider the stages of the life course to be a universal process; that is, all people experience these stages in the same way. (89)

FILL-IN QUESTIONS

1. Sociologists are interested in studying how the _____ influence(s) human experience. (72)
2. _____ is the process by which people learn the characteristics of their group—the attitudes, values, and actions thought appropriate for them. (74)

3.   Charles H. Cooley coined the term _____ to describe the process by which a sense of self develops. (74)

4.   _____ is the term Mead used to describe someone, such as a parent and/or a sibling, who plays a major role in our social development. (74)

5.   According to George Herbert Mead, the development of the self through role-taking goes through three stages: (1) _____ ; (2) _____; and (3) _____. (75)

6.   The idea that personality consists of the id, ego, and superego was developed by _____. (77)

7.   We refer to the behaviors and attitudes which are considered appropriate for females and males as _____. (78)

8.   Television, music, and advertising are all types of _____ which reinforce society's expectations of gender. (80-81)

9.   _____ include the family, school, religion, peers, mass media, and workplace. (81)

10. Transmitting skills of reading, writing, and arithmetic is part of the _____ of education. (82)

11. The _____ refers to values that may not be taught explicitly, but nevertheless form an inherent part of a school's "message." (82-83)

12. _____ are made up of individuals the same age linked by common interests. (83)

13. The mental rehearsal for some future activity, or learning to play a role before actually entering it, is referred to as _____. (83-84)

14. Resocialization generally takes place in _____ such as boot camps, prisons, and concentration camps. (85)

15. _____ refers to the attempt to remake the self by stripping away an individual's self-identity and stamping a new identity in its place. (85)

MATCH THESE SOCIAL SCIENTISTS WITH THEIR CONTRIBUTIONS

__1. Erving Goffman
__2. George Herbert Mead
__3. Charles H. Cooley
__4. Jean Piaget
__5. Harry and Margaret Harlow
__6. Sigmund Freud
__7. Melissa Milkie

a. *coined the term "looking-glass self"*
b. *conducted studies of isolated rhesus monkeys*
c. *coined the term "generalized other"*
d. *studied total institutions*
e. *asserted that human behavior is based on unconscious drives*
f. *discovered that there are four stages in cognitive development*
g. *studied the impact of media messages on adolescent males*

ESSAY QUESTIONS

1.   Explain what is necessary in order for us to develop into full human beings.
2.   Why do sociologists argue that socialization is a process and not a product?
3.   How would you answer the question "What is the sociological significance of the life course?"

"DOWN-TO-EARTH SOCIOLOGY"

1. Think about learning the emotions that are appropriate for you because of your age, race or ethnicity, gender, and social class background. How were you socialized into emotions; for example, "little boys don't cry" and "little girls don't fight"?

2. Have you ever played video games? Have you ever thought about the images of gender that these games convey? Would you agree that they contain disturbing gender messages (p. 80)?

3. What kinds of things did you do in anticipation of being in college? In you first few months in school, what kinds of things did you have to learn that were new or different?

4. What are some of the ways in which private school resocializes students (p. 86)? What are some examples of degradation ceremonies? What is the point of subjecting new students to this experience?

5. What are some of the challenges facing you at whatever stage in the life course you are at right now? How have changes in society contributed to these challenges?

CHAPTER 5

SOCIAL STRUCTURE AND SOCIAL INTERACTION

☞ CHAPTER SUMMARY

- There are two levels of sociological analysis; macrosociology investigates the large-scale features of social structure, while microsociology focuses on social interaction. Functional and conflict theorists tend to use a macrosociological approach while symbolic interactionists and postmodernists are more likely to use a microsociological approach.
- The term social structure refers to a society's framework, which forms an envelope around us and sets limits on our behavior.
- Social institutions are the organized and standard means that a society develops to meet its basic needs. Functionalists view social institutions as established ways of meeting universal group needs; however, conflict theorists see social institutions as the primary means by which the elite maintains its privileged position.
- Over time, social structure undergoes changes—sometimes very dramatic—as illustrated by Durkheim's concepts of mechanical and organic solidarity, and Tönnies' constructs of *Gemeinschaft* and *Gesellschaft* at the macro-level of society.
- An individual's location in the social structure affects his or her perceptions, attitudes, and behaviors. Culture, social class, social status, roles, groups, and institutions are the major components of the social structure.
- Groups are the essence of life in society. By standing between the individual and the larger society, groups help to prevent anomie. An essential feature of a group is that its members have something in common and that they believe what they have in common makes a difference. Society is the largest and most complex group that sociologists study.
- The following types of groups exist within society: primary groups, secondary groups, in-groups and out-groups, reference groups, and social networks. Changed technology has given birth to a new type of group—the electronic community.
- Group dynamics concern the ways in which individuals affect groups and the ways in which groups affect individuals. Group size is a significant aspect of group dynamics. Leaders can be either instrumental (task-oriented) or expressive (socioemotional); both are essential for the functioning of the group. Three main leadership styles are: authoritarian, democratic, and laissez-faire.
- The Asch experiment demonstrates the influence of peer groups over their members, while the Milgram experiment shows how powerfully people are influenced by authority. Groupthink, which occurs when political leaders become isolated, poses a serious threat to society's well-being.
- In contrast to functionalist and conflict theorists, who as macrosociologists focus on the "big picture," symbolic interactionists tend to be microsociologists who look at social interaction in everyday life. They examine how people look at things and how that, in turn, affects their behavior.
- Stereotypes, assumptions we make about others based on their visible characteristics, guide our behavior toward them; they, in turn, are influenced to behave in ways that reinforce our stereotypes.

- Symbolic interactionists note that each of us is surrounded by a "personal bubble" that we carefully protect. The size of the bubble varies from one culture to another. North Americans have four different "distance zones": intimate, personal, social, and public.
- The dramaturgical analysis provided by Erving Goffman analyzes everyday life in terms of the stage. At the core of this approach is the analysis of the impressions we attempt to make on others by using sign-vehicles (setting, appearance, and manner), teamwork, and face-saving behavior.
- Ethnomethodologists try to uncover our background assumptions which provide us with basic ideas about the way life is. The social construction of reality refers to how we each create a view, or understanding, of how our world is.
- Both macrosociology and microsociology are needed to understand human behavior because we must grasp both social structure and social interaction.

☞ LEARNING OBJECTIVES

As you read Chapter 5, use these learning objectives to organize your notes. After completing your reading, briefly state an answer to each of the objectives, and review the text pages in parentheses.

1. Differentiate between macrosociology and microsociology and indicate which is most likely to be used by functionalists, conflict theorists, and symbolic interactionists. (94)
2. Discuss social structure and explain why a person's location in this structure affects his or her perceptions, attitudes, and behaviors. (95-96)
3. Explain what social institutions are, identify the social institutions common to all industrialized societies, and summarize the basic features of each. (96)
4. Compare and contrast functionalists' and conflict theorists' views of social institutions. (98-99)
5. Use Durkheim's concepts of mechanical and organic solidarity and Tönnies' typologies of *Gemeinschaft* and *Gesellschaft* to explain what holds societies together, and discuss their continuing relevance. (99-100)
6. Define the following concepts: culture, social class, social status, roles, and groups. (100-104)
7. Explain why groups are so important to individuals and to societies. (103)
8. Distinguish between a group, an aggregate, and a category. (104)
9. Define each of the following: primary groups, secondary groups, in-groups and out-groups, reference groups, and social networks. (104-107)
10. Identify the changes that have contributed to the emergence of the electronic community. (107)
11. Explain the concept of group dynamics and indicate how group size affects interaction. (108-110)
12. Describe the two types of leaders in groups, the three basic styles of leadership and why researchers have concluded that democratic leaders are more effective than authoritarian or laissez-faire ones. (110-111)
13. Discuss the impact of peer pressure on conformity by analyzing the Asch experiment. (111-112)
14. Explain the following about the Milgram experiment: purpose of study, how it was conducted, conclusions reached, and why the methodology was questioned. (112-113)
15. Discuss groupthink, explain how it can be dangerous for a society, and identify how this can be prevented. (113-114)
16. State the key assumptions of the symbolic interaction perspective regarding social life. (114)
17. Explain how stereotypes influence an individual's expectations and behavior. (114)
18. Explain the concepts of personal space and touching and discuss how they are used differently in different cultures. (114-116)
19. Outline the key components of the dramaturgical view of everyday life and discuss how we manage our impression using sign-vehicles, teamwork, and face-saving behavior. (116-120)
20. Discuss what background assumptions are, according to ethnomethodology. (120)

21. Explain what "the social construction of reality" means and how this is related to the Thomas theorem. (120-122)
22. Indicate why macrosociology and microsociology are both needed to understand social life. (122)

☞ CHAPTER OUTLINE

I.   **Levels of Sociological Analysis**
    A.   Macrosociology places the focus on large-scale features of social structure. It investigates large-scale social forces and the effects they have on entire societies and the groups within them. It is utilized by functionalist and conflict theorists.
    B.   Microsociology places the emphasis on social interaction and language, or what people do when they come together and how they communicate with each other. Symbolic interactionism and postmodernism are examples.

II.   **The Macrosociological Perspective: Social Structure**
    A.   Social structure is defined as the patterned relationships between people that persist over time. Behaviors and attitudes are determined by our location in the social structure. Components of social structure are culture, social class, social status, roles, groups, and institutions.
    B.   Social institutions are society's standard ways of meeting its basic needs.
        1.   The family, religion, law, politics, economics, education, science, medicine, and the military all are social institutions.
        2.   Social institutions are sociologically significant because they set limits and provide guidelines for our behavior.
    C.   The mass media is an emerging social institution; it influences our attitudes toward social issues, other people, and even our self-concept. Of interest is who controls the mass media. Functionalists would say that the mass media represent the varied interests of the many groups that make up the nation, while conflict theorists would see that the interests of the political elite are represented.
    D.   The functionalists and conflict theorists differ in how they see social institutions.
        1.   Functionalists view social institutions as established ways of meeting universal group needs, including replacing members; socializing new members; producing and distributing goods and services; preserving order; and providing a sense of purpose.
        2.   Conflict theorists look at social institutions as the primary means by which the elite maintains its privileged position.
    E.   Changes in social structure occur as a result of changes in culture, globalization, shifts in social classes and racial and ethnic groups, and so forth.
    F.   Many sociologists have tried to find an answer to the question of what holds society together.
        1.   Social cohesion is the degree to which members of a society feel united by shared values and other social bonds.
        2.   Emile Durkheim used mechanical solidarity and organic solidarity to explain what holds society together. Mechanical solidarity is a collective consciousness that people experience as a result of performing the same or similar tasks while organic solidarity is a collective consciousness based on the interdependence brought about by the division of labor—how people divide up tasks.
        3.   Ferdinand Tönnies analyzed how intimate community (*Gemeinschaft*) was being replaced by impersonal associations (*Gesellschaft*). *Gemeinschaft* is a society in

which life is intimate; a community in which everyone knows everyone else and people share a sense of togetherness. *Gesellschaft* is a society dominated by impersonal relationships, individual accomplishments, and self-interest.

    4.   These concepts are still relevant today, helping us to understand contemporary events such as the rise of Islamic fundamentalism.

G.   Culture refers to a group's language, beliefs, values, behaviors, and gestures. It includes the material objects used by a group. It determines what kind of people we will become.

H.   Social class is based on income, education, and occupational prestige. Large numbers of people who have similar amounts of income and education and who work at jobs that are roughly comparable in prestige make up a social class.

I.   Social status refers to the positions that an individual occupies.

    1.   Status set refers to all the statuses or positions that an individual occupies.

    2.   Ascribed statuses are positions an individual either inherits at birth or receives involuntarily later in life. Achieved statuses are positions that are earned, accomplished, or involve at least some effort or activity on the individual's part.

    3.   Status symbols are signs that identify a status.

    4.   A master status—such as being male or female—cuts across the other statuses that an individual occupies. Status inconsistency is a contradiction or mismatch between statuses.

J.   Roles are the behaviors, obligations, and privileges attached to a status. The individual occupies a status, but plays a role. Roles are an essential component of culture because they lay out what is expected of people, and as individuals perform their roles, those roles mesh together to form the society.

III.   Social Groups and Societies

A.   Groups are the essence of life in society; the groups to which we belong help to determine our goals and values, how we feel about ourselves, and even how we feel about life itself.

B.   An essential element of a social group is that its members have something in common and that they believe what they have in common makes a difference.

C.   Society, which consists of people who share a culture and a territory, is the largest and most complex group that sociologists study.

IV.   Groups Within Society

A.   Groups are viewed as a buffer between individuals and society.

    1.   Durkheim believed that small groups serve as a sort of lifeline that helps to prevent anomie.

    2.   Sociologists distinguish aggregates and categories from groups. An aggregate is made up of individuals who temporarily share the same physical space but do not have a sense of belonging together; a category is a collection of people who have similar characteristics. Unlike groups, the individuals who make up aggregates or categories do not interact with one another or take one another into account.

B.   Sociologist Charles H. Cooley used the term "primary group" to refer to groups characterized by cooperative, intimate, long-term, face-to-face relationships.

    1.   The primary group becomes part of the individual's identity and the lens through which to view life.

    2.   Primary groups are essential to an individual's psychological well-being, since humans have an intense need for associations that provide feelings of self-esteem.

    3.   Some primary groups can be dysfunctional. Examples are families whose members quarrel and humiliate one another and gangs that purposely set themselves against

society. Groups can become dysfunctional if they break down throughout society and cease to serve a purpose.

C. Secondary groups are larger, relatively temporary, more anonymous, formal, and impersonal than are primary groups, and are based on some interest or activity.
    1. Members are likely to interact on the basis of specific roles, such as president, manager, worker, or student.
    2. In industrial societies, secondary groups have multiplied and become essential to our welfare.
    3. Secondary groups tend to break down into primary groups within the larger group, such as friendship cliques at school or work. The primary group serves as a buffer between the individual and the needs of the secondary group.

D. Groups toward which individuals feel loyalty are called in-groups, while those toward which they feel antagonisms are called out-groups.
    1. The division is significant sociologically because in-groups provide a sense of identification or belonging and exercise a high degree of control over their members.
    2. In-groups also foster ethnocentrism, encouraging members to judge their own accomplishments and characteristics as superior. Sociologist Robert K. Merton identified a double standard that this produces: the behaviors of an in-group's members are seen as virtues, while the same behaviors by members of an out-group are viewed as vices.
    3. Dividing the world into "we" and "them" can sometimes lead to acts directed against the out-groups.

E. Reference groups are the groups we use as standards to evaluate ourselves, whether or not we actually belong to those groups.
    1. They exert great influence over our behavior; people may change their clothing, hair style, speech, and other characteristics to match what the reference group would expect of them.
    2. Having two reference groups that clearly conflict with each other can produce intense internal conflict.

F. Social networks consist of people linked by various social ties.
    1. Interaction takes place within social networks that connect us to the larger society.
    2. Stanley Milgram did an experiment which demonstrated how small our social world really is; he found that social networks are so interrelated that almost everyone in the U.S. is connected by just five links.
    3. The term "networking" refers to the conscious use or even cultivation of contacts that people think will be helpful to them, for instance, by joining and belonging to clubs. Many networks are hard to break into; the "old boy" network, for instance, tends to keep the best positions available to men only, rather than women.

G. In the 1990s, due to technology, an entirely new type of human group made its appearance—the electronic community.
    1. Through the Internet, people around the world interact with one another in news groups.
    2. While most news groups are only an interesting, new way of communicating, some meet our definition of a group, because the people who use them have established relationships and think of themselves as belonging together.

V.   Group Dynamics
A. How individuals affect groups and groups affect individuals is known as group dynamics.
    1. The study of group dynamics focuses on group size, leadership, conformity and decision making.

2. Sociologists recognize a small group as one that is small enough for everyone in it to interact directly with all the other members.

B. As sociologist Georg Simmel (1858-1918) noted, the size of the group is significant for its dynamics.

1. A dyad is a social group containing two members. It is the smallest and most fragile of all human groupings. Marriages and love affairs are examples: if one member loses interest, the dyad collapses.

2. A triad is a group of three persons—a married couple with a first child, for example. Triads basically are stronger than dyads, but still are extremely unstable. It is not uncommon for the bonds between two members to seem stronger, with the third person feeling hurt and excluded.

3. As more members are added to a group, intensity decreases and stability increases, for there are more linkages among more people within the group. The groups develop a more formal structure to accomplish their goals, for instance, by having a president, treasurer, etc. This structure enables groups to survive over time.

4. Research by Darley and Latané found that as groups grow larger, they tend to break into smaller groups, people are less willing to take individual responsibility (diffusion of responsibility), and they interact more formally towards one another.

C. A leader may be defined as someone who influences the behavior of others.

1. There are two types of group leaders. Instrumental (task-oriented) leaders are those who try to keep the group moving toward its goals, reminding the members of what they are trying to accomplish. Expressive (socioemotional) leaders are those who are less likely to be recognized as leaders but help with the group's morale. These leaders may have to minimize the friction that instrumental leaders necessarily create.

2. There are three types of leadership styles. Authoritarian leaders are those who give orders and frequently do not explain why they praise or condemn a person's work. Democratic leaders are those who try to gain a consensus by explaining proposed actions, suggesting alternative approaches, and giving "facts" as the basis for their evaluation of the members' work. Laissez-faire leaders are those who are very passive and give the group almost total freedom to do as it wishes.

3. Psychologists Ronald Lippitt and Ralph White discovered that the leadership styles produced different results when used on small groups of young boys. Under authoritarian leaders the boys became either aggressive or apathetic; under democratic leaders they were more personal and friendly; and under laissez-faire leaders they asked more questions, made fewer decisions, and were notable for their lack of achievement.

4. Different situations require different leadership styles.

5. Sociologists would disagree that people are born to be leaders. Rather, they find that people with certain characteristics are more likely to become leaders—those who represent the group's values, are seen as capable of leading the group out of crisis, are more talkative, express determination and self-confidence, are taller or are judged better looking.

D. A study by Dr. Solomon Asch indicates that people are strongly influenced by peer pressure. Asch was interested in seeing whether individuals would resist the temptation to change a correct response to an incorrect response because of peer pressure.

1. Asch held cards up in front of small groups of people and asked them which sets of cards matched; one at a time, they were supposed to respond aloud. All but one of the group members were confederates, having been told in advance by the researcher how to answer the question.

2.   After two trials in which everyone answered correctly, the confederates intentionally answered incorrectly, as they had been previously instructed to do.

3.   Of the fifty people tested, 33 percent ended up giving the incorrect answers of the rest of the group at least half of the time, even though they knew the answers were wrong; only 25 percent always gave the right answer despite the peer pressure.

E.   Dr. Stanley Milgram sought to determine why otherwise "good people" apparently participated in the Nazis' slaughter of Jews and others.

1.   He conducted experiments in which one person (the "teacher") was instructed to administer an electric shock to the other person (the "learner") for each wrong answer given to certain questions, and to increase the voltage of the shock after each wrong answer.

2.   In fact, the "learner" was playing a role, intentionally giving wrong answers but only pretending to be receiving an electrical shock.

3.   Since a person in apparent authority (scientist, white coat, university laboratory) continually stated that the experiment had to go on, most of the "teachers" gave in to that authority and continued to administer the "shocks" even when they appeared to produce extreme pain.

4.   The scientific community was disturbed not only by Milgram's findings but also by his methods. Associations of social researchers accordingly adopted codes of ethics to require that subjects be informed of the nature and purpose of social research, and almost all deception was banned.

F.   Sociologist Irving Janis coined the word "groupthink" to refer to situations in which a group of people think alike and any suggestion of alternatives becomes a sign of disloyalty. Even moral judgments are put aside for the perceived welfare of the group.

1.   The Asch and Milgram experiments demonstrate how groupthink can develop.

2.   Groupthink can be prevented only by insuring that leaders regularly are exposed to individuals who have views conflicting with those of the inner circle.

VI.   The Microsociological Perspective: Social Interaction in Everyday Life

A.   The microsociological approach places emphasis on face-to-face social interaction, or what people do when they are in the presence of one another.

B.   Symbolic interactionists are interested in the symbols that people use to define their worlds, how people look at things, and how that affects their behavior. Included within this perspective are studies of stereotypes, personal space and touching.

1.   Stereotypes are used in everyday life. First impressions are shaped by the assumptions one person makes about another person's sex, race, age, and physical appearance. Such assumptions affect one's ideas about the person and how one acts toward that person. Stereotypes tend to bring out the very kinds of behavior that fit the stereotype.

2.   Personal space refers to the physical space that surrounds us and that we claim as our own. The amount of personal space people prefer varies from one culture to another.

3.   Anthropologist Edward Hall found that North Americans use four different distance zones: (1) Intimate distance—about 18 inches from the body—for lovemaking, wrestling, comforting and protecting. (2) Personal distance—from 18 inches to 4 feet—for friends, acquaintances, and ordinary conversations. (3) Social distance— from 4 feet to 12 feet—for impersonal or formal relationships such as job interviews. (4) Public distance—beyond 12 feet—for even more formal relationships such as separating dignitaries and public speakers from the general public.

4.   From our culture we learn rules about touching. Both the frequency and the meaning of touching vary from one culture to the next. Men and women react differently to being touched.

C.   Dramaturgy is an analysis of how we present ourselves in everyday life.

1.   Dramaturgy is the name given to an approach pioneered by Erving Goffman analyzing social life in terms of drama or the stage.

2.   According to Goffman, socialization prepares people for learning to perform on the stage of everyday life. Front stage is where performances are given (wherever lines are delivered). Back stage is where people rest from their performances, discuss their presentations, and plan future performances.

3.   Role performance is the particular emphasis or interpretation that an individual gives a role, the person's "style." Role conflict occurs when the expectations attached to one role are incompatible with the expectations of another role—in other words, conflict between roles. Role strain refers to conflicts that someone feels within a role.

4.   Impression management is the person's efforts to manage the impressions that others receive of her or him.

5.   Three types of sign-vehicles are used to communicate information about the self: (1) social setting—where the action unfolds, which includes scenery (furnishings used to communicate messages); (2) appearance—how a person looks when he or she plays his or her role, and this includes props which decorate the person; and (3) manner—the attitudes demonstrated as an individual plays her or his roles.

6.   Teamwork, when two or more players work together to make sure a performance goes off as planned, shows that we are adept players.

7.   When a performance doesn't come off, we engage in face-saving behavior—ignoring flaws in someone's performance.

D.   Ethnomethodology involves the discovery of rules concerning our views of the world and how people ought to act.

1.   Ethnomethodologists try to uncover people's background assumptions, which form the basic core of one's reality, and provide basic rules concerning our view of the world and of how people ought to act.

2.   Harold Garfinkel founded the ethnomethodological approach.

E.   The social construction of reality refers to what people define as real because or their background assumptions and life experiences.

1.   Symbolic interactionists believe that people define their own reality and then live within those definitions.

2.   The Thomas theorem (by sociologist W. I. Thomas) states, "If people define situations as real, they are real in their consequences."

VII.   **The Need for Both Macrosociology and Microsociology**

A.   To understand human behavior, it is necessary to grasp both social structure (macrosociology) and social interaction (microsociology).

B.   Both are necessary for us to understand social life fully because each in its own way adds to our knowledge of human experience.

☞ KEY TERMS

After studying the chapter, review the definitions of the following terms.

achieved statuses: positions that are earned, accomplished, or involve at least some effort or activity on the individual's part

aggregate: individuals who temporarily share the same physical space but do not see themselves as belonging together

appearance: how an individual looks when playing a role

ascribed statuses: positions an individual either inherits at birth or receives involuntarily later in life

authoritarian leader: a leader who leads by giving orders

back stage: where people rest from their performances, discuss their presentations, and plan future performances

background assumptions: deeply embedded common understandings, or basic rules, concerning our view of the world and how people ought to act

category: people who have similar characteristics

clique: clusters of people within a larger group who choose to interact with one another; an internal faction

coalition: the alignment of some members of a group against others

definition of the situation: the way we look at matters in life; the way we define reality or some particular situation

democratic leader: a leader who leads by trying to reach a consensus

division of labor: the splitting of a group's or a society's tasks into specialties

dramaturgy: the name given to an approach, pioneered by Erving Goffman, analyzing social life in terms of drama or the stage; also called dramaturgical analysis

dyad: the smallest possible group, consisting of two persons

electronic community: individuals who more or less regularly interact with one another on the Internet

"electronic primary group": individuals who regularly interact with one another on the Internet, who see themselves as a group. and who develop close ties with one another

ethnomethodology: the study of how people use background assumptions to make sense of life

exchange theory: a theory of behavior that assumes human actions are motivated by a desire to maximize rewards and minimize costs

expressive leader: an individual who increases harmony and minimizes conflict in a group; also known as a socioemotional leader

face-saving behavior: techniques used to salvage a performance that is going sour

front stage: where performances are given

functional requisites: the major tasks that a society must fulfill if it is to survive

Gemeinschaft: a type of society in which life is intimate; a community in which everyone knows everyone else and people share a sense of togetherness

Gesellschaft: a type of society dominated by impersonal relationships, individual accomplishments, and self-interests

group: defined differently by various sociologists, but in a general sense, people who have something in common and who believe that what they have in common is significant; also called a social group

group dynamics: the ways in which individuals affect groups and the ways in which groups affect individuals

groupthink: Irving Janis's term for a narrowing of thought by a group of people, leading to the perception that there is only one correct answer, in which the suggestion of alternatives becomes a sign of disloyalty

impression management: the term used by Erving Goffman to describe people's efforts to control the impressions that others receive of them

in-groups: groups toward which one feels loyalty

instrumental leader: an individual who tries to keep the group moving toward its goals; also known as a task-oriented leader

involuntary memberships (or involuntary associations): groups in which people are assigned membership rather than choosing to join

laissez-faire leader: an individual who leads by being highly permissive

leader: someone who influences the behaviors of others

leadership styles: ways in which people express their leadership

macrosociology: analysis of social life focusing on broad features or social structure, such as social class and the relationships of groups to one another; an approach usually used by functionalist and conflict theorists

manner: the attitudes that people show as they play their roles

master status: a status that cuts across the other statuses that an individual occupies

mechanical solidarity: a shared consciousness that people experience as a result of performing the same or similar tasks

microsociology: analysis of social life focusing on social interaction; an approach usually used by symbolic interactionist

networking: the process of consciously using or cultivating networks for some gain

organic solidarity: solidarity based on the interdependence brought about by the division of labor

out-groups: groups toward which one feels antagonisms

primary group: a group characterized by intimate, long-term, face-to-face association and cooperation

reference group: Herbert Hyman's term for the groups we use as standards to evaluate ourselves

role: the behaviors, obligations, and privileges attached to a status

role conflict: conflict that someone feels *between* roles because the expectations attached to one role are incompatible with the expectations of another role

role performance: the ways in which someone performs a role within the limits that the role provides; showing a particular "style" or "personality"

role strain: conflicts that someone feels *within* a role

secondary group: compared with a primary group, a larger, relatively temporary, more anonymous, formal, and impersonal group based on some interest or activity, whose members are likely to interact on the basis of specific roles

sign-vehicles: the term used by Goffman to refer to how people use social setting, appearance, and manner to communicate information about the self

small group: a group small enough for everyone to interact directly with all the other members

social class: a large number of people with similar amounts of income and education who work at jobs that are roughly comparable in prestige

social cohesion: the degree to which members of a group or society feel united by shared values and other social bonds

social construction of reality: the process by which people use their background assumptions and life experiences to define what is real for them

social institutions: the organized, usual, or standard ways by which society meets its basic needs

social interaction: what people do when they are in the presence of one another

social network: the social ties radiating outward from the self that link people together

social setting: the place where the action of everyday life unfolds

social structure: the framework that surrounds us, consisting of the relationship of people and groups to one another which give direction to and set limits on behavior

society: people who share a culture and a territory

status: the position that someone occupies in society or a social group

status symbols: items used to identify a status

status set: all of the statuses or positions that an individual occupies

status inconsistency (or discrepancy): a contradiction or mismatch between statuses

stereotype: assumptions of what people are like, based on previous associations with them or with people who have similar characteristics, or based on information, whether true or false

teamwork: the collaboration of two or more persons interested in the success of a performance to manage impressions jointly

Thomas theorem: William I. Thomas's classic formulation of the definition of the situation: "If people define situations as real, they are real in their consequences."

triad: a group of three persons

voluntary memberships (or voluntary associations): groups that people choose to join

☞ KEY PEOPLE

Review the major theoretical contributions or findings of these people.

Solomon Asch: Asch is famous for his research on conformity to group pressure.

William Chambliss: Chambliss used macro- and microsociology to study high school gangs and found that social structure and interaction explained the patterns of behavior in these groups.

Charles H. Cooley: It was Cooley who noted the central role of primary groups in the development of one's sense of self.

John Darley and Bibb Latané: These researchers investigated what impact the size of the group has on individual members' attitudes and behaviors. They found that as the group grew in size, individuals' sense of responsibility diminished, their interactions became more formal, and the larger group tended to break down into smaller ones.

Emile Durkheim: Durkheim identified mechanical and organic solidarity as the keys to social cohesion. Durkheim also viewed the small group as a buffer between the individual and society, helping to prevent anomie.

Harold Garfinkel: Garfinkel is the founder of ethnomethodology; he conducted experiments in order to uncover people's background assumptions.

Erving Goffman: Goffman developed dramaturgy, the perspective within symbolic interactionism that views social life as a drama on the stage.

Edward Hall: This anthropologist found that personal space varied from one culture to another and that North Americans use four different "distance zones."

Lloyd Howells and Selwyn Becker: These social psychologists found that factors such as location within a group underlie people's choices of leaders.

Irving Janis: Janis coined the term "groupthink" to refer to the tunnel vision that a group of people sometimes develop.

Ronald Lippitt and Ralph White: These social psychologists carried out a class study on leadership styles and found that the style of leadership affected the behavior of group members.

Robert K. Merton: Merton observed that the traits of in-groups become viewed as virtues, while those same traits in out-groups are seen as vices.

Joshua Meyrowitz: This sociologist stresses that the media should not be considered as passable channels of information, but rather, they shape our lives.

Stanley Milgram: Milgram's research has contributed greatly to sociological knowledge of group life. He did research on social networks as well as individual conformity to group pressure.

Georg Simmel: This early sociologist was one of the first to note the significance of group size; he used the terms dyad and triad to describe small groups.

Mark Snyder: Snyder carried out research in order to test whether or not stereotypes are self-fulfilling; he found that subjects were influenced to behave in a particular way based on their stereotypes.

W. I. Thomas: This sociologist was known for his statement, "If people define situations as real, they are real in their consequences."

Ferdinand Tönnies: Tönnies analyzed different types of societies that existed before and after industrialization. He used the terms *Gemeinschaft* and *Gesellschaft* to describe the two types of societies.

☞ SELF-TEST

After completing this self-test, check your answers against the Answer Key at the back of this Study Guide and against the text on page(s) indicated in parentheses.

MULTIPLE CHOICE QUESTIONS

1. Which of the following statements applies to microsociology? (94)
    a. It focuses on social interaction.
    b. It investigates large-scale social forces.
    c. It focuses on broad features of social structure.
    d. It is used by functionalists and conflict theorists.

2. Which level of analysis do sociologists use to study social class and group structure? (94)
    a. dramaturgy
    b. ethnomethodology
    c. macrosociology
    d. microsociology

3. You want to study how homeless mothers care for their children. Which would you use? (94)
    a. macrosociology
    b. microsociology
    c. functionalism
    d. conflict perspective

4. The term social structure refers to: (95-96)
    a. the framework of society.
    b. the patterns of society.
    c. relationships between individuals or groups within a society.
    d. all of the above.

5. Of what are religion, politics, education, and the military all examples? (96)
    a. involuntary groups
    b. voluntary associations
    c. social institutions
    d. social fixtures

6. What term do sociologists use to describe activities such as the replacement of members and the socialization of new members of a society? (98)
    a. functional necessities
    b. functional requisites
    c. functional prerequisites
    d. dysfunctional prerequisites

7. Which perspective states that social institutions are controlled by an elite that uses them to its own advantage? (98)
    a. functionalist
    b. conflict
    c. symbolic interactionist
    d. dramaturgy

8. Which of the following would be found in a society characterized by organic solidarity? (99)
    a. a highly specialized division of labor
    b. members who are interdependent on one another
    c. a high degree of impersonal relationships
    d. all of the above

9. What type of society is it where everyone knows everyone else, people conform because they are very sensitive to the opinions of others and want to avoid being gossiped about, and people draw comfort from being part of an intimate group? (99)
    a. *Gemeinschaft*
    b. *Gesellschaft*
    c. mechanical society
    d. organic society

10. Which of the following refers to the position that an individual holds in a social group? (100)
    a. social class
    b. social status
    c. social role
    d. social location

11. A person is simultaneously a daughter, a wife, and a mother. All together, what are these? (100)
    a. social status
    b. social class
    c. status position
    d. status set

12. Which of the following describes an individual's race, sex, and inherited social class? (101)
    a. ascribed statuses
    b. achieved statuses
    c. status inconsistencies
    d. status incongruities

13. Wedding rings, military uniforms, and clerical collars are all examples of what? (101)
    a. social stigma
    b. social class
    c. status symbols
    d. achieved statuses

14. Which of the following statements regarding status symbols is incorrect? (101-102)
    a. Status symbols are signs that identify a status.
    b. Status symbols often are used to show that people have "made it."
    c. Status symbols are always positive signs or people would not wear them.
    d. Status symbols are used by people to announce their statuses to others.

15. What is a master status? (102)
    a. It is always an ascribed status.
    b. It is a status that cuts across the other statuses that a person holds.
    c. It can be fairly easily changed.
    d. It is a status that identifies high ranking members of a society.

16. Under what conditions is status inconsistency most likely to occur? (102)
    a. When a contradiction or mismatch between statuses exists.
    b. When we know what to expect of other people.
    c. When a person wears too many status symbols at once.
    d. When a society has few clearly defined master statuses.

17. What do we call the behaviors, obligations, and privileges attached to statuses? (102)
    a. status sets
    b. master statuses
    c. status differentiations
    d. roles

18. Why are roles of sociological significance? (102)
    a. Sociologists need something concrete to study.
    b. Roles are an essential component of culture.
    c. Most deviant behavior occurs in roles.
    d. So many people are engaged in performing roles every day.

19. What do people make up when they have something in common and believe that what they have in common is significant? (103)
    a. assembly
    b. aggregate
    c. category
    d. group

20. Which of the following do we use to describe people who have similar characteristics? (104)
    a. group
    b. aggregate
    c. category
    d. society

21. According to Emile Durkheim, what is the value of small groups? (104)
    a. They promote diversity.
    b. They generate change.
    c. They prevent anomie.
    d. They encourage conformity.

22. According to Cooley, which is essential to an individual's psychological well-being? (104)
    a. primary groups
    b. secondary groups
    c. therapy groups
    d. interpersonal groups

23. Secondary groups: (104)
    a. have members who are likely to interact on the basis of specific roles.
    b. are characteristic of industrial societies.
    c. are essential to the functioning of contemporary societies.
    d. All of the above.

24. Attacks against immigrants or a national anti-immigration policy is an example of: (105)
    a. homophobia.
    b. arachnophobia.
    c. agoraphobia.
    d. xenophobia.

25. Why are reference groups important? (105-106)
    a. They meet our intense need for face-to-face interaction.
    b. They are an efficient way in which to achieve goals or complete tasks.
    c. They provide us with standards we use to evaluate ourselves.
    d. They are groups towards which we feel an intense sense of loyalty.

26. What term describes the social ties radiating out from the self, linking people together? (106)
    a. social networks
    b. reference groups
    c. cliques
    d. inner-circles

27. Sociologists refer to the conscious use or cultivation of networks for some gain as: (106)
    a. networking.
    b. group dynamics.
    c. social climbing.
    d. being a user.

28. Dyads: (109)
    a. are the most intense or intimate of human groups.
    b. require continuing active participation and commitment of both members.
    c. are the most unstable of social groups.
    d. All of the above.

29. Personal space might be a research topic for a sociologist using which type of perspective? (114)
    a. macro-level analysis
    b. functional analysis
    c. symbolic interactionism
    d. the conflict perspective

30. According to Goffman, where do we go when we want to be ourselves? (116)
    a. front stage
    b. back stage
    c. inside the drama
    d. outside the drama

31. Susan is able to go to college and work full-time because she takes classes in the evenings after work. One day her boss asks her to move from working days to working evenings; he wants her to work during the same hours she is supposed to be in class. In this situation what is Susan experiencing? (117)
    a. role strain
    b. role performance
    c. role demands
    d. role conflict

32. The professor poses a question in class. You know the answer and want to raise your hand, but are afraid that if you do, you will show up the other students in the class. What are you experiencing in this situation? (117)
    a. role strain
    b. role conflict
    c. role distance
    d. role performance

33. Which of the following statements applies to social setting, appearance, and manner? (118)
    a. They are less important than role performance for impression management.
    b. They are sign-vehicles used by individuals for managing impressions.
    c. They are more important for females than males.
    d. They are techniques for saving face when a performance fails.

34. Which of the following reflects the views of ethnomethodologists? (120)
    a. Background assumptions are so deeply embedded in our consciousness that it is virtually impossible for sociologists to ever determine what they are.
    b. Background assumptions can be easily understood and change frequently.
    c. People use commonsense understandings to make sense out of their lives.
    d. Background assumptions are fairly stable from one culture to another.

35. Within which sociological perspective would you place the Thomas theorem? (120)
    a. functionalism
    b. conflict theory
    c. symbolic interactionism
    d. exchange theory

TRUE-FALSE QUESTIONS

T F   1.   Social structure has little impact on the typical individual. (95-96)
T F   2.   Sociologists have identified five basic social institutions in contemporary societies. (96)
T F   3.   There is agreement within sociology that the mass media is a social institution. (96)
T F   4.   According to Emile Durkheim, as a society's division of labor becomes more complex, it becomes much more difficult to achieve social cohesion. (99)
T F   5.   *Gemeinschaft* society is characterized by impersonal, short-term relationships. (99)
T F   6.   A person's ideas, attitudes, and behaviors largely depend on his or her social class. (100)
T F   7.   To sociologists, the terms "social class" and "social status" mean the same thing. (100)
T F   8.   Being a student is an example of an achieved status. (101)
T F   9.   The purpose of status symbols is to tell the world that you've made it to a particular place in society. (101)

T F   10. Being male or female is not considered a master status. (102)

T F   11. You occupy a status, but you play a role. (102)

T F   12. Groups generally don't have that much control over many aspects of our behavior. (103)

T F   13. Society is the largest and most complex group that sociologists study. (103)

T F   14. Anomie is most likely to occur in the absence of ties to primary groups. (104)

T F   15. Members of primary groups are likely to interact on the basis of specific roles. (104)

T F   16. Robert Merton observed that traits of our in-groups tend to be viewed as virtues, while those same traits are seen as vices when found among members of out-groups. (104)

T F   17. Reference groups are the groups we use as standards to evaluate ourselves. (106)

T F   18. Research by Stanley Milgram demonstrates how small our social world really is. (106)

T F   19. Networking refers to the conscious use or even cultivation of networks. (106)

T F   20. Dyads are more intimate and stable than triads. (109)

T F   21. As a small group grows larger, its intensity decreases and its stability increases. (109)

T F   22. The Asch experiment used fake shocks to demonstrate that people would do anything for authority figures. (111-112)

T F   23. We have a tendency to make assumptions about a person based on his or her visible features; these stereotypes may affect how we act toward that person. (114)

T F   24. The amount of personal space people prefer varies from one culture to another. (115)

T F   25. Researchers have found that lower-status individuals tend to touch more, because touching is a way of claiming more status. (116)

T F   26. According to Erving Goffman, back stages are where we can let our hair down. (116)

T F   27. The same setting will rarely serve as both a back and a front stage. (117)

T F   28. Role conflict is a conflict that someone feels within a role. (117)

T F   29. A face-saving technique in which people give the impression that they are unaware of a flaw in someone's performance is known as impression management. (118)

T F   30. Symbolic interactionists assume that reality has an independent existence, and people must deal with it. (120)

FILL-IN QUESTIONS

1. _____ investigates such things as social class and how groups are related to one another. (94)

2. The level of sociological analysis used by symbolic interactionists and postmodernists is _____. (94-95)

3. The _____ perspective states that societies must replace their members, teach new members, produce and distribute goods and services, preserve order, and provide a sense of purpose. (98)

4. A society's basic needs, which are required in order to guarantee survival, are called _____. (98)

5. Durkheim referred to a collective consciousness that people experience due to performing the same or similar tasks as _____. (99)

6. _____ is all of the statuses or positions that an individual occupies. (100)

7. A social position that a person assumes voluntarily is _____. (101)

8. _____ are signs used to identify a status. (101)

9. Groups in which people are assigned membership rather than choosing to join are _____. (103)

10. The term _____ is used to describe individuals who temporarily share the same physical space but do not see themselves as belonging together. (104)

11. A _____ group is characterized by relatively temporary, more anonymous, formal, and impersonal relationships. (104)

12. _____ provide a sense of identification or belonging while producing feelings of antagonism towards _____. (104)

13. The groups we use as standards to evaluate ourselves are _____. (106)

14. Individuals who interact with one another on the Internet, whether on a regular basis or not, are known as a(n) _____. (107)

15. The smallest possible group is a(n) _____. (109)

16. Someone who influences the behavior of others is a(n) _____. (110)

17. An individual who tries to keep the group moving toward its goals is a(n) _____ leader. An individual who increases harmony and minimizes conflict is a(n) _____ leader. (110)

18. A(n) _____ leader is one who gives orders; a(n) _____ leader is one who tries to gain consensus among group members; and a(n) _____ leader is one who is highly permissive. (110)

19. _____ is a narrowing of thought by a group of people, which results in overconfidence and tunnel vision. (113)

20. _____ focuses on face-to-face social interactions. (114)

21. Erving Goffman believed that in order to communicate information about the self, individuals use three types of _____. (118)

22. Goffman called the sign-vehicle that refers to the attitudes that we demonstrate as we play our roles _____. (118)

23. _____ are the ideas that we have about the way life is and the way things ought to work. (120)

24. What people define as real because of their background assumptions and life experiences is the _____. (121)

25. The _____ states, "If people define situations as real, they are real in their consequences." (122)

MATCH THESE SOCIAL SCIENTISTS WITH THEIR CONTRIBUTIONS

__1. Emile Durkheim
__2. Ferdinand Tönnies
__3. Edward Hall
__4. Erving Goffman
__5. W. I. Thomas
__6. Irving Janis
__7. Georg Simmel
__8. Emile Durkheim
__9. Stanley Milgram
__10. Solomon Asch
__11. Charles H. Cooley
__12. Robert K. Merton
__13. Ronald Lippitt and Ralph White

a. *described* Gemeinschaft *and* Gesellschaft *societies*
b. *wrote about mechanical and organic solidarity*
c. *analyzed everyday life in terms of dramaturgy*
d. *studied the concept of personal space*
e. *wrote a theorem about the nature of social reality*
f. *primary groups*
g. *obedience to authority*
h. *dyads*
i. *classic study on leadership styles*
j. *small groups and anomie*
k. *groupthink*
l. *conformity to peer pressure*
m. *in-group prejudice leads to double standard*

ESSAY QUESTIONS

1. Choose a research topic and discuss how you approach this topic using both macrosociological and microsociological approaches.

2. Today we can see many examples of people wanting to re-create a simpler way of life. Using Tönnies' framework, analyze this tendency.

3. Discuss the benefits and drawbacks to in-groups and out-groups.

4. Explain the three different leadership styles and suggest reasons why the democratic leader is the best style of leader for most situations.

5. Assume that you have been asked to give a presentation to your sociology class on Goffman's dramaturgy approach. Describe what information you would want to include in such a presentation.

"DOWN-TO-EARTH SOCIOLOGY"

1. Can you identify the social structure of some group to which you belong? What conclusions can you draw about the importance of social structure?

2. Are you a member of an electronic community like the ones described on pages 107-108? If you are, how would you describe your relationships with others within your particular community? Do you find yourself in closer, more personal relationships with your electronic friends than those you see every day? Why do you think that is? If you have never participated in an electronic community, why not?

3. After reading about the Milgram experiments (pages 112-113), consider how you would have reacted if you had been selected to participate. Under what conditions would you have carried out the orders? Under what conditions would you have disobeyed? Did the fact that Milgram was able to discover an important aspect of human behavior justify the methods which he used?

4. After reading on page 119 about the mass media and the presentation of the body in everyday life, think about your own sense of your body. How do you see yourself? How do you think others see you? To what degree do you think that your views reflect cultural expectations? Do you think that our cultural standards concerning body image are tougher on women than men?

5. After reading this chapter, try and analyze the statuses, roles, and so on in your own life. How does when and where you were born affect your life? What are your current statuses and roles? What kinds of role conflict or role strain have you experienced in these roles?

CHAPTER 6

SOCIAL INEQUALITY: GLOBAL AND NATIONAL PERSPECTIVES

☞ CHAPTER SUMMARY

- Social stratification is a system in which people are divided into layers according to their relative power, property, and prestige. The nations of the world, as well as people within a nation, are stratified into groups based on relative power, prestige, and property.
- Four major systems of social stratification include: (1) slavery—owning other people; (2) caste—lifelong status determined by birth; (3) clan—status depends on lineage; and (4) class—based on possession of money or material possessions. Class systems are characteristic of industrialized societies.
- Early sociologists disagreed about the meaning of social class in industrialized nations. Karl Marx argued that a person's relationship to the means of production was the only factor determining social class. Max Weber argued that three elements—property, prestige, and power—dictate an individual's standing in society.
- Most sociologists have adopted Weber's definition of social class as a large group of people who rank closely to one another in terms of wealth, power, and prestige. Social class can be measured in three different ways: subjective method, reputational method, and objective method. Most sociologists prefer the objective method.
- The three criteria for measuring social class are wealth, consisting of property and income; power, consisting of the ability to carry out one's will despite the resistance of others; and prestige, consisting of the regard or respect accorded an individual or social position. Most people are status consistent, meaning that they rank high or low on all three dimensions of social class. People who rank high on some dimensions and low on others are status inconsistent. The frustration of status inconsistency tends to produce political radicalism.
- Various arguments have been developed to explain the universal presence of stratification. Kingsley Davis and Wilbert Moore argued that society must offer rewards in order to assure that important social positions are filled by the most competent people.
- To maintain stratification within a nation, the ruling class controls ideas and information, depends on social networks, and relies on force.
- The model of global stratification presented in this text divides nations into three groups: the "Most Industrialized," the "Industrializing," and the "Least Industrialized" nations.
- Four theories explaining the origins of global stratification are imperialism and colonialism, world system theory, dependency theory, and the culture of poverty. International stratification is maintained through neocolonialism, the ongoing dominance of the Least Industrialized Nations by the Most Industrialized nations, and multinational corporations which operate across national boundaries. The new technology gives advantage to the world's Most Industrialized nations.
- Sociologists use two models to portray the social class structure. Erik Wright developed a four class model based on the ideas of Karl Marx. Dennis Gilbert and Joseph Kahl developed a six class model based on the ideas of Max Weber.
- Social class leaves no aspect of life untouched. Class membership affects life chances, physical and mental health, family life, politics, religion, education, and contact with crime and the criminal justice system.
- In studying the mobility of individuals within society, sociologists look at intergenerational mobility, individual changes in social class from one generation to the next; exchange mobility,

the movement of large numbers of people from one class to another; and structural mobility, the social and economic changes that affect the social class position of large numbers of people.

- Poverty is unequally distributed across Canada. While poverty is related to geography, however, the greatest predictors of poverty are race/ethnicity, education, and the sex of the person who heads the family. Sociologists generally focus on structural factors, such as employment opportunities, in explaining poverty.

- The Horatio Alger myth encourages people to strive to get ahead, and blames failures on individual shortcomings.

☞ LEARNING OBJECTIVES

As you read Chapter 6, use these learning objectives to organize your notes. After completing your reading, briefly state an answer to each of the objectives, and review the text pages in parentheses.

1. Define social stratification and explain why it is of sociological significance. (129)
2. Describe the characteristics of slavery and note the uses of slavery in the New World. (130)
3. Identify the features of caste systems. Give examples of different ones. (130-131)
4. List the characteristics of a class system and contrast its features with those of other systems of stratification. (131)
5. Identify the basic assumptions of Karl Marx regarding what determines social class. (131-132)
6. Explain why Max Weber was critical of Marx's perspective, and summarize Weber's views regarding social class position. (132-133)
7. Compare the three ways of measuring social class. (134)
8. Outline and explain the components of social class. (134-138)
9. Define status inconsistency and discuss the consequences for individual behavior. (138-139)
10. State the basic assumptions of functionalists like Davis and Moore, and present Tumin's criticisms of this viewpoint. (139-140)
11. Explain the mechanisms by which the elite maintains stratification. (140-141)
12. Describe the major characteristics of the three worlds of development, name the regions that fit in each category, and summarize some of the problems presented by this classification. (142-143)
13. Outline the major theories of how the world's nations became stratified and explain how global stratification has been maintained. (143-146)
14. Explain Erik Wright's updated model of Marx's class theory. (146)
15. Discuss Gilbert and Kahl's updated model of Weber's perspective. (146-149)
16. Examine the consequences of social class for new technology, physical and mental health, family life, education, religion, politics, and the criminal justice system. (149-151)
17. Discuss the patterns of social mobility within Canada and note the role that technology has played in terms of mobility, both upward and downward. (151-153)
18. Indicate how the poverty line is drawn and state the major characteristics of the poor in Canada. (153-156)
19. Assess individual versus structural explanations of poverty. (158-160)
20. Identify the social functions of the Horatio Alger myth. (160)

☞ CHAPTER OUTLINE

I.   **What is Social Stratification?**
    A.   Social stratification is a system in which large groups of people are divided into layers according to their relative power, property, and prestige.

B.   Stratification exists within a society and among nations and affects our life chances and our orientations to life.

II.   Systems of Social Stratification

A.   Slavery is a form of social stratification in which some people own other people.
   1.   Initially, slavery was based on debt, punishment for violation of the law, or defeat in battle.
   2.   Slavery could be temporary or permanent and was not necessarily passed on to one's children. Typically, slaves owned no property and had no power; however, this was not universally true.
   3.   The first form of slavery in the New World was indentured service—a contractual system in which someone voluntarily sold his or her services for a specified period of time; at the end of that time the individual was freed.
   4.   Given the shortage of indentured servants, American colonists first tried to enslave Indians and then turned to Africans, who were being brought to North and South America by the British, Dutch, English, Portuguese, and Spanish.
B.   In a caste system, status is determined by birth and is lifelong.
   1.   Ascribed status is the basis of a caste system. Societies with this form of stratification try to make certain that boundaries between castes remain firm by practicing endogamy (marriage within their own group) and developing rules about ritual pollution—teaching that contact with inferior castes contaminates the superior caste.
   2.   Although abolished by the Indian government in 1949, the caste system remains part of everyday life in India, as it has for almost three thousand years. This system is based on religion and is made up of four main castes, or *varnas*, which are subdivided into thousands of specialized subcastes or *jati*. The lowest caste is considered to be "untouchable," and ablutions—washing rituals—are required to restore purity for those contaminated by individuals from this group. India's caste system is finally breaking down because of industrialization and urbanization.
C.   Clan systems used to be common in agricultural societies. Each individual is linked to a large network of relatives. A clan system is one in which the individual's status depends on lineage linking him or her to an extended network of relatives.
   1.   Although clan membership is determined by birth and is lifelong, interclan marriage is permitted and is sometimes used to forge alliances between clans.
   2.   Industrialization and urbanization are making clans more fluid, even replacing them by social classes.
D.   A class system is a form of social stratification based primarily on the possession of money or material possessions.
   1.   Initial social class position is based on that of one's parents (ascribed status).
   2.   With relatively fluid boundaries, a class system allows for social mobility—movement up or down the social class ladder—based on achieved status.

III.   What Determines Social Class?

A.   According to Karl Marx, social class is determined by one's relationship to the means of production—the tools, factories, land, and investment capital used to produce wealth.
   1.   The bourgeoisie (capitalists) own the means of production; the proletariat (workers) are the people who work for those who own the means of production.
   2.   As capital becomes more concentrated, the two classes will become increasingly more hostile to one another.

3.   Class consciousness—awareness of a common identity based on position in the means of production—will develop; it is the essential basis of the unity of workers, according to Marx.

4.   Marx believed that the workers would revolt against the capitalists, take control of the means of production, and usher in a classless society. However, the workers' unity and revolution are held back by false consciousness—the mistaken identification of workers with the interests of capitalists.

B.   Unlike Marx, Max Weber did not believe that property was the sole basis of a person's position in the stratification system, but rather that property, prestige, and power determine social class.

1.   Property is an essential element; however, powerful people, like managers of corporations, control the means of production although they do not own them.

2.   Prestige may be derived from ownership of property; however, it also may be based on other factors such as athletic skills.

3.   Power is the ability to control others, even over their objections.

C.   Social class can be defined as a large group of people who rank close to each other in wealth, power, and prestige.

D.   There are three ways of measuring social class.

1.   The subjective method consists of asking people what their own social class is; however, most people give the wrong answer.

2.   The reputation method consists of asking people what class other people belong to, based on their reputations. It generally is useful only in smaller cities, where people know each other's reputations.

3.   The objective method consists of ranking people according to objective criteria such as wealth, power and prestige. Most sociologists use the objective method.

IV.   The Components of Social Class

A.   Wealth consists of property (what we own) and income (money we receive). Wealth and income are not always the same—a person may own much property yet have little income, or vice versa. Usually, however, wealth and income go together.

1.   Ownership of property (real estate, stocks and bonds, etc.) is not distributed evenly: 80% of all corporate stocks and bonds are owned by fewer than 1000 individuals. These "super-rich" make up less than 2% of the Canadian population.

2.   Income is also distributed disproportionately: over 40% of families earn less than $40,000 and almost 60% earn less than the national average of $55,000. Only 9.4% of Canadian families earn more than $100,000. The poorest 20% of Canadians receives less of the nation's income today than it did in the 1940s.

3.   The most affluent group in Canadian society is the executive officers of the largest corporations. Their median income (excluding stock options) is $862,000 a year. The ten top-earning CEO's took home over $10 million in 1997.

B.   Power is the ability to carry out your will despite resistance. Power is concentrated in the hands of a few—the "power elite"—who share the same ideologies and values, belong to the same clubs, and reinforce each other's world view. No major decision in government is made without their approval.

C.   Prestige is the respect or regard people give to various occupations and accomplishments.

1.   Occupations are the primary source of prestige, although some people gain prestige through inventions, feats, or doing good to others. Occupations with the highest prestige pay more, require more education, entail more abstract thought, and offer greater autonomy.

2.   For prestige to be valuable, people must acknowledge it. The elite traditionally has made rules to emphasize its higher status.

3.   Status symbols, which vary according to social class, are ways of displaying prestige. They may include designer label clothing, expensive cars, and prestigious addresses.

D.   Status inconsistency is the term used to describe the situation of people who have a mixture of high and low rankings in the three components of social class (wealth, power, and prestige).

1.   Most people are status consistent—they rank at the same level in all three components. People who are status inconsistent want others to act toward them on the basis of their highest status, but others tend to judge them on the basis of their lowest status.

2.   Sociologist Gerhard Lenski determined that people suffering the frustrations of status inconsistency are more likely to be radical and approve political action aimed against higher status groups.

V.   Why Is Social Stratification Universal?

A.   According to the functionalist view expressed by Kingsley Davis and Wilbert Moore, stratification is inevitable.

1.   Society must make certain that its important positions are filled; to guarantee that the more important positions are filled by the more qualified people, society must offer them greater rewards.

2.   Davis and Moore argued that society offers greater rewards for its more responsible, demanding, and accountable positions.

B.   Melvin Tumin was the first to present a number of criticisms to the Davis and Moore thesis.

1.   He asked how the importance of a position is measured (e.g., "Is a surgeon really more important to society than a garbage collector?"). Rewards can not be used to measure the importance of a job; there must be some independent measure of importance.

2.   He noted that if stratification worked as Davis and Moore describe it, society would be a meritocracy—a form of social stratification in which all positions are awarded on the basis of merit—but it does not work this way (e.g., the best predictor of college entrance is family income, not ability).

3.   He also argued that money and fringe benefits are not the only reasons people take jobs.

4.   Finally, he noted that stratification is dysfunctional to many people, thus not functional.

C.   Conflict theorists stress that conflict, not function, is the basis of social stratification.

1.   Every society has only limited resources to go around, and in every society groups struggle with one another for those resources.

2.   Whenever a group gains power, it uses that power to extract what it can from the groups beneath it. The dominant group takes control of the social institutions, using them to keep other groups weak and to preserve the best resources for itself. Ruling classes develop an ideology to justify people's relative positions.

3.   Modern conflict theorists such as C. Wright Mills, Ralf Dahrendorf, and Randall Collins stress that conflict between capitalists and workers is not the only important conflict in contemporary society, but rather, that groups within the same class compete for scarce resources, resulting in conflict between many groups (e.g., young vs. old; women vs. men).

VI.   How Do Elites Maintain Social Inequality?

A.   Social stratification is maintained within a nation by elites who control ideas and information, maintain social networks, and use force.

B.   The control of ideas and information can be remarkably more effective than the use of brute force and is used by elites everywhere to maintain their positions of power—whether in dictatorships or in democracies.

C.   Social networks are also critical in maintaining social stratification because they supply valuable information and tend to perpetuate social inequality.

D.   Technology, especially monitoring devices, helps the elite maintain its position.

E.   Underlying the maintenance of stratification is control of social institutions—the legal establishment, the police, and the military.

VII.   Global Stratification: Three Worlds of Development

A.   Until the 1980s, a simple model was used, consisting of the First World (industrialized, capitalistic nations), Second World (communist nations), and Third World (any nations that didn't fit the other categories). A more neutral way is to use terms related to a nation's level of industrialization: "Most Industrialized," "Industrializing," and "Least Industrialized."

B.   Classifying the nations of the world into these three categories creates certain problems.

1.   How much industrialization does a nation need in order to be classified as Most Industrialized or Industrializing?

2.   Does the fact that some nations have become "postindustrial" mean that a separate classification needs to be created?

3.   While the oil-rich nations of the world are immensely wealthy, they are not industrialized. How are they classified?

VIII.   How the World's Nations Become Stratified

A.   The explanation of how the world became stratified focuses on how European nations exploited weaker nations.

1.   Imperialism (the pursuit of unlimited geographic expansion) was practiced by European powers over the centuries. Industrialized nations needed consumers elsewhere; through conquests, markets expanded and businessmen gained access to new markets and raw materials. Nations that industrialized first got ahead of the rest of the world and became the most powerful.

2.   Colonization occurred when industrialized nations made colonies of weaker nations and exploited their labor/natural resources. European nations tended to focus on Africa, while the U.S. concentrated on Central and South America.

B.   According to world system theory as espoused by Immanuel Wallerstein, countries are politically and economically tied together.

1.   There are four groups of interconnected nations: (1) core nations, where capitalism first developed; (2) semi-periphery (Mediterranean area), highly dependent on trade with core nations; (3) periphery (eastern Europe), mainly limited to selling cash crops to core nations, with limited economic development; (4) external area (most of Africa/Asia) left out of growth of capitalism, with few economic ties to core nations.

2.   A capitalist world economy (capitalist dominance) results from relentless expansion: even external area nations are drawn into the commercial web.

3.   Globalization (the extensive interconnections among nations resulting from the expansion of capitalism) has speeded up because of new forms of communication and transportation. The consequence is that no nation is able to live in isolation.

C.   Dependence theory attributes the Least Industrialized nations' low economic development to dominance by the Most Industrialized nations. The Most Industrialized nations turned the Least Industrialized nations into their plantations and mines, taking whatever they needed; many of the Least Industrialized nations thus specialized in a single cash crop.

D.   John Kenneth Galbraith argued that some nations remained poor because they were crippled by a culture of poverty, a way of life based on traditional values and religious beliefs that perpetuated poverty from one generation to the next and kept some of the Least Industrialized nations from developing.

E.   Most sociologists find imperialism, world system, and dependency theory explanations preferable to the culture of poverty theory because the last places the blame on the victim, but each theory only partially explains global stratification.

IX.   Maintaining Global Stratification

A.   Neocolonialism is the economic and political dominance of the Least Industrialized nations by the Most Industrialized nations. Michael Harrington assets that the Most Industrialized nations control the Least Industrialized nations because they control markets, sets prices, etc. The Most Industrialized nations move hazardous industries to the Least Industrialized nations. The Most Industrialized nations sell weapons and manufactured goods to the Least Industrialized nations, preventing them from developing their own industrial capacity.

B.   Multinational corporations contribute to exploitation of the Least Industrialized nations.
1.   Some exploit the Least Industrialized nations directly by controlling national and local politics, running them as a fiefdom.
2.   The Most Industrialized nations are primary beneficiaries of profits made in the Least Industrialized nations.
3.   They often work closely with the elite of the Least Industrialized nations, many times in informal partnerships that are mutually beneficial.
4.   In some situations, multinational corporations may bring prosperity to the Least Industrialized nations because new factories provide salaries and opportunities which otherwise would not exist for workers in those countries.

C.   The new technology favors the Most Industrialized nations, enabling them to maintain their global domination.
1.   The profits of multinational corporations can be invested in developing and acquiring the latest technology, thereby generating even greater profits.
2.   Many of the Least Industrialized nations do not have the resources to invest in new technology, creating an even gap between the levels of industrialization globally.

X.   Applying Sociological Models of Social Class

A.   How many classes exist in industrial society is a matter of debate, but there are two main models, one that builds on Marx and the other on Weber.

B.   Sociologist Erik Wright realized that not everyone falls into Marx's two broad classes (capitalists and workers, which were based upon a person's relationship to the means of production). For instance, although executives, managers, and supervisors would fall into Marx's category of workers, they act more like capitalists.
1.   Wright resolved this problem by regarding some people as simultaneously members of more than one class, which he called contradictory class locations.
2.   Wright identified four classes: capitalists (owners of large enterprises); petty bourgeoisie (owners of small businesses); managers (employees, but who have authority over others); and workers.

C. Using the model originally developed by Weber, sociologists Dennis Gilbert and Joseph Kahl created a model to describe class structure in the U.S. and other capitalist countries.

1. The capitalist class (1.1% of the population) is composed of investors, heirs, and a few executives; it is divided into "old" money and "new" money. The children of "new" money move into the old money class by attending the right schools and marrying "old" money.

2. The upper-middle class is composed of professionals and upper managers, almost all of whom have attended college or university and frequently have postgraduate degrees.

3. The lower-middle class is composed of lower managers, craftspeople and foremen. They have at least a high school education.

4. The upper- and lower-middle class constitute 26.5% of the population.

5. The working class is composed of factory workers and low-paid white collar workers. Most have high school education.

6. The working poor is composed of relatively unskilled blue-collar and white-collar workers, and those with temporary and seasonal jobs. If they graduated from high school, they probably did not do well in school.

7. The working class and working poor constitute 63.7% of the population.

8. The lower class and underclass (8.7% of the population) is concentrated in the inner cities and has little connection with the job market. Welfare is their main support.

D. The homeless are so far down the class structure that their position must be considered even lower than the underclass. They are the "fallout" of industrialization, especially the postindustrial developments that have contributed to a decline in the demand for unskilled labor.

XI. Consequences of Social Class

A. The new technology does not affect social classes in the same way.

1. The higher one is on the social class ladder, the more likely they are to benefit from technology. For the capitalist class, the new technology is a means to extensive, worldwide profits.

2. The upper-middle class also benefit because the new technology enables them to achieve in their chosen professions, and their education prepares them to take a leading role in managing in the new global system.

3. Below these top two classes, technology creates much more uncertainty, with uncertainty increasing as you move down the ladder. Those at the bottom have few technological skills.

B. The lower a person's social class, the more likely that person is to die at an earlier age than people in higher classes; this is true at all ages. As well, mental health is worse for the lower classes because of stresses associated with their class position.

C. Social class also plays a role in family life.

1. Children of the capitalist class are under great pressure to select the right mate in order to assure the continuity of the family line. Parents in this social class play a large role in mate selection.

2. Marriages are more likely to fail in the lower social classes; the children of the poor thus are more likely to live in single-parent households.

3. Child rearing varies by class, with each class raising its children with attitudes and behaviors suited to the kinds of occupations they will eventually hold. Lower class families teach children to defer to authority, as is required in their jobs. Higher class families encourage freedom, creativity, and self-expression, as is found in their jobs.

D.   Education levels increase as one moves up the social class ladder. The change occurs not only in terms of the amount of education you obtain, but also in terms of the type of education, with the capitalist class bypassing public schools in favor of exclusive private schools, where its children are trained to take a commanding role in society.

E.   All aspects of religious orientation follow class lines. Social classes tend to cluster around different denominations. Lower classes are attracted to spontaneous worship services and louder music, while higher classes prefer more restrained worship services.

F.   Political views and involvement are influenced by social class. However, there is no class majority supporting any one party.
1.   The rich and the poor take divergent political paths, with people in lower social classes more likely to vote New Democrat, while those in higher classes vote Progressive Conservative; the parties are seen as promoting different class interests.
2.   People in working classes are more likely to be liberal on economic issues and more conservative on social issues.
3.   Political participation is not equal: the higher classes are more likely to vote and get involved in politics than those in lower social classes.

G.   The criminal justice system is not blind to class: members of lower classes are more likely to be arrested, are more likely to be on probation, parole, or in jail, and more crimes occur in lower class neighborhoods.

XII.   Social Mobility
A.   There are three basic types of social mobility: intergenerational, structural, and exchange.
1.   Intergenerational mobility is the change that family members make in their social class from one generation to the next. As a result of individual effort, a person can rise from one level to another; in the event of individual failure, the reverse can be true.
2.   Structural mobility involves social changes that affect large numbers of people. By way of example, when computers were invented, many opportunities opened up for people to switch from blue-collar to white-collar work. While individual effort played a role, the major reason for the change in position was structural.
3.   Exchange mobility is movement of people up and down the social class system, where, on balance, the system remains the same. The term refers to general, overall movement of large numbers of people that leaves the class system basically untouched.

B.   Women have been largely ignored in studies of occupational mobility. Studies of social mobility among men indicate that about one-half of sons have moved beyond their fathers; about one-third have stayed at the same level; and about one-sixth have fallen down the ladder.
1.   With the large numbers of women now working for pay, studies of their mobility patterns have appeared.
2.   One study indicated that women that did move up were encouraged by their parents to postpone marriage and get an education.

C.   Technology is responsible for much of the uncertainty and downward mobility of Canadian workers. Computers and instantaneous communications enable companies to relocate production worldwide, locating in areas with lower paid, non-unionized work forces.

XIII.   Poverty
A.   Statistics Canada uses the Low-Income Cut-Off (LICO) to identify the poverty line. The LICO assumes that poor families are those whose income requires them to spend more than 56.2% of their gross income on food, clothing, and shelter.

B.   Poverty is not evenly distributed across Canada. The greatest predictors of whether Canadians are poor are race/ethnicity, education, and sex of the person who heads the family.

    1.   Reflecting differences in the local economies, poverty rates in Canada range from a high of 20.3% in Newfoundland to a low of 12.1% in Prince Edward Island.

    2.   In 1995, more than one-third of the visible minority population in Canada and 45% of children under age six in visible-minority families were living on low incomes. These figures were even greater for Aboriginal peoples.

    3.   The chances of being poor decrease as the amount of education increases. However, many heads of poor families have education beyond high school.

    4.   The sex of the person who heads a family is another major predictor of whether or not a family is poor. Most poor families are headed by women. They are several times more likely to be poor than families headed by two parents. The major causes of this phenomenon, called the feminization of poverty, are divorce, births to unwed mothers, and the lower wages paid to women.

    5.   The percentage of poor people over age 65 declined dramatically during the latter years of the 20th century. However, unattached women over 65 still had a poverty rate of 42% in 1997 and a substantial number of seniors are struggling below the LICO levels.

C.   In 1997, there were over one million children living in poverty in Canada.

XIV.   The Dynamics of Poverty

A.   In the 1960s Michael Harrington and Oscar Lewis suggested that the poor get trapped in a "culture of poverty" as a result of having values and behaviors that make them "fundamentally different" from others.

    1.   National statistics indicate that most poverty is short, lasting one year or less.

    2.   Since the number of people who live in poverty remains fairly constant, this means that as many people move into poverty as move out of it.

B.   In trying to explain poverty, the choice is between focusing on individual explanations or on social structural explanations.

    1.   Sociologists look to such factors as inequalities in education, access to learning job skills, racial, ethnic, age, and gender discrimination, and large-scale economic change to explain the patterns of poverty in society.

    2.   The other explanation is individualistic, focusing on the characteristics of individuals that are assumed to contribute to their poverty.

    3.   Recent welfare reforms across Canada have dramatically cut back on income supports for those facing economic stress.

C.   Because the poor don't see the future as different from the past, they find it difficult to defer gratification—give up things now for the sake of greater gains in the future.

D.   Real-life examples of people from humble origins who climbed far up the social ladder encourage the widely held belief that anyone has a chance of getting ahead.

    1.   The Horatio Alger myth obviously is a statistical impossibility. Despite this, functionalists would stress that this belief is functional for society because it encourages people to compete for higher positions, while placing the blame for failure squarely on the individual.

    2.   As Marx and Weber both noted, social class affects our ideas of life and our proper place in society. At the same time, the dominant ideology often blinds us to these effects in our own lives.

☞ KEY TERMS

After studying the chapter, review the definition for each of the following terms.

bourgeoisie: Karl Marx's term for the people who own the means of production

capitalist world economy: the dominance of capitalism in the world along with the international interdependence that capitalism has created

caste system: a form of social stratification in which one's status is determined by birth and is lifelong

clan: an extended network of relatives

clan system: a form of social stratification in which individuals receive their social standing through belonging to an extended network of relatives

class consciousness: Karl Marx's term for awareness of a common identity based on one's position in the means of production

class system: a form of social stratification based primarily on the possession of money or material possessions

colonization: the process by which one nation takes over another nation, usually for the purpose of exploiting its labor and natural resources

contradictory class location: Erik Wright's term for a position in the class structure that generates contradictory interests

culture of poverty: a culture that perpetuates poverty from one generation to the next

deferred gratification: forgoing something in the present in the hope of achieving greater gains in the future

dependency theory: the belief that lack of industrial development in the Least Industrialized nations is caused by the industrialized nations dominating the world economy

divine right of kings: the idea that the king's authority comes directly from God

downward social mobility: movement down the social class ladder

endogamy: marriage within one's own group

exchange mobility: about the same numbers of people moving up and down the social class ladder, such that, on balance, the social class system shows little change

false consciousness: Karl Marx's term to refer to workers identifying with the interests of capitalists

feminization of poverty: a trend in Canadian poverty whereby most poor families are headed by women

globalization: the extensive interconnections among world nations due to the expansion of capitalism

ideology: beliefs about the way things ought to be that justify social arrangements

imperialism: a nation's attempt to create an empire; its pursuit of unlimited geographical expansion

indentured service: a contractual system in which someone sells his or her body (services) for a specified period of time in an arrangement very close to slavery, except that it is voluntarily entered into

intergenerational mobility: the change that family members make in social class from one generation to the next

means of production: the tools, factories, land, and investment capital used to produce wealth

meritocracy: a form of social stratification in which all positions are awarded on the basis of merit

multinational corporations: companies that operate across many national boundaries; also called transnational corporations

neocolonialism: the economic and political dominance of the Least Industrialized nations by the Most Industrialized nations

objective method (of measuring social class): a system in which people are ranked according to objective criteria such as their wealth, power, and prestige

power: the ability to get your way in spite of the desires of other people

power elite: C. Wright Mills's term for the top people in Canadian corporations, military, and politics who make the nation's major decisions

poverty line: the official measure of poverty; calculated to include those whose incomes are less than three times a low-cost food budget

prestige: respect or regard

proletariat: Karl Marx's term for the people who work for those who own the means of production

reputational method (of measuring social class): a system in which people who are familiar with the reputations of others are asked to identify their social class

slavery: a form of social stratification in which some people own other people

social class: according to Weber, a large group of people who rank close to one another in wealth, power, and prestige; according to Marx, one of two groups: capitalists who own the means of production and workers who sell their labor

social mobility: movement up or down the social class ladder

social stratification: the division of large numbers of people into layers according to their relative power, property, and prestige; applies both to nations and to people within a nation, society, or other group

status: social ranking

status consistency: ranking high or low on all three dimensions of social class

status inconsistency (or status discrepancy): a condition in which a person ranks high on some dimensions of social class and low on others

structural mobility: movement up or down the social class ladder that is attributable to changes in the structure of society, not to individual efforts

subjective method (of measuring social class): a system in which people are asked to state the social class to which they belong

underclass: a small group of people for whom poverty persists year after year and across generations

upward social mobility: movement up the social class ladder

wealth: property and income

world system: economic and political connections that tie the world's countries together

☞ KEY PEOPLE

Review the major theoretical contributions or findings of these people.

Wallace Clement: Clement studied the distrubtion of wealth and power in Canada.

Kingsley Davis and Wilbert Moore: These functionalists developed a theory of stratification that suggests inequality is universal because it helps societies survive by motivating the most qualified members of society to strive to fill the most important social positions.

William Domhoff: Drawing upon the work of C. Wright Mills, Domhoff analyzed the workings of the ruling class.

John Kenneth Galbraith: This economist argued that the Least Industrialized nations remain poor because their own culture holds them back.

Dennis Gilbert and Joseph Kahl: These sociologists developed a more contemporary stratification model based on Max Weber's work.

Ray Gold: In research on status inconsistency, Gold studied tenant reactions to janitors who earned more than they did. He found that the tenants acted "snooty" to the janitors, and the janitors took pleasure in knowing the intimate details of the tenants' lives.

Michael Harrington: Harrington saw that colonialism has been replaced by neocolonialism.

Elizabeth Higgenbotham and Lynn Weber: These sociologists studied the mobility patterns for women. They found that those women who experienced upward mobility were most likely to have strong parental support to defer marriage and get an education.

Melvin Kohn: Kohn studied social class differences in child-rearing patterns.

Gerhard Lenski: Lenski noted that everyone wants to maximize their status, but that others often judge them on the basis of their lowest status despite the individual's efforts to be judged on the basis of his highest status.

Karl Marx: Marx concluded that social class depended exclusively on the means of production; an individual's social class was determined by whether or not he owned the means of production.

C. Wright Mills: Mills used the term power elite to describe the top decision-makers in the nation.

John Porter: Porter demonstrated the ways in which wealth and power are concentrated in Canada.

Melvin Tumin: Tumin was the first to offer a criticism of the functionalist view on stratification.

Immanuel Wallerstein: This historian proposed a world system theory to explain global stratification.

W. Lloyd Warner: Warner did a classic study of stratification using the reputational method.

Max Weber: Weber argued that social class was based on three components—class, status, and power.

Erik Wright: Wright proposed an updated version of Marx's theory of stratification.

☞ SELF-TEST

After completing this self-test, check your answers against the Answer Key at the back of this Study Guide and against the text on page(s) indicated in parentheses.

MULTIPLE CHOICE QUESTIONS

1. What is the division of large numbers of people into layers according to their relative power, property, and prestige? (129)
   a. social distinction
   b. social stratification
   c. social distance
   d. social diversification

2. What is a form of social stratification in which some people own other people? (130)
   a. a caste system
   b. slavery
   c. a class system
   d. apartheid

3. In which stratification system are individuals linked into a large network of relatives? (131)
   a. clan system
   b. caste system
   c. slavery system
   d. class system

4. Which of the following characterizes class systems? (131)
   a. social mobility
   b. geographic mobility
   c. distribution of social standings belonging to an extended network of relatives
   d. fixed boundaries between layers of the stratification system

5. According to Marx, on what does social class depend? (131-132)
   a. wealth, power, and prestige
   b. the means of production
   c. where one is born in the social stratification system
   d. what a person achieves during his or her lifetime

6. According to Max Weber, what determines social class? (132-133)
   a. one's property, prestige, and power
   b. one's relationship to the means of production
   c. one's tasks and how important they are to society
   d. one's political power

7. Which of the ways of measuring social class asks people to identify their own social class? (134)
   a. objective
   b. reputational
   c. subjective
   d. individualistic

8. With which social class do the vast majority of Canadians identify? (134)
   a. upper
   b. middle
   c. working
   d. lower

9. On what is the objective method of measuring social class based? (134)
   a. asking people who are familiar with the reputations of others to judge their social class
   b. ranking people according to criteria such as wealth, power, and prestige
   c. asking people to define their own social class
   d. None of the above

10. According to Paul Samuelson, if an income pyramid were made out of a child's blocks, where would most people be? (135)
    a. near the top of the pyramid
    b. near the middle of the pyramid
    c. near the bottom of the pyramid
    d. None of the above

11. Which of the statements regarding jobs that have the most prestige is not true? (137)
    a. They pay more.
    b. They require more education.
    c. They require special talent or skills.
    d. They offer greater autonomy.

12. What term did Mills use to refer to decision makers at the top of society? (137)
    a. the decision elite
    b. the power elite
    c. the power corps
    d. the power brokers

13. Which of these statements is consistent with the functionalist view of stratification? (139)
    a. Stratification is dysfunctional for society.
    b. Stratification is the outcome of conflict between different social classes.
    c. Stratification will disappear in societies that are characterized by a meritocracy.
    d. Stratification is an inevitable feature of social organization.

14. Which of these is *not* one of Tumin's criticisms of the functionalist theory of stratification? (139-140)
    a. The importance of a social position cannot be measured by the rewards it carries.
    b. The functionalists ignore the impact of family background.
    c. Stratification is not functional for everyone.
    d. The functionalists focus too much on status and power and not enough on income.

15. A form of social stratification in which positions are awarded based on merit is called a(n): (140)
    a. meritocratic system.
    b. egalitarian system.
    c. socialistic system.
    d. democratic system.

16. According to conflict theorists, the basis of social stratification is: (140)
    a. functional necessity in society.
    b. conflict over limited resources.
    c. ascribed statuses.
    d. the way in which individuals perceive their social class position.

17. The majority of the world's population lives in _____ nations. (142)
    a. Most Industrialized
    b. Industrializing
    c. Least Industrialized
    d. old-rich

18. Why is it difficult to know how to classify some nations into a global system of stratification? (143)
    a. It is difficult because the dividing line between levels—Most Industrialized, Industrializing, and Least Industrialized—are soft.
    b. Some nations have moved beyond industrialization.
    c. Some nations have not yet industrialized but are still extremely wealthy.
    d. All of the above reflect problems with classifying nations into a global system.

19. Imperialism is: (143)
    a. a nation's pursuit of unlimited geographical expansion.
    b. the process in which one nation takes over another nation, usually for the purpose of exploiting its labor and natural resources.
    c. the extensive interdependence among the nations of the world which results from the expansion of capitalism.
    d. All of the above.

20. According to world system theory, all of the following are groups of interconnected nations, except: (144)
    a. core nations.
    b. nations on the semiperiphery.
    c. nations on the periphery.
    d. nations in the internal area which have extensive connections with the core nations.

21. The culture of poverty theory was used to analyze global stratification by: (144)
    a. Immanuel Wallerstein.
    b. Max Weber.
    c. John Kenneth Galbraith.
    d. Karl Marx.

22. Neocolonialism refers to: (145)
    a. recent efforts by the Most Industrialized nations to colonize Least Industrialized nations.
    b. the economic policies of the Most Industrialized nations that are designed to control the markets of the Least Industrialized nations.
    c. programs like the Peace Corps that attempt to teach residents of the Least Industrialized countries the skills necessary to survive in an industrial society.
    d. the economic policy of the Least Industrialized nations in which they hold the Most Industrialized nations hostage by controlling access to national resources like oil.

23. Multinational corporations: (145-146)
    a. are companies that operate across many national boundaries.
    b. always exploit the Least Industrialized nations directly.
    c. benefit the Least Industrialized nations as much as the Most Industrialized nations.
    d. All of the above.

24. How did Erik Wright update Marx's class categories in response to criticisms that they were too broad? (146)
    a. He divided each of the two classes into three sub-classes, making six classes in all.
    b. He created an open scale in which people place themselves into classes.
    c. He recommended listing people's different associations and then classifying them on the basis of their most important one.
    d. He recognized that some people can be members of more than one class at the same time.

25. According to Gilbert and Kahl, all of the following are characteristics of the working class, *except*: (148)
    a. most are employed in relatively unskilled blue-collar and white-collar jobs.
    b. most have attended college for one or two years.
    c. most hope to get ahead by achieving seniority on the job.
    d. about thirty percent of the population belong to this class.

26. Which class or classes benefit from technology? (149-150)
    a. working class and the working poor
    b. upper and lower middle classes
    c. lower middle and working classes
    d. capitalist and upper middle classes

27. According to Melvin Kohn lower class parents are concerned that their children be: (150)
    a. creative.
    b. independent.
    c. conformists.
    d. all of the above.

28. Which class tends to bypass public schools entirely, in favor of exclusive private schools? (151)
    a. capitalist
    b. upper-middle
    c. middle
    d. all of the above

29. Members of the _____ class are more likely to be robbed, burglarized, or murdered. (151)
    a. upper
    b. middle
    c. lower
    d. none of the above

30. A homeless person whose father was a physician has experienced: (151)
    a. exchange mobility.
    b. structural mobility.
    c. upward mobility.
    d. downward mobility.

31. As compared with their fathers, most Canadian men: (152)
    a. have a status higher than that of their fathers.
    b. have the same status their fathers did.
    c. have a status lower than their fathers'.
    d. The relative statuses of fathers and sons can't be compared because of structural mobility.

32. Higgenbotham and Weber found that for career women from working class backgrounds: (152)
    a. intergenerational mobility was greater for sons than for daughters.
    b. upwardly mobile women achieved higher positions despite their parents' reservations.
    c. upwardly mobile women achieved higher class positions because of parental
        encouragement that began when they were just little girls.
    d. any upward mobility was due entirely to structural changes in the economy rather than
        individual effort or parental influences.

33. The measure of poverty that is based on a percentage of gross income relative to spending on
    food, clothing, and shelter is: (153)
    a. adjusted income level.
    b. the welfare distribution scale.
    c. the low-income cut-off.
    d. the welfare line.

34. Which factors are the greatest predictors of poverty? (154)
    a. race/ethnicity
    b. education
    c. sex of person who heads the family
    d. all of the above

35. In trying to explain poverty, sociologists are most likely to stress: (158)
    a. individual characteristics that are assumed to contribute to poverty.
    b. features of the social structure that contribute to poverty.
    c. decisions made by the poor that prevent them from ever moving out of poverty.
    d. that poverty is intergenerational, so that most who are born poor will remain poor.

TRUE-FALSE QUESTIONS

T F   1.   Social stratification refers only to individuals. (129)

T F   2.   Throughout history, slavery has always been based on racism . (130)

T F   3.   The first form of slavery in the New World was indentured service. (130)

T F   4.   A caste system is a form of social stratification in which individual status is determined by birth and is lifelong. (130)

T F   5.   A class system is based primarily on money or material possessions. (131)

T F   6.   According to Karl Marx, the means of production is the only factor in determining social class. (131)

T F   7.   According to Max Weber, class standing is a combination of power, prestige, and property. (132)

T F   8.   The reputation method of measuring social class involves asking people to define their own social class. (134)

T F   9.   Wealth and income are the same thing. (134-135)

T F   10.   The most affluent group in Canadian society consists of the chief executive officers of the nation's largest corporations. (136)

T F   11.   Occupational prestige rankings vary widely across countries and over time. (137)

T F   12.   Functionalists believe that people should be rewarded for their unique abilities and the type of position they hold in society is not important. (139)

T F   13.   According to conflict theorists, the oppressed often support laws even when the laws operate against their own interests. (140)

T F   14.   The idea of the divine right of kings is an example of how the ruling elite uses ideas to maintain stratification. (141)

T F   15.   In maintaining stratification, elites find that technology is not particularly useful, because everyone can access technology. (141)

T F   16.   Colonization generally accompanied imperialism. (143)

T F   17.   Most industrialized nations rejected imperialism as a strategy for expanding their economic markets and gaining access to cheap raw materials. (143-144)

T F   18.   The expansion of capitalism resulted in a capitalist world economy dominated by the core nations. (144)

T F   19.   The culture of poverty thesis is generally preferred by sociologists as an explanation of global stratification. (144)

T F   20.   Neocolonialism is the economic and political dominance of the Least Industrialized nations by the Most Industrialized nations. (145)

T F   21.   According to Gilbert and Kahl, the capitalist class has the ability to shape the consciousness of the nation. (147)

T F   22.   The underclass is concentrated in the inner city and has little or no connection with the job market. (148)

T F   23.   The homeless are the "fallout" of industrialization, especially of postindustrial developments. (149)

T F   24.   Social class affects a person's chances of living and dying. (150)

T F   25.   Marriages of the poor are more likely to fail and their children to group up in broken homes. (150-151)

T F   26.   Members of the lower classes are more likely to be on probation, on parole, or in jail than members of the upper classes. (151)

T F   27.   Structural mobility refers to social and economic changes that affect the status of large numbers of people. (151-152)

T F   28.   Exchange mobility leaves the class system basically untouched. (152)

T F   29.   The majority of the poor live below the poverty line for long periods of time. (158)

T F   30. Sociological explanations of poverty tend to focus on structural features of society more than on any particular characteristics of poor individuals. (158-159)

FILL-IN QUESTIONS

1. _____ is a system in which people are divided into layers according to their relative power, property, and prestige. (129)
2. A form of social stratification in which some people own other people is _____. (130)
3. A(n) _____ system is a form of social stratification in which individual status is determined by birth and is lifelong. (130)
4. Sociologists refer to movement up or down the social class ladder as _____. (131)
5. According to Marx, the tools, factories, land, and investment capital used to produce wealth is _____. (131)
6. According to Marx, the awareness of a common identity based on one's position in the means of production is _____. (132)
7. According to Max Weber, the three dimensions of social class are: (1)_____; (2)_____; and (3)_____. (132)
8. Most sociologists use the _____ method of measuring social class in which people are ranked according to objective criteria such as wealth, power, and prestige. (134)
9   Property and income together make up an individual's _____. (134)
10. According to C. Wright Mills, the _____ makes the big decisions in society. (137)
11. A _____ is a form of social stratification in which all positions are awarded on the basis of merit. (140)
12. The _____ is the idea that the king's authority comes directly from God. (141)
13. _____ is the process in which one nation takes over another nation, usually for the purpose of exploiting its labor and natural resources. (143)
14. _____ is the extensive interconnections among world nations resulting from the expansion of capitalism. (144)
15. _____ is a way of life that perpetuates poverty from one generation to the next. (144)
16. _____ refers to the economic and political dominance of the Least Industrialized nations by the Most Industrialized Nations. (145)
17. Companies that operate across many national boundaries are _____. (145)
18. Erik Wright referred to a position in the class structure that generates inconsistent interests as _____. (146)
19. According to Gilbert and Kahl, the capitalist class can be divided into two groups: (1) _____ and (2) _____. (147)
20. _____ is movement up the social class ladder. (151)
21. An official measure of poverty is referred to as the _____; it is a calculation based on a ratio of gross income to family spending on food, clothing, and shelter. (153)
22. _____ is a trend whereby most poor families in Canada are headed by women. (155)
23. Sociologists focus on _____ as the source of poverty. (158)
24. The _____ are people who, in the public mind, are poor through no fault of their own, while the _____ are viewed as having brought on their own poverty. (159)
25. Forgoing something in the present in hope of achieving greater gains in the future is _____. (159)

MATCH THESE SOCIAL SCIENTISTS WITH THEIR CONTRIBUTIONS

__1. Karl Marx
__2. Kingsley Davis & Wilbert Moore
__3. Immanuel Wallerstein
__4. Michael Harrington
__5. John Kenneth Galbraith
__6. Max Weber
__7. Melvin Tumin
__8. Gerhard Lenski
__9. C. Wright Mills
__10. Erik Wright
__11. Gilbert & Kahl
__12. W. Lloyd Warner
__13. Melvin Kohn

a. *world system theory*
b. *criticism of functional view of stratification*
c. *stressed culture of poverty*
d. *false consciousness*
e. *stated functionalist view of stratification*
f. *neocolonialism*
g. *class based on property, prestige and power*
h. *power elite*
i. *social class patterns of child rearing*
j. *status inconsistency*
k. *updated Marx's model*
l. *pioneered the reputational model*
m. *updated Weber's model*

ESSAY QUESTIONS

1. Compare Marx's theory of stratification with Weber's theory.
2. Assume that you carry out a study of social class. Review the different ways that social class can be measured and select the one that would be most appropriate for your study. Explain your selection.
3. Consider why ideology is a more effective way of maintaining stratification than brute force.
4. In the 1960s most former colonies around the globe won their political independence. Since that time the position of these countries has remained largely unchanged within the global system of stratification. Provide some explanation as to why political independence alone was not enough to alter their status.
5. Describe which groups are a greatest risk of poverty and then suggest ways in which poverty can be reduced by targeting these populations.

"DOWN-TO-EARTH SOCIOLOGY"

1. Why do you think the income per person is so much higher in highly industrialized nations than in the least industrialized nations? Does money just "go a lot farther" in less industrialized nations or do people in these countries have much lower standards of living than people in highly industrialized nations? Could you live on $1,000 a year?
2. Study the figure on page 135 and then explain the consistency of income distribution across the years to someone who is unfamiliar with Canadian society.
3. What was your reaction after reading about children in the least industrialized nations who are growing up in poverty? (pp. 142-143) How does the image of life in the slums compare with your image of the lives of Canada's poor? Do you think that people in highly industrialized nations should do anything about this situation? If yes, what?
4. Which myths about the poor that are listed on pages 154-155 reflect your own ideas about poverty? Did the facts help you in understanding the realities of poverty?
5. After reading "Children in Poverty" (pp. 157-158), is child poverty a concern only for the poor or is it everyone's concern? What should be done to relieve the problem?
6. Do you often distinguish the deserving poor from the undeserving poor (p. 159)? Why do you think we do this? What are the social characteristics of both groups? What are the social conditions that contribute to their poverty? What can be done about it?

CHAPTER 7

INEQUALITIES OF GENDER

☞ **CHAPTER SUMMARY**

- Gender stratification refers to unequal access to power, property, and prestige on the basis of sex. Each society establishes a structure that, on the basis of sex and gender, opens and closes access to privileges. Sex refers to biological distinctions between males and females; gender refers to behaviors and attitudes thought to be socially acceptable for males and females. In the "nature versus nurture" debate, almost all sociologists take the side of nurture. In recent years the door to biology has opened somewhat.
- George Murdock found a pattern of sex-typed activities among premodern societies, with greater prestige given to those activities performed by males.
- The dominant theory to explain the status of women as a minority group focuses on the physical limitations imposed by childbirth.
- Although feminist movements have battled to eliminate some of the most blatant forms of gender discrimination, there are still many areas of inequality. More females than males now attend college, but both generally end up in gender-biased academic fields although there are some signs of change today. Two indicators of gender inequality in everyday life are the general devaluation of femininity and the male dominance of conversation.
- In the workplace women's problems include discrimination in pay and sexual harassment.
- Traditional gender patterns still exist in regard to violent behavior. Female circumcision is a special case of violence against women.
- Women in Canada have the numerical capacity to take over politics and transform society, but continue to encounter obstacles to their full participation as elected officials.
- As females come to play a larger role in decision-making processes of Canadian social institutions, stereotypes and role models will be broken. It is possible that a new concept of the human personality—one that allows males and females to pursue their individual interests unfettered by gender—might occur.

☞ **LEARNING OBJECTIVES**

As you read Chapter 7, use these learning objectives to organize your notes. After completing your reading, briefly state an answer to each of the objectives, and review the text pages in parentheses.

1. Define gender stratification and differentiate between sex and gender. (166-167)
2. Discuss the continuing controversy regarding the biological and cultural factors which come into play in creating gender differences in societies. (167)
3. Summarize findings of research studies that suggest biology does play a role in gender behavior. (167-169)
4. Describe the global nature of male dominance. (169-170)
5. Discuss the dominant theories about the origins of discrimination against women. (170-172)
6. Describe the major factors which contributed to the two "waves" of feminism in Canada and note how successful this movement has been up to this point in time. (172-174)
7. Discuss ways in which educational systems may perpetuate gender inequality. (174-177)
8. Describe how gender inequality is expressed in everyday life. (177-178)
9. Explain gender relations in the workplace, including the pay gap, the glass ceiling, the "mommy track," and sexual harassment. (178-182)

10. Explain what the authors mean when they say gender violence is a "one-way street." (182-184)
11. Explain why women historically have not taken over politics and transformed Canadian life. (184-185)
12. Describe what the future looks like in terms of gender relations in Canada. (186)

☞ **CHAPTER OUTLINE**

I. **Issues of Sex and Gender**
    A. Gender stratification refers to men's and women's unequal access to power, prestige, and property.
    B. Sex and gender reflect different bases.
        1. Sex is biological characteristics distinguishing males and females—primary sex organs (organs related to reproduction) and secondary sex organs (physical distinctions not related to reproduction).
        2. Gender is a social characteristic which varies from one society to another and refers to what the group considers proper for its males and females. The sociological significance of gender is that it is the means by which society controls its members; it sorts us, on the basis of sex, into different life experiences.
    C. Some researchers argue that biological factors (two X chromosomes in females, one X and one Y in males) result in differences in conduct, with men being more aggressive and domineering and women being more comforting and nurturing.
    D. The dominant sociological position is represented by the symbolic interactionists, who stress that people in every society determine what physical differences mean to them: males and females take the positions that society assigns to them.
    E. Alice Rossi suggested that women are better prepared biologically for "mothering" than are men: nature provides biological predispositions which are overlaid with culture.
    F. Real-life cases provide support for the argument that men's and women's behaviour is influenced by both culture and biology.
        1. A medical accident led to a young boy being reassigned to the female sex. Reared as a female, the child behaved like a girl; however, by adolescence she was unhappy and having a difficult time adjusting to being a female.

II. **Gender Inequality in Global Perspective**
    A. Historian and feminist Gerda Lerner has concluded that women as a group have never held decision-making power over men as a group. This was true even in the earliest known societies, in which there was much less gender discrimination.
    B. George Murdock, who surveyed 324 premodern societies, found activities to be sex-typed in all of them, although activities considered female in one society may be male in another. There is nothing about anatomy that requires this.
    C. Universally, greater prestige is given male activities regardless of what they are. If caring for cattle is men's work, it carries high prestige; if it is women's work, it has less prestige.
    D. Globally, gender discrimination occurs in the areas of education, politics, paid employment, and violence.

III. **Gender Inequality in Theoretical Perspective**
    A. Around the world, gender is the primary division between people. Because society sets up barriers to deny women equal access, they are referred to as a minority even though they outnumber men.
    B. Although the origin of patriarchy (male dominance) is unknown, the dominant theory

assumes that patriarchy is universal and that biology along with social factors plays a role in male dominance.

1.   In early societies, life was short and many children needed to be born in order for the group to survive. Consequently, women were pregnant or nursing young children for much of their adult lives. As a result of these biologically driven activities, women were limited in terms of alternatives and assumed tasks associated with the home and child care.

2.   Men took over tasks requiring greater strength and longer absences, such as hunting animals. This enabled men to make contact with other tribes, trade with those other groups, and wage war and gain prestige by returning home with prisoners of war or with large animals to feed the tribe; little prestige was given to women's more routine tasks.

C.   The answer as to the accuracy of this theory is buried in human history and there is no way of testing either this one or others suggested by Marvin Harris, Frederick Engels, or Gerda Lerner. Whatever the origin, male dominance continues into the present.

IV.   **Gender Inequality in Canada**

A.   A society's culture and institutions both justify and maintain its customary forms of gender inequality.

B.   Until this century, Canadian women did not have the right to vote, hold property, testify in court, or serve on a jury; if a woman worked outside the home, she handed the wages she earned over to her father or husband.

1.   Males did not willingly surrender their privileges; rather, greater political rights for women resulted from a prolonged and bitter struggle waged by a first wave of feminists in the 19th and early 20th centuries.

2.   A second wave of feminism began in the 1960s. As more women gained an education and began to work outside the home, they compared their wages and working conditions to those of men. As awareness of gender inequalities grew, protest and struggle emerged. The goals of this second wave of feminism are broad, from changing work roles to changing policies on violence against women.

3.   Both waves of feminism were characterized by two branches—one conservative and the other liberal—each of which has had different goals and different tactics.

4.   While women enjoy more rights today, gender inequality still exists.

C.   Despite evidence of educational gains made by women—more females than males are enrolled in Canadian universities and females earn 59% of all bachelor's and first professional degrees—some traditional male-female distinctions persist.

1.   At university males and females are channeled into different fields; 94% of bachelor's degrees in nursing are awarded to females; 81% of engineering degrees are awarded to males.

2.   The proportion of females decreases in graduate school.

3.   There is gender stratification in both the rank and pay within higher educational institutions. Women are less likely to be in the higher ranks of academia, and at all levels are paid less than their male counterparts.

4.   Changes are occurring. The proportion of women earning professional degrees has increased sharply.

D.   Patterns of gender discrimination continue to exist in everyday life.

1.   Females' capacities, interests, attitudes, and contributions are not taken as seriously as those of males. For example, the worst insult that can be thrown at a male is that he is a sissy, or they he does things like a girl.

2.   Patterns of conversation reflect inequalities between men and women. Men are more likely than women to interrupt a conversation and to control a change in topics.

V.   Gender Relations in the Workplace

A.   Men continue to earn more than women in the Canadian work force, although the gap is closing.

1.   At all levels of educational achievement women earn less than men.

2.   Women in the work force are more likely to be excluded from the inner circle and average only 73.4% of men's wages.

3.   Research by Fuller and Schoenberger found that upon entry to a career, women averaged lower pay than men, even when they have more qualifications than their male counterparts; five years after graduation from college, the pay gap was even wider than it was upon entering the job market.

4.   A 1993 *Financial Post* survey found that less than 2% of all CEOs are women.

B.   The "glass ceiling" describes an invisible barrier that women face in trying to reach the executive suites.

1.   Researchers find that women are not in the positions like marketing, sales, and production—positions from which top executives are recruited. Rather they are in human resources and public relations; their work is not appreciated to the same degree because it does not bring in profits.

2.   Much of the blame for this situation rests with the male corporate culture. Those in power look for potential leaders who have the same characteristics as themselves; they steer white males into the "pipeline" for promotions and women and minorities into other positions.

3.   Another explanation for the situation is that women lack mentors; male executives are reluctant to mentor them because they fear the gossip and sexual harassment charges if they get too close to female subordinates, or because they see women as weak.

4.   There are cracks in the glass ceiling as women learn to play by "men's rules" and develop a style with which men feel comfortable.

5.   Men who go into nontraditional fields do not encounter a glass ceiling; rather they find a "glass escalator"—they move up more quickly than female co-workers.

C.   Since most wives spend more time and take greater responsibility in caring for the children, it has been suggested that corporations offer women a choice of two parallel career paths.

1.   The "fast track" (may require 60 or 70 hours of work per week, unexpected out-of-town meetings, etc.); or the "mommy track" (stresses both career and family).

2.   Critics suggest that the mommy track would encourage women to be satisfied with lower aspirations and fewer promotions, it would perpetuate or increase the executive pay gap, and it would confirm stereotypes about female executives.

3.   Felice Schwartz, who first proposed these alternatives, counters critics with the idea of a "zigzag" track, in which both men and women would slow down during the time that their children were small, picking up speed once again when the children were older.

4.   Critics suggest that a better way than the mommy track is for husbands to share responsibility at home and for firms to provide day care.

D.   Until the 1970s, women did not draw a connection between unwanted sexual advances on the job and their subordinate positions at work.

1. As women began to discuss the problem, they named it (sexual harassment) and came to see such unwanted sexual advances by men in powerful positions as a structural problem. The change in perception resulted from reinterpreting women's experiences—giving them a name.

2. As more women have moved into positions of power, sexual harassment has not been exclusively a woman's problem, although male victims are less frequent than female victims and are less likely to find sympathy for their situation.

VI.   Gender and Violence

A. Most victims of violence are females.

1. Women are more likely than men to experience assault from an intimate male partner, while men are more likely to be assaulted by a stranger. In both Canada and the United States, convicted rapists are almost exclusively young males.

2. Date rape—sexual assault in which the assailant is acquainted with the victim—is not an isolated event and is most likely to occur between couples who have known each other for about a year.

3. Males are more likely than females to commit murder and be the victim of murder.

4. Other forms of violence against women include battering, spousal abuse, incest and female circumcision.

B. Feminists use symbolic interactionism to understand violence against women. They stress that Canadian culture promotes violence by males. It teaches men to associate power, dominance, strength, virility and superiority with masculinity. Men use violence to try and maintain a higher status.

C. To solve violence we must first break the link between violence and masculinity.

VII.   Gender and Change

A. Despite the gains Canadian women have made in recent elections, they continue to be underrepresented in political office, especially in higher office. Reasons for this include:

1. Women are still underrepresented in law and business, the careers from which most politicians are drawn.

2. Women do not see themselves as a voting bloc who need political action to overcome discrimination.

3. Women still find the roles of mother and politician incompatible.

4. Males seldom incorporate women into the centers of decision making or present them as viable candidates.

5. Trends in the 1990s indicate that women will participate in political life in far greater numbers than in the past.

B. Canadian women are developing a notable presence in professional, amateur, and school-sponsored sports of all types, at all levels.

1. Women's sports continue to be underfunded, however, and are often marginalized.

2. Images of lean, muscular bodies and competitive spirits conflict with dominant conceptions of femininity and motherhood.

3. Despite these obstacles, women's participation in organized sports is increasing.

C. As women have challenged gendered norms, men have begun to adapt.

1. More men are working outside the home and undertaking unpaid housekeeping duties.

2. Awareness of men's concerns over body image has been raised in recent studies.

3. The men's cosmetic industry has experienced a boom in recent years and men's clothing lines have grown.

VIII. Glimpsing the Future—With Hope
   A.   As women play a fuller role in the decision-making processes, further structural obstacles to women's participation in society will give way.
   B.   As gender stereotypes are abandoned, both males and females will be free to feel and express their needs and emotions, something that present arrangements deny them.

☞ KEY TERMS

After studying the chapter, review the definition for each of the following terms.

feminism: the philosophy that men and women should be politically, economically, and socially equal, and organized activity on behalf of this principle

gender: the social characteristics that a society considers proper for its males and females; masculinity or femininity

gender stratification: males' and females' unequal access to power, prestige, and property on the basis of their sex

matriarchy: a society in which women dominate men

minority group: a group that is discriminated against on the basis of its members' physical or cultural characteristics

patriarchy: a society in which men dominate women

sex: biological characteristics that distinguish females and males, consisting of primary and secondary sex characteristics

sex-typing: the association of behaviors with one sex or the other

sexual harassment: the abuse of one's position of authority to force unwanted sexual demands on someone

☞ KEY PEOPLE

Review the major theoretical contributions or findings of these people.

Janet Chafetz: Chafetz studied the second wave of feminism in the 1960s, noting that as large numbers of women began to work in the economy, they began to compare their working conditions with those of men.

Frederick Engels: Engels argued that male dominance developed with the origin of private property.

Cynthia Fuchs: Epstein: Epstein is a proponent of the view that differences between males' and females' behavior is solely the result of social factors such as socialization and social control.

Douglas Foley: This sociologist's study of sports lends support to the view that things feminine are generally devalued.

Rex Fuller and Richard Schoenberger: These economists examined the starting salaries of business majors and found that women averaged 11 percent lower pay than men right out of college, and that the gap grew to 14 percent after five years in the work force.

Steven Goldberg: This sociologist's view is that the differences between males and females are not due to environment but to inborn differences that direct the emotions and behaviors of the two genders.

Marvin Harris: This anthropologist suggested that male dominance grew out of the greater strength that men had which made them better suited for the hand-to-hand combat of tribal societies; women became the reward to entice men into battle.

Gerda Lerner: Lerner concluded that in all societies women—as a group—have never had decision-making power over men.

Catharine McKinnon: McKinnon is an activist lawyer who published a book identifying sexual harassment as a structural problem in workplaces.

George Murdock: This anthropologist surveyed 324 premodern societies around the world and found that in all of them activities were sex-typed.

Alice Rossi: This feminist sociologist has suggested that women are better prepared biologically for "mothering" than are men.

Felice Schwartz: Schwartz is associated with the notion of dual career tracks — one for women who want to combine work and motherhood (the mommy track) and the other for women who want to devote their time and energies to a career (the fast track).

Jean Stockard and Miriam Johnson: These sociologists observed boys playing basketball and heard them exchange insults that reflect a disrespect and devaluation of women.

Samuel Stouffer: In his classic study of combat soldiers during World War II, Stouffer noted the general devaluation of things associated with women.

Christine Williams: Williams found that men in non-traditional careers and occupations often experience a glass escalator — moving more quickly than women into desirable work assignments, higher-level positions, and larger salaries.

☞ SELF-TEST

After completing this self-test, check your answers against the Answer Key at the back of this Study Guide and against the text on page(s) indicated in parentheses.

MULTIPLE CHOICE QUESTIONS

1. Which of the following statements about gender stratification is *incorrect*? (166)
    a. It cuts across all aspects of social life.
    b. It cuts across all social classes.
    c. It refers to the unequal access to power, prestige, and property on the basis of sex.
    d. Unlike class stratification, it is not a structured feature of society.

2. To what does the term "sex" refer? (166)
    a. the social characteristics that a society considers proper for its males and females
    b. the biological characteristics that distinguish females and males
    c. masculinity and femininity
    d. All of the above

3. If biology is the principal factor in human behavior, around the world what would we find? (167)
    a. Things to be just like they are.
    b. Men and women to be much more like each other than they currently are.
    c. Women to be one sort of person and men another.
    d. None of the above.

4. Patriarchy: (168)
    a. is a society in which men dominate women.
    b. has existed throughout history.
    c. is universal.
    d. All of the above.

5. What is the association of behaviors with one sex or the other called? (169)
    a. sex-typing
    b. sex-association
    c. sex-discrimination
    d. sex-orientation

6. When anthropologist George Murdock surveyed 324 premodern societies, which of the following was *not* one of his findings? (169)
    a. Activities were sex-typed in all of them.
    b. Every society associates activities with one sex or the other.
    c. Biological requirements were the basis for men and women being assigned different tasks.
    d. Activities considered "female" in one society may be considered "male" activities in another.

7. In regard to the prestige of work: (170)
    a. greater prestige is given to activities which are considered to be of great importance to a society, regardless of whether they are performed by females or males.
    b. greater prestige goes to female activities that males can't do, like pregnancy and lactation.
    c. greater prestige is given to male activities.
    d. None of the above.

8. Which statement concerning global discrimination is *incorrect*? (170)
    a. Of about 1 billion adults around the world who can't read, two-thirds are women.
    b. Canada leads the world in the number of women who hold public office.
    c. Around the globe, women average less pay than men.
    d. A global human rights issue has become violence against women.

9. In which of the following do women still not have the right to vote? (170)
    a. Kenya
    b. Kuwait
    c. Bosnia
    d. Vietnam

10. Which of the statements below applies to minority groups? (170)
    a. A minority group is a politically correct way of referring to those who feels that life has treated them unfairly.
    b. A minority group is of little interest to sociologists, who study dominant groups instead of minority ones.
    c. A minority group is a group that is discriminated against on the basis of its smaller size.
    d. A minority group is a group that is discriminated against on the basis of its members' physical or cultural characteristics.

11. Historically in Canada, women: (172)
    a. did not have the right to vote until the 1950s.
    b. were allowed to make legal contracts but had to be represented by an attorney because it was assumed that they were like children.
    c. could not serve on juries or hold property in their own name.
    d. could spend their own wages but had to tell their fathers how the money was spent.

12. A "second wave" of protest and struggle against gender inequalities: (174)
    a. occurred when women began to compare their working conditions with those of men.
    b. began in the 1960s.
    c. had as its goals everything from changing work roles to changing policies on violence against women.
    d. All of the above.

13. Gender inequality in education: (174-177)
    a. has virtually disappeared today.
    b. is allowed by law.
    c. is perpetuated by the use of sex to sort students into different academic disciplines.
    d. disappears by the time men and women enter graduate school.

14. Researchers who have studied conversation patterns between men and women conclude that: (177-178)
    a. women talk more and interrupt men more frequently than the other way around.
    b. men and women are social equals when it comes to everyday conversation.
    c. even in everyday conversation, the talk between a man and a woman reflects social inequality.
    d. men interrupt more in conversations, but women control the topics that are discussed.

15. The pay gap between men and women: (178)
    a. is found primarily among those with less than a high school education.
    b. is found primary among those with college and graduate education.
    c. is found at all educational levels.
    d. largely has disappeared.

16. The glass ceiling: (179)
    a. keeps both men and women out of non-traditional occupations.
    b. has largely been shattered by today's generation of business women.
    c. refers to the invisible barrier that keeps women from reaching the executive suite.
    d. All of the above.

17. Which of the following is *not* a reason for women's absence from core corporate positions? (179)
    a. The male corporate culture stereotypes potential leaders as people who look like themselves; women are seen as better at providing "support."
    b. Women do not seek out opportunities for advancement and do not spend enough time networking with powerful executives.
    c. Women lack mentors who take an interest in them and teach them the ropes.
    d. Women are generally steered away from jobs that are stepping stones to top corporate office; instead they are recruited for jobs in human resources and public relations.

18. Felice Schwartz suggested that corporations create two parallel career paths. These are: (181)
    a. the college-bound and the vocational-technical.
    b. the "partner-material" path and the "non-partner-material" path.
    c. the "mommy track" and the "daddy track."
    d. the "mommy track" and the "fast track."

19. Sexual harassment: (181-182)
   a. is still exclusively a female problem.
   b. is rooted in individual relationships rather than the structure of the workplace.
   c. involves a person in authority using the position to force unwanted sex on subordinates.
   d. means male victims of sexual harassment receive more sympathy than female victims.

20. The pattern of date rape shows: (183)
   a. that it is not an isolated event.
   b. that it is more likely to happen with couples who have dated for a period of time.
   c. it is difficult to prosecute.
   d. all of the above.

21. Which of the following is *not* among feminist explanations for gender violence? (184)
   a. higher testosterone levels in males
   b. males reassert their declining power and status
   c. the association of strength and virility with violence
   d. cultural traditions that are patriarchal

22. Women continue to be underrepresented in politics because: (184)
   a. they are not really interested in pursuing political careers.
   b. they are not viewed as serious candidates by the voters.
   c. their roles as mothers and wives are incompatible with political roles.
   d. they lack the proper educational backgrounds.

23. In many parts of Canada today, the primary concern of voters is: (185)
   a. the gender of the candidate.
   b. whether the candidate can win.
   c. whether the candidate is the primary caregiver of young children.
   d. how much money the candidate spends.

24. What is most likely to break the stereotypes locking us into traditional gender activities? (186)
   a. stricter laws
   b. equal pay
   c. increased female participation in the decision-making processes of social institutions
   d. increased male participation in nurturing activities

25. What is it that keeps most males and females locked into fairly rigid gender roles? (186)
   a. social structural obstacles
   b. socialization
   c. stereotypes
   d. all of the above

TRUE-FALSE QUESTIONS

T F   1. The terms sex and gender basically mean the same thing to sociologists. (166-167)
T F   2. The study of the medical accident that led to the sex change operation conclusively supports the view that biology is destiny. (169)
T F   3. Universally, there is great variability in terms of the amount of prestige accorded to male and female activities. (170)

T F   4.   Although female circumcision was once common in parts of Africa and southeast Asia, it is quite rare today. (170)

T F   5.   As China has begun the cautious transition to capitalism, the situation of women within that country has improved. (171)

T F   6.   Men, who are reluctant to abandon their privileged positions, use various cultural devices to keep women subservient. (172)

T F   7.   In Canada women's political rights were gained only after a prolonged and bitter struggle. (173)

T F   8.   In the second wave of the Canadian women's movement, women began to challenge the gender inequalities experienced in the workplace. (174)

T F   9.   In the past, some educators have claimed that women's wombs dominated their minds. (174)

T F   10. Today women and men have equal levels of achievement in higher education. (175)

T F   11. Women are less likely to hold the rank of full professor in colleges and universities, and if they do, they are likely to get paid less than male counterparts. (175)

T F   12. In a study of World War II combat soldiers, Samuel Stouffer reported that officers used feminine terms as insults to motivate soldiers. (177)

T F   13. Women are more likely to interrupt a conversation and to control changes in topics. (177-178)

T F   14. Research by Fuller and Schoenberger found that women college graduates were able to close the income gap within five years of graduating. (178)

T F   15. The "glass ceiling" and "mommy track" both have a more negative impact on women than on men in corporations and the professions. (179-181)

T F   16. The "glass escalator" refers to the opportunities that women have to advance quickly in traditional male occupations. (179-180)

T F   17. Once sexual harassment was defined as a problem, women saw some of their experiences in a different light. (181-182)

T F   18. In Canada, males are as likely as females to be victims of violence. (182)

T F   19. Women in Canada are greatly outnumbered by men in political office. (184)

T F   20. The only reason there are not more women in public office is because men keep them out. (184-185)

FILL-IN QUESTIONS

1.   Males' and females' unequal access to power, prestige, and property on the basis of sex reflects _____. (166)

2.   _____ refers to biological characteristics that distinguish females and males, consisting of primary and secondary sex characteristics. (166)

3.   The social characteristics that a society considers proper for its males and females make up an individual's _____. (167)

4.   You inherit your _____, but you learn your _____ as you are socialized into specific behaviors and attitudes. (167)

5.   A society in which women dominate men is called a _____. (168)

6.   When activities become associated with one sex or the other they are said to be _____. (169)

7.   _____, the burning of a living widow with her dead husband's body, is an example of violence against women that is embedded in social customs. (170)

8.   _____ is a particular form of violence directed exclusively against women. (170)

9.   A _____ is a group that is discriminated against on the basis of its members' physical characteristics. (170)

10.   _____ is the philosophy that men and women should be politically, economically, and socially equal. (173)

11.   The _____ prevents women from advancing to top executive positions. (179)

12.   Men who move into traditionally female occupations are likely to climb onto a _____, moving very quickly into more desirable work assignments, higher level positions, and larger salaries. (179-180)

13.   The proposed _____ would address the stresses that many working women experience when they attempt to combine careers and families. (181)

14.   The abuse of one's position of authority to force unwanted sexual demands on someone is referred to as _____. (181)

15.   _____ most commonly occurs between couples who have known each other about a year. (183)

MATCH THESE SOCIAL SCIENTISTS WITH THEIR CONTRIBUTIONS

__1. Janet Chafetz

__2. Alice Rossi

__3. Felice Schwartz

__4. Christine Williams

__5. Gerda Lerner

__6. Catharine McKinnon

__7. George Murdock

__8. Samuel Stouffer

__9. Marvin Harris

__10. Steven Goldberg

__11. Frederick Engels

__12. Douglas Foley

a.   *surveyed 324 societies and found evidence of sex-typed activities*

b.   *men in non-traditional occupations often experience a glass escalator*

c.   *male dominance grew out of the greater strength that men had*

d.   *study supports the view that things feminine are generally devalued*

e.   *associated with the notion of the mommy tack and the fast track*

f.   *differences between males and females are due to inborn differences*

g.   *women are better prepared biologically for "mothering" than are men*

h.   *identified sexual harassment as a structural problem in work places*

i.   *patriarchy may have had different origins around the globe*

j.   *male dominance developed with the origin of private property*

k.   *noted the devaluation of things associated wth women among soldiers*

l.   *studied the second wave of feminism in the 1960s*

ESSAY QUESTIONS

1.   Summarize the sociobiology argument concerning behavioral differences between men and women. Explain which position most closely reflects your own — biological, sociological, or sociobiological.

2.   Compare and contrast the two waves of the feminist movement in Canada by identifying the forces that contributed to both waves.

3.   Evaluate Felice Schwartz's proposed "mommy track," stating both the strengths and weaknesses of this approach to the problem of gender inequality.

"DOWN-TO-EARTH SOCIOLOGY"

1. Read "Thinking Critically About Social Controversy" on pages 167-168. Select one view or the other to adopt (at least temporarily) as your own and prepare a statement in which you justify your position. If you have taken the side of nurture, consider all of the forces that shape our behavior and attitudes as men or women. On the other hand, if you take the side of nature, consider whether or not this mean that male dominance and discrimination against women is inevitable. After you have considered one side, try doing the same thing with the opposing side. Then come up with an argument that combines elements of both.

2. After reading about the experiences of women in China (p. 171), what do you see as some of the factors that make it difficult for women there to improve their status today? Which do you think is a more powerful force in shaping women's position in society—economics or politics?

3. Did you realize before reading "Making the Invisible Visible" on pages 174-175 that physicians often do not take women's medical complaints as seriously as those of men? How can this type of problem be a matter of life or death? Do you think gender bias ever affects your own perceptions and behavior?

4. One of the central issues raised by contemporary Canadian feminists is that women should be granted reproductive rights—that their bodies are their own and they alone should have the right to decide what happens to them. Yet after reading about reproductive technologies on page 182, you can see that there are still areas in which women do not have this right. How do you feel—should women have exclusive control, or do men and the state have certain rights?

5. What is your view on the recent incidents involving sexual harassment in the military in the United States (p. 183)? After reading this chapter, do you think that the problem is between individuals—young men with overactive sex drives—or social structural—related to society and the inequalities based on gender?

CHAPTER 8

INEQUALITIES OF RACE AND ETHNICITY

☞ CHAPTER SUMMARY

- Race is a complex and often misunderstood concept. Race is a reality in the sense that inherited physical characteristics distinguish one group from another. However, race is a myth in the sense of one race being superior to another and of there being pure races. The idea of race is powerful, shaping basic relationships between people. Ethnic and ethnicity refer to a group of people who identify with one another on the basis of common ancestry and cultural heritage. A minority group is defined as one singled out for unequal treatment by members of the dominant group and that regards itself as the object of collective discrimination. Both race and ethnicity can be a basis for unequal treatment.

- Prejudice refers to an attitude and discrimination to unfair treatment. Individual discrimination is the negative treatment of one person by another, while institutional discrimination is discrimination built into society's social institutions.

- Psychological theories explain the origin of prejudice in terms of stress frustration that gets directed towards scapegoats and in terms of the development of authoritarian personalities. Sociologists emphasize how different social environments affect levels of prejudice. They look at the benefits and costs of discrimination, the exploitation of racial-ethnic divisions by those in power, and the self-fulfilling prophecies that are the outcome of labeling.

- Dominant groups typically practice one of six policies toward minority groups: genocide, population transfer, internal colonialism, segregation, assimilation, or pluralism.

- The major classifications in Canada are: the Native peoples, including status Indians, Métis, and Inuit; the two "Charter Groups," the French and English white settlers; and immigrant groups from other regions of the world.

- Canadian society has been described as a "vertical mosaic"—a pyramid in which the apex is composed of one dominant group, the English.

- The primary issues in Canada today around questions of race and ethnicity are demands for greater political autonomy from Quebec and new challenges of racial and ethnic diversity due to the immigration of people from the less developed nations of the world.

☞ LEARNING OBJECTIVES

As you read Chapter 8, use these learning objectives to organize your notes. After completing your reading, briefly state an answer to each of the objectives, and review the text pages in parentheses.

1. Explain how race can be both a reality and a myth and distinguish between the concepts of race and ethnicity. (192-194)
2. Define the term "minority group," explain the process by which a group becomes a minority, and identify five characteristics shared by minority groups worldwide. (194-195)
3. Differentiate between prejudice and discrimination. (195)
4. Provide examples of prejudice and discrimination among racial and ethnic groups and relate these examples to the concept of racism. (195)
5. Compare and contrast individual and institutional discrimination and give examples of each type of discrimination. (195-196)
6. Discuss the different psychological perspectives on prejudice. (196)

7.   Outline the functionalist, conflict, and symbolic interactionist perspectives on prejudice. (196-197)
8.   List and describe the six patterns of intergroup relations. (198-200)
9.   Discuss Canadian government policy with respect to Native peoples. (201-202)
10. Identify the two Charter Groups and explain why John Porter termed Canada a "vertical mosaic." (202-204)
11. Compare and contrast the experiences of immigrants from Europe, Africa, Latin and Central America, and Asia. (204-205)
12. Identify the key issues facing Canadians tied to race and ethnicity. (205)

☞ CHAPTER OUTLINE

I.   **Laying the Sociological Foundation**
     A.   Race, a group with inherited physical characteristics that distinguish it from another group, is both a myth and a reality.
          1.   It is a reality in the sense that humans come in different colors and shapes.
          2.   It is a myth because there are no pure races; what we call "races" are social classifications, not biological categories. In addition, it is a myth that any one race is superior to another.
          3.   The myth makes a difference for social life because people believe these ideas are real and they act on their beliefs.
     B.   Race and ethnicity are often confused due to the cultural differences people see and the way they define race. Ethnicity and ethnic refers to cultural characteristics that distinguish a people. Physical or cultural differences can lead to unfair treatment.
     C.   Minority groups are people singled out for unequal treatment and who regard themselves as objects of collective discrimination.
          1.   They are not necessarily in the numerical minority. Sociologists refer to those who do the discriminating as the dominant group—they have greater power, more privileges, and higher social status. The dominant group attributes its privileged position to its superiority, not to discrimination.
          2.   A group becomes a minority through expansion of political boundaries by another group. Another way for a group to become a minority is by migration into a territory, either voluntarily or involuntarily.
          3.   Shared characteristics of minorities worldwide: (1) membership is ascribed involuntarily through birth; (2) the physical or cultural traits that distinguish them are held in low esteem by the dominant group; (3) they are unequally treated by the dominant group; (4) they tend to marry within their own group; and (5) they tend to feel strong group solidarity.
     D.   Prejudice and discrimination exist throughout the world, in, for example, Canada, Israel, and Japan.
          1.   Discrimination is unfair treatment directed toward someone. When based on race, it is known as racism. It also can be based on features such as age, sex, sexual preference, religion, or politics.
          2.   Prejudice is prejudging of some sort, usually in a negative way.
          3.   Ethnocentrism is so common that each racial/ethnic group views other groups as inferior in at least some way. Studies confirm that there is less prejudice among the more educated and among younger people.
     E.   Sociologists distinguish between individual discrimination (negative treatment of one person by another) and institutional discrimination (negative treatment of a minority group that is built into a society's institutions).

II.   **Theories of Prejudice**
    A.   Psychological Perspectives
        1.   According to John Dollard, prejudice results from frustration: people unable to strike out at the real source of their frustration find scapegoats to unfairly blame.
        2.   According to Theodor Adorno, highly prejudiced people are insecure, intolerant people who long for the firm boundaries established by strong authority; he called this complex of personality traits the authoritarian personality.
        3.   Subsequent studies have generally concluded that people who are older, less educated, less intelligent and from a lower social class are more likely to be authoritarian.
    B.   Sociological Perspectives
        1.   To functionalists, the social environment can be deliberately arranged to generate either positive or negative feelings about people. Prejudice is functional in that it creates in-group solidarity and out-group antagonism. Functionalists do not justify what they discover but simply identify functions and dysfunctions of human action.
        2.   To conflict theorists, the ruling class systematically pits group against group; by splitting workers along racial ethnic lines the ruling class benefits, because solidarity among the workers is weakened. The higher unemployment rates of minorities creates a reserve labor force from which owners can draw when they need to expand production temporarily. The existence of the reserve labor force is a constant threat to white workers, who modify their demands rather than lose their jobs to unemployment.
        3.   To symbolic interactionists, the labels people learn color their perception, leading people to see certain things and be blind to others. Racial and ethnic labels are powerful because they are shorthand for emotionally laden stereotypes. Symbolic interactionists stress that people learn prejudices in interactions with others.
        4.   The stereotypes that we learn not only justify prejudice and discrimination, but they also lead to a self-fulfilling prophecy—stereotypical behavior in those who are stereotyped.

III.   **Global Patterns of Intergroup Relations**
    A.   Genocide is the actual or attempted systematic annihilation of a race or ethnic group that is labeled as less than fully human. The Holocaust is an example.
    B.   Population transfer is involuntary movement of a minority group. Indirect transfer involves making life so unbearable that members of a minority then leave; direct transfer involves forced expulsion. A combination of genocide and population transfer occurred in Bosnia, in the former Yugoslavia, as Serbs engaged in the wholesale slaughter of Muslims and Croats, with survivors forced to flee the area.
    C.   Internal colonialism is a society's policy of exploiting a minority, by using social institutions to deny it access to full benefits. Slavery is an extreme example.
    D.   Segregation is the formal separation of groups. It accompanies internal colonialism.
    E.   Assimilation is the process by which a minority is absorbed into the mainstream. Forced assimilation occurs when the dominant group prohibits the minority from using its own religion, language, customs. Permissive assimilation is when the minority adopts the dominant group's patterns in its own way and/or at its own speed.
    F.   Multiculturalism, also called pluralism, permits or encourages ethnic variation.

IV.   **The Major Classifications in Canada**
    A.   Canadians can be classified into three categories: Native peoples; the two "Charter Groups" (French and English); and all the other ethnic groups that have settled in Canada through immigration over the past century.

B. Native peoples in Canada comprise a rich diversity of customs, languages, and cultural differences that stretch back to pre-European contact.
   1. Native peoples constitute approximately 3.7% of Canada's population.
   2. These include status Indians, non-status Indians, Métis, and Inuit.
   3. The Charter of Rights and Freedoms recognizes the "existing Aboriginal and treaty rights" of Indians, Inuit, and Métis. This recognition has not resolved land claims disputes, however, as many of the land rights sought by Native peoples are contested by provincial governments and political parties.
C. The two "Charter Groups" refers to the linguistic and culturally distinct white "settler" groups, the French and British.
   1. The early history of French-English relations was characterized by struggles over the colonization of North America.
   2. The century leading up to Confederation witnessed the growth of the two Charter Groups. Each controlled its own institutional elite: the British controlled commerce, while the French Catholics held onto the professions (lawyers, doctors, clergy) and farming.
   3. As Canada developed politically and economically, it developed into a "vertical mosaic": a pyramid in which the apex was composed of one dominant Charter Group, the English.
D. Canada also includes a rich diversity of immigrants and refugees from different parts of the world. Today, the majority of Canadians have neither British nor French ancestry.
   1. New immigrants create more jobs than they fill, rather than taking employment away from other Canadians.
   2. Faced with unemployment and discrimination, however, up to 20% of some immigrant groups have returned to their native countries.

V. **Looking Toward the Future**
A. There will be two major issues facing Canadians in relation to questions of race and ethnicity. First, the continued demands for political autonomy from within Quebec. Second, new challenges of racial and ethnic diversity due to immigration, and arrivals of refugees, from less developed nations of the world.

☞ **KEY TERMS**

After studying the chapter, review the definition for each of the following terms.

assimilation: the process of being absorbed into the mainstream culture
authoritarian personality: Theodor Adorno's term for people who are prejudiced and rank high on scales of conformity, intolerance, insecurity, respect for authority, and submissiveness to superiors
Charter Groups: the term used to define the two linguistic and culturally distinct white settler groups, the French and the British
civil disobedience: the act of deliberately but peacefully disobeying laws considered unjust
compartmentalize: to separate acts from feelings or attitudes
discrimination: an act of unfair treatment directed against an individual or a group
dominant group: the group with the most power, greatest privileges, and highest social status
ethnic (and ethnicity): having distinctive cultural characteristics
ethnic cleansing: a policy of population elimination, including forcible expulsion and genocide. The term emerged in 1992 among the Serbians during their planned policy of expelling Croats and Muslims from territories claimed by them during the Yugoslav wars.
ethnic work: activities designed to discover, enhance, or maintain ethnic/racial identification

genocide: the systematic annihilation or attempted annihilation of people based on their presumed race or ethnicity

individual discrimination: the negative treatment of one person by another on the basis of that person's perceived characteristics

institutional discrimination: negative treatment of a minority group that is built into a society's institutions; also called *systemic discrimination*

internal colonialism: the policy of economically exploiting a minority group

minority group: people who are singled out for unequal treatment, and who regard themselves as objects of collective discrimination

multiculturalism (also called pluralism): a philosophy or political policy that permits or encourages ethnic variation

Native peoples: includes status Indians, non-status Indians, Métis, and Inuit

pluralism: a philosophy that permits or encourages ethnic variation

population transfer: involuntary movement of a minority group

prejudice: an attitude or prejudging, usually in a negative way

race: inherited physical characteristics that distinguish one group from another

racism: prejudice and discrimination on the basis of race

reserve labor force: the unemployed; unemployed workers are thought of as being "in reserve"—capitalists take them "out of reserve" (put them back to work) during times of high production and lay them off (put them back in reserve) when they are no longer needed

rising expectations: the sense that better conditions are soon to follow, which, if unfulfilled, creates mounting frustration

scapegoat: an individual or group unfairly blamed for someone else's troubles

segregation: the policy of keeping racial or ethnic groups apart

selective perception: seeing certain features of an object or situation but remaining blind to others

split-labor market: workers split along racial, ethnic, gender, age, or any other lines; this split is exploited by owners to weaken the bargaining power of workers

vertical mosaic: the term used by John Porter to describe the dominant position of the English Charter Group in Canadian society

☞ KEY PEOPLE

Review the major theoretical contributions or findings of these people.

Theodor Adorno: Adorno identified the authoritarian personality type.

Emery Cowen, Judah Landes and Donald Schaet: In an experiment these psychologists found that students directed frustrations onto people who had nothing to do with their problem.

John Dollard: This psychologist first suggested that prejudice is the result of frustration and scapegoats become the targets for frustration.

Raphael Ezekiel: This sociologist did participant observation of neo-Nazis and the Ku Klux Klan in order to examine racism from inside racist organizations.

John Porter: Porter studied patterns of economic inequality in Canadian society and noted the dominant position of the English Charter Group

Muzafer and Carolyn Sherif: The Sherifs researched the functions of prejudice and found that it builds in-group solidarity.

W.I. Thomas: Thomas observed that once people define a situation as real, it is real in its consequences.

Charles Wagley and Marvin Harris: These anthropologists identified the characteristics of minorities worldwide.

Louis Wirth: Wirth offered a sociological definition of minority group.

☞ **SELF-TEST**

After completing this self-test, check your answers against the Answer Key at the back of this Study Guide and against the text on page(s) indicated in parentheses.

MULTIPLE CHOICE QUESTIONS

1. Race: (192)
    a. means having distinctive cultural characteristics.
    b. means having inherited physical characteristics that distinguish one group from another.
    c. means people who are singled out for unequal treatment.
    d. is relatively easy to determine.

2. People often confuse race and ethnicity because: (194)
    a. they dislike people who are different from themselves.
    b. of the cultural differences people see and the way they define race.
    c. they are unaware of the fact that race is cultural and ethnicity is biological.
    d. All of the above.

3. A minority group: (194)
    a. is discriminated against because of physical or cultural differences.
    b. is discriminated against because of personality factors.
    c. does not always experience discrimination.
    d. All of the above.

4. To what does the dominant group in a society almost always considers its position to be due? (194)
    a. its own innate superiority
    b. its ability to oppress minority group members
    c. its ability to control political power
    d. all of the above

5. Prejudice and discrimination: (195)
    a. are less prevalent in Canada than in other societies.
    b. are more prevalent in Canada than in other societies.
    c. appear to characterize every society, regardless of size.
    d. appear to characterize only large societies.

6. Prejudice: (195)
    a. is an attitude.
    b. may be positive or negative.
    c. often is the basis for discrimination.
    d. All of the above.

7. Racism is: (195)
    a. unique to the United States.
    b. an example of individual discrimination.
    c. present only in people with authoritarian personalities.
    d. discrimination based on race.

8. The negative treatment of one person by another on the basis of personal characteristics is: (195)
    a. individual discrimination.
    b. individual prejudice.
    c. institutional discrimination.
    d. institutional prejudice.

9. What do the findings of Hartley's research on prejudice confirm? (196)
    a. prejudice is almost always based on a negative experience with a different racial or ethnic group
    b. people tend to be prejudiced against only one ethnic or racial group
    c. people are never prejudiced against groups they have never encountered
    d. prejudice does not depend on negative experiences with others

10. Sociologists encourage researchers to examine: (196)
    a. how discrimination is woven into the fabric of society.
    b. how discrimination is routinized.
    c. how discrimination sometimes becomes a matter of social policy.
    d. All of the above.

11. Why do functionalists consider prejudice functional for social groups? (196)
    a. It is a useful weapon in maintaining social divisions.
    b. It contributes to the creation of scapegoats.
    c. It helps to create solidarity within the group by fostering antagonisms directed against other groups.
    d. It affects how members of one group perceive members of other groups.

12. According to conflict theorists, prejudice: (197)
    a. benefits capitalists by splitting workers along racial or ethnic lines.
    b. contributes to the exploitation of workers, thus producing a split-labor market.
    c. keeps workers from demanding higher wages and better working conditions.
    d. All of the above.

13. Symbolic interactionists stress that prejudiced people: (197)
    a. are born that way.
    b. have certain types of personalities.
    c. learn their prejudices in interaction with others.
    d. None of the above.

14. From his research on racist groups, Raphael Ezekiel concluded that the leaders of these movements: (198)
    a. are basically ignorant people who want to stir up problems.
    b. take advantage of the masses' anxieties concerning economic insecurity and of their tendency to see the "Establishment" as the cause of economic problems.
    c. are able to distinguish clearly the nuances of racial classification, but exploit the masses perceptions that "black is black, and white is white."
    d. use race as a handy concept for recruiting followers, but that it is not really very useful in understanding why people are the way they are.

15. Genocide: (198)
    a. occurred when Hitler attempted to destroy all Jews.
    b. is the systematic annihilation of a race or ethnic group.
    c. often requires the cooperation of ordinary citizens.
    d. All of the above.

16. When a minority is expelled from a country or from a particular area of a country, the process is called: (199)
    a. population redistribution.
    b. direct population transfer.
    c. indirect population transfer.
    d. expelled population transfer.

17. A society's policy of exploiting a minority group, using social institutions to deny the minority access to the society's full benefits, is referred to as: (199)
    a. segregation.
    b. pluralism.
    c. internal colonialism.
    d. genocide.

18. The process of being absorbed into the mainstream culture is: (199)
    a. pluralism.
    b. assimilation.
    c. cultural submersion.
    d. internal colonialism.

19. Another term for pluralism is: (199)
    a. assimilation.
    b. melting pot.
    c. ethnic unity.
    d. multiculturalism.

20. The term "Charter Groups" refers to: (200)
    a. status and non-status Indians.
    b. French and English white settlers.
    c. Métis and Inuit.
    d. all of the above.

21. According to your text, the Charter of Rights and Freedoms remains unsatisfactory to many Native groups because: (201)
    a. it does not recognize the rights of Métis.
    b. it only recognizes "existing" aboriginal treaty rights.
    c. many rights to Native land claims are not recognized by some provincial governments.
    d. only the Nisg'a in British Columbia have been able to successfully negotiate land claims under the Charter.

22. The unequal distribution of economic power between the two Charter Groups was meant to be balanced by: (203)
    a. recognition of the need for special status in Quebec.
    b. government-subsidized industrialization in Quebec.
    c. laissez-faire capitalist development.
    d. political accommodation at the federal level.

23. According to John Porter, Canadian society is a "vertical mosaic" because: (204)
    a. it is structured like a pyramid, with the English at the top.
    b. it is a diverse society, representative of the interests of many ethnic groups.
    c. each of the major ethnic groups in Canada has representatives in the political elite.
    d. All of the above.

24. Which of the following statements about the economic elite in Canada is incorrect? (204)
    a. It has become more insular.
    b. It has become more integrated with the economic interests of the United States.
    c. It has become more culturally diverse.
    d. It has become more exclusive.

25. According to Metta Spencer, what factor(s) contribute to some immigrants deciding to return to their native countries? (205)
    a. policies of assimilation
    b. differences in educational requirements for some professions
    c. lack of formal protection under the Charter of Rights and Freedoms
    d. unemployment and discrimination

TRUE-FALSE QUESTIONS

T F   1. Scientists generally agree on just how many races there are in the world. (193)
T F   2. Sociologists often use the terms race and ethnicity interchangeably. (194)
T F   3. Physical or cultural differences can be a basis of unequal treatment in societies. (194)
T F   4. A group must represent a numerical minority to be considered a minority group. (194)
T F   5. Certain characteristics are shared by minorities worldwide. (195)
T F   6. Minorities often have a shared sense of identity and of common destiny. (195)
T F   7. Discrimination is unfair treatment based solely on racial characteristics. (195)
T F   8. Although prejudice can be either positive or negative, most prejudice is negative, involving a prejudging of other groups as inferior. (195)
T F   9. Discrimination often results from prejudicial attitudes. (195)
T F   10. Sociologists believe that individual discrimination is an adequate explanation for discrimination. (195-196)
T F   11. Hartley found that people who are prejudiced against one racial or ethnic group tend to be prejudiced against other groups. (196)
T F   12. Persons with an authoritarian personality are characterized by prejudice and high rankings on scales of conformity, intolerance, insecurity, and excessive respect for authority. (196)
T F   13. The Sherif study demonstrates that the social environment can be deliberately arranged to generate either positive or negative feelings about people. (197)
T F   14. Functionalists focus on the role of the capitalist class in exploiting racism and ethnic inequalities. (197)

T F 15. Symbolic interactionists stress that prejudiced people learn their prejudices in interaction with others. (197)

T F 16. Genocide often relies on labeling and compartmentalization. (198)

T F 17. Segregation allows the dominant group to exploit the labor of the minority while maintaining social distance. (199)

T F 18. Native Canadians did not consent to the patriation of the Canadian constitution because they feel that the Charter of Rights and Freedoms does not sufficiently recognize treaty rights. (201)

T F 19. Porter found that members of the English Charter Group dominate Canada's political and media elites. (204)

T F 20. Spencer found that while British and American immigrants tend to do well in Canada, others are apt to be less successful. (205)

FILL-IN QUESTIONS

1. _____ is inherited physical characteristics that distinguish one group from another. (192)

2. Membership in a minority group is a(n) _____ status; that is, it is not voluntary, but comes through birth. (194)

3. _____ is discrimination on the basis of race. (195)

4. _____ discrimination is the negative treatment of a minority group that is built into a society's institutions. (195-196)

5. Theodor Adorno's term for people who are prejudiced and rank high on scales of conformity, intolerance, insecurity, respect for authority, and submissiveness to superiors is _____. (196)

6. _____ theorists believe that prejudice can be both functional and dysfunctional. (197)

7. Dual labor market is used by _____ theorists to explain how racial and ethnic strife can be used to pit workers against one another. (197)

8. The term used to describe the unemployed who can be put to work during times of high production and then discarded when no longer needed is _____. (197)

9. _____ is the ability to see certain points but remain blind to others. (197)

10. The systematic annihilation or attempted annihilation of a race or ethnic group is _____. (198)

11. The types of population transfer are: (1) _____ and (2) _____. (199)

12. The policy of forced expulsion and genocide is referred to as _____. (199)

13. _____ is the process of being absorbed into the mainstream culture. (199)

14. _____ is a philosophy or political policy that permits or even encourages ethnic variation. (199)

15. _____ is Porter's term to describe the economic and political dominance of Canada by the English Charter Group. (204)

MATCH THESE SOCIAL SCIENTISTS WITH THEIR CONTRIBUTIONS

__1. Theodor Adorno   a. *suggested that prejudice is the result of frustration*

__2. W.I. Thomas   b. *offered a sociological definition of minority group*

__3. John Dollard   c. *observed that defining a situation as real makes it real in its consequences*

__4. Raphael Ezekiel   d. *identified the authoritarian personality type*

__5. Louis Wirth   e. *studied racism in neo-Nazis and the KKK organizations*

ESSAY QUESTIONS

1. Explain what the authors mean when they say that race is both a myth and a reality.
2. Using the experiences of different racial and ethnic groups in Canada, identify and discuss the six patterns of intergroup relations.
3. Explore how both psychological and sociological theories can be used together to gain a deeper understanding of prejudice and discrimination.

"DOWN-TO-EARTH SOCIOLOGY"

1. After reading about "The Racist Mind" (p. 198), why do you think hate groups have recently grown in number? What social changes have contributed to the emergence of such groups? How do Ezekiel's research findings fit with Adorno's concept of the authoritarian personality?
2. What were the rationales given by the Canadian federal government to support the relocation of Inuit peoples (pp. 201-202)? What were the impacts of these relocations? Is some form of restitution in order? What would be an appropriate form of compensation?
3. What does the history of Louis Riel (pp. 203-204) tell us about French-English relations? About relations with Native peoples? To what extent is Riel's legacy still felt today?

CHAPTER 9

INEQUALITIES OF AGE

☞ CHAPTER SUMMARY

- There are no universal attitudes, beliefs or policies regarding the aged; attitudes and practices range from exclusion and killing to integration and honour. Today there is a trend for people to live longer. In Canada, the rising proportion of older people in the population is referred to as the "graying of Canada." Because of this trend, the cost of health care for the elderly has become a social issue, and sentiment about the elderly seems to be shifting.

- The symbolic interaction perspective identifies four factors that influence when people label themselves as "old": biological changes, biographical events, gender roles, and cultural timetables. Ageism is based on stereotypes that are influenced by the mass media.

- The functionalist perspective analyzes the withdrawal of the elderly from positions of responsibility. Disengagement and activity theories are two functional theories arising from research in this area.

- Conflict theorists study the potential for conflict created by issues related to aging (e.g., struggles by seniors to protect pension programs).

- Problems of dependency for the elderly include inadequate nursing homes, elder abuse, and poverty. About one-third of elderly men and one-half of women will spend at least some time in nursing homes.

- Industrialization has changed the individual's experience with death. The process of dying involves denial, anger, negotiation, depression, and acceptance. Hospices, a recent cultural device, are intended to provide dignity in death, to reduce the emotional and physical burden on relatives, to reduce costs, and to make people comfortable during the living-dying interval. Suicide increases with age and shows sharply different patterns by sex and race.

☞ LEARNING OBJECTIVES

As you read Chapter 9, use these learning objectives to organize your notes. After completing your reading, briefly state an answer to each of the objectives, and review the text pages in parentheses.

1. Explain what the "social construction of aging" means and how industrialization affects the aged population. (210-212)
2. Examine what the term "graying of Canada" means and discuss differences in aging based on gender and ethnicity. (213-214)
3. Discuss the major conclusions drawn by symbolic interactionists regarding aging. (214-216)
4. Use cross-cultural comparisons to show how societies vary widely in their perceptions of what makes a person old, what it means to grow old, and how the elderly are viewed. (216-217)
5. Review how the meaning of old age has changed over time in Canada and consider some of the factors that contributed to this change. (217)
6. Discuss ways in which the mass media perpetuate these ideas. (217-218)
7. Summarize the functionalist perspective on aging and explain disengagement and activity theories. (219-220)
8. Explain why conflict theorists see social life as a struggle between groups for scarce resources, note how this impacts different age cohorts, and discuss senior empowerment. (220-224)

9.   State some of the problems of dependency, especially in regard to isolation, nursing homes, elder abuse, and poverty. (224-227)

10. Examine the effects of industrialization and new technology on the process of death and dying. (227)

11. Outline the stages people go through when they are told they have an incurable disease. (227-228)

12. Explain the functions of hospices in modern societies. (228)

13. Give reasons for the high rate of suicide among the elderly. (228-229)

☞ **CHAPTER OUTLINE**

I.   **Aging in Global Perspective**

A.   Every society must deal with the problem of people growing old; as the proportion of the population that is old increases, those decisions become more complex and the tensions between the generations grow deeper.

B.   Attitudes about aging are socially constructed—related to how a society views the aged—and the aging process depends on culture, not on biology.

1.   The Abkhasians may be the longest-lived people in the world, with many claiming to live past 100.

2.   The main factors that appear to account for their long lives are diet, lifelong physical activity, and a highly developed sense of community.

C.   As a country industrializes, more of its people reach older ages.

1.   This reflects the higher standard of living, better public health measures, and successes in fighting deadly diseases.

2.   As the proportion of elderly increases, so does the bill that younger citizens must pay in order to provide for their needs. Among industrialized nations, this bill has become a major social issue.

D.   In Canada, the "graying of Canada" refers to the proportion of older persons in Canada's population.

1.   Today over 12% of the population has achieved age 65; there are now 3.5 million seniors in Canada.

2.   While life expectancy—the number of years an average newborn can expect to live—has increased, the life span—maximum length of life—has not.

3.   Women's life expectancy is higher than that of men. The life expectancy of Native Canadians is less than that of non-Native Canadians.

II.   **The Symbolic Interactionist Perspective**

A.   There are several factors that push people to apply the label.

1.   Biology changes how a person looks and feels; the person adopts the role of "old" (acts the way old people are thought to act) upon experiencing these changes.

2.   Personal history (an injury that limits mobility) or biography (becoming a grandmother at an early age) may affect self-concept regarding age.

3.   Gender age also plays a part. The relative values that culture places on men's ages is less than that of women's ages.

4.   When a particular society defines a person as "old," the person is likely to feel "old." These timetables are not fixed; groups sometimes adjust expectations about the onset of old age.

B.   Aging is relative; when it begins and what it means varies from culture to culture.

1.   The Tiwi tribe is a gerontocracy (a society run by the elderly) where older men are so entrenched in power that they control all of the wealth and all of the women.

2. To grow old in traditional Inuit society meant voluntary death. Inuit society was so precarious that a person no longer able to pull his or her own weight was expected to simply go off and die.

C. Robert Butler coined the term ageism to refer to prejudice, discrimination, and hostility directed at people because of their age.

1. With the coming of industrialization, the traditional bases of respect for the elderly eroded. The distinctiveness of age was lost and new ideas of morality made the opinions of the elderly outmoded. The meaning of old age was transformed—from usefulness to uselessness, from wisdom to foolishness, from an asset to a liability.

2. The meaning of old age is being transformed with the increasing wealth of Canadian elderly and the coming of age of the Baby Boom generation. The Baby Boom generation, given their vast numbers and economic clout, are likely to positively affect our images of the elderly.

D. The mass media communicate messages about the aged, not only reflecting their devalued status, but also reinterpreting and refining it.

1. On TV, in advertisements, and in most popular magazines the elderly are likely to be stereotyped in unflattering terms; the message is that they are past their prime and of little consequence.

2. Because of the negative images of aging, people try to deny that they are growing old; the media then exploit this fear of aging to sell things asserted to avoid even the appearance of age.

3. The Canadian Association of Retired Persons provides a mechanism through which to lobby for more positive images of seniors.

III. The Functionalist Perspective

A. Functionalists examine age from the standpoint of how those persons who are retiring and those who will replace them in the work force make mutual adjustments.

B. Elaine Cumming and William Henry developed disengagement theory to explain how society prevents disruption to itself when the elderly retire. The elderly are rewarded in some way (pensions) for giving up positions rather than waiting until they become incompetent or die; this allows for a smooth transition of positions. This theory is criticized because it assumes that the elderly disengage and then sink into oblivion.

C. Activity theory examines people's reactions to exchanging one set of roles for another. Older people who maintain a high level of activity tend to be more satisfied with life than those who do not. Level of activity is connected to key factors such as social class, health, and individual orientation.

1. Most research findings support the hypothesis that more active people are more satisfied people.

2. Underlying people's activities are finances, health, and individual orientation.

IV. The Conflict Perspective

A. Conflict theorists examine social life as a struggle between groups for scarce resources. Pension legislation is an example of that struggle.

1. Since the 1920s, the federal and provincial governments have increasingly introduced policies to provide some measure of economic security for seniors. Currently Canadian seniors are supported by a three-level retirement system which includes the Old Age Security System, the Canada and Quebec Pension Plan, and registered retirement savings plans.

2. Conflict theorists state that pension legislation was not a result of generosity, but rather of competition among interest groups.

B.   Since equilibrium is only a temporary balancing of social forces, some form of continuing conflict between the younger and the older appears inevitable.

1.   The huge costs of government pension funds have become a national concern. The dependency ratio (number of workers compared with number of recipients) is currently four working-age Canadians paying to support each person over 65, but is expected to drop to a ratio of 2-to-1 by 2030.

2.   Sociologists are new drawing attention to the tension between younger and older generations due to a perception among younger Canadians that they are being denied the opportunities enjoyed by their parents and grandparents.

C.   Empowering the elderly, some organizations today work to protect the hard-won gains of the elderly.

1.   The Gray Panthers was organized in the 1960s to encourage persons of all ages to work for the welfare of both the elderly and the young. On the micro level, the goal is to develop positive self concepts; on the macro level, the goal is to build a power base with which to challenge all institutions that oppress the poor, whether young or old.

2.   To protect their gains, older Canadians have organized groups such as the Fédération de l'Age d'Or du Québec, the Alberta Council of Aging, Grandparents Raising Grandchildren, and the Ontario Network for the Prevention of Elder Abuse. The most telling example of the ability of Canadian seniors to mobilize effectively and quickly around a social issue was the seniors' response to the 1985 government efforts to de-index government pensions.

V.   Problems of Dependency

A.   The elderly are not as isolated as stereotypes would lead us to believe.

1.   Most elderly are not isolated; 62% live with their immediate family and 7% live with their extended family.

2.   Because of women's longevity and patterns of marriage age, women are more likely to end up on their own than men.

B.   A large number of Canadians living at home report at least one chronic health problem; one-third of seniors living at home report cognitive difficulties.

C.   Currently, care for ill or disabled seniors is provided by an uneven mix of home care, hospital care, and institutional care. Seniors make up 74% of all institutionalized Canadians.

1.   Individuals who continue to live in their communities must rely on informal caregivers. Such individuals often become the responsibilities of daughters and elderly wives.

D.   Elder abuse may come from professional caregivers or family members. One reason for abuse from family members may be due to stress from caring for a highly dependent person. Feminist researchers also point to the need to understand elder abuse in relation to patterns of gender inequalities and the subordination of women.

E.   A major fear of the elderly is that their money may not last as long as their life does.

1.   Despite improvements due to increased government income support, many seniors still live near the poverty line.

2.   Almost half of unattached senior women live in poverty.

VI.   The Sociology of Death and Dying

A.   In preindustrial societies, the sick were cared for at home and died at home. With the coming of modern medicine, dying was transformed into an event to be managed by professionals; most people never have personally seen anyone die.

1. The process of dying has become strange to most people; we hide from the fact of death, we even construct a language of avoidance—a person is "gone" or "at peace now," rather than dead.
2. New technology has produced "technological lifespace." This refers to a form of existence that is neither life nor death; the person is brain dead, but the body lives on.

B. Elisabeth Kübler-Ross identified the stages a person passes through when told that she or he has an incurable disease: (1) denial; (2) anger; (3) negotiation; (4) depression; and (5) acceptance. Kübler-Ross noted that not everyone experiences all of these stages and not everyone goes through them in order.

C. Elderly persons want to die with dignity in the comforting presence of friends and relatives. Due to advances in medical technology, most deaths in Canada occur after the age of 65.
1. Hospitals are awkward places to die, surrounded by strangers in hospital garb in an organization that puts routine ahead of individual needs. Patients experience what sociologists call "institutional death."
2. Hospices have emerged as a solution to these problems, providing greater dignity and comfort at less cost.

D. The elderly have been a part of the general trend towards an increasing suicide rate from the 1920's to the 1980's.
1. The suicide rate for senior men is six times higher than that for women.
2. To explain seniors' suicide rates, research has suggested that some seniors may have stronger feelings of lack of meaning in life, and feelings of isolation and loneliness. Ill health may contribute as well.

☞ KEY TERMS

After studying the chapter, review the definition for each of the following terms.

activity theory: the view that satisfaction during old age is related to a person's level and quality of activity

age cohort: people born at roughly the same time who pass through the life course together

ageism: prejudice, discrimination, and hostility directed against people because of their age; can be directed against any age group, including youth

dependency ratio: the number of workers required to support dependent persons—those 64 and older and those 15 and younger

disengagement theory: the view that society prevents disruption by having the elderly vacate (or disengage from) their positions of responsibility so that the younger generation can step into their shoes

gender age: the relative values of men's and women's ages in a particular culture

gerontocracy: a society (or other group) run by the elderly

graying of Canada: a term that refers to the rising proportion of older persons as a percentage of the Canadian population

hospice: a place, or services brought into someone's home, for the purpose of bringing comfort and dignity to a dying person

life expectancy: the number of years that an average newborn can expect to live

life span: the maximum length of life of a species

☞ KEY PEOPLE

Review the major theoretical contributions or findings of these people.

Robert Butler: Butler coined the term "ageism" to refer to prejudice, discrimination and hostility directed against people because of their age.

Karen Cerulo and Janet Ruane: These sociologists have suggested that new technologies have brought on new experiences of death; they use the term "technological lifespace" to refer to an existence that is neither life nor death.

Elaine Cumming and William Henry: These two developed disengagement theory to explain how society prevents disruption when the elderly vacate their positions of responsibility.

Dorothy Jerrome: This anthropologist is critical of disengagement theory, pointing out that it contains implicit bias against old people.

Elisabeth Kübler-Ross: This psychologist found that coming face-to-face with one's own death sets in motion a five-stage process.

☞ SELF-TEST

After completing this self-test, check your answers against the Answer Key at the back of this Study Guide and against the text on page(s) indicated in parentheses.

MULTIPLE CHOICE QUESTIONS

1. The Abkhasians are an interesting example regarding age because they: (210)
   a. live such short lives.
   b. live such long lives.
   c. have so many words in their language for "old people."
   d. quit working when they were quite young.

2. Which of the following contributes to an increase in the number of people who reach older ages? (212)
   a. changing social attitudes about aging
   b. reduction in warfare
   c. later retirement
   d. industrialization

3. The process by which older persons make up an increasing proportion of Canada's population is referred to as: (213)
   a. the aging process.
   b. the graying of Canada.
   c. the gentrification process.
   d. None of the above.

4. What explains the fact that Native Canadians have lower life expectancy? (213)
   a. different cultural attitudes about aging
   b. biological differences and susceptibility to disease
   c. the presence or absence of networks of support within each group's community
   d. higher rates of unemployment, economic marginalization, homelessness, and inadequate housing

5.   The relative value that a culture places on men's and women's ages is: (215)
     a.   cultural aging.
     b.   ageism.
     c.   gender age.
     d.   relative age.

6.   Factors that may push people to apply the label of old to themselves include: (215-216)
     a.   personal history or biography.
     b.   cultural signals about when a person is old.
     c.   biological factors.
     d.   All of the above.

7.   A local miniature golf course bars children under the age of 16 from playing golf after 6 p.m. What does this policy reflect? (217)
     a.   sound business practices
     b.   ageism
     c.   the graying of Canada
     d.   misguided efforts to control juvenile customers

8.   It has been suggested that _____ will have a positive effect on Canadian social images of the elderly in the years to come, given their numbers and economic clout. (217)
     a.   Parliament
     b.   the Baby Boom generation
     c.   Generation X
     d.   seniors living on RRSPs

9.   The mass media: (217-218)
     a.   communicate messages that reflect the currently devalued status of the elderly.
     b.   tell us what people over 65 should be like.
     c.   often treat the elderly in discourteous and unflattering terms.
     d.   All of the above.

10. Some researchers believe that the process of disengagement begins: (219)
     a.   when a person first starts a job.
     b.   during middle age.
     c.   at retirement.
     d.   about one year after retirement.

11. _____ suggests that satisfaction in old age depends on one's level/quality of activity. (219)
     a.   Activity theory
     b.   Recreational theory
     c.   Satisfaction theory
     d.   None of the above.

12. Conflict theorists believe that pension legislation is the result of: (221)
     a.   generous hearts in Parliament.
     b.   a struggle between competing interest groups.
     c.   many years of hard work by elderly Canadians.
     d.   None of the above.

13. As the population of Canada grays, there is concern that: (221)
    a. participation in the electoral process will decline because older citizens are less likely to vote.
    b. the ratio of working people to retired people will become smaller, making it more difficult to support programs like pension benefits.
    c. there will be a shortage of affordable housing for widowed individuals living on a fixed income.
    d. All of the above.

14. Isolation is a problem for many people over 65, especially for: (224)
    a. women.
    b. minorities.
    c. the disabled.
    d. immigrants.

15. Drawbacks to current family-based elder care include: (226)
    a. caring responsibilities fall disproportionately on women.
    b. few adult women and men can afford the time and energy necessary to provide informal care.
    c. responsibility for an ailing senior may be too emotionally and physically exhausting.
    d. All of the above.

16. Researchers have found that elder abuse: (226)
    a. occurs less frequently than one might think, given the level of abuse shown in the media.
    b. is fairly extensive.
    c. is most often caused by workers in nursing homes.
    d. is easy to study because the victims are so visible.

17. The percentage of Canadians aged 65 and older living below the poverty line: (227)
    a. has declined since the 1980s.
    b. has increased relative to the population under 65 who live below the poverty line.
    c. has remained unchanged since the 1980s.
    d. has become increasingly more male, as men's life expectancy has improved.

18. Karen Cerulo and Janet Ruane use the term _____ to describe a form of existence that is neither life nor death—the brain is dead but the body lives on. (227)
    a. institutional death
    b. technological lifespace
    c. technological fix
    d. living death

19. In preindustrial societies, the sick: (227)
    a. were taken care of at home.
    b. were taken care of in hospitals.
    c. were taken care of in hospices.
    d. did not live long enough to have to be taken care of by anyone.

20. In trying to explain suicide rates of seniors, sociologists point out: (229)
     a.   feelings of lack of meaning in life.
     b.   feelings of isolation and loneliness.
     c.   ill health.
     d.   All of the above.

TRUE-FALSE QUESTIONS

T F   1.   When sociologists say that aging is socially constructed, what they mean is that attitudes about aging reflect cultural values rather than biological factors. (210)

T F   2.   Industrialization is less important than cultural attitudes in influencing the growth in the number of elderly within a society. (212)

T F   3.   Life expectancy and life span describe the same thing. (213)

T F   4.   According to the symbolic interactionists, a person's perception of "old" and what it means to be old is influenced by stereotypes and societal definitions of age. (214-215)

T F   5.   That older male news anchors are likely to be retained by news stations while female anchors who turn the same age are more likely to be transferred to a less visible position is an example of gender age. (215)

T F   6.   A gerontocracy is a society run by younger people on behalf of the elderly. (216)

T F   7.   In Canada today, the elderly are underrepresented on TV, in ads, and even in popular magazines. (218)

T F   8.   Disengagement theory is used to explain how society prevents disruption by having the elderly vacate their positions of responsibility. (219)

T F   9.   Activity theorists believe that older people who maintain a high level of activity tend to be more satisfied with life than those who do not. (219)

T F   10. According to conflict theorists, the passage of pension legislation is an example of the struggle between the young and old in society. (221)

T F   11. The dependency ratio is the number of workers compared to the number of QPP/CPP recipients. (221)

T F   12. The elderly are more isolated than stereotypes would lead us to believe. (224)

T F   13. Elder abuse includes abuse from both professional caregivers and family members. (226)

T F   14. The income level of Canada's seniors has declined since 1980. (227)

T F   15. Industrialization radically altered the circumstances of dying. (227)

FILL-IN QUESTIONS

1.   The process by which older persons make up an increasing proportion of Canada's population is called _____. (213)

2.   The _____ of an average newborn is the number of years he or she can expect to live. (213)

3.   While experts may disagree on the actual number, _____ refers to the maximum length of life of a species. (213)

4.   The relative value that a culture places on men's and women's ages is referred to as _____. (215)

5.   _____ is a society (or other group) run by the old. (216)

6.   _____ is the discrimination against the elderly because of their age. (217)

7.   The _____ not only communicate messages about the devalued status of the elderly in Canadian society but also contribute to the ideas. (217-218)

8. An _____ is people born at roughly the same time who pass through the life course together. (219)

9. The belief that society prevents disruption by having the elderly vacate their positions of responsibility is _____. (219)

10. _____ theory asserts that satisfaction during old age is related to a person's level and quality of activity. (219)

11. The number of workers required to support the portion of the population aged 64 and older is the _____. (221)

12. Founded in the 1960s by Margaret Kuhn, the _____ encourages people of all ages to work for the welfare of both the old and the young. (222)

13. Resistance to government efforts to _____ provides a telling example of the ability of seniors to mobilize effectively. (223)

14. Sociologists Cerulo and Ruane use the term _____ to describe a form of existence in which, due to technology, the body lives on even after brain function is gone. (227)

15. _____ is a place, or services brought into someone's home, for the purpose of bringing comfort and dignity to a dying person. (228)

MATCH THESE SOCIAL SCIENTISTS WITH THEIR CONTRIBUTIONS

__1. Robert Butler   a. *use the term "technological lifespace" for life sustained by technology*
__2. Dorothy Jerrome   b. *developed disengagement theory*
__3. E. Kübler-Ross   c. *coined "ageism" to refer to prejudice or discrimination based on age*
__4. Cerulo & Ruane   d. *criticized disengagement theory for its implicit bias against the old*
__5. Cumming & Henry   e. *suggested that facing death sets in motion a five-stage process*

ESSAY QUESTIONS

1. Choose one of the three different perspectives and discuss how that perspective approaches the subject of aging. Consider both the strengths as well as the weaknesses of the perspective you chose.

2. Discuss the impact that industrialization and technology has had on aging as well as dying.

"DOWN-TO-EARTH SOCIOLOGY"

1. "Aging From a Feminist Perspective" on pages 221-222 discusses the gendered character of aging. What specific issues face women as they age? In what ways does feminist analysis construct aging as a positive experience? What types of social change are needed to ensure that aging does not result in marginalization?

2. Do you think the QPP/CPP system will still be there when you retire? How might we change the current system so that it not only provides for today's retired workers but will also provide for future retirees?

3. Have you ever known someone with Alzheimer's disease (p. 225)? What kind of living arrangement were they in? What do you see as the advantages of the Swedish arrangement for the individual and his/her family?

4. What kind of life do you hope to have when you reach your senior years? Given the current conditions, do you think your view will remain accurate?

CHAPTER 10

BUREAUCRACY AND FORMAL ORGANIZATIONS

☞ CHAPTER SUMMARY

- The rationalization of society refers to a major transformation in the way people think—from a desire to protect time-honored ways to a concern with efficiency and practical results. Max Weber traced the rationalization of society to Protestantism, while Marx attributed it to capitalism.

- As a result of the emphasis on rationality, formal organizations—secondary groups designed to achieve explicit objectives—have proliferated. Their most common form is a bureaucracy, which Weber characterized as having a hierarchy of authority, a division of labor, written rules, written communications, and impersonality. Weber's characteristics of bureaucracy are an "ideal type" which may not accurately describe any real organization.

- The dysfunctions of bureaucracies include alienation, red tape, lack of communication between units, goal displacement, and incompetence. In Weber's view, the impersonality of bureaucracies tends to produce alienation among workers. In Marx's view, workers experience alienation when they lose control of the work process and are cut off from the finished product of their labor.

- In Canada voluntary associations—groups made up of volunteers who organize on the basis of some mutual interest—also have proliferated. The iron law of oligarchy—the tendency of formal organizations to be dominated by a small, self-perpetuating elite—is a problem in voluntary associations.

- The concept of corporate culture refers to the organization's traditions, values, and norms. Much of this culture is invisible. It can affect its members, either negatively or positively, depending upon the members' available opportunities to achieve.

- Humanizing work settings involves strategies to develop human potential. Among the characteristics of more humane bureaucracies are expanded opportunities on the basis of ability and contributions rather than personal characteristics, a more even distribution of power, less rigid rules, and more open decision-making. Conflict theorists claim that these efforts conceal the fundamental goal of employers to exploit workers.

- The Japanese corporate model provides a contrast to the North American corporate model, although the reality of life in the Japanese corporation is at variance with the model that is generally presented.

☞ LEARNING OBJECTIVES

As you read Chapter 10, use these learning objectives to organize your notes. After completing your reading, briefly state an answer to each of the objectives, and review the text pages in parentheses.

1. Explain what is meant by the "rationalization of society," and differentiate between the views of Max Weber and Karl Marx on this process. (234-236)
2. State the definition of formal organizations and list the characteristics of bureaucracies. (236-237)
3. Describe the difference in "ideal" versus "real" bureaucracy. (239-240)
4. Discuss the dysfunctions of bureaucracies, and give examples of each type of problem. (240-242)
5. Explain the sociological significance of bureaucracies. (243)
6. Indicate the roles of voluntary associations, the different motivations for joining, and explain how the problem of oligarchy occurs in such organizations. (243-244)
7. Identify the consequences of hidden values in the corporate culture, especially noting their impact on women and minority participants. (245-246)

8. Discuss the characteristics of management strategies, focusing on scientific management, humanizing work, quality circles, employee stock ownership, small work groups, and workplace day care. (246-248)
9. Discuss an alternative to corporate capitalism. (248-249)
10. Explain the criticisms made by conflict theorists of the move to humanize the workplace. (249)
11. Describe how computer technology can be used to control workers. (249-250)
12. Compare and contrast the Japanese and North American corporate organizational models. (250-252)

☞ CHAPTER OUTLINE

I.   **The Rationalization of Society**
     A. Rationality—the acceptance of rules, efficiency, and practical results as the right way to approach human affairs—is a characteristic of industrial societies.
     B. The contribution of Max Weber
         1. Historically, the traditional orientation to life had been based on the idea that the past is the best guide for the present; however, this orientation stood in the way of industrialization.
         2. In *The Protestant Ethic and the Spirit of Capitalism* Weber proposed that a set of behaviors rooted in Protestantism led to the development of capitalist activity and the rationalization of society.
         3. Weber argued that because of the Calvinistic belief in predestination, people wanted to show they were among the chosen of God. Financial success in life became a sign of God's approval; however, money was not to be spent on oneself. Rather, the investment of profits became an outlet for people's excess money, while the success of those investments became a further sign of God's approval.
         4. Because capitalism demanded rationalization (the careful calculation of practical results), traditional ways of doing things, if not efficient, had to be replaced, for what counted were the results.
     C. Marx on rationalization
         1. Unlike Weber, Karl Marx attributed the growth of rationality to capitalism instead of religion.
         2. Marx said that the development of capitalism caused people to change their way of thinking, not the other way around. Because capitalism was more efficient, and it produced the things that they wanted in greater abundance, people changed their ideas.

II. **Formal Organizations and Bureaucracy**
     A. Formal organizations—secondary groups designed to achieve explicit objectives—have become a central feature of contemporary life.
     B. The essential characteristics of bureaucracies are:
         1. a hierarchy where assignments flow downward and accountability flows upward;
         2. a division of labor;
         3. written rules;
         4. written communications and records; and
         5. impersonality.
     C. Weber's characteristics of bureaucracy describe an ideal type—a composite of characteristics based on many specific examples. The real nature of bureaucracy often differs from its ideal image.

D.   Weber's model only accounts for part of the characteristics of bureaucracies. Dysfunctions can also be identified.

1.   Red tape, or the strict adherence to rules, often results in nothing getting accomplished.

2.   A lack of communication between units means that they are sometimes working at cross purposes; sometimes one unit "undoes" what another unit has accomplished because the two fail to inform one another of what each is doing.

3.   Bureaucratic alienation, a feeling of powerlessness and normlessness, occurs when workers are assigned to repetitive tasks in order for the corporation to achieve efficient production, thereby cutting workers off from the product of their labor.

4.   To resist alienation, workers form primary groups within the larger secondary organization, relating to one another not just as workers, but as people who value one another.

5.   The alienated bureaucrat is one who feels trapped in the job, does not take initiative, will not do anything beyond what she or he is absolutely required to do, and uses rules to justify doing as little as possible.

6.   Goal displacement occurs when an organization adopts new goals after the original goals have been achieved and there is no longer any reason for it to continue.

7.   Bureaucratic incompetence is reflected in the Peter principle—members of an organization are promoted for good work until they reach their level of incompetence. In reality, bureaucracies are remarkably successful.

E.   To the sociologist, bureaucracies are significant because they represent a fundamental change in how people relate to one another. Prior to this rationalization, work focused on human needs—for instance, making sure that everyone had an opportunity to earn a living; with rationalization, the focus shifts to efficiency in performing tasks and improving the bottom line.

III.   Voluntary Associations

A.   Voluntary associations are groups made up of volunteers who have organized on the basis of some mutual interest.

B.   Voluntary associations represent no single interest or purpose. The idea of mutual interest is characteristic of all voluntary associations; a shared interest in some view or activity is the tie that binds members together.

1.   The motivation for joining a group differs widely among its members, from the expression of strong convictions to the cultivation of personal contacts.

2.   Because of this, membership turnover tends to be high.

C.   Within voluntary associations is an inner core of individuals who stand firmly behind the group's goals and are firmly committed to maintaining the organization. Robert Michels used the term "iron law of oligarchy" to refer to the tendency of this inner core to dominate the organization by becoming a small, self-perpetuating elite.

IV.   Careers in Bureaucracies

A.   Rosabeth Moss Kanter's organizational research demonstrates that the corporate elite maintain hidden values. These function to keep the elite in power and also provide better access to information, networking, and "fast tracks" for workers like themselves, usually white and male.

1.   Workers who fit in are given opportunities to advance; they outperform others and are more committed.

2.   Those who are judged outsiders and experience few opportunities think poorly of themselves, are less committed, and work below their potential.

3. These hidden values create this self-fulfilling prophecy and contribute to the iron law of oligarchy.

B. Women and minorities do not match the hidden values of the corporate culture and may by treated differently. They may experience "showcasing"—being put in highly visible positions with little power so that the company is in compliance with affirmative action—and "slow-track" positions—jobs where promotions are slow because accomplishments in these areas seldom come to the attention of top management.

C. Morale is influenced by the level one achieves in an organization; the higher people go, the higher their morale.

V.   Management Strategies and the Corporate Culture

A. Corporations have developed many strategies to manage work forces, harness people's energies to specific goals, and monitor progress to those goals.

B. Management strategies include:

1. Scientific Management. This is a strategy used to establish management control over the pace of work, the level of production, and all decisions pertaining to the labor process. Scientific management involves dividing complex work tasks into simple sub-tasks and separating conceptual work from the execution of work tasks.

2. Humanizing Work. This refers to efforts to organize the workplace in such a way that it develops rather than impedes human potential. Characteristics of more humane work are: the availability of opportunities on the basis of ability and contributions rather than personal characteristics; the more equal distribution of power; and less rigid rules and more open decision-making.

3. Quality Circles. These are small groups of workers and a manager or two who meet regularly to try to improve the quality of the work setting and the product.

4. Employee Stock Ownership. This does not mean that working conditions and employee-management relations are friction-free because profitability still is the key.

5. Small Work Groups. Within these groups workers are able to establish primary relationships with other workers so that their identities are tied up with their group; the group's success becomes the individual's success.

6. Workplace Day Cares. These ease the strain on parents, leading to reduced turnover, less absenteeism, and shorter maternity leaves.

C. The cooperative represents an alternative to bureaucracy. These are collectives owned by members who collectively make decisions, determine goals, evaluate resources, set salaries, and assign work tasks. The economic results of cooperatives have been mixed— some are more profitable than private organizations, some are less.

D. Conflict theorists point out that the basic relationship between workers and owners is confrontational regardless of how the work organization is structured.

E. While the computer has the capacity to improve the quality of people's lives, it also holds the potential of severe abuse.

1. Computers allow managers to increase surveillance without face-to-face supervision.

2. Computers can create the "maximum-security workplace," potentially keeping track of every movement a worker makes while on the job. Some worry that it is only a short step from this type of workplace to the "maximum-security society."

VI.   The Japanese Corporate Model

A. The Japanese production technique is often referred to as *lean production*. Lean production uses a just-in-time (JIT) strategy to reduce the need for large warehouses and work stations. Lean production relies on flexible work assignments and a strategy of continuous improvement, which may result in job elimination and work intensification. William Ouchi lists five ways in which this model differs from the North American system:

B.   1.   Hiring and promotion: The Japanese model features a team approach; a starting cohort of workers gets the same salary, is rotated through the organization, and develops intense loyalty to one another and to the organization. In the North American model, employees are hired on the basis of what the individual can contribute; the emphasis is on competition; and individual loyalty is to the individual himself or herself, not to the company.

     2.   Lifetime security: The Japanese model takes lifetime security for granted; the company is loyal to the employee, and expects the employee to be loyal to the company. In the North American model, lifetime security is unusual; continued employment is based on good and/or bad economic conditions; and workers are expected to look out for themselves.

     3.   Almost total involvement: Work is like a marriage in Japan in that the company and the employee are committed to each other. In North America, the work relationship is highly specific; fulfill your job obligations and the rest of your time is your private life, separated from the firm.

     4.   Broad training: In Japan, workers move from one job to another within the corporation. In North America, employees are expected to perform one job well and then be promoted to a job with more responsibility.

     5.   Decision-making by consensus: In Japan, decision-making occurs after lengthy deliberations in which each person to be affected by a decision is included in the process. In North America, the individual responsible for the unit does as much consulting as she or he thinks necessary and then makes the decision.

C.   Research on Japanese corporations suggests that the Japanese corporate model fails to adequately reflect the reality of Japanese corporate life.

☞   **KEY TERMS**

After studying the chapter, review the definition for each of the following terms.

assimilation: the process by which the dominant group absorbs a minority group

alienation: Marx's term for the experience of being cut off from the product of one's labor, which results in a sense of powerlessness and normlessness

bureaucracy: a formal organization with a hierarchy of authority; a clear division of labor; emphasis on written rules, communications, and records; and impersonality of positions

capitalism: the investment of capital with the goal of producing profits

corporate culture: the orientations that characterize corporate work settings

formal organization: a secondary group designed to achieve explicit objectives

goal displacement: a goal displaced by another, in this context, the adoption of new goals by an organization; also known as *goal replacement*

humanizing a work setting: organizing a workplace in such a way that it develops rather than impedes human potential

ideal type: a composite of characteristics based on many specific examples ("ideal" in this case means a description of the abstract characteristics, not what one desires to exist)

iron law of oligarchy: Robert Michels's phrase for the tendency of formal organizations to be dominated by a small, self-perpetuating elite

just-in-time (JIT): a strategy to reduce parts inventories to the amount needed at the time, thereby reducing the demand for huge parts warehouses and large work stations

kaizen: means continuous improvement; a system where production techniques are constantly evaluated in search of more efficient and improved methods

lean production: a production technique developed in Japan that uses just-in-time (JIT) methods, and relies on flexible work assignments and a strategy of continuous improvement

Peter Principle: a bureaucratic "law," according to which the members of an organization are promoted for good work until they reach their level of incompetence, the level at which they can no longer do good work

rationality: the acceptance of rules, efficiency, and practical results as the right way to approach human affairs

rationalization of society: a widespread acceptance of rationality and a social organization built around this idea

scientific management: a strategy used to establish management control over the pace of work, the level of production, and all decisions pertaining to the labor process

traditional orientation: the idea, characteristic of tribal, peasant, and feudal societies, that the past is the best guide for the present

voluntary association: a group made up of volunteers who have organized on the basis of some mutual interest

☞ KEY PEOPLE

Review the major theoretical contributions or findings of these people.

Rosabeth Moss Kanter: Kanter studied the "invisible" corporate culture, which for the most part continually reproduces itself by promoting those workers who fit the elite's stereotypical views.

Gary Marx: Marx has written about the "maximum security" workplace, given the increased use of computers to control workers.

Karl Marx: Marx believed that the emergence of rationality was due to capitalism. Capitalism changed the way people thought about life, rather than people's orientation to life producing capitalism.

Robert Michels: Michels first used the term "the iron law of oligarchy" to describe the tendency for the leaders of an organization to become entrenched.

William Ouchi: Ouchi studied the Japanese corporation and identified defining qualities of this corporate model.

George Ritzer: Ritzer coined the term the "McDonaldization of society" to describe the increasing rationalization of modern social life.

Joyce Rothchild and Allen Whitt: These sociologists researched the history of cooperatives

Max Weber: Weber studied the rationalization of society by investigating the link between Protestantism and capitalism and identifying the characteristics of bureaucracy.

Shoshana Zuboff: Zuboff has researched the degree to which computer technology increases managers' ability to carry out surveillance on workers without face-to-face interaction.

☞ SELF-TEST

After completing this self-test, check your answers against the Answer Key at the back of this Study Guide and against the text on page(s) indicated in parentheses.

MULTIPLE CHOICE QUESTIONS

1. What is rationality? (234)
    a. the idea that the past is the best guide for the present
    b. making excuses for bureaucratic incompetence
    c. the acceptance of rules, efficiency, and practical results as the right way to approach human affairs
    d. None of the above

2. The idea that the past is the best guide for the present is referred to as: (235)
    a. traditional orientation.
    b. modern orientation.
    c. status quo.
    d. rationalization.

3. What was one of the major obstacles to industrialization? (235)
    a. the medieval church
    b. a traditional orientation
    c. money lenders
    d. the traditional family

4. According to Max Weber, capitalism: (235-236)
    a. is the investment of capital in the hopes of producing profits.
    b. became an outlet for the excess money of Calvinists.
    c. produced success for many that became a sign of God's approval.
    d. All of the above.

5. In reconciling Weber's and Marx's views on rationality, sociologists feel that: (236)
    a. Weber was most correct.
    b. Marx was most correct.
    c. Weber and Marx were both incorrect.
    d. no analyst has yet reconciled the opposing views satisfactorily.

6. A secondary group designed to achieve explicit objectives is the sociological definition of: (236)
    a. a social institution.
    b. a formal organization.
    c. a rationalized system.
    d. None of the above.

7. All of the following are characteristics of bureaucracy, *except*: (237)
    a. a division of labor.
    b. a hierarchy with assignments flowing upward and accountability flowing downward.
    c. written rules, communications and records.
    d. impersonality.

8. Ideal types: (239)
    a. are composites of characteristics based on many specific examples.
    b. are the model or perfect way to do something.
    c. largely are not used in sociology because they are unrealistic.
    d. All of the above.

9. George Ritzer used the term "the McDonaldization of society" to refer to: (239)
    a. the preference for McDonald's over Burger King.
    b. the spread of McDonald's world-wide.
    c. the increasing rationalization of daily living.
    d. All of the above.

10. What is the force behind "the McDonaldization of society"? (239)
    a. the desire to control the marketplace with uniform products
    b. the increased efficiency which contributes to lower prices
    c. the security that comes from knowing the product
    d. corporate greed

11. Dysfunctions of bureaucracies include: (240-242)
    a. alienation.
    b. goal displacement.
    c. red tape.
    d. All of the above.

12. As a worker in a large corporation, Linda is often unhappy. At work she often feels that no one appreciates her and that the work she does is boring and repetitive. Which of the following best describes Linda's situation? (241)
    a. bureaucratic incompetence
    b. alienation
    c. goal displacement
    d. goal frustration

13. How do workers resist alienation? (241)
    a. by forming primary groups
    b. by praising each other and expressing sympathy when something goes wrong
    c. by putting pictures and personal items in their work areas
    d. All of the above

14. According to your text, what is the alienated bureaucrat likely to do? (241-242)
    a. quit his or her job once unhappiness and dissatisfaction sets in
    b. seek counseling to overcome the problem
    c. not do anything for the organization beyond what he or she is required to do
    d. return to school for further training in order to move up in the organization

15. When does goal displacement occur? (242)
    a. When a bureaucrat has the inability to see the goals of the organization and to function as a cooperative, integrated part of the whole.
    b. When goals conflict with one another.
    c. When an organization adopts new goals.
    d. When members of an organization are promoted until they reach their level of incompetence.

16. The Peter Principle: (242)
    a. states that each employee of a bureaucracy is promoted to his or her level of competence.
    b. states that each employee of a bureaucracy is promoted to his or her level of incompetence.
    c. is generally true and explains why so many bureaucracies fail.
    d. was first stated by Max Weber.

17. Voluntary associations: (243)
    a. are groups made up of volunteers who organize on the basis of some mutual interest.
    b. include political parties, unions, professional associations, and churches.
    c. have been an important part of American life.
    d. All of the above.

18. Why do voluntary associations exist in Canada? (243)
    a. They meet people's basic needs.
    b. People are required to belong to these organizations.
    c. People don't have anything to do other than work.
    d. They take the place of government agencies.

19. What is the term that describes the tendency for organizations to be dominated by a small, self-perpetuating elite? (244)
    a. the Peter Principle
    b. bureaucratic engorgement
    c. the iron law of oligarchy
    d. the corporate power struggle

20. According to Rosabeth Moss Kanter, what is the nature of the corporate culture? (245)
    a. The corporate culture determines an individual's corporate fate.
    b. The people with the best qualifications typically will rise to the top of an organization.
    c. The employees who work the hardest and are the most cooperative have the greatest likelihood of being promoted.
    d. All of the above.

21. What does it mean to humanize a work setting? (247)
    a. Employees bring plants, pictures, and other personal items to the office.
    b. Having a period of time in which workers visit with each other, tell jokes, and get to know each other more personally.
    c. Purchasing furniture which is more comfortable for employees.
    d. Organizing a workplace so that human potential is developed rather than impeded.

22. Research on the costs and benefits of employer-financed day care demonstrated that: (248)
    a. such a benefit is costly to the employer because of strict government regulations that must be met.
    b. such a benefit cuts into stockholders' dividends by eating up profits.
    c. few employees took advantage of the benefit.
    d. such a benefit can save the employer money by reducing turnover and absenteeism.

23. Which type of organization attempts to allow members to work towards their own goals? (249)
    a. corporations
    b. cooperatives
    c. collectives
    d. small businesses

24. Which of the following reflects the views of conflict theorists? (249)
   a. quality circles, employee stock ownership, and small work groups are excellent ways to solve the problems encountered in bureaucracies
   b. the interests of workers and owners both may be met by humanizing the work setting
   c. the interests of workers and owners are fundamentally opposed and, in the final analysis, workers are always exploited
   d. there is less conflict in the Japanese corporate model than in the North American model

25. Computers in the workplace: (249-250)
   a. have the potential of improving the quality of work life.
   b. could lead to more surveillance of workers by managers.
   c. may be the first step towards a society in which every move a citizen makes is recorded.
   d. All of the above.

TRUE-FALSE QUESTIONS

T F   1. Rationality involves the acceptance of rules, efficiency, and practical results as the right way to approach human affairs. (234)

T F   2. Traditional orientation is based on the idea that the present is the best guide for the future. (235)

T F   3. Max Weber believed that the growth of capitalism contributed to the rise of the Protestant ethic. (235-236)

T F   4. Calvinists believed that thrift was a virtue and that money should not be spent on the luxuries of life. (235-236)

T F   5. Marx argued that rationality was the result of economics. (236)

T F   6. Either primary or secondary groups can be formal organizations. (236)

T F   7. Weber identified five essential characteristics of bureaucracy. (237)

T F   8. Most colleges and universities do not have written systems of accountability for faculty members. (237)

T F   9. In a bureaucracy, each worker is a replaceable unit. (237)

T F   10. The characteristics of bureaucracy identified by Max Weber are ideal types. (239)

T F   11. Marx coined the term alienation. (241)

T F   12. Workers can successfully resist becoming alienated if they work at it. (241-242)

T F   13. The Peter Principle has been proven to be true. (242)

T F   14. Voluntary associations are made up of volunteers who have organized on the basis of some mutual interest. (243)

T F   15. Voluntary associations can be reactionary or can demand social change. (243-244)

T F   16. The iron law of oligarchy was defined by Robert Michels. (244)

T F   17. Bureaucracies are likely to disappear as our dominant form of social organization in the near future. (246)

T F   18. Scientific management, quality circles, employee stock ownership, and small work groups are four examples of management strategies. (246-248)

T F   19. Conflict theorists believe that bureaucracies exploit workers regardless of the way in which work is set up. (249)

T F   20. Like the North American corporate model, the Japanese corporate model emphasizes lifetime job security. (251)

FILL-IN QUESTIONS

1. _____ is the acceptance of rules, efficiency, and practical results as the right way to approach human affairs. (234)
2. The idea that the past is the best guide for the present is known as _____. (235)
3. _____ was written by Max Weber and emphasizes that religion holds the key to understanding the development of certain types of economic systems. (235)
4. The investment of capital in the hope of producing profits is called _____. (236)
5. A secondary group designed to achieve explicit objectives is referred to as a(n) _____. (236)
6. George Ritzer has coined the term _____ to refer to the increasing rationalization of life's routine tasks. (239)
7. _____ is a feeling of powerlessness and normlessness; the experience of being cut off from the product of one's labor. (241)
8. _____ occurs when new goals are adopted by an organization to replace previous goals which may have been fulfilled. (242)
9. A group made up of volunteers who have organized on the basis of some mutual interest is called a(n) _____. (243)
10. _____ refers to the tendency of formal organizations to be dominated by a small, self-perpetuating elite. (244)
11. The orientation that characterizes corporate work settings is referred to as _____. (245)
12. Women and minorities are often _____, which means that they are placed in highly visible positions with little power in order to demonstrate to the public and affirmative action officials how progressive the company is. (246)
13. _____ consist of perhaps a dozen workers and a manager or two who meet regularly to try to improve the quality of the work setting and of the company's products. (248)
14. Humanizing a work setting is just another attempt to manipulate workers into active cooperation in their own exploitation, according to _____ theorists. (249)
15. Lean production, almost total involvement, broad training, and collective decision making are characteristics of the _____ model. (250-251)

MATCH THESE SOCIAL SCIENTISTS WITH THEIR CONTRIBUTIONS

__1. Max Weber
__2. Robert Michels
__3. William Ouchi
__4. Karl Marx
__5. Rosabeth Moss Kanter
__6. George Ritzer

a. *the iron law of oligarchy*
b. *the McDonaldization of society*
c. *hidden values in the corporate culture*
d. *exploitation of workers by capitalists*
e. *rationalization of society*
f. *Japanese corporate model*

ESSAY QUESTIONS

1. Explain what an ideal type is and why such constructs are useful.
2. Define the iron law of oligarchy and discuss why this problem occurs in voluntary associations.
3. Evaluate whether or not the use of technology to control workers is an inevitable aspect of bureaucracy.

"DOWN-TO-EARTH SOCIOLOGY"

1. Acquire a copy of the organizational chart for your own college or university. Compare it with Figure 10.1 (p. 238) to determine ways in which the charts are similar and ways in which they differ. What are some of your own experiences with bureaucratic dysfunctions?

2. What was your reaction to the "Down-to-Earth Sociology" box on pp. 239-240? Can you see evidence of McDonaldization in your own life? What do you see as the advantages of this trend? What do you see as the disadvantages? Do you agree with the author when he says that "to resist [this trend] will be futile?"

3. Why did the female insurance executive say that women in her work organization have no other choice than to play corporate games in order to achieve their objectives (p. 245)? Do you agree or disagree? What has been your own experience with the hidden culture in offices in which you have worked?

4. After reading about diversity training on page 247, what would you say are the advantages of these types of programs? What are the drawbacks?

5. After reading "Cracks in the Corporate Facade" (p. 252), how has your thinking about the Japanese corporate model changed? What are the forces behind the changes in corporate Japan? How does this compare with the situation in North America?

CHAPTER 11

THE ECONOMY: MONEY AND WORK

☞ CHAPTER SUMMARY

- The earliest hunting and gathering societies were characterized by subsistence economies; economic systems became more complex as people discovered first how to domesticate and cultivate (horticultural and pastoral societies), then to farm (agricultural societies) and finally to manufacture (industrial societies).
- In the least complex societies, people exchanged goods and services through barter. As societies and economies evolved, certain items were assigned uniform value and became the mediums of exchange. Today we rely increasingly on electronic transfer of funds with credit and debit cards.
- The two major economic systems are capitalism, in which the means of production are privately owned, and socialism, in which the means of production are state owned. There are different forms of both capitalism (laissez-faire capitalism and welfare capitalism) and socialism (democratic socialism). In recent years each system has adopted features of the other.
- Corporations dominate modern capitalism; an inner circle—a group of leaders from the major corporations—are mutually interested in making certain that corporate capitalism is protected. The sociological significance of global capitalism is that the interests of the inner circle extend beyond national boundaries.
- Symbolic interactionists analyze such things as factors that distinguish professions from jobs and the aspects that lead to work satisfaction. Functionalists state that work is a fundamental source of social solidarity; preindustrial societies foster mechanical solidarity while industrial societies, with their more complex division of labor, are characterized by organic solidarity. Conflict theorists focus on power, noting how the new technologies and global capitalism affect workers and owners; workers lose jobs while the inner circle maintains it power and profits.
- Most Canadian workers today are employed in the tertiary sector, as opposed to either the primary or secondary sectors. A quiet revolution has occurred due to the dramatic increase in the number of married women who work for pay. The underground economy, economic activity that is not reported to the government, runs perhaps 15 to 20 percent of the regular economy. Initially, the amount of leisure decreased as the economy changed from preindustrial to industrial; with unionization workers gained back some leisure.
- Work will continue to be restructured as a result of downsizing, new technologies, and the expansion of global capitalism.

☞ LEARNING OBJECTIVES

As you read Chapter 11, use these learning objectives to organize your notes. After completing your reading, briefly state an answer to each of the objectives, and review the text pages in parentheses.

1. Trace the transformation of the economic systems through each of the historical stages and state the degree to which social inequality existed in each of the economies. (258-260)
2. Explain what the "medium of exchange" means and how it is vital to society. (260-261)
3. State the essential features of capitalism and socialism. (261-265)
4. Identify variations on models of "pure" capitalism and socialism and explain why these exist. (262-265)
5. State criticisms of capitalism and socialism. (265)

6.   Describe the recent changes in both capitalist and socialist economies, and explain why some theorists believe the two systems are converging. (265-267)
7.   Explain the significance of the following terms: the corporation, stockholders' revolts, oligopolies, and corporate capitalism. (267-268)
8.   Discuss how the wealthy use interlocking directorates to maintain power. (268)
9.   Define the concepts "multinational corporations" and explain why the emergence of global capitalism has sociological significance. (268-270)
10. Explain the difference between a profession and a job, using the symbolic interactionist perspective. (271)
11. Contrast mechanical and organic solidarity as Durkheim originally envisioned them, discuss changes in the global economy that have contributed to a new meaning of organic solidarity, and explain the consequences of this new form of interdependency. (272)
12. Outline the conflict perspective on economic life and explain the role of the inner circle. (272)
13. Review recent changes in the Canadian economy, including the shift in employment among the three economic sectors, the employment of women outside the home, the growth of the underground economy, the decline in real wages, and patterns of work and leisure. (273-277)
14. Consider what impact expanding global trade, new technologies, and downsizing will have on the Canadian economy and society in the years to come. (277-279)

☞ **CHAPTER OUTLINE**

I.   **The Transformation of Economic Systems**
      A.   Market, or economy, is the mechanism by which values are established in order to exchange goods and services.
           1.   The economy, which may be one of our most important social institutions, is the system of distribution of goods and services.
           2.   The economy today is radically different from that of the past; it is impersonal and global in nature.
      B.   As societies developed, a surplus emerged which fostered social inequality.
           1.   Earliest hunting and gathering societies had subsistence economies, characterized by little trade with other groups, and a high degree of social equality.
           2.   In pastoral and horticultural economies, people created more dependable food supplies. The creation of a surplus allowed groups to grow in size, to settle in a single place, to develop a specialized division of labor, and to trade with other groups, all of which fostered social inequality.
           3.   Agricultural economies brought even greater surpluses, magnifying prior trends in social, political and economic inequality. More people were freed from food production, a more specialized division of labor developed, and trade expanded.
      C.   The surplus (and greater inequality) grew in industrial societies. As the surplus increased emphasis changed from production of goods to consumption (Thorstein Veblen coined the term conspicuous consumption).
      D.   The "information explosion" and the global village are key elements of postindustrial society.
           1.   According to Daniel Bell, postindustrial economies have six traits: (1) extensive trade among nations; (2) a large surplus of goods; (3) a service sector employing the majority of workers; (4) a wide variety and amount of goods available to the average person; (5) an information explosion; and (6) a global village with instantaneous, worldwide communications.

2.   Consequences of the information explosion are uneven. Due to political and economic arrangements, some will prosper while others suffer.

3.   Overall, the postindustrial economy has brought a greater availability of goods, it has not resulted in income equality.

II.   The Transformation of the Medium of Exchange

A.   A medium of exchange is the means by which people value and exchange goods and services.

B.   One of the earliest mediums of exchange was barter, the direct exchange of one item for another.

C.   In agricultural economies, people came to use gold and silver coins. Deposit receipts which transferred ownership of a specified amount of gold or bushels of wheat, etc., on deposit somewhere were used. Toward the end of this period, the receipts were formalized into currency (paper money). Currency represented stored value; no more could be issued than the amount of gold or silver the currency represented.

D.   In industrial economies, bartering largely disappeared and gold was replaced by paper currency. The gold standard (a dollar represents a specified amount of gold) kept the number of dollars that could be issued to a specific limit. When "fiat money" came into existence, the currency no longer could be exchanged for gold or silver.

1.   Even without a gold standard, the amount of paper money that can be issued is limited: prices increase if a government issues currency at a rate higher than the growth of its gross national product. Issuing more produces inflation: each unit of currency will purchase fewer goods and services.

2.   Checking accounts and credit cards have become common in industrial economies, largely replacing currency.

E.   In postindustrial economies paper money is being replaced by checks, credit cards, and debit cards. Spending eventually becomes an electronic transfer of numbers residing in computer memory banks.

III.   World Economic Systems

A.   Capitalism has three essential features: (1) the private ownership of the means of production; (2) the pursuit of profit; and (3) market competition.

1.   Pure (laissez-faire) capitalism exists only when market forces are able to operate without interference from the government.

2.   Canada today has welfare (or state) capitalism. Private citizens own the means of production and pursue profits, but do so within a vast system of laws designed to protect the public welfare.

3.   Under welfare capitalism the government supports competition but establishes its own monopoly over "common good" items, e.g., those presumed essential for the common good of the citizens.

B.   Socialism also has three essential features: (1) the public ownership of the means of production; (2) central planning; and (3) the distribution of goods without a profit motive.

1.   Under socialism, the government owns the means of production, and a central committee determines what the country needs instead of allowing market forces (supply and demand) to control production and prices. Socialism is designed to eliminate competition, to produce goods for the general welfare, and to distribute them according to people's needs, not their ability to pay.

2.   Socialism does not exist in pure form. Although the ideology of socialism calls for resources to be distributed according to need rather than position socialist nations found it necessary to offer higher salaries for some jobs in order to entice people to take greater responsibilities.

3.   Some nations (e.g., Sweden and Denmark) have adopted democratic or welfare socialism: both the state and individuals engage in production and distribution, although the state owns certain industries (steel, mining, forestry, telephones, television stations, and airlines) while retail stores, farms, and most service industries remain in private hands.

C.   The primary criticism of capitalism is that it leads to social inequality (a top layer of wealthy, powerful people, and a bottom layer of people who are unemployed or underemployed). Socialism has been criticized for not respecting individual rights, and for not being capable of producing much wealth (thus the greater equality of socialism actually amounts to almost everyone having an equal chance of being poor).

D.   In recent years, fundamental changes have taken place in these two economic systems.

1.   Over the years Canada has adopted many public welfare policies – universal health care, accessible and free public education, employment insurance, the Canada Pension Plan, and Old Age Security.

2.   In 1989, the former Soviet Union concluded that its system of central planning had failed. It began to reinstate market forces, including private ownership of property and profits for those who produce and sell goods.

3.   Despite the firm stand that Chinese leaders took in regard to Tiananmen Square, they too began to endorse capitalism, soliciting western investment, allowing the use of credit cards, and approving a stock market. The result of such measures has been an increasing standard of living.

4.   As the two systems continue to adopt features of each other, convergence theory predicts that they will eventually converge, creating a hybrid economic system. The reality is that the two remain far from "converged" and the struggles between them continue, although they are more muted than in the past. With the pullback of socialism around the world, capitalism—in its many varieties—has a strong lead.

IV.   Capitalism in a Global Economy

A.   The corporation (joint ownership of a business enterprise, whose liabilities are separate from those of its owners) has changed the face of capitalism.

1.   Corporate capitalism refers to economic domination by giant corporations.

2.   Oligopolies, several large companies that dominate a single industry, dictate pricing, set the quality of their products, and protect the market. Often they use their wealth and connections for political purposes (e.g., favorable legislation giving them special tax breaks or protecting their industry from imports).

3.   One of the most significant aspects of large corporations is the separation of ownership and management, producing ownership of wealth without appreciable control, and control of wealth without appreciable ownership. A stockholders' revolt (stockholders of a corporation refuse to rubber stamp decisions made by the management) is likely to occur if the profits do not meet expectations.

B.   Interlocking directorates occur when individuals serve as directors of several companies, concentrating power and minimizing competition.

C.   As corporations have outgrown national boundaries, the result is the creation of multinational corporations, detached from the interests and values of their country of origin with no concern other than making a profit.

D.   The sociological significance of global capitalism is that the multinational corporations are reshaping the globe as no political force has been able to do. Furthermore, they have loyalty to profit and market share rather than to a regional or cultural value system.

E.   On the positive side, global interconnections, which transcend national loyalties, may promote global peace. On the negative side, the world's market may come to be dominated by a handful of corporate leaders.

V.   Applying Sociological Theories
   A.   The symbolic interactionist perspective is useful in understanding the distinctions between a job and a profession.
      1.   The characteristics that make work a profession include: (1) rigorous education including graduate school and an admission examination; (2) the education is theoretical, not practical or "how to do it"; (3) self-regulation by the profession; (4) authority over clients based on specialized education and theoretical understanding; and (5) service to society.
   B.   The functionalist perspective states that work is functional for society because important tasks are accomplished.
      1.   It binds people together according to Durkheim's principles of mechanical solidarity (unity from being involved in similar occupations or activities) and organic solidarity (interdependence resulting from mutual need as each individual fulfills his or her job).
      2.   Today organic solidarity has expanded far beyond anything Durkheim envisioned, creating interdependencies that span the globe. These global interdependencies suggest the need for a new term—perhaps "superorganic solidarity."
      3.   The world's nations are dividing into three primary trading blocs: North and South America dominated by the U.S., Europe dominated by Germany, and Asia dominated by Japan.
      4.   If free trade is achieved within each of these trading blocs, competition will increase and prices will decrease, resulting in a higher standard of living. At the same time, there will be an enormous loss of production jobs in the most industrialized nations and a possible decrease in nationalistic ties.
   C.   Conflict theorists are concerned that the wealthy will benefit from changing technology at the expense of workers and that an inner circle of corporate and government leaders will wield too much economic and political power.
      1.   With the introduction of new technologies, low-level workers, living from paycheck to paycheck, are most directly affected by the uncertainty, the loss of jobs and the lower wages. The result is that profits increase by lowering production costs.
      2.   The multinationals are headed by an inner circle. This group, while in competition with one another, are united by a mutual interest in preserving capitalism. Sometimes this leads to a misuse of their enormous power, as was the case when ITT plotted with the CIA to unseat the democratically elected president of Chile because he was a socialist.
      3.   The inner circle develops a close relationship with high-level politicians, such that the interests of the corporations and those of the top political leaders often converge and much of the activity of the latter is dedicated to promoting the interests of the economic elite.

VI.   Work in Canadian Society
   A.   Sociologists divide economic life into primary (extracting natural resources), secondary (turning raw materials into goods), and tertiary (service-oriented) sectors. In postindustrial societies, most of the labor force works in the tertiary sector.
   B.   A sharp increase in the number of women working outside the home has occurred in Canada.
      1.   How likely a woman is to work depends on several factors, such as her education, marital status, and the age of her children; race and ethnicity have little influence.
      2.   Men and women have different work experiences and different models for success.

3.   The quiet revolution refers to the continually increasing proportions of women in the labor force. This transformation affects consumer patterns, relations at work, self concepts, and familial relationships.

C.   The underground (informal) economy is exchange of goods and services not reported to the government, including income from work done "on the side" and from illegal activities (e.g., drug dealing). Estimates place the underground economy at 15 to 20% of the regular economy, which means it may run close to $100 billion. As a result, Revenue Canada loses millions of dollars in taxes a year.

D.   In Canada, household income growth declined during the past two decades. For some, trying to stay even has meant having to work more hours or more jobs.

E.   Different societies have had differing amounts of leisure (time not taken up by work or required activities such as eating/sleeping).

1.   Early societies had a lot of time for leisure. Industrialization brought changes: bosses and machines now control people's time.

2.   It is not the activity itself that makes something leisure, but rather its purpose (e.g., driving a car for pleasure or driving it to work). Patterns of leisure change with the life course, with both the young and the old enjoying the most leisure and parents with young children having the least.

3.   Compared with early industrialization, workers today have far more leisure (shorter work weeks, for example). In recent decades, the trend for more leisure has been reversed in Canada.

VII.   The Future: Facing the Consequences of Global Capitalism

A.   Predictions for a shorter work week and more meaningful jobs have not yet materialized.

1.   Jobs are being transformed and new jobs created, particularly in the knowledge/ information services sector. However, this change has also meant thousands of lost jobs.

B.   There is a great deal of uncertainty with respect to the future of work for Canadians. Will there be enough good service jobs created by the private sector? What would it take to rescue the dream of the "Leisure Revolution"?

☞ KEY TERMS

After studying the chapter, review the definition for each of the following terms.

barter: the direct exchange of one item for another

capitalism: an economic system characterized by the private ownership of the means of production, the pursuit of profit, and market competition

conspicuous consumption: Thorstein Veblen's term for a change from the Protestant ethic to an eagerness to show off wealth by the elaborate consumption of goods

convergence theory: the view that as capitalist and socialist economic systems each adopt features of the other, a hybrid (or mixed) economic system may emerge

corporate capitalism: the domination of the economic system by giant corporations

corporation: the joint ownership of a business enterprise, whose liabilities and obligations are separate from those of the owners

credit card: a device that allows its owner to purchase goods but be billed later

currency: paper money

debit card: a device that allows its owner to charge purchases against his or her bank account

democratic socialism: a hybrid economic system in which capitalism is mixed with state ownership

deposit receipts: a receipt stating that a certain amount of goods is on deposit in a warehouse or bank; the receipt is used as a form of money

divest: to sell off

economy: a system of distribution of goods and services

fiat money: currency issued by a government that is not backed by stored value

gold standard: **paper money backed by gold**

gross national product (GNP): the amount of goods and services produced by a nation

inflation: an increase in prices

interlocking directorates: the same people serving on the board of directors of several companies

laissez-faire capitalism: unrestrained manufacture and trade (literally, "hands off" capitalism)

leisure: time not taken up by work or required activities such as eating, sleeping, commuting, childcare, and housework

market: any process of buying and selling; on a more formal level, the mechanism that establishes values for the exchange of goods and services

market competition: the exchange of items between willing buyers and sellers

market forces: the law of supply and demand

market restraints: laws and regulations that limit the capacity to manufacture and sell products

mechanical solidarity: Durkheim's term for the unity that comes from being involved in similar occupations or activities

medium of exchange: the means by which people value goods and services in order to make an exchange, for example, currency, gold, and silver

money: any item (from sea shells to gold) that is used as a medium of exchange; today, currency is the most common form

monopoly: the control of an entire industry by a single company

oligopoly: the control of an entire industry by several large companies

organic solidarity: Durkheim's term for the interdependence that results from people's needing others to fulfill their job

primary sector: that part of the economy that extracts raw materials from the environment

private ownership of the means of production: the ownership of machines and factories by individuals, who decide what shall be produced

profession: an occupation characterized by rigorous education, a theoretical perspective, self-regulation, authority over clients, and service to society (as opposed to a job)

quiet revolution (the): the fundamental changes in society that occurred as a result of vast numbers of women entering the work force

secondary sector: that part of the economy in which raw materials are turned into manufactured goods

socialism: an economic system characterized by the public ownership of the means of production, central planning, and the distribution of goods without a profit motive

stockholders' revolt: the refusal of a corporation's stockholders to rubber-stamp decisions made by its managers

stored value: the backing of a currency by goods that are stored and held in reserve

subsistence economy: the type of economy in which human groups live off the land with little or no surplus

tertiary sector: that part of the economy that consists of service-oriented occupations

underemployment: the condition of having to work at a job beneath one's level of training and abilities, or of being able to find only part-time work

underground economy: exchanges of goods and services that are not reported to the government and thereby escape taxation

welfare (state) capitalism: an economic system in which individuals own the means of production but the state regulates many economic activities for the welfare of the population

☞ KEY PEOPLE

Review the major theoretical contributions or findings of these people.

Daniel Bell: Bell identified six characteristics of the postindustrial society.

Wallace Clement: Followed in John Porter's footsteps and showed the increasing concentration of corporate power in Canada.

Emile Durkheim: Durkheim contributed the concepts of mechanical and organic solidarity to our understanding of social cohesion.

John Porter: The first Canadian sociologist to identify the highly concentrated character of Canada's corporate elite.

R. Jack Richardson: Compared corporate concentration in several developed economies.

Michael Useem: Using a conflict perspective, Useem studied the activities of the "inner circle" of corporate executives.

Thorstein Veblen: Veblen created the term "conspicuous consumption" to refer to the eagerness to show off one's wealth through the elaborate consumption of material goods.

☞ SELF-TEST

After completing this self-test, check your answers against the Answer Key at the back of this Study Guide and against the text on page(s) indicated in parentheses.

MULTIPLE CHOICE QUESTIONS

1. What is a market? (258)
   a. It is any process of buying and selling.
   b. It is the mechanism that establishes values for the exchange of goods and services.
   c. It means the movement of vast amounts of goods across international borders.
   d. All of the above.

2. Which of the following characterize hunting and gathering societies? (258)
   a. market economy
   b. surplus economy
   c. subsistence economy
   d. maintenance economy

3. Which of the following took place in pastoral and horticultural economies? (258)
   a. a subsistence economy exists
   b. a more dependable food supply led to the development of a surplus
   c. the plow was used extensively
   d. trade expanded

4. Which of the following is *not* a feature of industrial economies? (259)
   a. Machines are powered by fuels.
   b. A surplus unlike anything the world had seen is created.
   c. The steam engine was invented and became the basis for the economy.
   d. A service sector developed and employed the majority of workers.

5.   What did Veblen label the lavishly wasteful spending of goods designed to enhance social prestige? (259)
    a.   prestigious consumption
    b.   wasteful consumption
    c.   conspicuous prestige
    d.   conspicuous consumption

6.   Which of the following is *not* a defining characteristics of postindustrial economies? (259-260)
    a.   a large surplus of goods
    b.   extensive trade among nations
    c.   machines powered by fuels
    d.   a "global village"

7.   In which type of society was money first used extensively? (261)
    a.   agricultural
    b.   industrial
    c.   postindustrial
    d.   pastoral and horticultural

8.   What term is used to describe the total goods and services that a nation produces? (261)
    a.   the gross national product
    b.   the net national product
    c.   the national debt
    d.   the medium of exchange

9.   The debit card came into existence in the: (261)
    a.   agricultural economy.
    b.   industrial economy.
    c.   postindustrial economy.
    d.   None of the above.

10.   Private ownership of the means of production is an essential feature of: (261)
    a.   communism.
    b.   socialism.
    c.   democracy.
    d.   capitalism.

11.   "Pure" capitalism is: (262)
    a.   the type of capitalism found in North America.
    b.   an ideal type used to develop models of capitalism in Western Europe.
    c.   a system where market forces operate without interference from government
    d.   a system where market forces are moderated by some government interference.

12.   Which system has public ownership, central planning, and no profit motive? (264)
    a.   democratic socialism
    b.   socialism
    c.   capitalism
    d.   communism

13. Dissatisfied with the greed of capitalism and the lack of individual freedom of socialism, some Western nations (Sweden, Denmark) developed: (264-265)
    a.   welfare capitalism.
    b.   democratic socialism.
    c.   postindustrialism.
    d.   laissez-faire capitalism.

14. Some critics believe that underemployment is a problem caused by: (265)
    a.   socialism.
    b.   capitalism.
    c.   democratic socialism.
    d.   communism.

15. Jointly owning an enterprise, with liabilities and obligations independent of its owners, is: (267)
    a.   an oligopoly.
    b.   a monopoly.
    c.   a corporation.
    d.   an interlocking directorate.

16. What is oligopoly? (267)
    a.   the control of an entire industry by several large companies
    b.   the control of an entire industry by a single company
    c.   illegal in Canada
    d.   None of the above

17. A stockholders' revolt occurs when: (267)
    a.   major stockholders dump their holdings in the open market.
    b.   stockholders lead workers in a protest against company policies.
    c.   stockholders refuse to rubber-stamp the recommendations made by management.
    d.   people boycott the stocks of certain companies that are socially irresponsible.

18. The elites who sit on the boards of directors of multiple companies are referred to as: (268)
    a.   vertical integrators.
    b.   interlocking trustees.
    c.   interlocking directorates.
    d.   oligopolies.

19. Which of the following characteristics describes a profession? (271)
    a.   rigorous educational training
    b.   authority over clients based on the specialized training
    c.   service to society rather than to the self
    d.   all of the above are among the characteristics of a profession

20. Which perspective views work as the tie which binds us together? (272)
    a.   functionalist
    b.   conflict
    c.   symbolic interactionist
    d.   ethnomethodological

21. As societies industrialize, they become based on: (272)
    a. mechanical solidarity.
    b. organic solidarity.
    c. social solidarity.
    d. None of the above.

22. According to conflict theory, which group bears the brunt of technological change? (272)
    a. middle management
    b. top-level executives
    c. low-level workers
    d. laborers in the least industrialized nations

23. Workers who package fish, process copper into electrical wire, and turn trees into lumber and paper are in the: (273)
    a. primary sector.
    b. secondary sector.
    c. tertiary sector.
    d. None of the above.

24. What term is used to describe the fundamental changes in society that follow the movement of vast numbers of women from the home to the work force? (274)
    a. the feminization of work
    b. the "mommy movement"
    c. the quiet revolution
    d. the backlash

25. What is the underground economy? (275)
    a. It is an exchange of goods and services that is not reported to the government.
    b. It helps many Canadians avoid what they consider exorbitant taxes.
    c. It includes illegal activities such as drug dealing.
    d. All of the above.

TRUE-FALSE QUESTIONS

T F 1. Hunting and gathering societies were the first economies to have a surplus. (258)
T F 2. In pastoral and horticultural economies, some individuals were able for the first time in human history to develop their energies to tasks other than food production. (258)
T F 3. The characteristics of postindustrial economies were identified by Daniel Bell. (259)
T F 4. Industrial economies are based on information processing and providing services. (259)
T F 5. The richest fifth of Canadians earn about 47 percent of all the income in Canada. (260)
T F 6. The gold standard was a medium of exchange in industrial economies. (261)
T F 7. Credit cards and debit cards are the same thing. (261)
T F 8. In welfare capitalism, private citizens own the means of production and pursue profits, but do so within a vast system of laws. (262)
T F 9. The Canadian government controls "common good" items. (264)
T F 10. Socialism involves the distribution of goods without a profit motive. (264)
T F 11. According to convergence theory, the world's nations are becoming more and more capitalistic. (266)

T F   12.   Oligopolies are formed when many different-sized companies all compete within a single industry. (267)

T F   13.   The sociological significance of multinational corporations is that they owe allegiance only to profits and market share, not to any nation, not even any particular culture. (269)

T F   14.   Members of a profession claim that only they possess sufficient knowledge to determine the profession's standards and to certify those qualified to be admitted. (271)

T F   15.   Durkheim's concept of organic solidarity is an adequate concept for understanding the interdependency that exists among the nations of the world today. (272)

T F   16.   The inner circle is made up of the heads of the largest multinational corporations. (272)

T F   17.   Researchers have found that both men and women workers are equally concerned with maintaining a balance between their work and family lives. (274)

T F   18.   The "quiet revolution" refers to the continually increasing proportions of women who have joined the ranks of paid labor. (274)

T F   19.   While Canada's banks and corporations report record profits, household income growth has declined dramatically over the past twenty years. (275)

T F   20.   In recent decades, Canada has followed the lead of the western nations in terms of a gradually shrinking work week and an increase in leisure. (276)

FILL-IN QUESTIONS

1.   _____ is the term for a system of distribution of goods and services. (258)

2.   The means (for example, currency, gold, and silver) by which people value goods and services in order to make an exchange is the _____. (260)

3.   A _____ allows its owners to purchase goods but to be billed later. A _____ allows its owners to charge purchases against his or her bank account. (261)

4.   The economic system where market forces operate without interference from government is called _____. (262)

5.   The law of supply and demand is referred to as _____. (264)

6.   _____ is the condition of having to work at a job beneath one's level of training and abilities, or of being able to find only part-time work. (265)

7.   The view that as capitalist and socialist economic systems each adopt features of the other, a hybrid (or mixed) economic system may emerge is _____. (266)

8.   One way in which the wealthy use corporations to wield power is by means of _____, or serving as directors of several companies simultaneously. (268)

9.   Durkheim's term for the unity that comes from being involved in similar occupations or activities is _____. (272)

10. Members of the _____ may compete with one another, but they are united by a mutual interest in preserving capitalism. (272)

11. That part of the economy in which raw materials are turned into manufactured goods is the _____. (273)

12. In the _____ sector, workers are primarily involved in providing services. (273)

13. The _____ has contributed to a transformation of consumer patterns, relations at work, self-concepts, and relationships with family and friends. (274-275)

14. The _____ consists of economic activities, whether legal or illegal, that people don't report to the government. (275)

15. _____ is time not taken up by work or required activities such as eating and sleeping. (276)

MATCH THESE SOCIAL SCIENTISTS WITH THEIR CONTRIBUTIONS

__1. Daniel Bell   a. *studied the activities of the "inner circle"*
__2. Emile Durkheim   b. *studied the concentration of corporate power in Canada*
__3. Michael Useem   c. *identified six characteristics of postindustrial society*
__4. Wallace Clement   d. *created the term "conspicuous consumption"*
__5. Thorstein Veblen   e. *contributed the concepts of mechanical and organic solidarity*

ESSAY QUESTIONS

1. Discuss the advantages and disadvantages of both capitalism and socialism as ideologies and as economic systems.
2. Identify the defining characteristics of professions and discuss the usefulness of this framework for understanding work.
3. The chapter discusses several different economic trends that have been occurring in the second half of this century. Discuss the role of technology in each of the following: the global corporation, the movement of women into the economy, unemployment and the shrinking paychecks, and patterns of work and leisure.

"DOWN-TO-EARTH SOCIOLOGY"

1. After reading "Advertising – The Creation of Discontent" (p. 265), can you think of ways in which advertising is able to increase your desire to consume products, even when you previously felt no need for them? How does advertising affect what you wear? What you eat? What you do for recreation? How does advertising affect the way you feel about yourself?
2. What forces do you think have contributed to the emergence of bartering in the former Soviet Union (p. 266)? Have there been times when you have engaged in bartering yourself? What were the circumstances that led you to barter? What conclusions can you draw about the social—or economic—factors associated with this form of exchange?
3. When you read "Finding Work" (p. 276), were you surprised to learn that trends of job security are different now than they were 40 years ago? What are the social implications of this change?
4. Do your concerns about technology and work mirror those voiced in "New Technology and the Restructuring of Work" (p. 278)? What kinds of social, political, and economic conditions would have to be present for either of the future alternatives to come true?

CHAPTER 12

POLITICS: POWER AND AUTHORITY

☞ **CHAPTER SUMMARY**

- The essential nature of politics is power, the ability to carry out one's will despite resistance; every group is political. Micropolitics refers to the exercise of power in everyday life while macropolitics refers to large-scale power, such as governing a nation.

- Authority refers to the legitimate use of power, while coercion is its illegitimate use. The state is a political entity that claims a monopoly on violence over a particular territory. Three types of authority, traditional, rational-legal, and charismatic, were identified by Max Weber as ideal type constructs. The orderly transfer of authority at the death, resignation, or incapacitation of a leader is critical for social stability.

- Three forms of government are monarchies (power is based on hereditary rule), democracies (power is given by the citizens), and dictatorships and oligarchies (power is seized by an individual or a small group).

- The Canadian system of government is a parliamentary democracy, where parliament is the highest political authority in the country. However, provincial governments also have separate and significant powers of their own. Many democracies in Europe have a system of proportional representation which encourages the formation of coalition governments.

- Functionalists and conflict theorists have very different views on who rules Canada. According to the functionalists, no one group holds power; the outcome is that the competing interest groups balance one another (pluralism). According to conflict theorists, Canada is governed by a ruling class made up of members drawn from the elite (power elite).

- War is a common means to implement political objectives; however, dehumanization of the enemy is a particularly high cost of war.

- The global expansion of communication, transportation, and trade, the widespread adoption of capitalism and the retreat of socialism, as well as the trend toward larger political unions suggest that a new international world order may be in the process of emerging. The oppositional trend is for fierce nationalism to emerge.

☞ **LEARNING OBJECTIVES**

As you read Chapter 12, use these learning objectives to organize your notes. After completing your reading, briefly state an answer to each of the objectives, and review the text pages in parentheses.

1. Define the term power and distinguish between micropolitics and macropolitics. (284)
2. Explain the difference between authority and coercion and why the state claims a monopoly on legitimate violence. (284-285)
3. Describe the sources of authority identified by Weber, indicate why these are "ideal types," and explain how the orderly transfer of authority is achieved under each type of authority. (285-287)
4. Differentiate between monarchies, democracies, and dictatorships and oligarchies. (287-288)
5. Explain how the political system is structured in Canada. (288-289)
6. Describe the Parliamentary system in Canada. (289-290)
7. Discuss the evolution of Canada's political party system. (291-292)
8. Analyze the impact of the Quiet Revolution and the Quebec sovereignty movement on Canadian politics. (292-293)

9.   Compare Canadian democracy with democratic systems found in Europe. (293-294)
10. Distinguish between the functionalist and conflict perspectives on how the Canadian political process operates, and discuss the power elite perspectives of C. Wright Mills and John Porter. (294-295)
11. Discuss the conditions that lead to war and analyze the dehumanizing aspects of war. (296-298)
12. Evaluate the possibility for global political and economic unity in the future and what impact the resurgence of nationalism could have on this new world order. (298-299)

☞ CHAPTER OUTLINE

I.   Micropolitics and Macropolitics
   A.   Power is the ability to carry out one's will despite resistance.
   B.   Symbolic interactionists use micropolitics to refer to exercise of power in everyday life. Macropolitics is the exercise of large-scale power over a broad group.

II.   Power, Authority, and Violence
   A.   Authority is legitimate power that people accept as right, while coercion is power that people do not accept as just.
   B.   The state is the source of legitimate force or violence in society; violence is the ultimate foundation of political order. A government that is viewed as legitimate is more stable than one that is not; revolution (armed resistance to overthrow a government) is a rejection by the people of a government's claim to rule and of its monopoly on violence.
   C.   Three sources of authority were identified by Max Weber.
        1.   Traditional authority (based on custom) is prevalent in preliterate groups, where custom sets relationships. When society changes, traditional authority is undermined, but does not die, even in postindustrial societies. For example, parental authority is a traditional authority.
        2.   Rational-legal authority (based on written rules, also called bureaucratic authority) derives from the position an individual holds, not from the person. Everyone (no matter how high the office) is subject to the rules.
        3.   Charismatic authority (based on an individual's personal following) may pose a threat. Because this type of leader works outside the established political system and may threaten the established order, the authorities are often quick to oppose this type of leader.
   D.   Weber's three types of authority are ideal types representing composite characteristics found in real life examples. In rare instances, traditional and rational-legal leaders possess charismatic traits, but most authority is one type or another.
   E.   Orderly transfer of authority upon death, resignation, or incapacity of a leader is critical for stability. Succession is more of a problem with charismatic authority than with traditional or rational-legal authority. Routinization of charisma refers to the transfer of authority from a charismatic leader to either traditional or rational-legal authority.

III.   Types of Government
   A.   A monarchy is a government headed by a king or queen.
        1.   As cities developed, each city-state (an independent city whose power radiated outward, bringing adjacent areas under its rule) had its own monarchy.
        2.   As city-states warred with one another, the victors would extend their rule, eventually over an entire region. As the size of these regions grew, people developed an identification with the region; over time this gave rise to the state.

B.   A democracy is a government whose authority derives from the people.

1.   Direct democracy (eligible voters meet to discuss issues and make decisions) emerged about 2,000 years ago in Athens.

2.   Representative democracy (voters elect representatives to govern and make decisions on their behalf) emerged as Canada became more populous, making direct democracy impossible.

3.   Today, citizenship (people have basic rights by virtue of birth or residence) is taken for granted in Canada; this idea is quite new to the human scene. Universal citizenship (everyone having the same basic rights) came into practice very slowly and only through struggle.

C.   Dictatorship is government where power is seized and held by an individual; oligarchy results when a small group of individuals seizes power. Dictators and oligarchies can be totalitarian; this is when the government exercises almost total control of a people.

IV.   **The Canadian Political System**

A.   Canada is a parliamentary democracy.

1.   Parliament is the highest political authority in the country.

2.   Provincial governments have a number of separate and significant powers of their own.

3.   Canada's system of government lies in-between the models of a unitary state (where all power resides with the central government) and a confederal union (where provinces have most power).

B.   The Parliamentary system in Canada is made up of three levels of national government: the Queen, the Senate, and Parliament.

1.   The Queen has no powers to make laws in Canada, and the Senate is a minor player in the lawmaking process.

2.   While Parliament is the highest lawmaking authority, there are limits to its powers; it cannot make laws in areas of provincial jurisdiction.

3.   Opposition parties play an adversarial role, debating the government's policies.

4.   The federal bureaucracy includes employees in the armed forces, the RCMP, various government agencies, and the public service.

5.   The Canadian government has enacted policies of employment equity to provide more opportunities for women, aboriginal peoples, visible minorities, and peoples with disabilities in the federal public service.

6.   Politics in Quebec are tied to the struggles over French language and French-Canadian culture.

C.   Not all democracies around the world are Parliamentary systems like ours.

1.   Most European countries use proportional representation (legislative seats divided according to the proportion of votes each political party received).

2.   The European system encourages minority parties. Non-centrist parties (representing marginal ideas) develop in European systems with proportional representation.

3.   Three main results follow from proportional representation: (1) minority parties can gain access to the media, which keeps their issues alive; (2) minority parties can gain power beyond their numbers; and (3) the government may be unstable due to the breakdown of coalitions (a coalition occurs when a country's largest party aligns itself with one or more smaller parties to get required votes to make national decisions).

V.   Who Rules Canada?

A.   The functionalists say that pluralism, the diffusion of power among interest groups, prevents any one from gaining control of the government. Functionalists believe pluralism helps keep the government from turning against its citizens.

1.   In order to get elected and re-elected, a political candidate must pay attention to groups representing special interests—ethnic groups, women, farmers, factory workers, bankers, bosses, and the retired, but to name a few.

2.   In this system, power is widely dispersed; as each group pursues its interests, it is balanced by others pursuing theirs.

B.   According to the conflict perspective, the power elite makes the decisions that direct the country and shape the world.

1.   As stated by C. Wright Mills, the power elite (heads of leading corporations, powerful generals and admirals in the armed forces, and certain elite politicians) rule Canada. The corporate heads are the most powerful, as all three sectors of the elite view capitalism as essential to the welfare of the country; thus, business interests come first.

2.   In addition to an economic elite, John Porter identified elites in the media, religion, organized labor, and Canadian politics.

3.   The Canadian economic elite attend the same schools and social clubs, and recruit one another to serve on various boards of directors.

VI.   War: A Means to Implement Political Objectives

A.   The state uses violence to protect citizens from individuals and groups, turning violence against other nations. War (armed conflict between nations or politically distinct groups) often is part of national policy.

B.   War is not characteristic of all human groups, but simply one option for settling disputes. At the same time, war is a fairly common occurrence; Pitirim Sorokin counted 967 wars between 500 B.C. and 1925 A.D., for an average of one war every two to three years.

C.   Nicholas Timasheff identified three essential conditions of war.

1.   There is a cultural tradition of war; because they have fought wars in the past, leaders see war as an option.

2.   An antagonistic situation exists, with two or more states confronting incompatible objectives.

3.   A "fuel" heats the antagonistic situation to the boiling point, so that people move from thinking about war to actually engaging in it; Timasheff identified seven fuels.

D.   Despite the fact war is costly to society, it continues to be a common technique for pursuing political objectives.

E.   The Most Industrialized Nations relentlessly pursue profits by selling powerful weapons to the Least Industrialized Nations—Russia and the United States are the chief merchants of death to the Least Industrialized Nations.

F.   Today terrorism directed against civilian populations is a danger.

1.   Suicide terrorism is one of the few options available to a weaker group that wants to retaliate against a powerful country.

2.   The real danger is from nuclear, chemical, and biological weapons.

G.   War has an effect on morality.

1.   Exposure to brutality and killing often causes dehumanization (reducing people to objects that do not deserve to be treated as humans).

2.   Characteristics of dehumanization include: (1) increased emotional distance from others; (2) an emphasis on following procedures; (3) inability to resist pressures; and (4) a diminished sense of personal responsibility.

3.   Tamotsu Shibutani stressed that dehumanization is helped along by the tendency for prolonged conflicts to be transformed into a struggle between good and evil.

4.   Dehumanization does not always insulate the self from guilt; after the war ends, returning soldiers often find themselves disturbed by what they did during the war. Although most eventually adjust, some live with the guilt forever.

VII.   A New World Order?

A.   Today the embrace of capitalism and worldwide flow of information, capital and goods has made national boundaries less meaningful. There are many examples of nations working together to solve mutual problems — the North American Free Trade Agreement (NAFTA), the European Union (EU), and the United Nations (UN).

B.   The resurgence of fierce nationalism represents a challenge to a new world order.

☞ KEY TERMS

After studying the chapter, review the definition for each of the following terms.

anarchy: a condition of lawlessness or political disorder caused by the abuse or collapse of governmental authority

authority: power that people accept as rightly exercised over them; also called *legitimate power*

centrist party: a political party that represents the center of political opinion

charismatic authority: authority based on an individual's outstanding traits, which attract followers

citizenship: the concept that birth (and residence) in a country impart basic rights

city-state: an independent city whose power radiates outward, bringing the adjacent areas under its rule

coalition government: a government in which a country's largest party aligns itself with one or more smaller parties

coercion: power that people do not accept as rightly exercised over them; also called *illegitimate power*

confederal union: a form of government where power resides in provinces, rather than a central government

dehumanization: the act or process of reducing people to objects that do not deserve the treatment accorded humans

democracy: a system of government in which authority derives from the people, derived from two Greek words that translate literally as "power to the people"

dictatorship: a form of government in which power is seized by an individual

direct democracy: a form of democracy in which the eligible voters meet together to discuss issues and make their decisions

macropolitics: the exercise of large-scale power, the government being the most common example

micropolitics: the exercise of politics in everyday life, such as deciding who is going to do the housework

monarchy: a form of government headed by a king or queen

nationalism: a strong identity with a nation, accompanied by the desire for the nation to be dominant

non-centrist party: a political party that represents marginal ideas

oligarchy: a form of government in which power is held by a small group of individuals; the rule of the many by the few

pluralism: the diffusion of power among many interest groups, preventing any single group from gaining control of the government

power: the ability to carry out one's will, even over the resistance of others

power elite: C. Wright Mills's term for those who rule Canada; the top people in the leading corporations, the most powerful generals and admirals of the armed forces, and certain elite politicians

proportional representation: an electoral system in which seats in a legislature are divided according to the proportion of votes each political party receives

rational-legal authority: authority based on law or written rules and regulations; also called *bureaucratic authority*

representative democracy: a form of democracy in which voters elect representatives to govern and make decisions on their behalf

revolution: armed resistance designed to overthrow a government

routinization of charisma: the transfer of authority from a charismatic figure to either a traditional or a rational-legal form of authority

ruling class: another term for the power elite

state: a political entity that claims a monopoly on the use of violence in some particular territory; commonly known as a country

totalitarianism: a form of government that exerts almost total control over the people

traditional authority: authority based on custom

unitary state: a state in which all power resides with the central government

universal citizenship: the idea that everyone has the same basic rights by virtue of being born in a country (or by immigrating and becoming a naturalized citizen)

voter apathy: indifference and inaction on the part of individuals or groups with respect to the political process

war: armed conflict between nations or politically distinct groups

☞ KEY PEOPLE

Review the major theoretical contributions or findings of these people.

Peter Berger: Berger argued that violence is the ultimate foundation of any political order.

Wallace Clement: Clement classified three components of Canada's corporate elite: a Canadian component, a foreign (mostly U.S.) component, and a "comprador" elite.

Everett Hughes: Hughes studied the industrialization of rural Quebec and the division of labour between English-speaking Protestants and French-speaking Catholics.

C. Wright Mills: Mills suggested that power resides in the hands of an elite made up of the top leaders of the largest corporations, the most powerful generals of the armed forces, and certain elite politicians.

John Porter: Porter identified an economic elite, as well as elites in the media, religion, organized labor, and the political sector of Canadian society.

Tamotsu Shibutani: Shibutani noted that the process of dehumanization is helped along by the tendency for prolonged conflicts to be transformed into a struggle between good and evil.

Pitirim Sorokin: Sorokin studied wars from 500 B.C. to 1925 A.D. and found that war was a fairly routine experience. There had been 967 wars during this time span, for an average of a war every two or three years.

Nicholas S. Timasheff: Timasheff identified three essential conditions of war—a cultural tradition of war, an antagonistic situation in which two or more countries have incompatible objectives, and a fuel which moves the antagonisms into conflict situations.

Max Weber: Weber identified three different types of authority: traditional, rational-legal, and charismatic.

☞ SELF-TEST

After completing this self-test, check your answers against the Answer Key at the back of this Study Guide and against the text on page(s) indicated in parentheses.

MULTIPLE CHOICE QUESTIONS

1. Which of the following relates to power? (284)
    a. The concept was defined by Max Weber.
    b. It is the ability to carry out one's will in spite of resistance from others.
    c. It is an inevitable part of everyday life.
    d. All of the above.

2. Governments, whether dictatorships or the elected forms, are examples of: (284)
    a. coercion.
    b. macropolitics.
    c. micropolitics.
    d. None of the above.

3. What did Peter Berger consider to be the ultimate foundation of any political order? (285)
    a. laws
    b. elections
    c. violence
    d. leaders

4. Traditional authority: (285)
    a. is the hallmark of preliterate groups.
    b. is based on custom.
    c. was identified by Max Weber.
    d. All of the above.

5. Pierre Elliott Trudeau: (287)
    a. was a rational-legal leader.
    b. was a charismatic leader.
    c. is an example of a leader who is difficult to classify in terms of ideal types.
    d. All of the above.

6. Which of the following is considered the least stable type of authority? (287)
    a. traditional
    b. rational-legal
    c. charismatic
    d. monarchy

7. An individual who seizes power and imposes his will onto the people is known as a: (288)
    a. charismatic leader.
    b. dictator.
    c. totalitarian leader.
    d. monarch.

8.   Which form of government exerts almost total control over the people? (288)
     a.   monarchy
     b.   dictatorship
     c.   totalitarian regime
     d.   oligarchy

9.   Canada's political system is: (288)
     a.   a parliamentary democracy.
     b.   a unitary state.
     c.   a confederal state.
     d.   None of the above.

10. What does the history of the political party system in Canada demonstrate? (291-292)
     a.   Third parties have generally promoted left-wing policies.
     b.   The party system evolved into a multi-party system during the 20th century.
     c.   The Liberals and Conservatives are the only important political parties.
     d.   All of the above.

11. What event(s) in Quebec have transformed Canadian politics? (292-293)
     a.   the Quiet Revolution
     b.   the rise of the sovereignty movement
     c.   (a) and (b)
     d.   the Meech Lake Accord

12. Most European countries base their elections on a system of: (293-294)
     a.   parliamentary democracy.
     b.   multi-party competition.
     c.   pluralism.
     d.   proportional representation.

13. Functionalists see that _____ prevent(s) any one group from having total government control. (294)
     a.   the existence of a powerful elite
     b.   pluralism
     c.   coalition governments
     d.   all of the above

14. Which perspective suggests that conflict is minimized as special-interest groups negotiate with one another and reach compromises? (294)
     a.   functionalists
     b.   conflict theorists
     c.   symbolic interactionists
     d.   political sociologists

15. Members of the power elite are drawn from: (295)
     a.   the largest corporations.
     b.   the armed forces.
     c.   top political offices.
     d.   all of the above.

16. According to conflict theorists, the ruling class is: (295)
    a. a group that meets together and agrees on specific matters.
    b. a group which tends to have complete unity on issues.
    c. made up of people whose backgrounds and orientations to life are so similar that they automatically share the same goals.
    d. a myth.

17. War: (296)
    a. is armed conflict between nations or politically distinct groups.
    b. is universal.
    c. is chosen for dealing with disagreements by all societies at one time or another.
    d. All of the above.

18. Which of the following is *not* one of the essential conditions of war identified by Nicholas Timasheff? (296)
    a. the existence of a strong, well-armed military force
    b. a cultural tradition of war
    c. an antagonistic situation in which two or more states confront incompatible objectives
    d. the presence of a "fuel" that heats the antagonistic situation to a boiling point

19. The act or process of reducing people to objects that do not deserve the treatment accorded humans is: (297)
    a. institutionalization.
    b. dehumanization.
    c. regimentation.
    d. totalitarianism.

20. Today, national boundaries are becoming less meaningful because of: (298)
    a. the embrace of capitalism by more and more nations.
    b. the worldwide flow of information, capital and goods.
    c. the formation of large economic and political units like the European Union.
    d. All of the above.

TRUE-FALSE QUESTIONS

T F   1.   In every group, large or small, some individuals have power over others. (284)
T F   2.   Coercion refers to legitimate power. (284)
T F   3.   The state claims a monopoly on violence within some designated territory. (285)
T F   4.   Even with industrialization some forms of traditional authority go unchallenged. (285-286)
T F   5.   Rational-legal authority derives from the position that an individual holds, not from the person who holds the position. (286)
T F   6.   Because the authority of charismatic leaders is based on their personal ability to attract followers, they pose no threat to the established political system. (286-287)
T F   7.   It is difficult to classify some leaders as having one specific type of authority. (287)
T F   8.   Routinization of charisma involves the transfer of authority from a charismatic leader to either traditional or rational-legal authority. (287)
T F   9.   The first type of government was that based on direct participation of all citizens. (287-288)

T F 10. Direct democracy was not possible in Canada as its population grew in number and spread out. (288)

T F 11. The concept of representative democracy based on citizenship revolutionized political systems. (288)

T F 12. The idea of universal citizenship caught on quickly in Canada. (288)

T F 13. Public sector employees constitute a very small fraction of the total labour force. (292)

T F 14. Employment equity initiatives have resolved problems of under-representation of women and visible minorities in the federal public service. (292)

T F 15. The European system of democracy is not that different from our own. (293-294)

T F 16. Functionalists believe that pluralism prevents any one group from gaining control of the government and using it to oppress the people. (294)

T F 17. According to C. Wright Mills, the three groups that make up the power elite share power equally. (295)

T F 18. War is universal. (296)

T F 19. Sociologists attribute the causes of war to human factors such as aggressive impulses. (296)

T F 20. Terrorism is one of the few options open to a weaker political group looking for ways to retaliate against a powerful country. (297)

FILL-IN QUESTIONS

1. The exercise of power in everyday life, such as deciding who is going to do the housework is referred to as _____. (284)

2. _____ is synonymous with government; the source of legitimate violence in society. (285)

3. A _____ is armed resistance designed to overthrow a government. (285)

4. _____ is authority based on custom. (285)

5. Bureaucratic authority is also called _____. (286)

6. An independent city whose power radiates outward, bringing the adjacent area under its rule, is a _____. (287)

7. _____ is a form of democracy in which the eligible voters meet together to discuss issues and make their decisions. (288)

8. The concept that birth and residence in a country impart basic rights is known as _____. (288)

9. A form of government that exerts almost total control over the people is _____. (288)

10. An electoral system in which seats in a legislature are divided according to the proportion of votes each political party receives is called _____. (294)

11. A _____ is a government where the party with the most seats aligns itself with one or more of the smaller parties to maintain power. (294)

12. A state of lawlessness or political disorder caused by the absence or collapse of governmental authority is _____. (294)

13. _____ is C. Wright Mills's term for the top people in leading corporations, the most powerful generals and admirals of the armed forces, and certain elite politicians. (295)

14. The act or process of reducing people to objects that do not deserve the treatment accorded humans is _____. (297)

15. Today _____, a strong identity with a nation, accompanied by the desire for that nation to be dominant, challenges efforts to forge a new world order. (299)

MATCH THESE SOCIAL SCIENTISTS WITH THEIR CONTRIBUTIONS

__1. Peter Berger
__2. John Porter
__3. C. Wright Mills
__4. Max Weber
__5. Nicholas Timasheff
__6. Tamotsu Shibutani
__7. Pitirim Sorokin

a. *war as a fairly routine experience*
b. *violence is the foundation of the political order*
c. *three types of authority*
d. *identified Canadian elite*
e. *the process of dehumanization*
f. *essential conditions of war*
g. *power elite*

ESSAY QUESTIONS

1. Distinguish between macropolitics and micropolitics, explaining what each is and which perspectives are associated with each, and provide your own examples to illustrate each.
2. Compare and contrast the systems of democracy found in Canada and Europe.
3. Discuss what you see as the future of the new world order.

"DOWN-TO-EARTH SOCIOLOGY"

1. What are your views of political parties, political leadership and the electoral process? Which perspective (functionalist, conflict) best reflects your own views? Do you vote? If not, why not?
2. Based on "The Rise of Nationalism Versus the Globalization of Capitalism: Implications for a New World Order," (pp. 298-299), do you agree that the next twenty years may be bloody if the world cannot find a better way to answer the demands of newly emboldened nations? Why or why not? How can the needs of these new nations for national identities be balanced against the demands of an increasingly global economy?

CHAPTER 13

THE FAMILY: INITIATION INTO SOCIETY

☞ CHAPTER SUMMARY

- Because there are so many cultural variations, family structure is hard to define. Nevertheless, family is defined broadly as two or more people who consider themselves related by blood, marriage or adoption. Marriage and family patterns vary remarkably across cultures, but four universal themes in marriage are mate selection, descent, inheritance, and authority.

- According to the functionalist perspective, the family is universal because it serves six essential functions: economic production, socialization of children, care of the sick and aged, recreation, sexual control, and reproduction. Conversely, conflict theorists focus on how changing economic conditions affect families, especially gender relations. Symbolic interactionists focus on the contrasting experiences and perspectives of men and women that are played out in marriage.

- The family life cycle is analyzed in terms of love and courtship, marriage, childbirth, child rearing, and the family in later life. Within Canada, marriage, childbirth, and child rearing all vary by social class.

- Family diversity in Canadian society is based on racial and ethnic differences, as well as social class. As well, one-parent families, childless families, blended families, and gay families represent some of the different types of families today.

- Trends in Canadian families include postponement of marriage, common-law marriage, and the emergence of the "sandwich generation" who are caught between caring for their own children and caring for their elderly parents.

- Various studies have focused on problems in measuring divorce, children of divorce, ex-spouses, and remarriage. Research suggests that children can suffer long-term negative effects from divorce. However, researchers have noted that the impacts of divorce are complex, not uniform.

- Violence and abuse—including child abuse, battering, marital rape, and incest —are the "dark side" of family life. Researchers have identified variables that help marriages last and be happy.

- The trends for the future include a continued increased in cohabitation, births to unmarried mothers, and postponement of marriage. The continuing growth in the numbers of working wives will impact on marital balance of power.

☞ LEARNING OBJECTIVES

As you read Chapter 13, use these learning objectives to organize your notes. After completing your reading, briefly state an answer to each of the objectives, and review the text pages in parentheses.

1. Explain why it is difficult to define the term "family," including the different ways in which family systems can be classified. (305)
2. Identify the common cultural themes that run through marriage and the family. (305-306)
3. Explain why is it important to avoid a "monolithic bias" when defining the family. (307-308)
4. Contrast the functionalist, conflict, and symbolic interaction perspectives regarding marriage and family. (308-313)
5. Outline the major developments in each stage of the family life cycle and discuss the social factors that produce variations within each of these stages. (313-316)
6. State examples of the impact of racial and ethnic diversity on Canadian family life. (316-318)

7. Identify the major concerns of one-parent families, families without children, blended families, gay families, and intentional families. (318-321)
8. Describe the current trends affecting marriage and family life in Canada. (321-325)
9. Outline the legislative changes in Canadian society that facilitated increased divorce rates. (323-324)
10. Note some of the adjustment problems of children of divorce. (324)
11. Explain the statement that "family life can be rewarding or brutal" and give examples of abuse within the family setting. (325-326)
12. List some of the characteristics which tend to be present in marriages that work. Explain why happy and unhappy couples approach problems differently. (326)
13. Summarize conclusions regarding the future of marriage and family in Canada. (326-327)

☞ **CHAPTER OUTLINE**

I.   **Marriage and Family in Global Perspective**
       A.   Defining Family
            1.   The term "family" is difficult to define because there are many types.
            2.   In some societies men have more than one wife (polygyny) or women have more than one husband (polyandry).
       B.   Common Cultural Themes
            1.   Each group establishes norms to govern whom you can and cannot marry. Endogamy is the practice of marrying within one's own group, while exogamy is the practice of marrying outside of one's own group. Some norms of mate selection are written into law, others are informal.
            2.   Three major patterns of descent (tracing kinship over generations) are: (a) bilateral (descent traced on both the mother's and the father's side); (b) patrilineal (descent traced only on the father's side); and (c) matrilineal (descent traced only on the mother's side).
            3.   Mate selection and descent are regulated in all societies in order to provide an orderly way of passing property, etc., to the next generation. In a bilateral system, property passes to males and females; in a patrilineal system, property passes only to males; in a matrilineal system, property passes only to females.
            4.   Patriarchy is a social system in which men dominate women, and runs through all societies. No historical records exist of a true matriarchy. In an egalitarian social system authority is more or less equally divided between men and women.
       C.   The Problem of Monolithic Bias
            1.   A broad definition of family is two or more people who consider themselves related by blood, marriage, or adoption, and live together (or have lived together).
            2.   A household, in contrast to a family, is all the people occupying the same housing unit.
            3.   The family of orientation is the family in which a person grows up, while the family of procreation is the family formed when a couple's first child is born. A person who is married but has not had a child is part of a couple, not a family.
            4.   Marriage is a group's approved mating arrangements, usually marked by a ritual.
            5.   Canadian sociologists have rejected a "monolithic" approach to studying families, and argue that the vision of the nuclear family supports a very limited view of family life.
            6.   They note that a monolithic bias can also contribute to a conservative bias, or a

"normalizing" of the heterosexual, nuclear family.

II.   **Marriage and Family in Theoretical Perspective**
    A.   The functionalist perspective stresses how the family is related to other parts of society and how it contributes to the well-being of society.
        1.   The family is universal because it serves functions essential to the well-being of society: economic production, socialization of children, care of the sick and aged, recreation, sexual control, and reproduction.
        2.   The incest taboo (rules specifying which people are too closely related to have sex or marry) helps the family avoid role confusion and forces people to look outside the family for marriage partners, creating a network of support.
        3.   Industrialization has made the family more fragile by weakening its functions and removing reasons for a family to struggle together against hardship, leading to higher rates of divorce.
        4.   The nuclear family has few people it can depend on for material and emotional support; thus, the members of a nuclear family are vulnerable to "emotional overload." The relative isolation of the nuclear family makes it easier for the "dark side" of families (incest and other types of abuse) to emerge.
    B.   Central to the conflict perspective is the struggle over scarce resources; in the family this struggle centers around housework.
        1.   Most men resist doing housework; consequently, working wives end up doing almost all of it. Wives are 8 times more likely than husbands to feel that the division of housework is unfair.
        2.   Arlie Hochschild found that after an 8-hour day at work, women typically work a "second shift" at home; this means that wives work an extra month of 24-hour days each year. The result is that working wives feel deep discontent.
    C.   Using the symbolic interactionist perspective, we can explore the different meaning that housework has for men and women and how each sex experiences marriage differently.
        1.   When men's and women's earnings are about the same, men are more likely to share in the housework; when women earn more than their husbands, the men are least likely to do housework. A wife's higher earnings tends to threaten a man's gender identity; doing "woman's work" is a further threat.
        2.   Men and women perceive their marriages differently. A gulf exists because each holds down different corners of the marriage. Jessie Bernard argued that every marriage actually contains two separate marriages—his and hers.

III.   **The Family Life Cycle**
    A.   Romantic love provides the ideological context in which Canadians seek mates and form families. Romantic love has two components: (1) emotional, a feeling of sexual attraction; and (2) cognitive, the feeling we describe as being "in love."
    B.   The social channels of love and marriage in Canada include age, education, social class, race, and religion.
        1.   Homogamy is the tendency of people with similar characteristics to marry one another usually resulting from propinquity (spatial nearness).
    C.   Facts contradict the popular image that having a baby makes a couple deliriously happy.
        1.   Marital satisfaction usually decreases with the birth of a child. Having a child usually means less time, less sleep, and heavier expenses.
    D.   As more mothers today are employed outside the home, child care has become an issue.
        1.   Over one half of infants and nearly two-thirds of toddlers spend at least part of the week in nonparental care. Research indicates that high-quality day care benefits

children, while low-quality harms them.

2. Nannies have become popular among upper-middle class parents. A recurring problem is tensions between parents and nanny.

3. Parents socialize children into the norms of their respective work worlds. Working-class parents want their children to conform to societal expectations. Middle-class parents are more concerned that their children develop curiosity, self-expression, and self-control.

4. Birth order is significant in child rearing: first-borns tend to be disciplined more than children who follow but also receive more attention; when the next child arrives, the first born competes to maintain attention.

E. Later stages of family life bring both pleasures and problems.

1. The empty nest is a married couple's domestic situation after the last child has left home. The empty nest is thought to signal a difficult adjustment for women; however Lillian Rubin argues that this syndrome is largely a myth because women's satisfaction generally increases when the last child leaves home. Many couples report a renewed sense of companionship at this time.

2. With prolonged education and a growing cost of establishing households, Canadian children are leaving home much later, or are returning after having left (boomerang kids).

3. Women are more likely than men to face the problem of adjusting to widowhood, for not only does the average woman live longer than a man but she has also married a man older than herself.

IV. Diversity in Canadian Families

A. Cultural diversity influences the structures and practices of Canadian families.

1. Diversity in the areas of clothing, religion, language, cultural beliefs and values has a profound impact on almost every aspect of family life.

2. For example, research suggests that recent immigrants, notably Asian immigrants, have brought with them a cultural tradition of living in a large, extended family system, and have transplanted that family configuration into the Canadian context.

B. The lives of Canadian families are also profoundly influenced by patterns of discrimination and economic inequality.

1. The family life of First Nations peoples is conditioned by long-standing patterns of economic and social marginalization.

2. Missionary-led residential schools and, later, non-Native child-welfare agencies have also undermined family life in First Nations communities.

3. Historically, immigration policies have intentionally blocked family formation among working-class Chinese, South Asian, and Japanese men and women, and more recently black Caribbean women. Government policies have ensured that these visible immigrants remained "single," provided temporary labour, and then returned to their country of origin.

C. There has been an increase in one-parent families.

1. This is due to the high divorce rate and the sharp increase in unwed motherhood.

2. Most of these families are poor; the reason for the poverty is that most are headed by women who earn less than men.

3. Children from one-parent families are more likely to have poorer scores in terms of academic achievement, health, behavior, and relationships.

D. Overall, about 35 percent of Canadian families never have children.

1. According to Kathleen Gerson, there are a number of reasons why couples choose to be childfree—unstable marriages, lost career opportunities, and the expenses

involved are among the reasons.

2. For many families, choice is not the reason they have no children; they are infertile. Some adopt, while a few turn to new reproductive technologies.

E. A blended family is one whose members were once part of other families (two divorced persons marry, bringing children into a new family unit). Blended families are increasing in number and often experience complicated family relationships.

F. In 1998, British Columbia became the first jurisdiction in North America to give same-sex couples the same privileges and obligations as opposite-sex couples (including custody, access, and child support). As with opposite-sex couples, same-sex couples maintain diverse patterns of family life. They also continue to face a hostile climate of legal and social discrimination in Canada.

G. To overcome the loneliness and isolation that often accompanies the segmented relationships of contemporary society, many people form intentional families.

V. Trends in Canadian Families

A. The average age of Canadian brides is the older than at any time in the twentieth century.

B. Common-law marriage is living together without a formal married union, and has increased about 300% between 1981 and 1996.

C. The "sandwich generation" refers to people who find themselves sandwiched between two generations, responsible for the care of their children and for their own aging parents. Corporations have begun to offer some kind of elder care assistance to their employees, including seminars, referral services, and flexible work schedules.

D. Divorce and Remarriage
1. Although many marriages end in divorce, most divorces end in remarriages.
2. Legislative changes over the past 3 decades have facilitated increases in divorce actions.
3. After rising for a century, the Canadian divorce rate leveled off and has even declined; the rate today is lower than it was in 1980.
4. Men are more likely to remarry and remarry more quickly than women.
5. Women who possess very high levels of education and income are less likely to remarry than their less-educated, less well-to-do counterparts.

E. The number of children affected by divorce increased by 300% from the 1970s to the 1990s. Divorce profoundly affects a child's world.
1. Children's reactions to divorce include confusion and insecurity, adherence to the idea that the parents will be reunited, or siding with one parent and rejecting the other.
2. The impact of divorce is complex, however, and depends in part on the level of conflict prior to the divorce and the economic impact of the divorce.

VI. Two Sides of Family Life

A. Child Abuse, battering, marital rape, and incest represent the dark side of family life.
1. Currently, we do not have statistics that capture the extent of child abuse across Canada. However, police statistics indicate that one-third of reported sexual assaults against children were perpetuated by a family member.
2. Marital rape involves women being forced into sexual activity by their partner through the use of threats or physical force. Sexual violence is often present in relationships characterized by other forms of abuse.
3. Incest is sexual relations between relatives, such as brothers and sisters or parents and children. It is most likely to occur in families that are socially isolated, and is more common than it previously was thought to be.

B. There are a number of factors that make marriages work. Variables related to happy marriages include: thinking of spouse as best friend; like spouse as a person; think of marriage as long-term commitment; believe that marriage is sacred; agree with spouse on aims and goals; believe that spouse has grown more interesting over the years; strongly want relationship to succeed; laugh together.

VII. **The Future of Marriage and Family**

A. It is likely that cohabitation will increase, as will the age at first marriage, and the number of women joining the work force, with a resulting shift in marital power. Finally, more families will struggle with the twin demands of raising children and caring for aging parents.

☞ KEY TERMS

After studying the chapter, review the definition for each of the following terms.

bilateral (system of descent): a system of reckoning descent that counts both the mother's and the father's side

blended family: a family whose members were once part of other families

cohabitation: an unmarried couple living together in a sexual relationship

egalitarian: authority more or less equally divided between people or groups, in this instance between husband and wife

empty nest: a married couple's domestic situation after the last child has left home

endogamy: the practice of marrying within one's own group

exogamy: the practice of marrying outside one's group

extended family: a nuclear family plus other relatives, such as grandparents, uncles and aunts, who live together

family: two or more people who consider themselves related by blood, marriage, or adoption

family of orientation: the family in which a person grows up

family of procreation: the family formed when a couple's first child is born

homogamy: the tendency of people with similar characteristics to marry one another

household: all persons who occupy the same housing unit

incest: sexual relations between specified relatives, such as brothers and sisters or parents and children

intentional family: people who declare themselves a family and treat one another as members of the same family; originated in the late twentieth century in response to the need for intimacy not met due to distance, divorce, and death

marriage: a group's approved mating arrangements, usually marked by a ritual of some sort

marriage squeeze: the difficulty a group of men or women have in finding marriage partners due to an imbalanced sex ratio

matriarchy: authority vested in females; female control of a society or group

matrilineal (system of descent): a system of reckoning descent that counts only the mother's side

nuclear family: a family consisting of a husband, wife, and child(ren)

patriarchy: authority vested in males; male control of a society or group

patrilineal (system of descent): a system of reckoning descent that counts only the father's side

polyandry: a marriage in which a woman has more than one husband

polygyny: a marriage in which a man has more than one wife

romantic love: feelings of erotic attraction accompanied by an idealization of the other

serial fatherhood: a pattern of parenting in which a father, after divorce, reduces contact with his own children, serves as a father to the children of the woman he marries or lives with, then ignores them after moving in with or marrying another woman; this pattern repeats

system of descent: how kinship is traced over the generations

☞ KEY PEOPLE

Review the major theoretical contributions or findings of these people.

Jessie Bernard: Bernard studied marriages and concluded that husbands and wives have different conceptions of marriage, resulting in two marriages within every union.

Andrew Cherlin: Cherlin notes that our society has not yet developed adequate norms for remarriage.

Donald Dutton and Arthur Aron: These researchers compared the sexual arousal levels of men who are in dangerous situations with men in safe situations and found that the former were more sexually aroused than the latter.

Margrit Eichler: Eichler suggested that the sociological definition of the nuclear family supports a very limited view of family life.

Kathleen Gerson: Gerson found that there are different reasons why some couples choose not to have children—weak marriages, expenses associated with raising children, diminished career opportunities.

Arlie Hochschild: Hochschild conducted research on families in which both parents are employed full-time in order to find out how household tasks are divided up. She found that women did more of the housework than their husbands, resulting in women putting in a *second shift* at home after their workday has ended.

William Jankowiak and Edward Fischer: These anthropologists surveyed data on 166 societies and found that the majority of them contained the ideal of romantic love.

Jeanette and Robert Lauer: These sociologists interviewed 351 couples who had been married fifteen years or longer in order to find out what makes a marriage successful.

Meg Luxton: studied the movement of women into the paid labour force in Canada and the effects on the division of labour within the household

Lillian Rubin: Rubin also interviewed both career women and homemakers found that the notion of the "empty nest" as being a difficult time for women is largely a myth and that most women's satisfaction increased when the last child left home.

Diana Russell: Russell found that incest victims who experience the most difficulty are those who have been victimized the most often, over longer periods of time, and whose incest was "more intrusive."

☞ SELF-TEST

After completing this self-test, check your answers against the Answer Key at the back of this Study Guide and against the text on page(s) indicated in parentheses.

MULTIPLE CHOICE QUESTIONS

1. Polyandry is: (305)
    a. a marriage in which a woman has more than one husband.
    b. a marriage in which a man has more than one wife.
    c. male control of a society or group.
    d. female control of a society or group.

2. Endogamy: (306)
    a. is the practice or marrying outside one's group.
    b. is the practice of marrying within one's own group.

    c. is the practice of marrying someone within one's own family.

    d. None of the above.

3.   In a matrilineal system: (306)

    a. descent is figured only on the mother's side.

    b. children are not considered related to their mother's relatives.

    c. descent is traced on both the mother's and the father's side.

    d. descent is figured only on the father's side.

4.   The family of orientation: (307)

    a. is the family formed when a couple's first child is born.

    b. is the same thing as an extended family.

    c. is the same as the family of procreation.

    d. None of the above.

5.   According to functionalists, the family: (308)

    a. serves very different functions from society to society.

    b. serves certain essential functions in all societies.

    c. has very few functions left.

    d. is no longer universal.

6.   The incest taboo: (308)

    a. is rules specifying the degrees of kinship that prohibit sex or marriage.

    b. helps families avoid role confusion.

    c. facilitates the socialization of children.

    d. All of the above.

7.   According to research findings, which of the following feels most threatened by doing housework, and consequently does the least? (309)

    a. men who earn significantly more money than their wives

    b. men who earn about the same amount of money as their wives

    c. men who earn less money than their wives

    d. men who are employed in occupations that are highly sex-typed as masculine

8.   According to Meg Luxton, men engage in strategies of resistance when it comes to doing housework. Which of the following is not one of the strategies she identified? (310-312)

    a. avoid cleaning while babysitting

    b. hiring someone else to do the work

    c. "forgetting" to do the work

    d. trying to get away with the minimum

9.   Why do husbands and wives disagree on an answer to such a basic question as how frequently they have sex? (313)

    a. Men are embarrassed to say the real answer for fear of being viewed as inadequate.

    b. Husbands and wives have different perspectives on the motivation for love-making.

    c. Women don't want to say how much sex they have because they think it is socially inappropriate.

    d. Husbands and wives won't tell the truth because they don't trust the interviewer and don't know what the purpose of the research really is.

10. The tendency of people with similar characteristics to marry one another is: (314)
    a. propinquity.
    b. erotic selection.
    c. homogamy.
    d. heterogamy.

11. According to Lillian Rubin, when does a woman's marital satisfaction increase? (315)
    a. during the initial stages of child rearing
    b. when the last child leaves home
    c. prior to childbirth
    d. when the first child leaves home

12. In regard to child rearing, sociologists have concluded that: (315)
    a. parents of all social classes socialize their children similarly.
    b. middle-class parents are more likely to use physical punishment than working-class parents.
    c. working-class parents are more likely to withdraw privileges or affection than middle-class parents.
    d. None of the above.

13. The empty nest syndrome: (315)
    a. is not a reality for most parents.
    b. causes couples to feel a lack of companionship.
    c. is easier for women who have not worked outside the home.
    d. None of the above.

14. According to your text, which of the following contributes to family diversity in Canada: (316-317)
    a. language
    b. cultural beliefs
    c. cultural values
    d. all of the above

15. Family formation within First Nations communities in Canada has been undermined by: (318)
    a. temporary labour policies.
    b. internment policies during the second world war.
    c. forced family relocation policies.
    d. missionary-led residential schools and non-Native child welfare agencies.

16. Since 1961, the number of one-parent families in Canada has: (318)
    a. doubled.
    b. increased by 316%.
    c. increased by 150%.
    d. grown only slightly.

17. Children from single-parent families are more likely to: (318)
    a. have lower levels of academic achievement.
    b. have poorer levels of health.
    c. have more difficulty with relationships.
    d. All of the above.

18. Sociologist Kathleen Gerson found that there were different reasons why couples choose not to have children. Which of the following is *not* one of the reasons identified by Gerson? (319)
    a. unstable relationships
    b. lost career opportunities
    c. selfish and immature attitudes
    d. financial considerations

19. A family whose members were once part of other families is known as a: (319)
    a. reconstituted family.
    b. mixed family.
    c. blended family.
    d. multiple nuclei family.

20. Common-law marriage: (322)
    a. is currently as frequent as marriage.
    b. has decreased dramatically during the past two decades.
    c. is viewed as a preliminary step in preparation for long-term marriage.
    d. means two people living together without a formal married union.

21. The "sandwich generation" refers to: (323)
    a. stay-at-home moms who spend their days making sandwiches for their preschoolers.
    b. people who are sandwiched between two sets of family relations because of the increase in divorce today.
    c. young children who consume a lot of sandwiches and whose needs are often overlooked by parents whose time is stretched by work and household responsibilities.
    d. people who find themselves caught between two generations, simultaneously responsible for the care of their children and their aging parents.

22. Which statement about divorce and remarriage is *incorrect*? (323-324)
    a. The divorce rate of remarried people without children is the same as that of people in first marriages.
    b. Divorced people tend to marry other divorced people.
    c. The divorce rate of remarried couples with children is higher than the divorce rate of people in their first marriages.
    d. The presence or absence of children makes no difference in a remarried couple's chances of divorce.

23. When confronted with the tensions of divorce, children of divorce may: (324)
    a. cling to the idea that their parents may be reunited.
    b. side with one parent and reject the other.
    c. become confused and insecure.
    d. All of the above.

24. According to research by Diana Russell, who is most likely to be the offender in incest? (326)
    a. brothers
    b. fathers/stepfathers
    c. first cousins
    d. uncles

25. According to the author, what trend(s) are likely to continue into the next century? (326)

    a.   increase in cohabitation
    b.   increase in age at first marriage
    c.   more equality in the husband-wife relationship
    d.   all of the above

TRUE-FALSE QUESTIONS

T F   1.   Polygyny is a marriage in which a man has more than one wife. (305)

T F   2.   Laws of endogamy in Canada prohibit interracial marriages. (306)

T F   3.   Families are people who live together in the same housing unit. (307)

T F   4.   The popular vision of the nuclear family supports a very limited view of family life. (307)

T F   5.   Functionalists believe that the incest taboo helps the family to avoid role confusion. (308)

T F   6.   Conflict theorists believe that one of the consequences of married women working for pay is a reshuffling of power in the home. (309)

T F   7.   Meg Luxton concluded that the majority of women with children under 12 were not in the paid labour force. (310)

T F   8.   According to Arlie Hochschild men willingly take on household duties. (311)

T F   9.   Symbolic interactionists have found that husbands and wives generally share the same meanings about their marriages. (312-313)

T F   10.   Love and marriage channels include age, education, social class, race, and religion. (313-314)

T F   11.   Social class does not affect the ways couples adjust to the arrival of children. (315)

T F   12.   Firstborns tend to be disciplined more than children who follow. (315)

T F   13.   Researchers have found that most husbands and wives experience the empty nest when their last child leaves home. (315)

T F   14.   Women are about as likely as men to face the problem of adjusting to widowhood. (316)

T F   15.   According to recent research, the majority of newlyweds now indicate intentions to remain childless. (319)

T F   16.   Two divorced people who marry and each bring their children into a new family unit become a blended family. (319)

T F   17.   Marriage between same-sex couples is legal in several provinces, including British Columbia. (321)

T F   18.   Today, common-law relationships are as common as marriage. (322)

T F   19.   The "sandwich generation" are people who must care for both their parents and their children. (323)

T F   20.   According to research, marital rape is often connected to broader patterns of wife battering. (326)

FILL-IN QUESTIONS

1.   A marriage in which a man has more than one wife is _____. (305)

2.   _____ is the practice of marrying outside one's group. (306)

3.   Female control of a society or group is a(n) _____. (306)

4.   _____ is a group who consider themselves related by blood, marriage, or adoption. (307)

5.   A(n) _____ is a family consisting of a husband, wife, and child(ren). (307)

6.   Rules specifying the degrees of kinship that prohibit sex or marriage are _____. (308)

7.   _____ is the tendency of people with similar characteristics to get married. (314)

8.   A married couple's domestic situation after the last child has left home is sometimes referred to as the _____. (315)

9. A household with grandparents, children, and grandchildren all living together is _____. (317)

10. Historically _____ have intentionally blocked family formation among working-class Chinese, South Asian, and Japanese men and women, and more recently black Caribbean women. (318)

11. In 1998, British Columbia became the first jurisdiction in North America to grant custody, access and child support rights to _____. (321)

12. In Canada, _____, living together without a formal marriage, increased 300% between 1981-1996. (322)

13. The term _____ refers to people who find themselves caught between two generations and responsible for the care of both. (323)

14. A situation in which a husband forces his wife to have sex through the use of threats or physical force is _____. (326)

15. Sexual relations between specified relatives, such as brothers and sisters or parents and children, is _____. (326)

MATCH THESE SOCIAL SCIENTISTS WITH THEIR CONTRIBUTIONS

__1. Jessie Bernard
__2. Andrew Cherlin
__3. Kathleen Gerson
__4. Margrit Eichler
__5. Lillian Rubin
__6. Diana Russell
__7. Meg Luxton

a. *noted the existence of two marriages within one union*
b. *found that women's satisfaction increased after last child moved out*
c. *studied incest victims*
d. *identified reasons why couples choose to be child-free*
e. *noted lack of norms regarding remarriage*
f. *studied the gendered division of household labor*
g. *suggested that the definition of the nuclear family supports a very limited view of family life*

ESSAY QUESTIONS

1. Identify the stages in the family life cycle, discussing what tasks are accomplished in each stage and what event marks the transition from one stage to the next.
2. Explain the social forces that have contributed to the emergence of intentional families.
3. Discuss the impact that divorce has on family members—men, women and children.

"DOWN-TO-EARTH SOCIOLOGY"

1. What was your reaction to the description of family life in Sweden (p. 307)? Do you think that such benefits should be available to new families in Canada? What consequences would this have for family life? What are some of the obstacles to implementing such a program in this country?

2. Do you think that male resistance to household labour (pp. 310-312) is a temporary problem or a long-range problem in many families? How will you resolve problems such as this in your family?

3. After reading about high-tech reproductive technologies on pages 319-320, what are your own views on the subject? Consider both the pluses (infertile couples are able to become parents) and the minuses (the ethical considerations, the costs of the procedures) and then develop a convincing argument in favor or opposition.

CHAPTER 14

EDUCATION AND RELIGION

☞ CHAPTER SUMMARY

- Industrialized societies have become credential societies; employers use diplomas and degrees to determine who is eligible for jobs, even when these qualifications may be irrelevant to the particular work. Educational certification provides evidence of a person's ability.

- In earlier societies, education consisted of informal learning and was synonymous with acculturation. Today, education is no longer the same as informal acculturation, for the term now refers to a group's formal system of teaching knowledge, values, and skills.

- Functionalists emphasize the functions of education, including teaching knowledge and skills, transmitting cultural values, social integration, gatekeeping, and promoting personal and social change.

- Conflict theorists view education as a mechanism for maintaining social inequality and reproducing the social class system. Accordingly, they stress such matters as the way in which education reflects the social structure of society (the correspondence principle), unequal funding of schools, culturally biased IQ tests, tracking, and the hidden curriculum.

- Symbolic interactionists examine classroom interaction. They study how teacher expectations cause a self-fulfilling prophecy, producing the very behavior the teacher is expecting.

- Problems facing the current Canadian educational system include cheating, illegal essay-writing services, grade inflation, social promotion, functional illiteracy, teen pregnancy and violence in schools. Suggestions to improve Canadian education include implementing and maintaining a secure and safe learning environment and reforms directed at the structure of the educational system.

- The sociological study of religion involves the analysis of the relationship between society and religion to gain insight into the role of religion in people's lives. For Durkheim, the key elements of religion are: beliefs separating the profane from the sacred, rituals, and a moral community.

- According to functionalists, religion meets basic human needs such as answering questions about ultimate meaning, providing emotional comfort, social solidarity, guidelines for everyday life, social control, adaptation, support for the government, and social change. Functionalists also believe religion has two main dysfunctions: war and religious persecution.

- Symbolic interactionists focus on how religious symbols communicate meaning and how ritual and beliefs unite people into a community.

- Conflict theorists see religion as a conservative force that serves the needs of the ruling class by reflecting and reinforcing social inequality.

- Unlike Marx, who asserted that religion impedes social change by encouraging people to focus on the afterlife, Weber saw religion as a powerful force for social change. He analyzed how Protestantism gave rise to an ethic that stimulated "the spirit of capitalism." The result was capitalism, which transformed society.

- The world's major religions include Judaism, Christianity, Islam, Hinduism, Buddhism, and Confucianism. Just as different religions have distinct teachings and practices, so within a religion different groups contrast sharply with one another.

- Sociologists have identified cults, sects, churches, and ecclesia as distinct types of religious organizations. All religions began as cults; although most ultimately fail, those that survive become sects. Both cults and sects represent belief systems that are at odds with the prevailing beliefs and values of the broader society. If a sect grows, and its members make peace with the rest of society, it changes into a church. Ecclesiae, or state religions, are rare.

- Religion in Canada is characterized by diversity and a degree of continuity with the past. As well, Canadians differ dramatically from Americans in terms of those expressing no religious affiliation.
- Feminist spirituality in both Judaism and Christianity questions the male dominance of these religious traditions.

☞ LEARNING OBJECTIVES

As you read Chapter 14, use these learning objectives to organize your notes. After completing your reading, briefly state an answer to each of the objectives, and review the text pages in parentheses.

1. Explain why Canada has become a credential society. (332-333)
2. Describe the development of modern education. (333-334)
3. Discuss the beginning of universal education in Canada. (334-335)
4. List and briefly explain the manifest and latent functions of education. (335-339)
5. Explain how education maintains social inequality using the conflict perspective. (339-342)
6. Summarize symbolic interaction research regarding teacher expectations and the self-fulfilling prophecy. (342-344)
7. Identify the major problems that exist within Canadian education today and discuss solutions. (344-346)
8. Define religion and Durkheim's concepts of sacred and profane elements of religion. (347)
9. Discuss the functionalist view of religion, and list the functions and dysfunctions of religion as a social institution. (348)
10. Discuss the importance of rituals, symbols, and beliefs for the creation of a community. (349-350)
11. Describe the conflict perspective on religion. (350-351)
12. Describe the relationship Weber proposed between religion and capitalism. (351)
13. Describe the history and characteristics of the world's major religions. (352-354)
14. Describe the differences among types of religious groups (cult, sect, church, and ecclesia) and their relationships to the dominant culture. (354-357)
15. Describe the main characteristics of religion in Canada today. (357-358)
16. Discuss feminist themes in the sociological study of religion. (358-359)
17. On the basis of sociological knowledge, speculate on the future of religion in human societies. (359-360)

☞ CHAPTER OUTLINE

I. **Today's Credential Society**
   A. A credential society is one in which employers use diplomas and degrees to determine job eligibility. The sheer size, urbanization and consequent anonymity of Canadian society is a major reason why credentials are required. Diplomas/degrees often serve as sorting devices for employers; because they don't know the individual personally, they depend on schools to weed out the capable from the incapable.
   B. Without the right credentials, a person will not get hired despite the person's ability to do the job better than someone else.

II. **The Development of Modern Education**
   A. In earlier societies, education was synonymous with acculturation (transmission of culture from one generation to the next), not with a separate institution.
      1. In societies where a sufficient surplus developed, a separate institution arose. Some individuals devoted themselves to teaching, while those who had leisure became

their students. Education gradually came to refer to a group's formal system of teaching knowledge, values, and skills.

2. During the Dark Ages, only the monks and a handful of the wealthy nobility could read and write.

3. Industrialization created a need for the average citizen to be able to read, write, and work with figures because of the new machinery and new types of jobs.

B. The development of universal education in Canada was linked to the development of the industrial economy.

1. Before Confederation (1867) it was religious groups that were the most involved in providing education. They used education to attempt to assimilate Native Canadians. Church influence over education ensured that guidance in Christian morality and obedience were taught.

2. The development of universities was also connected to religious bodies, such as the Church of England.

3. The beginnings of a system of universal education were entrenched by the time of Confederation. Education became a matter of political socialization.

4. By 1920 most provinces had compulsory education laws that required children to attend school until they had either completed eighth grade or turned 16.

5. As industrialization developed, graduating with a postsecondary certificate or degree has become more common.

6. Those who do not complete high school experience higher rates of unemployment, lower earnings, and are less likely to hold secure jobs.

III.   The Functionalist Perspective: Providing Social Benefits

A. Manifest and latent functions of education include: (1) teaching knowledge and skills; (2) cultural transmission of values (individualism, competition, and patriotism); (3) social integration (molding students into a more or less cohesive unit); (4) gatekeeping (determining who will enter what occupations, through tracking and social placement); (5) promoting personal change through critical thinking; (6) promoting social change through research; (7) mainstreaming (incorporating people with disabilities into regular social activities); and (8) assuming many functions previously fulfilled by the family (e.g., child care and sex education).

B. Other functions include: (1) matchmaking (people finding a future spouse in school); (2) social networking; and (3) helping stabilize employment (keeping unskilled individuals out of the labor market).

IV.   The Conflict Perspective: Reproducing the Social Class Structure

A. Conflict theorists see that the educational system is a tool used by those in the controlling sector of society to maintain their dominance.

B. The hidden curriculum is unwritten rules of behavior and attitude (e.g., obedience to authority, conformity to cultural norms) taught in school in addition to the formal curriculum. Such values and work habits teach the middle and lower classes to support the capitalist class.

C. Conflict theorists criticize IQ (intelligence quotient) testing because it not only measures intelligence but also culturally acquired knowledge.

1. The tests focus only on certain components of intelligence—mathematical, spatial, symbolic, and linguistic abilities—while ignoring others.

2. By focusing on these factors, IQ tests reflect a cultural bias that favors the middle class and discriminates against minority and lower class students.

D. Because public schools are largely financed by local property taxes, there are rich and poor school districts. Unequal funding stacks the deck against minorities and the poor.

E. The correspondence principle is how schools correspond to (or reflect) the social structure of society. The educational system reinforces the status quo, because what is taught in a nation's schools corresponds to the characteristics of that society. Thus education perpetuates society's prevailing inequalities.

F. Schools reproduce social class inequalities, as children of the wealthy are more likely to attend university than poorer students. The education system helps pass privilege (or lack thereof) across generations.

V. The Symbolic Interaction Perspective: Teacher Expectations and the Self-Fulfilling Prophecy

A. Symbolic interactionists study face-to-face interaction inside the classroom. They have found that expectations of teachers are especially significant in determining what students learn.

B. The Rist research (participant observation in an African-American grade school with an African-American faculty) found tracking begins with teachers' perceptions.

1. After eight days—and without testing for ability—teachers divided the class into fast, average, and slow learners; social class was the basis for the assignments.

2. Students from whom more was expected did the best; students in the slow group were ridiculed and disengaged themselves from classroom activities.

3. The labels applied in kindergarten tended to follow the child through school. What occurred was a self-fulfilling prophecy (Robert Merton's term for an originally false assertion that becomes true simply because it was predicted).

C. Teachers shaped the experiences the students had within the classroom.

1. Teachers' own middle-class backgrounds influence their interactions: when middle-class students ask probing questions they are seen by the teachers as intelligent, but when lower-class students do they are defined as smart alecks.

VI. Rethinking Schools: Problems and Solutions

A. A variety of factors have been identified as the major problems facing the Canadian educational system today. These problems include: cheating and illegal essay-writing services; grade inflation, and how it relates to social promotion and functional illiteracy; violence in schools; and teenage pregnancy.

B. A number of solutions have been offered to address these problems, including implementing and maintaining a secure and safe learning environment and reforms directed at the structure of the educational system.

VII. What Is Religion?

A. According to Durkheim, religion is the beliefs/practices separating the profane from the sacred, uniting the adherents into a moral community. Sacred refers to aspects of life having to do with the supernatural that inspire awe, reverence, deep respect, or deep fear. Profane refers to the ordinary aspects of everyday life. Durkheim defined religion by three elements: (1) beliefs that some things are sacred (forbidden, set off from the profane); (2) practices (rituals) concerning things considered sacred; (3) a moral community (a church) resulting from a group's beliefs and practices.

VIII. The Functionalist Perspective

A. Religion performs certain functions: (1) answering questions about ultimate meaning (the purpose of life, why people suffer); (2) providing emotional comfort; (3) uniting believers into a community that shares values and perspectives; (4) providing guidelines for life; (5) controlling behavior; (6) helping people adapt to new environments; (7) providing support for the government; and (8) spearheading social change on occasion (as in the civil rights movement in the 1960s).

B.   War and religious persecution are dysfunctions of religion.

IX.   The Symbolic Interactionist Perspective

A.   Religions use symbols to provide identity and social solidarity for members. For members, these are not ordinary symbols, but sacred symbols evoking awe and reverence, which become a condensed way of communicating with others.

B.   Rituals are ceremonies or repetitive practices helping unite people into a moral community by creating a feeling of closeness with God and unity with one another.

C.   Symbols, including rituals, develop from beliefs. A belief may be vague ("God is") or specific ("God wants us to prostrate ourselves and face Mecca five times each day"). Religious beliefs not only include values (what is considered good and desirable) but also a cosmology (unified picture of the world).

D.   Shared meanings that come through symbols, rituals, and beliefs unite people into a moral community, which is powerful. It provides the basis for mutual identity and establishes norms that govern the behavior of members. Not only are members bound together by shared beliefs and rituals but they are also separated from those who do not share their symbolic world.

X.   The Conflict Perspective

A.   Conflict theorists are highly critical of religion. Karl Marx called religion the "opium of the people" because he believed that the workers escape into religion. He argued that religion diverts the energies of the oppressed from changing their circumstances because believers focus on the happiness they will have in the coming world rather than on their suffering in this world.

B.   Religious teachings and practices reflect a society's inequalities. Gender inequalities are an example: when males completely dominated Canadian society, women's roles in churches and synagogues were limited to "feminine" activities, a condition which is beginning to change.

C.   Religion legitimates social inequality; it reflects the interests of those in power by teaching that the existing social arrangements of a society represent what God desires.

XI.   Religion and the Spirit of Capitalism

A.   Weber saw religion as a force for social change, observing that European countries industrialized under capitalism. Thus, religion held the key to modernization (transformation of traditional societies into industrial societies).

B.   Weber concluded that:

1.   The spirit of capitalism (desire to accumulate capital as a duty, as an end in itself) was a radical departure from the past.

2.   Religion (including a Calvinistic belief in predestination and the need for reassurance as to one's fate) is the key to why the spirit of capitalism developed in Europe.

3.   A change in religion (from Catholicism to Protestantism) led to a change in thought and behavior (the Protestant ethic), which resulted in the "spirit of capitalism."

C.   Today the spirit of capitalism and the Protestant ethic are by no means limited to Protestants; they have become cultural traits that have spread throughout the world.

XII.   The World's Major Religions

    A.   The founding of Judaism marked a fundamental change in religion, in that it was the first religion based on monotheism, the belief in only one God.

        1.   Contemporary Judaism has three main branches: Orthodox (adheres to the laws espoused by Moses), Reform (more liberal, uses the vernacular in religious ceremonies, and has reduced much of the ritual); and Conservative (falling somewhere between).

        2.   The history of Judaism is marked by conflict and persecution (anti-Semitism).

    B.   Christianity developed out of Judaism and is based on the belief that Christ is the Messiah God promised the Jews.

        1.   During the first 1,000 years of Christianity, there was only one church organization, directed from Rome; during the 11th century, Greek Orthodoxy was established.

        2.   In the Middle Ages, the Roman Catholic church, aligned with the political establishment, grew corrupt. The Reformation of the 16th century, led by Martin Luther, was a reaction to the church's corruption.

        3.   The Reformation marked the beginning of a splintering of Christianity; today there are over one billion Christians, divided into hundreds of groups.

    C.   Islam (whose followers are known as Muslims) began in the same part of the world as Judaism and Christianity; like the Jews, Muslims trace their ancestry to Abraham.

        1.   The founder, Muhammad, established a theocracy, a government based on God being the ruler, his laws the statutes of the land, and priests his earthly administrators.

        2.   After Muhammad's death, a struggle for control split Islam into two branches that remain today: the Shi'ite which is more conservative and inclined to fundamentalism (the belief that true religion is threatened by modernism and that faith as it was originally practiced should be restored), and the Sunni which is generally more liberal.

    D.   Hinduism, the chief religion of India, goes back about 4,000 years, but has no specific founder or canonical scripture (texts thought to be inspired by God). Instead several books expound on the moral qualities people should strive to attain.

        1.   Hindus are polytheists (believe there are many gods) and believe in reincarnation, a cycle of life, death, and rebirth.

    E.   About 600 B.C., Siddhartha Gautama founded Buddhism, which emphasizes self-denial and compassion.

        1.   Buddhism spread rapidly into many parts of Asia. Today it flourishes in Ceylon, Burma, Tibet, Laos, Cambodia, Thailand, China, Korea, and Japan.

    F.   Confucius (China 551-479 B.C.) urged social reform and developed a system of morality based on peace, justice, and universal order.

        1.   The basic moral principle of Confucianism is to maintain jen (sympathy or concern for other humans). The basic principle is to treat those who are subordinate to you as you would like to be treated by those superior to you.

        2.   Originally, Confucianism was atheistic; however, as the centuries passed, local gods were added to the teachings, and Confucius himself was declared a god.

XIII.   Types of Religious Groups

    A.   A cult is a new religion with few followers, whose teachings and practices put it at odds with the dominant culture and religion.

        1.   All religions began as cults. Cults often begin with the appearance of a charismatic leader (exerting extraordinary appeal to a group of followers).

2. Each cult meets with rejection from society. The message given by the cult is seen as a threat to the dominant culture.

3. The cult demands intense commitment, and its followers confront a hostile world.

4. Although most cults ultimately fail because they are unable to attract a large enough following, some succeed and make history.

B. A sect is larger than a cult, but still feels substantial hostility from and toward society.

1. At the very least, members remain uncomfortable with many of the emphases of the dominant culture; nonmembers feel uncomfortable with sect members.

2. Sects usually are loosely organized, emphasize personal salvation (an emotional expression of one's relationship with God), and recruitment of new members (evangelism).

3. If a sect grows, its members tend to become respectable in society, and the sect is changed into a church.

C. A church is a large, highly organized religious group with formal, sedate services and less emphasis on personal conversion. The religious group is highly bureaucratized (including national and international offices that give directions to local congregations). Most new members come from within the church, from children born to existing members, rather than from outside recruitment.

D. An ecclesia is a religious group so integrated into the dominant culture that it is difficult to tell where one begins and the other leaves off.

1. Ecclesiae are also called state religions. The government and religion work together to try to shape the society.

E. Not all religions go through all stages, although all religions began as cults, not all varieties of a religion have done so.

1. Some die out because they fail to attract members; some remain sects. Few become ecclesia.

2. A denomination is a "brand name" within a major religion (e. g., Methodist).

F. Three major patterns of adaptation occur when religion and the culture in which it is embedded find themselves in conflict.

1. Members of a religion may reject the dominant culture and withdraw from it socially, although they continue to live in the same geographic area.

2. A cult or sect rejects only specific elements of the prevailing culture.

3. The society rejects the religious group entirely, and may even try to destroy it.

XIV.   Characteristics of Religion in Canada

A. Religion in Canada is very diverse and changing, but reflects a degree of continuity with the past.

1. Canada has been, historically, predominantly Christian. The population has been divided between Protestants, living outside Quebec, and Roman Catholics, living within Quebec.

2. The only religious groups that have grown significantly in recent years are the eastern non-Christian religions of Islam, Hinduism, and Buddhism.

3. Since the 1961 census, the number of Canadians reporting "no religion" has increased dramatically. Since the post-World War II period, attendance at religious services has dropped. Nonetheless, a vast majority still indicate a belief in God.

B. Feminist studies of spirituality have examined the positive spiritual experiences of women; the deeply personal character of women's spirituality; patterns of male domination in religious systems; the need to avoid Western male epistemologies that separate rationality and spirituality; and the need to include women in religious studies.

1. Four categories of feminist spirituality have been identified: revisionists – those

who believe that the basic message of religion is liberating; reformists – those who advocate revealing the "liberating core" of religious teachings with female imagery; revolutionaries – those who seek to change the established orthodoxy by importing language, images, and rituals from other traditions; and rejectionists – those who judge traditional teachings to be hopelessly sexist and have left to establish new spiritual traditions.

2. Christian feminists have attempted to overcome sexism in Christianity by taking account of women's experiences in the church, and have attempted to address ethical questions regarding abortion, homophobia, power and sexuality, and suffering and evil.

3. Jewish feminists have questioned the male dominance of their religion and have sought to change Judaism from within.

XV.   The Future of Religion
A. Marx was convinced religion would crumble when the workers threw off the chains of oppression; however, after communist countries were established (and despite persecution) people continued to be religious.
B. Neither science nor political systems can replace religion, and religion will last as long as humanity lasts.

☞ KEY TERMS

After studying the chapter, review the definition for each of the following terms.

acculturation: the transmission of culture from one generation to the next

animism: the belief that all objects in the world have spirits, some of which are dangerous and must be outwitted

anti-Semitism: prejudice, discrimination, and persecution directed against Jews

born again: a term describing Christians who have undergone a life-transforming religious experienc so radical that they feel they have become new persons

charisma: literally, an extraordinary gift from God; more commonly, an outstanding, "magnetic" personality

charismatic leader: literally, someone to whom God has given a gift; more commonly, someone who exerts extraordinary appeal to a group of followers

church: according to Durkheim, one of the three essential elements of religion—a moral community of believers; a second definition is a type of religious organization described on page 506—a large, highly organized religious group with formal, sedate worship services and little emphasis on personal conversion

correspondence principle: the sociological principle that schools correspond to (or reflect) the social structure of society

cosmology: teachings or ideas that provide a unified picture of the world

credential society: the use of diplomas and degrees to determine who is eligible for jobs, even though the diploma or degree may be irrelevant to the actual work

cult: a new religion with few followers, whose teachings and practices put it at odds with the dominan culture and religion

cultural transmission: in reference to education, the ways in which schools transmit a society's culture especially its core values

denomination: a "brand name" within a major religion, for example, Methodist or Baptist

ecclesia: a religious group so integrated into the dominant culture that it is difficult to tell where the one begins and the other leaves off; also called a *state religion*

education: a formal system of teaching knowledge, values, and skills

evangelism: an attempt to win converts

functional illiterate: a high school graduate who has difficulty with basic reading and math

fundamentalism: the belief that true religion is threatened by modernism and that the faith as it was originally practiced should be restored

gatekeeping: the process by which education opens and closes doors of opportunity; another term for the social placement function of education

grade inflation: higher grades given for the same work; a general rise in student grades without a corresponding increase in learning or test scores

hidden curriculum: the unwritten goals of schools, such as obedience to authority and conformity to cultural norms

latent functions: unintended consequences of people's actions

mainstreaming: helping people to become part of the mainstream of society

manifest functions: intended consequences of people's actions

modernization: the transformation of traditional societies into industrial societies

monotheism: the belief that there is only one God

political socialization: the way young people are inculcated with beliefs, ideas, and values to ensure they embrace the civil order

polytheism: the belief that there are many gods

profane: Durkheim's term for common elements of everyday life

Protestant ethic: Weber's term to describe the ideal of a self-denying, highly moral life, accompanied by hard work and frugality

reincarnation: in Hinduism and Buddhism, the return of the soul after death in a different form
religion: according to Durkheim, beliefs and practices that separate the profane from the sacred and unite adherents into a moral community

rituals: ceremonies or repetitive practices; in this context, religious observances or rites often intended to evoke a sense of awe of the sacred

sacred: Durkheim's term for things set apart or forbidden, that inspire fear, awe, reverence, or deep respect

sect: a group larger than a cult that still feels substantial hostility from and toward society

secular: belonging to the world and its affairs

self-fulfilling prophecy: Robert Merton's term for an originally false assertion that becomes true simply because it was predicted

social placement: a function of education that funnels people into a society's various positions

social promotion: passing students to the next grade even though they have not mastered basic materials

spirit of capitalism: Weber's term for the desire to accumulate capital as a duty—not to spend it, but as an end in itself—and to constantly reinvest it

state religion: a government-sponsored religion (also ecclesia)

tracking: the sorting of students into different educational programs on the basis of real or perceived abilities

☞ KEY PEOPLE

Review the major theoretical contributions or findings of these people.

Samuel Bowles and Herbert Gintis: Bowles and Gintis used the term correspondence principle to refer to the ways in which schools reflect the social structure of society.

Randall Collins: Collins studied the credential society.

Kingsley Davis and Wilbert Moore: Davis and Moore argue that a major task of society is to fill social positions with capable people and that one of the functions of schools is gatekeeping — the funneling of people into these positions based on merit.

Emile Durkheim: Durkheim investigated world religions and identified elements that are common to all religions—separation of sacred from profane, beliefs about what is sacred, practices surrounding the sacred, and a moral community.

Harry Gracey: Gracey conducted a participant observation study of kindergarten and concluded that the purpose of kindergarten is to socialize students into the student role. He referred to kindergarten as a boot camp.

John Hostetler: Hostetler is known for his research and writings on the Amish.

Benton Johnson: Johnson analyzed types of religious groups—cults, sects, churches, and ecclesiae.

William Kephart and William Zellner: These sociologists also investigated the Amish religion and way of life.

Karl Marx: Marx was critical of religion, calling it the opium of the masses.

Robert Merton: Merton coined the expression "self-fulfilling prophecy" to refer to an originally false assumption of what is going to happen that comes true simply because it is predicted.

Talcott Parsons: Another functionalist who suggested that a function of schools is to funnel people into social positions.

Liston Pope: Another sociologist who studied types of religious groups.

Ray Rist: This sociologist's classic study of an African-American grade school uncovered some of the dynamics of educational tracking.

Johanna Stuckey: Stuckey outlined four main categories of the feminist study of spirituality: revisionists, reformists, revolutionaries, and rejectionists.

Ernst Troeltsch: Yet another sociologist who is associated with types of religious groups from cults to eccelsiae.

Max Weber: Weber studied the link between Protestantism and the rise of capitalism and found that the ethic associated with Protestant denominations was compatible with the early needs of capitalism.

☞ SELF-TEST

After completing this self-test, check your answers against the Answer Key at the back of this Study Guide and against the text on page(s) indicated in parentheses.

MULTIPLE CHOICE QUESTIONS

1. Using diplomas to hire employees, even when diplomas are irrelevant to the work, is: (332)
   a. a credential society.
   b. a certification mill.
   c. employer discretion in hiring.
   d. None of the above.

2. In earlier societies: (333)
   a. there was no separate social institution called education.
   b. education was synonymous with acculturation.
   c. persons who already possessed certain skills taught them to others.
   d. All of the above.

3. Education: (334)
    a. is a formal system of teaching knowledge, values, and skills.
    b. is the same as informal acculturation.
    c. is very similar in countries throughout the world.
    d. All of the above.

4. According to functionalists, all of the following are functions of education, *except*: (335-339)
    a. maintaining social inequality.
    b. transmitting cultural values.
    c. helping to mold students into a more or less cohesive unit.
    d. teaching patriotism.

5. The function of education that sorts people into various positions on the basis of merit is: (338)
    a. functional placement.
    b. social placement.
    c. railroading.
    d. social promotion.

6. The hidden curriculum refers to: (339)
    a. the extra curriculum costs that are buried in school budgets.
    b. the lessons that teachers hide from the eyes of prying school boards.
    c. the unwritten rules of behavior and attitudes that are taught in school.
    d. All of the above.

7. Public schools are largely supported by: (341)
    a. provincial funding.
    b. federal funding.
    c. local property taxes.
    d. None of the above.

8. The ways in which schools correspond to, or reflect, the social structure of society is: (342)
    a. the reproduction of social class.
    b. the correspondence principle.
    c. the status quo quotient.
    d. the status maintenance process.

9. From a conflict perspective, the real purpose of education is to: (342)
    a. reproduce existing social inequalities.
    b. provide educational opportunities for students from all types of backgrounds.
    c. teach patriotism, teamwork, and cooperation.
    d. replace family functions which most families no longer fulfill.

10. Teacher expectations and the self-fulfilling prophecy are of interest to _____ theorists. (342)
    a. functionalist
    b. conflict
    c. symbolic interaction
    d. educational

11. Ray Rist found that _____ was the underlying basis for assigning children to different tables in a kindergarten classroom. (342-343)
    a. ability
    b. maturity level
    c. social class
    d. gender

12. A self-fulfilling prophecy: (343)
    a. is an originally false assertion that becomes true simply because it was predicted.
    b. is an originally true assertion that becomes false because a person decides to prove that the label is incorrect.
    c. is a term coined by Ray Rist.
    d. All of the above.

13. When compared to grades of forty years ago, today's grades: (344)
    a. are lower.
    b. are higher.
    c. have remained about the same.
    d. None of the above.

14. High school graduates who have difficulty with basic reading and writing are known as: (344)
    a. "boneheads."
    b. functional literates.
    c. functional illiterates.
    d. underachievers.

15. What was Durkheim's purpose in writing *The Elementary Forms of the Religious Life*? (347)
    a. He wanted to explain the development of Protestantism.
    b. He set out to chart the history of world religions.
    c. He wanted to study the development of religion from sect to church.
    d. He wanted to identify elements common to all religions.

16. According to Durkheim, a church: (347)
    a. is a large, highly organized religious group.
    b. has little emphasis on personal conversion.
    c. is a group of believers with a set of beliefs and practices regarding the sacred.
    d. All of the above.

17. All of the following are functions of religion, *except*: (348)
    a. encouraging wars for holy causes.
    b. support for the government.
    c. social change.
    d. social control.

18. War and religious persecution are: (348)
    a. manifest functions of religion.
    b. latent functions of religion.
    c. dysfunctions of religion.
    d. functional equivalents of religion.

19. Religion is the opium of the people according to some: (350)
    a. conservatives.
    b. functionalists.
    c. conflict theorists.
    d. symbolic interactionists.

20. An example of the use of religion to legitimize social inequalities is: (351)
    a. the divine right of kings.
    b. a declaration that the Pharaoh or Emperor is god or divine.
    c. the defense of slavery as being God's will.
    d. All of the above.

21. Weber believed that religion held the key to: (351)
    a. modernization.
    b. bureaucratization.
    c. institutionalization.
    d. socialization.

22. The spirit of capitalism is: (351)
    a. the desire to accumulate capital so one can spend it to show how one "has it made."
    b. Marx's term for the driving force in the exploitation of workers.
    c. the ideal of a highly moral life, hard work, industriousness, and frugality.
    d. None of the above.

23. Polytheism is the belief: (352)
    a. that God is a woman.
    b. that there is only one God.
    c. that there are many gods.
    d. that God does not exist.

24. What was an unanticipated outcome of the Reformation? (352)
    a. the splintering of Christianity
    b. the reunification of the Catholic Church
    c. the elimination of corruption in the Church
    d. the downgrading of women's status in the Church hierarchy

25. The religion with no specific founder is: (353)
    a. Islam.
    b. Hinduism.
    c. Buddhism.
    d. Confucianism.

26. Reincarnation: (353)
    a. is found only in Buddhism.
    b. is the return of the soul after death in the same form.
    c. is the return of the soul after death in a different form.
    d. None of the above.

27. A cult: (354)
   a. is a new religion with few followers.
   b. has teachings and practices which put it at odds with the dominant culture.
   c. often is at odds with other religions.
   d. All of the above.

28. Although larger than a cult, a _____ still feels substantial hostility from society. (355)
   a. commune.
   b. ecclesia.
   c. sect.
   d. church.

29. Churches: (356)
   a. are highly bureaucratized.
   b. have more sedate worship services.
   c. gain new members from within, from children born to existing members.
   d. All of the above.

30. In Canada, the only religious group that grew in any significant degree between 1986 and 1996 was: (357)
   a. eastern non-Christian religions.
   b. Christians.
   c. Atheists.
   d. those who believe in God but don't attend church.

TRUE-FALSE QUESTIONS

T F 1. Canada is a credential society. (332-333)
T F 2. In earlier societies there was a separate social institution called education. (334)
T F 3. By 1920, most Canadian provinces had compulsory education laws. (334)
T F 4. The rates of high school graduation are approximately equal across the provinces. (335)
T F 5. Education's most obvious manifest function is to teach knowledge and skills. (335)
T F 6. Canadian schools discourage individualism and encourage teamwork. (336)
T F 7. Students everywhere are taught that their country is the best country in the world. (336)
T F 8. Parental influence is strong enough to challenge the influence of peer culture when it comes to molding students' appearance, ideas, speech patterns, and interactions with the opposite sex. (336)
T F 9. Functional theorists believe that social placement is harmful to society. (338)
T F 10. Matchmaking is a latent function of education. (339)
T F 11. Functionalists emphasize the hidden curriculum in their analysis of Canadian education. (339)
T F 12. According to conflict theorists, unequal funding for education automatically stacks the deck against children from lower income families. (341)
T F 13. The correspondence principle states that schools correspond to the social structure of society. (342)
T F 14. Research by Ray Rist concluded that the child's journey through school was preordained by the end of the first year of kindergarten. (342-343)
T F 15. Teacher expectations of student ability are not related to the class background of teachers or students. (343)

T F   16. The goal of the sociological study of religion is to determine which religions are most effective in people's lives. (347)

T F   17. According to Durkheim, all religions separate the sacred from the profane. (347)

T F   18. Functionalists believe that religion is universal because it meets basic human needs. (348)

T F   19. The Crusades are an example of the dysfunctions of religion. (348)

T F   20. Karl Marx believed that religion is the opium of the people. (350)

T F   21. Conflict theorists believe that religion reduces social inequalities and social conflict. (350-351)

T F   22. Emile Durkheim wrote The Protestant Ethic and the Spirit of Capitalism. (351)

T F   23. Contemporary Judaism comprises two main branches. (352)

T F   24. Fundamentalism is the belief that modernism threatens religion and that the faith as it was originally practiced should be restored. (352)

T F   25. Reincarnation is a term used by Hindus to describe being born again. (353)

T F   26. Cults often begin with the appearance of a charismatic leader. (354)

T F   27. Unlike cults, sects do not stress evangelism. (355)

T F   28. Islam in Iran and Iraq is an example of ecclesia. (356)

T F   29. In Canada, the incidence of those reporting "no religion" has not changed over the past 4 decades. (357)

T F   30. Feminist approaches to spirituality advocate for a maintenance of women's traditional roles within religious traditions. (358)

FILL-IN QUESTIONS

1.   Using diplomas and degrees to determine eligibility for jobs occurs in a _____. (332)

2.   _____ is the transmission of culture from one generation to the next. (333)

3.   A formal system of teaching knowledge, values, and skills is the definition for _____. (334)

4.   Tracking and social placement both contribute to the _____ function of education. (337-338)

5.   A new function of education today is _____, incorporating people with disabilities into regular social activities. (338)

6.   The unwritten rules of behavior and attitude, such as obedience to authority and conformity to cultural norms, is referred to as the _____. (339)

7.   _____ theorists believe that culturally biased IQ tests favor the middle classes and discriminate against minorities and students from lower-class backgrounds. (341)

8.   The idea that schools reflect the social structure of society is the _____. (342)

9.   _____ theorists found that the expectations of teachers are especially significant for determining what students learn. (342)

10. _____ refers to the trend of giving higher grades for the same work, so that there is a general rise in student grades despite the fact that learning may be declining. (344)

11. It is not uncommon today for schools to practice _____, which involves passing students to the next grade even though they have not mastered basic material. (344)

12. Someone who has graduated from high school but still has difficulties with reading and writing is considered _____. (344)

13. Durkheim's term for common elements of everyday life was _____. (347)

14. Answering questions about ultimate meaning, providing emotional comfort, and uniting believers into a community are _____ of religion. (348)

15. Ceremonies or repetitive practices that help unite people into a moral community are_____ (349)
16. _____ is teachings or ideas that provide a unified picture of the world. (350)
17. According to conflict theorists, religion is the _____. (350)
18. _____ is Weber's term to describe the ideal of a highly moral life, hard work, industriousness, and frugality. (351)
19. The belief that there is only one God is _____. (352)
20. The belief that all objects in the world have spirits, many of which are dangerous and must be outwitted is _____. (352)
21. _____ is the belief that true religion is threatened by modernism and that the faith as it originally was practiced should be restored. (352)
22. A(n) _____ is someone who exerts extraordinary appeal to a group of followers. (354-355)
23. A group larger than a cult that still feels substantial hostility from and toward society is a(n) _____. (355)
24. A(n) _____ is a religious group so integrated into the dominant culture that it is difficult to tell where the one begins and the other leaves off. (356)
25. Within the categories of feminist spirituality, _____ seek to change the established orthodoxy by importing language, images, and rituals from other traditions. (358)

MATCH THESE SOCIAL SCIENTISTS WITH THEIR CONTRIBUTIONS

__1. Randall Collins
__2. Bowles and Gintis
__3. Ray Rist
__4. Coleman and Hoffer
__5. Harry Gracey
__6. Davis and Moore
__7. George Farkas
__8. Emile Durkheim
__9. Johanna Stuckey
__10. Max Weber
__11 John Hostetler
__12. Ernst Troeltsch
__13. Karl Marx

a. *gatekeeping sorts people on the basis of merit*
b. *credential society*
c. *correspondence principle*
d. *tracking and expectations of kindergarten teachers*
e. *kindergarten as boot camp*
f. *student performance linked to setting higher standards*
g. *students are rewarded for signals they send teachers*
h. The Protestant Ethic and the Spirit of Capitalism
i. *"religion is the opium of the people"*
j. The Elementary Forms of Religious Life
k. *outlined four categories of feminist spirituality*
l. *studied "shunning"*
m. *cult-sect-church-ecclesia typology*

ESSAY QUESTIONS

1. Explain the link between democracy, industrialization and universal education.
2. Select one of the three perspectives and design a research project to test the claims of that perspective about the nature of education.
3. Assume that you have been asked to make a presentation about religion to a group of people who have absolutely no idea what religion is. Prepare a speech in which you define religion and explain why it exists.
4. Discuss the process by which a religion matures from a cult into a church.

"DOWN-TO-EARTH SOCIOLOGY"

1. After reading "Kindergarten as Boot Camp" (p. 340), do you agree with Harry Gracey's ideas? Did you attend kindergarten? If so, which experiences do you remember the most vividly? Do you think it would be accurate to refer to college as a "boot camp?"

2. Have you ever been involved in a distance learning course like the ones described on pages 343-344? If you have, what aspects of the course did you like? What aspects did you dislike? What changes would have improved the course? In what ways might distance learning change the way in which education is organized and instruction is delivered? Thinking about the different sociological perspectives on education, analyze how each might "see" this new development in terms of addressing problems as well as creating new problems.

3. After reading this chapter, and particularly the box on Heaven's Gate (p. 355), do you understand why some people are attracted to cults and willing to give their lives for them? Why do you think cults rise up at certain points in history—like the 1970s and the 1990s? What is going on in society that would make them especially attractive?

4. Why do you think that attendance at religious services has declined in Canada in the post-World War II period (pp. 357-358)? What could explain the differences between the religious affiliations of Canadians and Americans?

CHAPTER 15

MEDICINE: HEALTH AND ILLNESS IN CANADA

☞ **CHAPTER SUMMARY**

- Sociologists study medicine as a social institution. In Canada, sociologists study how the health care sector is influenced by ideas of self-regulation, the bureaucratic structure, and public policy. Sociologists also study the social construction of illness and health.
- Symbolic interactionists view health and illness as intimately related to cultural beliefs and practices; definitions of illness vary from one group to the next. Functionalists study the sick role and the ways in which the rules governing this role excuse people from normal responsibilities but obligate them to get well in order to resume those responsibilities. The conflict perspective stresses that health care is one of the scarce resources over which groups compete.
- In Canada, universal government-funded medical, hospital and health insurance has been available since 1971. The purpose of the national health system is to eliminate financial barriers to health care. The Canada Health Act was enacted in 1984, setting out provisions for national standards. The Act outlines five basic criteria: comprehensive scope, universal coverage, public administration, portability, and accessibility.
- Current issues in medical and health care include depersonalization, sexism, gendered differences in experiences of health and illness, the medicalization of society, and questions related to medically assisted suicide.
- Major threats to health today include AIDS, the globalization of disease, smoking, alcohol abuse, and disabling environments.
- Alternatives to the current health-care system include individuals taking more responsibility for their health and a fundamental shift in the medical establishment toward "wellness" and preventive medicine.

☞ **LEARNING OBJECTIVES**

As you read Chapter 15, use these learning objectives to organize your notes. After completing your reading, briefly state an answer to each of the objectives, and review the text pages in parentheses.

1. Define the sociological perspective in studying medicine. (366)
2. Discuss the symbolic interactionist perspective on the role of culture in defining health and illness. (366-367)
3. Explain the components of health. (367)
4. Identify the functionalist perspective on the purpose of the sick role and explain why everyone is not given the same right to claim this role. (367-368)
5. Consider the conflict perspective on consequences of global stratification in terms of health, illness, and access to medical treatment. (368-369)
6. Answer the question, "Were Canadians healthier in the past?" (370)
7. Outline and briefly explain the major issues in Canadian health and health care. (370-375)
8. Discuss these threats to health: AIDS, drugs, and disabling environments. (375-379)
9. Analyze the prospects for change in medicine which might be possible through preventive medicine. (379-380)

☞ CHAPTER OUTLINE

I.   **Sociology and the Study of Medicine**
   A.   Medicine is a society's standard way of dealing with illness and injury. In Canada, medicine is a profession, a bureaucracy, and a publicly funded institution.
   B.   Sociologists study how medicine is influenced by ideals of professional self-regulation, the bureaucratic structure, and the profit motive; they also are interested in how illness and health are related to cultural beliefs, lifestyle, and social class.

II. **The Symbolic Interactionist Perspective**
   A.   Health is affected by cultural beliefs. In Western culture a person who hears voices and sees visions might be locked up; in a tribal society, such an individual might be a shaman, the healing specialist who attempts to control the spirits thought to cause a disease or injury.
   B.   Health is a human condition measured by four components: physical, mental, social, and spiritual. What makes someone healthy varies from culture to culture. Sociologists analyze the effects that people's ideas of health and illness have on their lives and even how people determine that they are sick.

III. **The Functionalist Perspective**
   A.   Functionalists point out that societies must set up ways to control sickness. They develop a system of medical care as well as make rules to keep too many people from "being sick."
   B.   The sick role is a social role that you are forced to play when you are not well.
   1.   It has four elements—you are not held responsible for being sick, you are exempt from normal responsibilities, you don't like the role, and you will get help so you can return to your usual routines. People who don't seek competent help are considered responsible for being sick and can not claim sympathy from others.
   2.   Often there is ambiguity between the well role and the sick role because most situations are not clear-cut examples, such as having a heart attack. A decision to claim the sick role typically is more of a social than a physical matter.
   3.   Parents and physicians are the primary mediators between children's feelings of illness and the right to be released from responsibilities.

IV. **The Conflict Perspective**
   A.   The primary focus of conflict theorists is the struggle over scarce resources, including medical treatment.
   B.   One consequence of global domination by the Developed Industrialized Nations is the international stratification of medical care.
   1.   The Least Industrialized Nations cannot afford the same life-saving technology available in highly industrialized nations. Differences in life expectancy and infant mortality rates illustrate the consequences of global stratification.
   2.   Global stratification even changes the face of diseases. People living in the Least Industrialized Nations located in the tropics face illness and death from four major sources: malaria, internal parasites, diarrhea, and malnutrition.

V.   **Historical Patterns of Health**
   A.   Epidemiology is the study of the distribution of medical disorders throughout a population; it provides answers about patterns of health and illness over time.

B.   Were Canadians healthier in the past? If being healthier is measured by life span, then Canadians are healthier than their ancestors.

C.   When it comes to mental health, no rational basis for comparisons exists. Perhaps there were fewer mental health problems in the past; however, it is also possible that there is greater mental health today than in the past.

VI.   **Issues in Health Care**

A.   The provision of health care in Canada is a provincial responsibility; however, the federal government has played a major role in providing funding.

1.   Universal government-funded health care has been available since 1971. The purpose of universal health care is to eliminate financial barriers to health care.

2.   Physicians are reimbursed on a fee-for-service basis; but these fees are determined by province-wide, uniform fee schedules.

3.   Private insurance companies offer coverage only for additional services not covered by federal funding.

4.   The Canada Health Act was introduced in 1984 to ensure that health services would be available to all Canadians. The Act sets out national standards for health care based on five basic criteria: comprehensive scope, universal coverage, public administration, portability, and accessibility.

B.   The sociology of health in Canada has passed through at least two major stages, the first focusing on issues related to the complexity of the health care system, and the second on issues such as the impact of population aging on the provision of health care.

1.   Research in the field of health care has used large surveys to determine the health status of Canadians.

2.   The ongoing National Population Health Survey has examined the causal links between social status and heath status, with a specific focus on factors such as socioeconomic status, gender, age, and ethnicity.

C.   Depersonalization is the practice of dealing with people as though they were cases and diseases, not individuals.

1.   Many patients get the impression that they are trapped by a cash machine—the physician watches the clock and calculates dollars while talking to the patient.

2.   Although students begin medical school wanting to "treat the whole person," as they progress through school, their feelings for patients are overpowered by the need to be efficient.

D.   Medicine is not immune to sexism; there is evidence that women and men are treated differently by the medical establishment.

1.   Physicians don't take women's health complaints as seriously as they do men's.

2.   Women may receive unnecessary surgery, such as total hysterectomy, as some male doctors work hard to "sell" the operation in order to make money.

3.   Male dominance of medicine in Canada underlies this sexism (less than 30% of Canadian physicians are women). The situation is improving, however, as today women earn 40.5% of all medical degrees in Canada.

E.   There are gendered differences in men's and women's experiences of health and illness. Sociologists have advanced five different theories to account for these gendered differences. These theories focus on (1) role accumulation; (2) role overload and role conflict; (3) gendered patterns of socialization; (4) caregiver responsibilities of women; (5) gendered differences in engagement in risky behavior.

F.   Medicalization is the transformation of something into a matter to be treated by physicians. Examples include balding, weight, wrinkles, small breasts and insomnia — yet, there is nothing inherently medical in such conditions.

G.   With modern technology, machines can perform most bodily functions even when the person's mind no longer works; this has created the question "Who has the right to pull the plug?"

    1.   A living will (that people in good health sign to make clear what they wish medical personnel to do should they become dependent on artificial life-support systems) is an attempt to deal with this issue.

VII.   Threats to Health

A.   AIDS (Acquired Immune Deficiency Syndrome) is probably the most pressing health issue in the U.S. and around the world.

    1.   Its exact origin is unknown.

    2.   AIDS is transmitted through the passing of bodily fluids such as blood and semen. AIDS cannot be transmitted by casual contact.

    3.   One of the most significant sociological aspects of AIDS is the stigma, which contributes to its spreading because people are afraid to be tested and stigmatized.

    4.   AIDS, a global problem, poses a public health problem. Africa has been the hardest hit, with life expectancy cut in half in some countries. AIDS cases are multiplying in the former Soviet Union due to increases in prostitution and drug use. AIDS is also flourishing in Asia.

    5.   Drugs have been found to slow the progress of AIDS, but there is no cure.

B.   With the vast increase in global travel, diseases have become globalized. AIDS is an example of a disease that has globalized; an outbreak of ebola in Zaire threatened to spread to other parts of the globe.

C.   Alcohol and tobacco are the most frequently used drugs in Canada.

    1.   Alcohol is the standard recreational drug in Canada. While limited amounts of alcohol reduce the risk of heart attacks and blood vessel diseases, alcohol consumption has been linked to increased risks of cancer and stroke.

    2.   Of all drugs, nicotine is the most harmful to health. Smoking doubles a person's risk of heart attack and causes progressive emphysema and several types of cancer. People continue to smoke despite harmful health effects for two major reasons: addiction and advertising.

D.   A disabling environment is one that is harmful to health.

    1.   Some occupations have high health risks which are evident (e.g., mining, construction, etc.). In others, the risk becomes evident only years after people have worked at what they thought was a safe occupation (e.g., laborers who worked with asbestos).

    2.   Industrialization not only increased the world's standard of living, but it has also led to the greenhouse effect—a warming of the earth that may change the globe's climate, melt its polar ice caps, and flood the earth's coastal shores. Use of fluorocarbon gases is threatening the ozone shield (the protective layer of the earth's upper stratosphere that screens out a high proportion of the sun's ultraviolet rays). In humans, this high-intensity ultraviolet radiation causes skin cancer.

VIII.   The Search for Alternatives

A.   Values and lifestyles have a major impact on health.

    1.   Many of the threats to health are preventable. Individuals can exercise regularly, eat nutritious food, maintain sexual monogamy, and avoid smoking and alcohol abuse in order to prevent disease.

    2.   Instead of treatment, the Canadian medical establishment should have "wellness" as its goal. To achieve such a goal the medical establishment must make a

fundamental change in its philosophy and the public must accept the benefits of "wellness."

3. On a broader scale, there needs to be a systematic attempt to eliminate disabling environments and the use of harmful drugs.

☞ KEY TERMS

After studying the chapter, review the definition for each of the following terms.

depersonalization: dealing with people as though they were objects; in the case of medical care, as though patients were merely cases and diseases, not persons

disabling environment: an environment that is harmful to health

epidemiology: the study of disease and disability patterns in a population

euthanasia: mercy killing

fee for service: payment to a physician to diagnose and treat the patient's medical problems

health: a human condition measured by four components: physical, mental, social, and spiritual

living will: a statement people in good health sign that clearly expresses their feelings about being kept alive on artificial life support systems

medicalization: the transformation of something into a matter to be treated by physicians

medicine: one of the major social institutions that sociologists study; a society's organized ways of dealing with sickness and injury

shaman: the healing specialist of a preliterate tribe who attempts to control the spirits thought to cause a disease or injury; commonly called a witch doctor

sick role: a social role that excuses people from normal obligations because they are sick or injured, while at the same time expecting them to seek competent help and cooperate in getting well

☞ KEY PEOPLE

Review the major theoretical contributions or findings of these people.

Sue Fisher: Fisher did participant observation in a hospital where she discovered doctors recommending total hysterectomies even when no cancer was present, because the reproductive organs were "potentially disease-producing" organs that were no longer needed once a woman had passed her child-bearing years.

Erich Goode: This sociologist compared the health of smokers and nonsmokers and found that smokers are three times as likely to die before reaching age 65.

Jack Haas and William Shaffir: These sociologists did a participant observation of medical students and discovered that, over the course of medical school, students' attitudes change from wanting to "treat the whole person" to needing to be efficient in treating the specific ailment.

Talcott Parsons: Parsons was the first sociologist to analyze the sick role, pointing out that it has four elements—not being responsible for your sickness, being exempt from normal responsibilities, not liking the role, and seeking competent help in order to return to daily routines.

Diana Scully: Scully interviewed residents about their attitudes towards surgical procedures involving women's reproductive organs and found that doctors try to "sell" women on the procedure, not because women need it, but because the doctor wants to make money.

Leonard Stein: This physician analyzed doctor-nurse interactions in terms of a game in which the nurse (lower-status role) disguises her recommendations about patient care to the doctor (higher-status role).

☞ SELF-TEST

After completing this self-test, check your answers against the Answer Key at the back of this Study Guide and against the text on page(s) indicated in parentheses.

MULTIPLE CHOICE QUESTIONS

1. Sociologists focus on medicine as: (366)
    a. a profession.
    b. a bureaucracy.
    c. a business.
    d. All of the above.

2. A _____ is the healing specialist of a preliterate tribe who tries to control the spirits thought to cause a disease or injury. (366-367)
    a. soothsayer
    b. high priest
    c. shaman
    d. medicine man

3. Which of the following is not one of the components of health? (367)
    a. physical
    b. social
    c. spiritual
    d. hereditary

4. How would a sick or injured person who can't fulfill normal role obligations be described? (367)
    a. a hypochondriac
    b. in the sick role
    c. deviant
    d. all of the above

5. The individual's claim to the sick role is legitimized primarily by: (368)
    a. demonstrating to others that he or she is ill.
    b. a doctor's excuse.
    c. employers, teachers, and sometimes parents.
    d. other workers or students who vouch for the fact that the individual is ill.

6. Life expectancy in the Least Developed Nations is lower than in the Developed Industrial Nations in part because of: (368-369)
    a. lack of access to affordable medical technology.
    b. malnutrition.
    c. higher risk of catching life-threatening disease.
    d. all of the above.

7. The field of epidemiology is the study of : (369)
    a. the development of medical knowledge.
    b. the professionalization of medicine.
    c. how medical disorders are distributed throughout a population.
    d. patterns of social stratification of medical care.

8. The top causes of death for Canadians are: (369)
    a. cancer, heart diseases, cerebrovascular diseases.
    b. related to cigarette and alcohol addictions.
    c. not related to physical health, but are due to mental disorders.
    d. a result of violent crimes.

9. The criteria of the Canada Health Act are: (371)
    a. comprehensive scope.
    b. universal coverage and public administration.
    c. portability and accessibility.
    d. all of the above.

10. The most significant findings of the National Population Health Survey point to the fact that: (372)
    a. Canadians are healthier than they have ever been.
    b. health care costs are currently reaching levels that are no longer affordable.
    c. social factors such as class, gender, age, and ethnicity influence health.
    d. the aging population is placing new strains on the provision of health care.

11. Which of the following statements about depersonalization is *incorrect*? (372-373)
    a. It is less common today because of the development of the Canada Health Act.
    b. It is the practice of dealing with people as though they were objects.
    c. It means treating patients as though they were merely cases and diseases.
    d. It occurs when an individual is treated as if he or she was not a person.

12. Doctor recommendations for total hysterectomies even when there is no cancer is present is an example of: (373)
    a. sexism in medicine.
    b. medicalization of society.
    c. monopolization of medicine.
    d. holistic medicine.

13. The pressures of the "double day," which lead to increased stress and excessive demands on women's time and energy, illustrate that there is/are: (374)
    a. different life expectations between men and women.
    b. demands on health created by role accumulation.
    c. gender differences in experiences of heath and illness.
    a. a social acceptability of women's role in the home.

14. The term medicalization refers to: (375)
    a. the increasing availability of public, accessible medical care.
    b. the growing awareness of new medical problems.
    c. the process of turning something that was not previously medical into a medical matter
    d. the use of medical procedures to treat criminal behavior.

15. AIDS is known to be transmitted by: (375)
    a. casual contact between a carrier and a non-carrier in which bodily fluids are exchanged.
    b. exchange of blood and/or semen.
    c. airborne passage of the virus from carrier to non-carrier through coughing or sneezing.
    d. all of the above.

16. A cure for AIDS: (377)
    a. has been found with drugs.
    b. can be found as soon as the one virus which causes AIDS is identified.
    c. has not been found.
    d. will never be found because pharmaceutical companies won't pool their research.

17. Why do diseases today have the potential of becoming truly global threats? (377-378)
    a. Viruses are stronger than they used to be.
    b. Medicine is less effective today than in the past.
    c. There are so many more viruses today than in the past, because of gene mutation.
    d. Contact between people of different countries has increased due to global travel.

18. Which of the following statements about smoking is *incorrect*? (378-379)
    a. Nicotine may be as addictive as heroin.
    b. The rate of cigarette smoking continues to climb, despite warnings about the dangers.
    c. The tobacco industry has a huge advertising budget to encourage people to smoke.
    d. When compared to nonsmokers, smokers are three times as likely to die before reaching age 65.

19. An environment that is harmful to health is referred to as a(n): (379)
    a. disabling environment.
    b. health hazard.
    c. harmful setting.
    d. crippling environment.

20. To implement a national policy of "prevention, not intervention" would require: (379-380)
    a. a fundamental change in the philosophy of the medical establishment.
    b. a change in the public's attitudes towards medicine and health care.
    c. eliminating disabling environments and reducing the use of harmful drugs.
    d. all of the above.

TRUE-FALSE QUESTIONS

T F 1. Health is a relative matter. (367)

T F 2. People who don't seek competent help when they are sick are just behaving as expected, according to the social definition of the sick role. (367-368)

T F 3. There is little ambiguity between the well role and the sick role. (368)

T F 4. In the Least Industrialized Nations, shorter life expectancy is related to patterns of global stratification. (369)

T F 5. Epidemiology is the study of mental illness within a population. (369)

T F 6. Gender differences in causes of death are most pronounced for suicide. (369)

T F 7. Because many people today live longer than their ancestors, it is possible to conclude that contemporary Canadians are healthier. (370)

T F 8. Commonsense beliefs that mental illness is more prevalent today than in the past represent perceptions, not measured reality. (370)

T F 9. In Canada, universal government-funded medical, hospital, and related health insurance has been available since the early years of the post-World War II period. (371)

T F 10. Canadian physicians are reimbursed on a fee-for-service basis, as are physicians in the United States. (371)

T F   11. The Canada Heath Act sets out guidelines for health care that vary across the provinces. (371)

T F   12. Studies on the health of Canadians have confirmed that the organization of work is an important predictor of health status. (372)

T F   13. Medicine in Canada is male dominated. (373)

T F   14. Role overload has been identified as a factor in creating gendered differences in experiences of health and illness. (374)

T F   15. There is a lack of consensus about the practice of euthanasia. (375)

T F   16. The globalization of AIDS has impacted upon Least Industrialized and Developed Industrial nations equally. (377)

T F   17. In Canada, the number of deaths due to AIDS has been increasing since the mid-1990s. (377)

T F   18. Alcohol consumption reduces the risk of heart attacks and blood vessel diseases and does not increase the risk for other diseases. (378)

T F   19. In general, people are very aware when they are working in a disabling environment, one that is harmful to their health. (379)

T F   20. Strategies for preventative medicine require both individual and group responsibility. (379)

FILL-IN QUESTIONS

1.   The healing specialist of a preliterate tribe who attempts to control the spirits thought to cause a disease or injury is a _____. (366-367)

2.   _____ is a human condition measured by four components: physical, mental, social, and spiritual. (367)

3.   The _____ is a social role that excuses people from normal obligations because they are sick or injured. (367)

4.   Parents and physicians are the primary _____ to the sick role. (368)

5.   One consequence of the inequitable distribution of economic and military power between nations is the _____ of medical care. (368)

6.   The study of disease and disability patterns in a population is _____. (369)

7.   In 1984, the _____ was enacted to ensure that health services would be available to all Canadians. (371)

8.   The practice of dealing with people as though they are cases, not individuals, is termed _____. (372)

9.   The fact that women are less likely than men to be given heart surgery, except in the more advanced stages of heart disease, is an example of _____ in medicine. (373)

10. The theory of _____ suggests that due to socialization women are more likely to accept help in dealing with their health problems. (374)

11. The term _____ refers to the process of turning something that was not previously considered medical into a medical matter. (375)

12. A(n) _____ is a statement people in good health sign that clearly expresses their feelings about being kept alive on artificial life-support systems. (375)

13. One of the most significant sociological aspects of AIDS is its _____. (375)

14. Of all drugs, _____ is the most harmful to health. (378)

15. Lumberjacking, mining, and the construction industry are all examples of _____. (379)

MATCH THESE SOCIAL SCIENTISTS WITH THEIR CONTRIBUTIONS

___1. Talcott Parsons   a. *compared health of smokers and nonsmokers*
___2. Erich Goode   b. *sick role*
___3. Haas/Shaffir   c. *transformation of medical students*
___4. Diana Scully   d. *sexism in medicine*
___5. Leonard Stein   e. *interaction games played by doctors and nurses*

ESSAY QUESTIONS

1. Describe the elements of the sick role and identify variations in the pattern of claiming this role.
2. Explain the pattern of the worldwide AIDS epidemic and suggest reasons why this threat to the health of the world's population has not be addressed more aggressively.
3. Discuss the obstacles to developing preventive medicine and suggest ways in which these obstacles can be overcome.

"DOWN-TO-EARTH SOCIOLOGY"

1. Do you think "The Doctor-Nurse Game" on page 374 is an accurate description of the relationship between most doctors and nurses today? If nurses spend more time with patients, why are they not in charge of determining what care the patients should receive? What function does this "game" that goes on between doctors and nurses serve?
2. After reading "Euthanasia in Holland" on page 376, what do you think about this subject? Why do you think leading Dutch physicians who practice euthanasia oppose its legalization in the United States? Do you agree?
3. What criteria do you think our society should use in providing access to new medical technologies (p. 376)? How would a conflict theorist answer this question? How would a functionalist?

CHAPTER 16

SOCIAL DEVIANCE AND SOCIAL CONTROL

☞ **CHAPTER SUMMARY**

- Deviance, which refers to violations of social norms, is relative; what people consider deviant varies from one culture to another and from group to group within a society. It is not the act itself, but the reaction to the act, that makes something deviant. To explain deviance, biologists and psychologists look for reasons within people, such as genetic predispositions or personality disorders, while sociologists look for explanations in social relationships.
- Symbolic interactionists use differential association theory, control theory, and labeling theory to analyze how group membership influences people's behaviors and views of the world.
- Many people succeed in neutralizing the norms of society and are able to commit deviant acts while thinking of themselves as conformists. Primary, secondary, and tertiary deviance refer to stages in people's reactions to their own socially unacceptable behaviors. Although most people resist being labeled deviant, there are those who embrace deviance.
- Functionalists state that deviance is functional, using strain theory and illegitimate opportunity structures to argue that widespread socialization into norms of material success accounts for much of the crime committed by the poor.
- Conflict theorists argue that the group in power imposes its definitions on other groups—the ruling class directs the criminal justice system against the working class, which commits highly visible property crimes, while it diverts its own criminal activities out of the criminal justice system. The conclusions of both symbolic interactionists and conflict theorists cast doubts on the accuracy of official crime statistics. Feminist theories of social deviance connect patterns of male violence against women to systems of patriarchy, which are rooted in ideologies of male superiority.
- Reactions to deviance include negative sanctions, degradation ceremonies, and imprisonment.
- Society may deal with deviance by medicalizing it and calling it mental illness. Thomas Szasz disagrees, claiming that deviance involves just problem behaviors, not mental illness.
- With deviance inevitable, the larger issues are how to protect people from deviant behaviors that are harmful to their welfare, to tolerate those that are not, and to develop systems of fairer treatment for deviants.

☞ **LEARNING OBJECTIVES**

As you read Chapter 16, use these learning objectives to organize your notes. After completing your reading, briefly state an answer to each of the objectives, and review the text pages in parentheses.

1. Explain what sociologists mean when they say that deviance is relative. (384)
2. Compare and contrast the functionalist and the conflict views on social control. (386)
3. Explain the importance of norms and their relation to a system of social order. (386-387)
4. Compare biological, psychological, and sociological explanations of deviance. (387-388)
5. State the key components of the symbolic interaction perspective on deviance, and briefly explain differential association theory, control theory, and labeling theory. (388-390)
6. Distinguish between primary, secondary, and tertiary deviance. Give examples of each. (390-391)
7. Summarize these reactions by deviants to their own behavior: neutralizing deviance and embracing deviance. (391-392)

8. Discuss the major reasons why functionalists view deviance as functional for society. (392)
9. Describe Merton's strain theory, and list and briefly explain the four types of responses to anomie. (392-393)
10. Identify the relationship between social class and crime by using the illegitimate opportunity theory and perspectives on white-collar crime. (393-395)
11. Explain the conflict view of the relationship between class, crime, and the criminal justice system. (395)
12. State why official statistics may not accurately reflect the nature and extent of crime. (395-396)
13. Discuss feminist theories of social deviance, focusing on issues of male violence against women and Canadian public policy. (396-397)
14. State why there is a need to use more than one theory of deviance in trying to explain this behavior and discuss how the different theories can be combined. (397)
15. Describe the reactions to deviance by explaining sanctions, degradation ceremonies, and imprisonment. (397)
16. Explain what is meant by the medicalization of deviance and discuss how social conditions like homelessness can contribute to mental illness, just as mental illness is seen as contributing to these same conditions. (399-400)

☞ CHAPTER OUTLINE

I.   **Gaining a Sociological Perspective of Deviance**
   A. Sociologists use the term deviance to refer to a violation of norms.
      1. According to sociologist Howard S. Becker, it is not the act itself that makes an action deviant, but rather how society reacts to it.
      2. Because different groups have different norms, what is deviant to some is not deviant to others.
      3. Deviants are people who violate rules, whether the infraction is minor (jaywalking) or serious (murder). To sociologists, all people are deviants because everyone violates rules from time to time.
      4. Erving Goffman used "stigma" to refer to attributes that discredit one's claim to a "normal" identity; a stigma (e.g., physical deformities, skin color) defines a person's master status, superseding all other statuses the person occupies.
   B. In trying to answer the question of where definitions of deviance come from, functional and conflict perspectives agree that social groups develop norms, along with a system of social control, with formal and informal means of enforcing them.
      1. In tribal societies, agreement on how life should be lived is relatively simple, because these societies are small with strong social bonds. In industrial societies, because there are many competing groups, techniques of social control are set up to enforce different groups' version of what is good.
      2. To functionalists, social control emerges as individuals and groups attempt to achieve a balance between competing interest groups. According to the pluralistic theory of social control, in societies like Canada, the central government often plays a mediating role between groups.
      3. To conflict theorists, the purpose of social control is to maintain power for an elite group, primarily consisting of wealthy, white males who work behind the scenes to control government. Official deviance (the statistics on victims, lawbreakers, and the outcome of criminal investigations and sentencing) reflects the elite's concern with protecting its interests.

C. Norms make social life possible by making behavior predictable. Without norms, social chaos would exist. The reason deviance is seen as threatening is because it undermines predictability. Thus, social control (the formal and informal means of enforcing norms) is necessary for social life.

D. Comparing Biological, Psychological, and Sociological Explanations

1. Psychologists and sociobiologists explain deviance by looking within individuals; sociologists look outside the individual.

2. Biological explanations focus on genetic predisposition—factors such as intelligence, "XYY" theory (an extra Y chromosome in men leads to crime), or body type (squarish, muscular persons more likely to commit street crimes). Psychiatrist Dorothy Lewis found that when compared with non-delinquents, delinquents had suffered significantly more head injuries.

3. Psychological explanations focus on personality disorders (e.g., "bad toilet training," "suffocating mothers," etc.). Yet these do not necessarily result in the presence or absence of specific forms of deviance in a person.

4. Sociological explanations search outside the individual: crime is a violation of norms written into law, and each society has its own laws against certain types of behavior, but social influences—such as socialization, subcultural group memberships, or social class (people's relative standing in terms of education, occupation, income and wealth)—may "recruit" some people to break norms.

II.   The Symbolic Interactionist Perspective

A. Differential association is Edwin Sutherland's term to indicate that those who associate with groups oriented toward deviant activities learn an "excess of definitions" of deviance and, thus, are more likely to engage in deviant activities.

1. The key to differential association is the learning of ideas and attitudes favorable to following the law or favorable to breaking it. Some groups teach members to violate norms (e.g., families involved in crime may set their children on a lawbreaking path; some friends and neighborhoods tend to encourage deviant behavior; even subcultures contain particular attitudes about deviance and conformity that are learned by their members).

2. Symbolic interactionists stress that people are not mere pawns, because individuals help produce their own orientation to life and their choice of association helps to shape the self.

B. Control Theory

1. According to control theory everyone is propelled towards deviance, but two control systems work against these motivations to deviate.

2. Inner controls are our capacity to withstand temptations toward deviance, and include internalized morality, integrity, fear of punishment, and desire to be good; while outer controls involve groups (e.g., family, friends, the police) that influence us to stay away from crime.

3. Sociologist Travis Hirschi noted that strong bonds to society lead to more effective inner controls; bonds are based on attachments, commitments, involvements, and beliefs.

C. Labeling theory is the view that the labels people are given affect their own and others' perceptions of them, thus channeling their behavior either into deviance or into conformity.

1. Gresham Sykes and David Matza use the term "techniques of neutralization" to describe the strategies deviants employ to resist society's label. These are (1) denial of responsibility ("I didn't do it"); (2) denial of injury ("Who really got hurt?"); (3)

denial of a victim ("She deserved it"); (4) condemnation of the condemners ("Who are you to talk?"); and (5) appeal to higher loyalty ("I had to help my friends").

2. Sometimes an individual's deviant acts begin casually, and he or she gradually slides into more serious deviance.

3. Edwin Lemert identified primary deviance as fleeting acts that are not absorbed into an individual's self-concept and secondary deviance as deviant acts that are absorbed into one's self-concept. As a consequence, the deviant individual often redefines deviant behavior as nondeviant; this is referred to as tertiary deviance.

4. Most people resist being labeled deviant, but some revel in a deviant identity (e.g., motorcycle gangs may pride themselves on getting into trouble, laughing at death, etc.).

5. William J. Chambliss's study of the Saints (boys from respectable middle class families) and the Roughnecks (boys from working class families who hang out on the streets) provides an excellent illustration of labeling theory—labels given to people affect how others perceive them and how they perceive themselves, thus channeling their behavior into deviance or conformity. The study showed how labels open and close doors of opportunity for the individuals involved.

III. **The Functionalist Perspective**
  A. Emile Durkheim stated that deviance, including crime, is functional, for it contributes to social order.
    1. Deviance clarifies moral boundaries (a group's ideas about how people should act and think) and affirms norms.
    2. Deviance promotes social unity (by reacting to deviants, group members develop a "we" feeling and collectively affirm the rightness of their own ways).
    3. Deviance promotes social change (if boundary violations gain enough support, they become new, acceptable behaviors).
  B. Robert Merton developed strain theory to analyze what happens when people are socialized to desire cultural goals but denied the institutionalized means to reach them.
    1. Merton used "anomie" (Durkheim's term) to refer to the strain people experience when they are blocked in their attempts to achieve those goals.
    2. The most common reaction to cultural goals and institutionalized means is conformity (using lawful means to seek goals society sets); most people in industrialized societies follow this socially acceptable road.
    3. Merton identified four types of deviant responses to anomie: innovation (using illegitimate means to achieve societal goals); ritualism (giving up on achieving cultural goals but clinging to conventional rules of conduct); retreatism (rejecting cultural goals, dropping out); and rebellion (seeking to replace society's goals).
    4. According to strain theory, deviants are not pathogenic individuals but the products of society.
  C. Illegitimate Opportunity Theory
    1. Social classes have distinct styles of crime due to differential access to institutionalized means.
    2. Illegitimate opportunity structures are opportunities for remunerative crime woven into the texture of life. According to sociologists Richard Cloward and Lloyd Ohlin, such structures may result when legitimate structures fail, thereby drawing the poor into certain crimes in unequal numbers.
    3. White-collar crime (crimes that people of respectable and high social status commit in the course of their occupations) results from an illegitimate opportunity structure among higher classes which makes other forms of crime functional. Such crimes

exist in greater numbers than commonly perceived, and can be very costly—may total several hundred billion dollars a year. They can involve physical harm and sometimes death; for instance, unsafe working conditions due to executive decisions to put profits ahead of workers' safety kill about 1000 Canadians each year.

    D.   There have been some recent changes in the nature of white-collar crime.

        1.   A major change is the growing ranks of female offenders. As women have become more involved in the professions and the corporate world, they too have been enticed by illegitimate opportunities. Today nearly as many women as men are arrested for fraud and embezzlement.

        2.   A second change is theft by computer; workers insert fictitious information into a company's computer system and divert corporate resources for their own use.

IV.   The Conflict Perspective

    A.   The state's machinery of social control represents the interests of the wealthy and powerful; this group determines the laws whose enforcement is essential for maintaining its power.

    B.   The law is an instrument of oppression, a tool designed to maintain the powerful in privileged positions and keep the powerless from rebelling and overthrowing the social order. When members of the working class get out of line, they are arrested, tried and imprisoned in the criminal justice system.

    C.   Caution is needed in interpreting official statistics because the reactions of authorities are influenced by social class of the offender.

    D.   The criminal justice system directs its energies against violations by the working class; while it tends to overlook the harm done by the owners of corporations, flagrant violations are prosecuted. The publicity given to this level of white-collar crime helps to stabilize the system by providing evidence of fairness.

V.   Feminist Theories and Male Violence Against Women

    A.   Feminist theories of social deviance argue that male violence against women is connected to patriarchal ideologies of control; men assault their female partners to maintain control over them.

    B.   Public policy strategies to address the problem of male violence against women include policing initiatives, job creation, social services, and anti-sexist male collectives.

VI.   The Need for Multiple Theories

    A.   All of the different theories have merit in helping to explain deviance.

VII.   Reactions to Deviance

    A.   Sanctions are either negative sanctions (punishments ranging from frowns and gossip to imprisonment, exile, and capital punishment) or positive sanctions (rewards for desired behavior, ranging from smiles to awards).

        1.   Most negative sanctions are informal.

        2.   Reacting to deviance is vital to the welfare of groups; by reacting, the boundaries that establish the unique identity of the group are maintained.

    B.   Degradation ceremonies are rituals designed to mark an individual with the status of an outsider. Typically, an individual is called before a group and denounced; when the individual is pronounced guilty, steps are taken to strip the individual of his/her identity as a group member. Such proceedings signal that the individual is no longer a group member.

    C.   Imprisonment—follows a degradation ceremony involving a public trial/pronouncement that the person is unfit to live among law-abiding people for a specified period of time.

    D.   Medicalization of deviance is the view of deviance as a symptom of some underlying illness that needs to be treated by physicians.

        1.   Thomas Szasz argues that mental illness is simply problem behaviors: some forms of "mental" illnesses have organic causes (e.g., depression caused by a chemical imbalance in the brain); while others are responses to troubles with various coping devices.

        2.   Some sociologists find Szasz's analysis refreshing because it indicates that social experiences, and not some illness of the mind, underlie bizarre behaviors.

        3.   Being mentally ill can sometimes lead to other problems like homelessness; but being homeless can lead to unusual and unacceptable ways of thinking that are defined by the wider society as mental illness.

VIII.   The Need for a More Humane Approach

    A.   With deviance inevitable, one measure of a society is how it treats its deviants.

    B.   The larger issues are how to protect people from deviant behaviors that are harmful to their welfare, to tolerate those that are not, and to develop systems of fairer treatment for deviants.

☞ KEY TERMS

After studying the chapter, review the definition for each of the following terms.

capitalist class: the wealthy who own the means of production and buy the labor of the working class

control theory: the idea that two control systems—inner controls and outer controls—work against our tendencies to deviate

crime: the violation of norms that are written into law

criminal justice system: the system of police, courts, and prisons set up to deal with people who are accused of having committed a crime

cultural goals: the legitimate objectives held out to the members of a society

degradation ceremonies: rituals designed to strip an individual of his or her identity as a group member; for example, a court martial or the defrocking of a priest

deterrence: creating fear so people will refrain from breaking the law

deviance: the violation of rules or norms

differential association: Edwin Sutherland's term to indicate that associating with some groups results in learning an "excess of definitions" of deviance, and, by extension, in a greater likelihood that one will become deviant

genetic predispositions: inborn tendencies, in this context, to commit deviant acts

illegitimate opportunity structures: opportunities for crimes woven into the texture of life

incapacitation: to take away someone's capacity to commit crimes, in this instance, by putting the offender in prison

institutionalized means: approved ways of reaching cultural goals

labeling theory: the view, developed by symbolic interactionists, that the labels people are given affect their own and others' perceptions of them, thus channeling their behavior either into deviance or into conformity

marginal working class: the most desperate members of the working class, who have few skills, little job security, and are often unemployed

medicalization of deviance: to make deviance a medical matter, a symptom of some underlying illness that needs to be treated by physicians

negative sanction: a punishment or negative reaction for disapproved behavior, for deviance

official deviance: a society's statistics on lawbreaking; its measures of crime, victims, lawbreakers, and the outcomes of criminal investigations and sentencing

personality disorders: the view that a personality disturbance of some sort causes an individual to violate social norms

pluralistic theory of social control: the view that society is made up of many competing groups, whose interests manage to become balanced

police discretion: the practice of the police, in the normal course of their duties, to arrest someone for an offense or to overlook the matter

positive sanction: reward or positive reaction for approved behavior, for conformity

primary deviance: Edwin Lemert's term for acts of deviance that have little effect on the self-concept

recidivism rate: the proportion of persons who are rearrested

rehabilitation: the resocialization of offenders so that they can become conforming citizens

retribution: the punishment of offenders in order to restore the moral balance upset by the offense

secondary deviance: Edwin Lemert's term for acts of deviance incorporated into the self-concept, around which an individual orients his or her behavior

social control: a group's formal and informal means of enforcing norms

social order: a group's usual and customary social arrangements, on which its members depend and on which they base their lives

stigma: "blemishes" that discredit a person's claim to a "normal" identity

strain theory: Robert Merton's term for the strain engendered when a society socializes large numbers of people to desire a cultural goal (such as success) but withholds from many the approved means to reach that goal; one adaptation to the strain is crime, the choice of an innovative means (one outside the approved system) to attain the cultural goal

street crime: crimes such as mugging, rape, and burglary

techniques of neutralization: ways of thinking or rationalizing that help people deflect society's norms

tertiary deviance: "normalizing" behavior considered deviant by mainstream society; relabeling behavior as nondeviant

white-collar crime: Edwin Sutherland's term for crimes committed by people of respectable and high social status in the course of their occupations; for example, bribery of public officials, securities violations, embezzlement, false advertising, and price fixing

working class: those who sell their labor to the capitalist class

☞ KEY PEOPLE

Review the major theoretical contributions or findings of these people.

Howard Becker: Becker observed that an act is not deviant in and of itself, but only when there is a reaction to it.

William Chambliss: Chambliss demonstrated the power of the label in his study of two youth gangs— the Saints and the Roughnecks.

Richard Cloward and Lloyd Ohlin: These sociologists identified the illegitimate opportunity structures that are woven into the texture of life in urban slums and provide an alternative set of opportunities for slum residents when legitimate ones are blocked.

Nanette Davis: Davis studied young girls in order to find out what led them to become prostitutes. She found that they had experienced a gradual slide from promiscuity to prostitution.

Emile Durkheim: Durkheim noted the functions that deviance has for social life.

Robert Edgerton: This anthropologist's studies document how different human groups react to similar behaviors, demonstrating that what is deviant in one context is not in another.

Harold Garfinkel: Garfinkel used the term degradation ceremonies to describe formal attempts to mark an individual with the status of an outsider.

Erving Goffman: Goffman wrote about the role of stigma in the definition of who and what is deviant.

Travis Hirschi: Hirschi studied the strength of the bonds an individual has to society in order to understand the effectiveness of inner controls.

Edwin Lemert: Lemert distinguished between different types of deviance—primary, secondary, and tertiary deviance—in terms of the degree to which the deviant label has been incorporated into the individual's identity.

Robert Merton: Merton developed strain theory to explain patterns of deviance within a society.

Walter Reckless: Reckless developed control theory, suggesting that our behavior is controlled by two different systems, one external (outer controls like the police, family and friends) and the other internal (inner controls like our conscience, religious principles, and ideas of right and wrong).

Edwin Sutherland: Sutherland not only developed differential association theory, but was the first to study and give a name to crimes that occur among the middle class in the course of their work—white collar crime.

Gresham Sykes and David Matza: These sociologists studied the different strategies delinquent boys use to deflect society's norms—techniques of neutralization.

Thomas Szasz: Szasz argued that mental illness represents the medicalization of deviance.

Mark Watson: Watson studied motorcycle gangs and found that these people actively embraced the deviant label.

☞ SELF-TEST

After completing this self-test, check your answers against the Answer Key at the back of this Study Guide and against the text on page(s) indicated in parentheses.

MULTIPLE CHOICE QUESTIONS

1. In sociology, to what does the term deviance refer? (384)
    a. behavior that sociologists believe is bad enough to warrant being punished by society
    b. all violations of social rules
    c. the violation of serious rules
    d. crime

2. According to Erving Goffman, what is the function of stigma? (384)
    a. to punish the person because she/he violates the norms
    b. to reward society for conforming to the norms
    c. to define the norm violator as deviant
    d. to regulate behavior

3. The view that different groups mediate and balance competing interests in order to achieve social stability is the _____ theory of social control. (386)
    a. conflict
    b. equilibrium
    c. mediation
    d. pluralistic

4. According to conflict theorists, social control: (386)
    a. is based on balancing tensions between competing groups in society.
    b. represents the interests of the wealthy and powerful.

c. represents the interests of the general public.

d. is important for mediation in a pluralistic society.

5. Differential association theory is based on the: (388)

a. functionalist perspective.

b. conflict perspective.

c. symbolic interactionist perspective.

d. psychological perspective.

6. The idea that two control systems—inner controls and outer controls—work against our tendencies toward deviance is called: (389)

a. conflict theory.

b. differential association theory.

c. control theory.

d. strain theory.

7. Which of the following is not one of the ways of neutralizing deviance? (390)

a. appeal to higher loyalties

b. denial of responsibility

c. denial of deviant labels

d. denial of injury and of a victim

8. What is the term for acts of deviance that have little effect on the self-concept? (390-391)

a. primary deviance

b. secondary deviance

c. tertiary deviance

d. none of the above

9. How do we describe deviant behavior that is normalized by relabeling it as nondeviant? (391)

a. primary deviance

b. secondary deviance

c. tertiary deviance

d. normalized deviance

10. What does William Chambliss's study of the Saints and the Roughnecks suggest? (391-392)

a. Labels are easy to cast off once a person gets away from the group doing the labeling.

b. People often live up to the labels that a community gives them.

c. People often rebel against the labels given them and lead a completely different life.

d. Sociological research on labeling has produced few conclusions.

11. For Chambliss, what factors influence whether or not people are seen as deviant? (392)

a. social class

b. the visibility of offenders

c. styles of interaction

d. All of the above

12. Which of the following perspectives stresses that deviance promotes social unity and social change? (392)

a. functionalist

b.   conflict
c.   symbolic interactionist
d.   differential association

13.   All of the following are responses to anomie as identified by Robert Merton, except: (393)
a.   ritualism.
b.   rebellion.
c.   retreatism.
d.   recidivism.

14.   According to strain theory, who gives up pursuit of success by abusing alcohol or drugs? (393)
a.   rebels
b.   retreatists
c.   neurotics
d.   ritualists

15.   The illegitimate opportunity structures theory is based on: (393)
a.   the conflict perspective.
b.   the symbolic interactionist perspective.
c.   the exchange perspective.
d.   the functionalist perspective.

16.   What are crimes committed by high status people in the course of their occupations called? (394)
a.   upper-class crime
b.   crimes of respectability
c.   white-collar crime
d.   tuxedo crime

17.   Why do conflict theorists see the law as an instrument of oppression? (395)
a.   it penalizes corporate executives
b.   it is used by the powerful to maintain their privileged position
c.   it facilitates male violence against women
d.   All of the above.

18.   According to official statistics: (395-396)
a.   middle-class boys and working-class boys are about equally prone toward delinquency.
b.   working-class boys are more delinquent than middle-class boys.
c.   middle-class boys are more delinquent that working-class boys.
d.   None of the above.

19.   Feminist theorists relate male violence against women to: (396)
a.   biological tendencies towards violent behavior within men.
b.   systemic inequality rooted in capitalist exploitation.
c.   patriarchal ideologies, which promote male superiority.
d.   lack of proper socialization.

20.   Public policy strategies to address male violence include: (396-397)
a.   job creation programs.
b.   expanded social services.

c. anti-sexist self-help groups for violent men.
d. all of the above.

21. Of what are frowns, gossip, and crossing people off guest lists all examples? (397)
a. retribution
b. degradation ceremonies
c. negative sanctions
d. institutionalized means to achieve goals

22. A court martial where the guilty officer is publicly stripped of his rank is an example of: (397)
a. degradation ceremonies.
b. humiliation ceremonies.
c. stigmatization.
d. deinstitutionalization.

23. What experience follows a public pronouncement that a person is "unfit to live among decent, law-abiding people"? (397)
a. retribution
b. imprisonment
c. rehabilitation
d. deterrence

24. The medicalization of deviance refers to: (399)
a. the castration of sex offenders.
b. use of lethal injections for the death penalty.
c. viewing deviance as a medical matter.
d. All of the above.

25. A more humane approach to dealing with social deviance is needed because: (400-401)
a. social deviance is inevitable.
b. deviance is often the result of systems of inequality.
c. a measure of a society is how it treats deviant behavior.
d. all of the above

TRUE-FALSE QUESTIONS

T F   1. Across all cultures, certain acts are considered to be deviant by everyone. (384)
T F   2. According to your text, a college student cheating on an exam and a mugger lurking on a dark street have nothing at all in common. (384)
T F   3. Social control includes both formal and informal means of enforcing norms. (386)
T F   4. Functionalists agree with the pluralistic theory of social control. (386)
T F   5. Conflict theorists maintain that an elite group of wealthy, white males maintains power by controlling the government. (386)
T F   6. Sociologists believe that while biological factors may influence deviant behavior, they are not the only source for deviance. (387)
T F   7. According to differential association theory, the source of deviant behavior may be found in a person's socialization, or social learning. (388)
T F   8. In secondary deviance, the deviance is normalized by relabeling it nondeviant. (390)
T F   9. No one embraces deviance or wants to be labeled with a deviant identity. (391)

T F   10.   Outlaw bikers hold the conventional world in contempt and take pride in getting into trouble. (391)

T F   11.   In the study by Chambliss, the Saints and the Roughnecks both turned out largely as their labels would have predicted. (391-392)

T F   12.   The functionalist perspective states that deviance contributes to the social order. (392)

T F   13.   According to strain theory, everyone has a chance to get ahead in society, but some people prefer to use illegal means to achieve their goals. (392-393)

T F   14.   According to strain theory, some people experience greater pressures to deviate from society's norms because of their social location. (392-393)

T F   15.   Illegitimate opportunity structures are readily available in poor urban neighbourhoods. (394)

T F   16.   White-collar crime is not as costly as street crime. (394)

T F   17.   Both functionalists and conflict theorists agree that the criminal justice system functions for the well-being of all citizens. (395)

T F   18.   Official statistics are accurate counts of the crimes committed in our society. (395-396)

T F   19.   Feminist theories connect male violence against women to patriarchal ideologies of male violence. (396)

T F   20.   The purpose of positive sanctions is to express disapproval of deviance from social norms. (397)

FILL-IN QUESTIONS

1.   _____ is the violation of rules or norms. (384)
2.   Erving Goffman used the term _____ to refer to attributes that discredit people. (384)
3.   Formal and informal means of enforcing norms constitute a system of _____. (386)
4.   According to the _____ perspective, society is made up of competing groups, and the group that holds power uses social control to maintain its position of privilege. (386)
5.   _____ make social life possible by making behavior predictable. (386)
6.   _____ is a group's usual and customary social arrangements, on which its members depend and on which they base their lives. (387)
7.   _____ theory is the idea that two control systems—inner controls and outer controls— work against our pushes and pulls toward deviance. (389)
8.   Labeling theory is based on the _____ perspective. (390)
9.   _____ occurs at the point when individuals incorporate a deviant identity into their self-concept. (390)
10.   Strain theory is based on the idea that large numbers of people are socialized into desiring _____ (the legitimate objects held out to everyone) but many do not have access to _____ in order to achieve those goals. (392-393)
11.   Robert Merton used the term _____ to describe a sense of normlessness — that some people are frustrated in their efforts to achieve success. (393)
12.   Edwin Sutherland used the term _____ to refer to crimes that people of respectable and high social status commit in the course of their occupations. (394)
13.   In combination the policy, courts, and prisons that deal with people who are accused of having committed crimes make up the _____. (395)
14.   Steps to strip an individual of his or her identity as a group member occur during _____. (397)
15.   The view that deviance, including crime, is the product of mental illness is referred to as _____. (399)

MATCH THESE SOCIAL SCIENTISTS WITH THEIR CONTRIBUTIONS

__1. Edwin Sutherland

__2. Robert Merton

__3. Erving Goffman

__4. Thomas Szasz

__5. Emile Durkheim

__6. William Chambliss

__7. Gresham Sykes and David Matza

__8. Walter Reckless

__9. Harold Garfinkel

a. *strain theory*

b. *control theory*

c. *degradation ceremonies*

d. *white-collar crime*

e. *functions of deviance*

f. *effects of labeling*

g. *importance of stigma*

h. *techniques of neutralization*

i. *myth of mental illness*

ESSAY QUESTIONS

1. Discuss how the different sociological perspectives could be combined in order to provide a more complete picture of deviance.

2. Explain how forms of deviance such as street gangs can be both functional and dysfunctional at the same time.

3. In light of the different explanations for deviance, evaluate the effectiveness of the various reactions to deviance.

"DOWN-TO-EARTH SOCIOLOGY"

1. What can we learn about deviance from a cross-cultural perspective (p. 385)? How would the typical Canadian feel about driving a hunting knife through his elderly father's heart at the father's command? What would happen in Canada if a wife gathered her friends around her husband's bed to beat him because he had not satisfied her sexually? Can you think of some examples of covert norms that represent the real norms in our own society?

2. How did the reading material on youth, crime, and unemployment (p. 394) fit with your own picture of youth crime? Do you agree when the authors say that prison time is not the answer to youth crime? Why or why not? What does this suggest about proposals to reduce criminal activity among Canadian youth?

3. How would you explain the differential rates of imprisonment between Canada and the United States (p. 398) in sociological terms, using the theories presented in this chapter?

CHAPTER 17

POPULATION, URBANIZATION, AND THE ENVIRONMENT

☞ CHAPTER SUMMARY

- Demography is the study of the size, composition, growth, and distribution of human populations. Almost 200 years ago Thomas Malthus observed that populations grow geometrically while food supplies increase arithmetically; he argued that the population of the world would eventually outstrip its food supply. Many demographers today are convinced that the world is on a collision course with its food supply. Today, the basic cause of famine is the maldistribution of food rather than world overpopulation; however, the fact remains that the Least Industrialized Nations are growing fifteen times faster the Most Industrialized Nations.

- People in the Least Industrialized Nations have large families because children are viewed as gifts from God, it costs little to rear them, and they represent parents' social security. To project population trends, demographers use three demographic variables: fertility, mortality, and migration. A nation's growth rate is also affected by unanticipated variables like wars, famines, plagues, and changing economic and political conditions. The greatest challenge today is how to use technology to help the Least Industrialized Nations control their population and guarantee adequate food supplies to avoid malnutrition, starvation, and resource depletion.

- Cities can only develop if there is an agricultural surplus; the primary impetus to the development of cities was the invention of the plow about five or six thousand years ago. Urbanization, the process by which an increasing proportion of a population lives in cities, is so extensive today that some cities have become metropolises; in some cases metropolises have merged to form a megalopolis. Three major models have been proposed to explain how cities expand: the concentric-zone, sector, and multiple-nuclei models. These models fail to account for medieval cities, as well as many European cities and those in the Least Industrialized Nations.

- Some people find a sense of community in cities; others find alienation. To develop community in the city, people personalize their shopping, identify with sports teams, and even become sentimental about objects in the city. An essential element in determining whether someone finds community or alienation in the city is that person's social networks.

- Forces such as suburbanization, deindustrialization, and globalization have transformed Canadian cities.

- Today we face such environmental problems as acid rain, global warming, and the greenhouse effect. Environmental problems are worldwide, brought about by industrial production and urbanization, the pressures of population growth, and inadequate environmental regulation; the world today is facing a basic conflict between the lust for profits through the exploitation of the world's resources and the need to produce a sustainable environment. In response, a worldwide environmental movement has emerged, which seeks solutions in education, legislation, and political activism. If we are to survive, we must seek harmony between technology and the environment.

☞ LEARNING OBJECTIVES

As you read Chapter 17, use these learning objectives to organize your notes. After completing your reading, briefly state an answer to each of the objectives, and review the text pages in parentheses.

1. Discuss the Malthus theorem and identify key issues in the debate between New Malthusians and Anti-Malthusians regarding the specter of overpopulation. (406-409)
2. Outline the feminist perspective on the population debates. (409)
3. Explain why there is starvation. (409-410)
4. Explain why people in the Least Industrialized Nations have so many children and note the implications of different rates of population growth. (410-411)
5. State the three demographic variables used in estimating population growth and explain why it is difficult to forecast population growth. (411-414)
6. Describe urbanization and outline the history of how cities came into existence. (415-416)
7. Identify the trends contributing to the emergence of metropolises and megalopolises. (416)
8. Discuss urban patterns in Canada. (416)
9. Review the three models of urban growth and critique each of them. (416-417)
10. Explain why many people feel a sense of alienation by living in large urban areas. (419)
11. Define the urban village and briefly describe the different types of people who live in the city as identified by sociologist Herbert Gans. (420)
12. Describe ways in which city people create a sense of intimacy for themselves in large urban areas (420)
13. Outline the major changes facing Canadian cities regarding suburbanization, deindustrialization, and globalization. (420-421)
14. Describe the environmental problems in past civilizations. (421)
15. State ways in which nations at different stages of industrialization may have contributed to global environmental problems. (421-422)
16. Discuss the goals and activities of the environmental movement. (423)
17. List the assumptions of environmental sociology. (424)
18. Describe some of the actions which would be necessary to reach the goal of harmony between technology and the environment. (424)

☞ CHAPTER OUTLINE

I. **A Planet with No Space to Enjoy Life?**
   A. Demography is the study of size, composition, growth, distribution of populations.
   B. Thomas Malthus wrote *An Essay on the Principle of Population* (1798) stating the Malthus theorem—population grows geometrically while food supply increases arithmetically; thus, if births go unchecked, population will outstrip food supplies.
   C. New Malthusians believe Malthus was correct. The world population is following an exponential growth curve (where numbers increase in extraordinary proportions): 1800, one billion; 1930, two billion; 1960, three billion; 1975, four billion; and 1987, five billion. Right now, the world population has reached six billion.
   D. Anti-Malthusians believe that people do not blindly reproduce until there is no room left.
      1. They cite three stages of the demographic transition in Europe as an example. Stage 1, a fairly stable population (high birth rates offset by high death rates); Stage 2, "population explosion" (high birth rates and low death rates); and Stage 3, population stability (low birth rates and low death rates).

2. They assert this transition will happen in the Least Industrialized Nations, which currently are in the second stage.

3. Population shrinkage (a country's population is smaller because birth rate and immigration cannot replace those who die and emigrate) has occurred in Europe.

E. Who is correct? Only the future will prove the accuracy of either the projections of the New Malthusians or the Anti-Malthusians.

1. The New Malthusians interpret population growth negatively, while the Anti-Malthusians view the figures positively.

F. Feminists reject the population control strategies advanced by the New Malthusians, such as forced sterilization of women in the industrializing and least industrialized countries. They claim that these policies deprive women of freedom to make decisions about their own bodies.

1. Feminists argue that women's rights, particularly the right to decide one's reproductive future, must be recognized as human rights.

2. Feminist strategies to achieve population control include providing economic opportunities, education about birth control, and improving women's rights.

G. Why are people starving?

1. Anti-Malthusians note that the amount of food produced for each person in the world has increased: famines are not the result of too little food production, but result from maldistribution of existing food.

2. Recently, famines have been concentrated in Africa. However, these famines are not due to too many people living on too little land. Rather, these famines are due to outmoded farming techniques and ongoing political instability that disrupt harvests and food distribution.

II. Population Growth

A. Today, the populations of the Least Industrialized Nations are growing at fifteen times the rate of the Most Industrialized Nations; at these rates, the population of the average Most Industrialized Nation will double in 564 years, while the population of the average Least Industrialized Nation will do so in just 38 years.

B. Three reasons poor nations have so many children are: (1) the status that parenthood provides; (2) the community supports this view; and (3) children are considered to be economic assets (the parents rely on the children to take care of them in their old age). People in the Most Industrialized Nations see children as economic liabilities.

1. The symbolic interactionist perspective stresses that we need to understand these patterns within the framework of the culture and society in which the behavior occurs.

2. Feminists stress that in the Least Industrialized Nations, men dominate women in all spheres of life, including that of reproduction. There is an emphasis on male virility and dominance, including the fathering of many children, as a means of achieving status in the community.

C. Estimated population growth is based on three demographic variables:

1. Fertility, measured by the fertility rate (number of children an average woman bears), is sometimes confused with fecundity (number of children a woman theoretically can bear). To compute a country's fertility rate, demographers use crude birth rate (annual number of births per 1,000 people).

2. Mortality is measured by the crude death rate (number of deaths per 1,000 people).

3. Migration is measured by the net migration rate (difference between the number of immigrants moving in and emigrants moving out per 1,000 population); it may be voluntary or forced. Push factors make people want to leave where they are living

(e.g., persecution, lack of economic opportunity); pull factors attract people (e.g., opportunities in the new locale).

D. The growth rate equals births less deaths, plus net migration.

   1. Economic changes, government policies, and behavioral changes make it difficult to forecast population growth. The primary unknown factor that influences a country's growth rate is its rate of industrialization—in every country that industrializes, the growth rate declines.

   2. Because of the difficulties in forecasting population growth, demographers formulate several predictions simultaneously, each depending on different assumptions.

III. The Challenge of the Twenty-First Century

A. Today modern technology could be used to solve problems such as malnutrition. starvation, resource depletion, unrest, enforced migration, and armed conflict.

B. Technological advances are occurring in the Most Industrialized Nations. where there is slow population growth. The areas of the world where populations are rapidly expanding, and where there are many problems produced by this rapid expansion, do not have access to the technology to solve the problems.

C. The challenge is how to make technology available to the Least Industrialized Nations.

IV. Urbanization

A. A city is a place in which a large number of people are permanently based and do not produce their own food. Small cities with massive defensive walls existed as far back as 10,000 years ago.

B. The Industrial Revolution drew people to cities to work. Today urbanization not only means that more people live in cities, but also that today's cities are larger; about 300 of the world's cities contain one million people or more.

C. Urbanization is the process by which an increasing proportion of a population lives in cities. There are specific characteristics of cities, such as size and anonymity, that give them their unique urban flavor.

   1. Metropolis refers to cities that grow so large that they exert influence over a region; the central city and surrounding smaller cities and suburbs are connected economically, politically, and socially.

   2. Megalopolis refer to an overlapping area consisting of at least two metropolises and their suburbs, connected economically, socially, and sometimes politically.

D. In 1871, only about 18 percent of Canadians lived in small cities; by 1921, almost 50 percent of the Canadian population lived in urban areas; today, over four-fifths of Canadians live in cities.

   1. There is a hierarchy of cities in Canada, as not all Canadian cities are the same size, nor do they carry the same commercial or financial weight.

   2. Between 1991 and 1998 five of the ten fastest-growing metropolitan areas were in Ontario: Oshawa, Toronto, Kitchener, Windsor, and Ottawa-Hull.

   3. Toronto has the largest urban population, followed by Montreal, Vancouver, Ottawa-Hull, and Edmonton.

V. Models of Urban Growth

A. Robert Park coined the term human ecology to describe how people adapt to their environment (known as "urban ecology"); human ecologists have constructed three models which attempt to explain urban growth patterns:

B.   Ernest W. Burgess proposed the concentric-zone model.
1.   The city consists of a series of zones emanating from its center, with each characterized by a different group of people and activity: Zone 1—central business district; Zone 2—in transition with deteriorating housing and rooming houses; Zone 3—an area to which thrifty workers have moved to escape the zone in transition while maintaining access to work; Zone 4—more expensive apartments, single-family dwellings, and exclusive areas where the wealthy live; and Zone 5—commuter zone consisting of suburban areas or satellite cities that have developed around rapid transit routes.
2.   Burgess intended this model to represent the tendency for towns and cities to expand outward from the central business district.
C.   The sector model sees urban zones as wedge-shaped sectors radiating out from the center.
1.   A zone might contain a sector of working-class housing, another sector of expensive housing, a third of businesses, and so on, all competing with one another for the same land.
2.   In an invasion-succession cycle poor immigrants move into a city, settling in the lowest-rent area available; as their numbers grow, they begin to encroach on adjacent areas. As the poor move closer to the middle class, the middle class leave, expanding the sector of lower-cost housing.
3.   Gentrification is the movement of middle-class people into rundown areas of a city. As a consequence of gentrification, the poor are often displaced from their neighborhoods.
D.   The multiple-nuclei model views the city as comprised of multiple centers or nuclei, each of which focuses on a specialized activity (e.g., retail districts, automobile dealers, etc.).
E.   These models tell only a partial story of how cities are constructed. They reflect both the time frame and geographical region of the cities that were studied. They can not explain medieval cities, nor cities in other industrialized and the Least Industrialized Nations.

VI.   **City Life**
A.   Cities provide opportunities but also create problems. Humans have a need for community, which some people have a hard time finding in cities.
B.   Louis Wirth argued that the city undermines kinship and neighborhood, which are the traditional bases of social control and social solidarity.
1.   Urban dwellers live in anonymity, their lives marked by segmented and superficial encounters which make them grow aloof from one another and indifferent to other people's problems.
2.   This is similar to the idea that *Gemeinschaft* (a sense of community that comes from everyone knowing everyone else) is ripped apart as a country industrializes, and *Gesellschaft* (a society characterized by secondary, impersonal relationships which result in alienation) replaces it.
C.   The city is made up of a series of smaller worlds, within which people find a sense of community, or belonging.
D.   Herbert Gans identified types of people who live in the city.
1.   Cosmopolites—intellectuals and professionals, students, writers, and artists who live in the inner city to be near its conveniences and cultural benefits.
2.   Singles—young, unmarried people who come seeking jobs and entertainment.
3.   Ethnic villagers—live in tightly knit neighborhoods that resemble villages and small towns, united by race and social class.

4. The trapped—who consist of four subtypes: those who could not afford to move when their neighborhood was invaded by another ethnic group; downwardly mobile persons who have fallen from a higher social class; elderly people who have drifted into the slums because they are not wanted elsewhere and are powerless to prevent their downward slide; and alcoholics and drug addicts.

E. The city is divided into worlds that people come to know down to the smallest detail.
1. City people create a sense of intimacy for themselves by personalizing their shopping (by frequenting the same stores and restaurants, people become recognized as "regulars").
2. Spectator sports also engender community identification.
3. City dwellers develop strong feelings for particular objects and locations in the city such as trees, buildings, rivers, lakes, parks, and even street corners.

F. An essential element in determining whether someone finds community or alienation in a city is that person's social networks; community is found in relationships, not in buildings and space.

G. Suburbanization is the movement from the city to the suburbs. For the past 100 years, people have moved to towns next to the cities in which they worked.

H. The development of a global market has led to deindustrialization. Manufacturing firms have relocated from the inner city to areas where production costs are lower.

1. Hundreds of thousands of manufacturing jobs were eliminated.

2. The inner-city economies have not been able to provide alternative employment for poor residents, thereby locking them out of the economy.

VII.   The Natural Environment

A. Environmental problems are not new to the human scene. Several civilizations were destroyed because the environment on which their existence depended was destroyed.

B. Industrialization led to a major assault on the environment. While it has been viewed as good for the nation's welfare, it has also contributed to today's environmental problems.
1. Many of our problems today—depletion of the ozone layer, acid rain, the greenhouse effect, and global warming—are associated with our dependence on fossil fuels.
2. There is an abundant source of natural energy that would provide low-cost power and therefore help to raise the living standards of human across the globe. More technology is needed to harness this energy supply. From a conflict perspective, such abundant sources of energy present a threat to the multinationals' energy monopoly. We cannot expect the practical development and widespread use of alternative sources of power until the multinationals have cornered the market on the technology that will harness them.

C. Environmental degradation is also a problem in the industrializing nations, as these countries rushed into global industrial competition without the funds to purchase expensive pollution controls.
1. Pollution was treated as a state secret in the former Soviet Union. With protest stifled, no environmental protection laws to inhibit pollution, and production quotas to be met, environmental pollution was rampant.
2. Almost one-half of Russia's arable land is unsuitable for farming, air pollution in cities is ten times higher than that which is permitted in the U.S., and half the tap water is unfit to drink.
3. The consequence of these conditions is that Russian life expectancy has dropped.

D. The combined pressures of population growth and almost nonexistent environmental regulations destine least industrialized nations to become the earth's major source of pollution. Some companies in industrialized nations use the least industrialized nations as a garbage dump for hazardous wastes and for producing chemicals no longer tolerated in their own countries.

1.   As tropical rain forests are cleared for lumber, farms and pastures, the consequence may be the extinction of numerous plant and animal species.

2.   As the rain forests disappear at a rate of nearly 2500 acres every hour, it is estimated that 10,000 species are made extinct each year.

E.   The globalization of capitalism underlies today's environmental decay.

1.   The highly industrialized nations continue to push for economic growth, the industrializing nations strive to achieve faster economic growth, and the least industrialized nations, anxious to enter the race, push for even faster growth.

2.   If our goal is a sustainable environment, we must stop turning the earth's natural resources into trash.

F.   Concern about the world's severe environmental problems has produced a worldwide social movement. In some countries, the environment has become a major issue in local and national elections. This movement seeks solutions in education, legislation, and political activism.

G.   Environmental sociology examines the relationship between human societies and the environment. Its basic assumptions include: (1) the physical environment is a significant variable in sociological investigation; (2) humans are but one species among many that are dependent on the environment; (3) because of intricate feedbacks to nature, human actions have many unintended consequences; (4) the world is finite, so there are potential physical limits to economic growth; (5) economic expansion requires increased extraction of resources from the environment; (6) increased extraction of resources leads to ecological problems; (7) these ecological problems place restrictions on economic expansion; and (8) the state creates environmental problems by trying to create conditions for the profitable accumulation of capital.

H.   If we are to have a world that is worth passing on to the coming generations, we must seek harmony between technology and the natural environment.

☞ KEY TERMS

After studying the chapter, review the definition for each of the following terms.

acid rain: rain containing sulfuric and nitric acid (produced by the reaction of sulfur dioxide and nitrogen oxide with moisture when released into the air with the burning of fossil fuels)

basic demographic equation: growth rate = births − deaths + net migration

city: a place in which a large number of people are permanently based and do not produce their own food

community: a place people identify with, where they sense that they belong and that others care what happens to them

crude birth rate: the annual number of births per 1,000 population

crude death rate: the annual number of deaths per 1,000 population

demographic transition: a three-stage historical process of population growth; first, high birth rates and high death rates; second, high birth rates and low death rates; and third, low birth rates and low death rates

demographic variables: the three factors that influence population growth: fertility, mortality, and net migration

demography: the study of the size, composition, growth, and distribution of human populations

environmental sociology: a subdiscipline of sociology that examines how human activities affect the physical environment and how the physical environment affects human activities

exponential growth curve: a pattern of growth in which numbers double during approximately equal intervals, thus accelerating in the latter stages

fecundity: the number of children that women are theoretically capable of bearing

fertility rate: the number of children that the average woman bears

gentrification: the displacement of the poor by the relatively affluent, who renovate the former's homes

global warming: an increase in the earth's temperature due to the greenhouse effect

greenhouse effect: the buildup of carbon dioxide in the earth's atmosphere that allows light to enter but inhibits the release of heat; believed to cause global warming

growth rate: the net change in a population after adding births, subtracting deaths, and either adding or subtracting net migration

human ecology: Robert Park's term for the relationship between people and their environment (natural resources such as land)

invasion-succession cycle: the process of one group of people displacing a group whose racial-ethnic or social class characteristics differ from their own

Malthus theorem: an observation by Thomas Malthus that although the food supply increases only arithmetically (from 1 to 2 to 3 to 4 and so on), population grows geometrically (from 2 to 4 to 8 to 16 and so forth)

megalopolis: an urban area consisting of at least two metropolises and their many suburbs

metropolis: a central city surrounded by smaller cities and their suburbs

metropolitan statistical area (MSA): a central city and the urbanized counties adjacent to it

net migration rate: the difference between the number of immigrants and emigrants per 1,000 population

population shrinkage: the process by which a country's population becomes smaller because its birth rate and immigration are too low to replace those who die and emigrate

suburb: the communities adjacent to the political boundaries of a city

suburbanization: the movement from the city to the suburbs

sustainable environment: a world system that takes into account the limits of the environment, produces enough material goods for everyone's needs, and leaves a heritage of a sound environment for the next generation

urbanization: the process by which an increasing proportion of a population live in cities

zero population growth: a demographic condition in which women bear only enough children to reproduce the population

☞ KEY PEOPLE

Review the major theoretical contributions or findings of these people.

Ernest Burgess: Burgess developed the concentric zone model of urban development.

William Faunce: Writing about the far-reaching implications of exponential growth, this sociologist's views are consistent with the New Malthusians'.

William Flanagan: Flanagan has suggested three guiding principles for finding solutions to pressing urban problems—use of regional planning, awareness of human needs, and equalizing the benefits as well as the impact of urban change.

Herbert Gans: Gans studied urban neighborhoods, with the result that he documented the existence of community within cities and identified the several different types of urban dwellers that live there.

Chauncey Harris and Edward Ullman: These two geographers developed the multiple-nuclei model of urban growth.

Homer Hoyt: Hoyt modified Burgess's model of urban growth with the development of the sector model.

David Karp and William Yoels: These sociologists note that identification with a city's sports teams can be so intense that even after an individual moves away from the city, he or she continues to root for the team.

Thomas Malthus: Malthus was an economist who made dire predictions about the future of population growth.

Steven Mosher: This anthropologist, an anti-Malthusian, predicts that the world's population will decline sharply after peaking at about 7 billion in the year 2030.

Robert Park: Park coined the term "human ecology" to describe how people adapt to their environment.

Kathleen Riel: Riel is a Canadian sociologist who studies matters affecting the environment.

Victor Rodriguez: This sociologist points out that many U.S. industries have abandoned local communities and moved their factories to places where labor costs are lower because of competitive pressures of a global market.

Julian Simon: Simon is an anti-Malthusian who believes people do not just reproduce blindly but act intelligently and plan rationally. Simon has also argued that immigrants are a net contributor on the U.S. economy.

Gregory Stone: Stone observed how city people create a sense of intimacy for themselves by personalizing their shopping.

Louis Wirth: Wirth wrote a classic essay, "Urbanism as a Way of Life," in which he argued that city life undermines kinship and neighborhood.

Richard Wohl and Anseim Strauss: These sociologists have pointed out that city dwellers even develop strong feelings for particular objects and locations in the city.

☞ SELF-TEST

After completing this self-test, check your answers against the Answer Key at the back of this Study Guide and against the text on page(s) indicated in parentheses.

MULTIPLE CHOICE QUESTIONS

1.   Who is it that studies the size, composition, growth, and distribution of human population? (406)
   a.   Population experts
   b.   Growth specialists
   c.   Demographers
   d.   Social development professionals

2.   The proposition that the population grows geometrically while food supply increases arithmetically is known as the: (406)
   a.   food surplus equation.
   b.   Malthus theorem.
   c.   exponential growth curve.
   d.   demographic transition.

3. Which of the following statements is consistent with beliefs of the anti-Malthusians? (407-409)
    a. People will blindly reproduce until there is no room left on earth.
    b. It is possible to project the world's current population growth into the indefinite future.
    c. Most people do not use intelligence and rational planning when it comes to having children.
    d. The demographic transition provides an accurate picture of what the future looks like.

4. The three-stage historical process of population growth is known as the: (408)
    a. demographic equation.
    b. demographic transition.
    c. exponential growth curve.
    d. implosion growth curve.

5. The process by which a country's population becomes smaller because its birth rate and immigration are too low to replace those who die and emigrate is: (408-409)
    a. population transfer.
    b. population annihilation.
    c. population shrinkage.
    d. population depletion.

6. Starvation occurs because: (409-410)
    a. there is not enough fertile land worldwide on which to grow food.
    b. some parts of the world lack food while other parts of the world produce more than they can consume.
    c. population is growing at a faster rate than the world's ability to produce food.
    d. forces in nature—droughts, pests, floods—wipe out food supplies.

7. Why do people in the Least Industrialized Nations have so many children? (410-411)
    a. parenthood provides status
    b. children are considered to be an economic asset
    c. the community encourages people to have children
    d. All of the above

8. What are the factors that influence population growth called? (411)
    a. demographic variables
    b. demographic transitions
    c. demographic equations
    d. demographic constants

9. _____ refers to the number of children the average women bears. (412)
    a. Fertility rate
    b. Fecundity
    c. Crude birth rate
    d. Real birth rate

10. The annual number of deaths per 1,000 population is the: (412)
    a. crude death rate.
    b. crude mortality rate.
    c. crude life expectancy rate.
    d. net death rate.

11. What factors might push someone to migrate? (412)
    a. poverty
    b. lack of religious and political freedom
    c. political persecution
    d. All of the above

12. According to your text, why is it difficult to forecast population growth? (412)
    a. Government programs may encourage or discourage women from having children.
    b. Government bureaus may be dishonest in reporting data.
    c. There is a lack of computer programs to deal with data adequately.
    d. Births, deaths, and migration are human behaviors and thus extremely difficult to predict.

13. The process by which an increasing proportion of a population lives in cities is: (415)
    a. suburbanization.
    b. gentrification.
    c. megalopolitanism.
    d. urbanization.

14. What does today's rapid urbanization mean? (416)
    a. More people live in cities.
    b. Today's cities are larger.
    c. About 200 of the world's cities contain at least one million people.
    d. All of the above.

15. Who first proposed the concentric-zone model? (416)
    a. Herbert Gans.
    b. Ernest Burgess.
    c. Robert Park.
    d. Homer Hoyt.

16. When a new group of immigrants enter a city, they tend to settle in low-rent areas. As their numbers increase, those already living in the area begin to move out; their departure creates more low-cost housing for the immigrants. How do sociologists refer to this process? (417)
    a. progressive population replacement.
    b. reverse gentrification.
    c. cycle of assimilation.
    d. invasion-succession cycle.

17. The model which suggests that land use in cities is based on several centers, such as a clustering of restaurants or automobile dealerships, is the: (417)
    a. sector model.
    b. concentric-zone model.
    c. multiple-nuclei model.
    d. commerce model.

18. While a sense of community is natural to *Gemeinschaft*, as a society industrializes *Gesellschaft* emerges, with relationships based on: (419)
    a. chaos.
    b. impersonality.
    c. alienation.
    d. disorientation.

19. According to Gans's typology, the trapped include: (420)
    a. downwardly mobile persons.
    b. elderly persons.
    c. alcoholics and drug addicts.
    d. All of the above.

20. What is suburbanization? (420)
    a. movement from the suburbs to edge cities
    b. movement from the city to the suburbs
    c. movement from rural areas to suburbs
    d. displacement of the poor by the relatively affluent, who renovate the former's homes

21. The consequence of burning fossil fuels is: (421)
    a. acid rain.
    b. the greenhouse effect.
    c. global warming.
    d. All of the above.

22. How do conflict theorists explain the energy shortage? (421-422)
    a. They note that the earth has a limited supply of energy, and that multinational corporations are rapidly depleting it.
    b. There is no reliable alternative to the internal combustion engine.
    c. They argue that multinational corporations are unwilling to develop alternative energy sources, because it would threaten their monopoly over existing fossil fuels and cut into their profits.
    d. As a result of the past exploitation of natural resources by profit-hungry multinational corporations, there are no longer alternative energy resources that are reliable.

23. Which of the following presents the greatest threat to the survival of numerous plant and animal species? (422)
    a. the continued burning of fossil fuels
    b. the dumping of toxic waste in the least industrialized nations
    c. the disappearance of the world's rain forests
    d. the greenhouse effect

24. Environmental sociology examines: (424)
    a. how the physical environment affects human activities.
    b. how human activities affect the physical environment.
    c. the unintended consequences of human actions.
    d. All of the above.

25. What is the goal of environmental sociologists? (424)
    a. to stop pollution
    b. to do research on the mutual impact that individuals and environments have on one another
    c. to empower those who are disadvantaged by environmental threats so that the quality of their lives will be improved
    d. to lobby for alternatives to fossil fuels

TRUE-FALSE QUESTIONS

T F 1. Thomas Malthus was a sociologist at the University of Chicago in the 192Os. (406)

T F 2. The exponential growth curve is based on the idea that if growth doubles during approximately equal intervals of time, it accelerates in the latter stages. (406)

T F 3. The Anti-Malthusians believe that people breed like germs in a bucket. (408)

T F 4. There are four stages in the process of demographic transition. (408)

T F 5. The main reason why there is starvation is because there are too many people in the world today and too little food to feed them all. (409-410)

T F 6. The major reason why people in the Least Industrialized Nations have so many children is because they do not know how to prevent conception. (410-411)

T F 7. Demographers study fertility, mortality, and migration to project population trends. (412)

T F 8. The fertility rate refers to the number of children that the average woman bears. (412)

T F 9. Migration rates do not affect the global population. (412)

T F 10. It is difficult for demographers to forecast population growth. (412)

T F 11. The rate and extent of urbanization in recent years is new to the world scene. (415)

T F 12. The concentric-zone model is based on the idea that cities expand radially from their central business district. (416)

T F 13. The multiple-nuclei model is the most accurate model of urban growth. (417)

T F 14. The Urban Villagers was written by Herbert Gans. (420)

T F 15. Sports teams often engender community identification in urban areas. (420)

T F 16. Environmental problems have only recently emerged on the human scene. (421)

T F 17. Rain containing sulfuric and nitric acid, released into the air with the burning of fossil fuels, is a cause of the greenhouse effect. (421)

T F 18. Scientists are in agreement that the problems of acid rain and the greenhouse effect must be solved quickly. (421)

T F 19. Environmental sociology examines the relationship between human societies and the environment. (424)

T F 20. The goal of environmental sociology is to reduce pollution levels on a global scale. (424)

FILL-IN QUESTIONS

1. _____ is the study of the size, composition, growth, and distribution of human populations. (406)

2. A pattern of growth in which numbers double during approximately equal intervals, thus accelerating in the latter stages is the _____. (406)

3. The Anti-Malthusians believe that Europe's _____, a three-stage historical process of population growth, provides an accurate picture of the future. (408)

4. When the people in a society do not produce enough children to replace the people who die, there is concern about _____. (409)

5. The _____ refers to the number of children that the average woman bears. (412)

6. The basic demographic equation is *growth* = _____ − _____ + _____. (412)

7. When women bear only enough children to replace the population, _____has been achieved. (412)

8. _____ is a place in which a large number of people are permanently based and do not produce their own food. (415)

9. _____ is the process by which an increasing number of people live in cities. (416)

10. A central city, surrounded by smaller cities and their suburbs, forming an interconnected urban area, is a _____. (416)

11. _____ is the relationship between people and their environment. (416)

12. The displacement of the poor by the relatively affluent, who renovate the former's homes, is _____. (417)
13. _____ exists when people identify with an area and with one another. (419)
14. The greenhouse effect is believed to produce _____. (421)
15. A world system that takes into account the limits of the environment, produces enough material goods for everyone's needs, and leaves a heritage of a sound environment for the next generation is the definition of _____. (423)

MATCH THESE SOCIAL SCIENTISTS WITH THEIR CONTRIBUTIONS

__1. Thomas Malthus   a. *theorem on population growth*
__2. Ernest Burgess   b. *human ecology*
__3. Herbert Gans   c. *concentric-zone model*
__4. Homer Hoyt   d. *urban villagers*
__5. Robert Park   e. *sector model*

ESSAY QUESTIONS

1. State the positions of the New Malthusians and the Anti-Malthusians and discuss which view you think is more accurate, based on the information provided about each position.
2. Identify the problems that are associated with forecasting population growth.
3. Discuss whether or not cities are impersonal *Gesellschafts* or communal *Gemeinschafts*.
4. Discuss the role that global stratification plays in the worldwide environmental problems.

"DOWN-TO-EARTH SOCIOLOGY"

1. What was your reaction after reading "Killing Little Girls" on page 414? Why is this practice common in certain cultures and not others? What social, economic or political changes would contribute to the elimination of this practice?
2. As we look to the 21st century, we need to find ways to use technology to improve the quality of life around the globe (p. 414-415). This might involve reproductive technologies or those that boost food production and create employment. If you lived in a least industrialized nation how would you view these things? Would you see them as enhancing your life, or threatening it?
3. How does the picture of urban living painted on page 418 match your own "picture" of what life is like in the Least Industrialized Nations? Do the lives of people in these nations have any bearing on your life? Why or why not?
4. Do you think "Ecosabotage," (pp. 423), is ever justified? Do you think radical acts can do more harm than good? Do they alienate or unite supporters of the movement?

CHAPTER 18
SOCIAL MOVEMENTS AND SOCIAL CHANGE

☞ CHAPTER SUMMARY

- Early theorists argued that individuals are transformed by crowds, losing all capacity for rationality. Terms such as "herd mentality," "collective mind," and "circular reaction" were developed to explain why people behaved as they did when in the midst of a crowd. According to Herbert Blumer, crowds go through five stages before they become an acting crowd: social unrest, an exciting event, milling, a common object of attention, and common impulses.

- Contemporary explanations emphasize the rationality of the crowd, the emergence of norms to govern behavior; collective behavior is seen as directed toward a goal, even if it is cruel and destructive behavior.

- Some of the major forms of collective behavior are riots, panics, moral panics, rumors, fads, fashions, and urban legends. Conditions of discontent and uncertainty provide fertile ground for collective behavior.

- Social movements usually involve more people, are more prolonged, are more organized, and focus on social change. Depending on whether their target is individuals or society and the amount of change desired is partial or complete, social movements can be classified as alternative, redemptive, reformative, or transformative.

- Tactics are chosen on the basis of a group's levels of membership, its publics, and its relationship to authority. Because the mass media are the gatekeepers, their favorable or unfavorable coverage greatly affects a social movement and tactics are chosen with the media in mind.

- Mass society theory, relative deprivation theory and ideological commitment theory all attempt to explain why people join social movements.

- Social movements go through distinct stages: initial unrest and agitation; resource mobilization; organization; institutionalization; organizational decline and possible resurgence. Resource mobilization is the crucial factor that enables social movements to make it past the first stage.

- Social change, the alteration of culture and society over time, is a vital part of social life.

- William Ogburn identified three processes of social change. Technology can lead to social change through innovation, discovery, and diffusion. Cultural lag refers to the changes in the symbolic culture in response to changes in technology.

- Technology is a driving force in social change, and it can shape an entire society by changing existing technology, social organization, ideology, values, and social relationships, as is evident when analyzing the impact that both the automobile and the computer have had on Canadian society.

- Other theories of social change include: evolutionary theories (both unilinear and multilinear), Marxist conflict theories, cyclical theories, feminist theories, and postmodern theories.

- Social movements rarely solve all of society's social problems. However, many have become powerful forces for social change.

☞ LEARNING OBJECTIVES

As you read Chapter 18, use these learning objectives to organize your notes. After completing your reading, briefly state an answer to each of the objectives, and review the text pages in parentheses.

1. Discuss early explanations of collective behavior and note how these explanations focused on the transformation of the individual. (430-432)

2.   Compare and contrast the minimax strategy and the emergent norm theory. (432-433)
3.   Describe the forms of collective behavior, including riots and demonstrations, panic, moral panic, rumors, fads and fashions, and urban legends. (433-437)
4.   Compare and contrast proactive and reactive social movements. (437)
5.   List the different types of social movements, classifying them according to their target and the amount of change they seek. (437-439)
6.   Describe the role that each of the following plays in influencing leadership choice of tactics: membership levels, publics, and relationships to authorities. (439-440)
7.   Define propaganda and discuss the role of the mass media in social movements. (440-442)
8.   Compare the different explanations of why people join social movements. (442-443)
9.   Discuss the role of the agent provocateur in social movements. (443)
10.   Identify the five stages that social movements go through as they grow and mature. (443-444)
11.   Identify the double meaning of technology and discuss the role of technology in postmodern societies. (445)
12.   Identify and define Ogburn's three processes of social change, explain what is meant by "cultural lag," and evaluate the utility of Ogburn's theory. (446)
13.   Using automobiles or computers, explain how technology transforms society. (446-449)
14.   State the impact that computers will have on social inequality in the 21st century. (449-450)
15.   Explain the relationship between technology and shifts in the global map and discuss threats posed by the resurgence of ethnic conflicts. (450-451)
16.   Outline the alternative theories of social change, including evolutionary, Marxist, cyclical, feminist, and postmodern theories. (451)

☞ CHAPTER OUTLINE

I.   **Early Explanations of Collective Behavior: The Transformation of the Individual**
        A.   Collective behavior is characterized by a group of people becoming emotionally aroused and engaging in extraordinary behavior, in which the usual norms do not apply.
        B.   In 1852, Charles Mackay concluded that when people were in crowds, they sometimes went "mad" and did "disgraceful and violent things;" just as a herd of cows will stampede, so people can come under the control of a "herd mentality."
        C.   Based on Mackay's idea, Gustave LeBon stressed that the individual is transformed by the crowd.
                1.   In a crowd, people feel anonymous, not accountable for what they do; they develop feelings of invincibility, believing that together they can accomplish anything. A collective mind develops.
                2.   They become highly suggestible; this paves the way for contagion, a kind of collective hypnosis, which releases the destructive instincts that society has so carefully repressed.
        D.   To LeBon's analysis, Robert Park added the ideas of social unrest, which is transmitted from one individual to another, and circular reaction, the back-and-forth communication between the members of a crowd whereby a "collective impulse" is transmitted.
        E.   Using symbolic interaction theory and synthesizing both LeBon's and Park's ideas, Herbert Blumer identified five stages of collective behavior.
                1.   A background condition of social unrest exists—when people's routine activities are thwarted or when they develop new needs that go unsatisfied.
                2.   An exciting event occurs—one so startling that people are preoccupied with it.
                3.   People engage in milling—the act of standing or walking around as they talk about the exciting event and circular reaction sets in.

4. A common object of attention emerges—people's attention becomes riveted on some aspect of the event.

5. Stimulation of the common impulses occurs—people collectively agree about what they should do. Social contagion, described as a collective excitement passed from one person to another, becomes the mechanism that stimulates these common impulses. The end result is an acting crowd—an excited group that collectively moves toward a goal, which may be constructive or destructive.

II. The Contemporary View: The Rationality of the Crowd

A. Richard Berk pointed out that people use a minimax strategy (trying to minimize their costs and maximize their rewards) whether in small groups or in crowds; the fewer the costs and the greater the rewards that people anticipate, the more likely they are to carry out a particular act.

B. Ralph Turner and Lewis Killian noted that human behavior is regulated by the normative order—socially approved ways of doing things that make up our everyday life —but when an extraordinary event occurs and existing norms do not cover the new situation, people develop new norms to deal with the problem (emergent norms).

1. There are five kinds of crowd participants: (1) the ego-involved, who feel a high personal stake in the event; (2) the concerned, who have a personal interest in the event, but less than the ego-involved; (3) the insecure, who have little concern about the issue but have sought out the crowd because it gives them a sense of power and security; (4) the curious spectators, who are inquisitive and may cheer the crowd on even though they do not care about the issue; and (5) the exploiters, who do not care about the issue but use it for their own purposes (e.g., hawking food or T-shirts).

2. The concept of emergent norms is important because it points to a rational process as the essential component of collective behavior.

III. Forms of Collective Behavior

A. Riots, such as the one which erupted in Los Angeles after the verdict in the Rodney King trial, are usually caused by frustration and anger at deprivation.

1. Frustration develops from a perception of being kept out of the mainstream society—limited to a meager education, denied jobs and justice, and kept out of good neighborhoods—and builds to such a boiling point that it takes only a precipitating event to erupt in collective behavior.

2. It is not only the deprived who participate in riots or demonstrations; others, who are not deprived, but who still feel frustration at the underlying social conditions that place them at a disadvantage, also get involved.

3. The event that precipitates a riot is much less important than the riot's general context.

B. Panic, like the one which occurred following the broadcast of H. G. Wells's "War of the Worlds," is behavior that results when people become so fearful that they cannot function normally.

1. One explanation as to why people panic is because they are anxious about some social condition.

2. This is why it is against the law to shout "Fire!" in a public building when no such danger exists—if people fear immediate death, they will lunge toward the nearest exit in a frantic effort to escape.

3. Sociologists have found that not everyone panics in these situations, and some employees, such as some of those at the supper club, engage in role extension—the incorporation of additional activities into a role—to try to help people to safety.

    C.   Moral panics occur when large numbers of people become intensely concerned, even fearful, about some behavior that is perceived as a threat to morality—the threat is seen as enormous and hostility builds toward those thought responsible.

        1.   Like other panics, moral panics center around a sense of danger. But, because they involve larger numbers of people and are fostered by the mass media, moral panics, as opposed to other forms of panic, do not arise as quickly.

        2.   Moral panics are often fed by rumor, information for which there is no discernible source and which is usually unfounded.

        3.   Moral panics also thrive on uncertainty and anxiety.

    D.   Rumors thrive in conditions of ambiguity, functioning to fill in missing information.

        1.   Most rumors are short-lived and arise in a situation of ambiguity, only to dissipate when they are replaced either by another rumor or by factual information. A few rumors have a long life because they hit a responsive cord (e.g., rumors of mass poisoning of soft drink products that spread to many countries).

        2.   Three main factors in why people believe rumors are that they: (1) deal with a subject that is important to an individual; (2) replace ambiguity with some form of certainty; and (3) are attributed to a creditable source.

    E.   A fad is a temporary pattern of behavior that catches people's attention, while fashion is a more enduring version of the same.

        1.   John Loftand identified four types of fads: (1) object fads, such as the hula hoop or pet rocks; (2) activity fads, such as eating goldfish or playing Trivial Pursuit: (3) idea fads, such as astrology; and (4) personality fads. such as Elvis Presley, Vanna White, and Michael Jordan.

        2.   Fashion is a behavior pattern that catches people's attention, lasting longer than a fad. Most often thought of in terms of clothing fashions, it can also refer to hairstyles, home decorating, design and colors of buildings, and language.

    F.   Urban legends are stories with an ironic twist that sound realistic but are false. Jan Brunvand, who studied the transmission of urban legends, concluded that urban legends are passed on by people who think that the event really happened to someone, such as a "friend of a friend"; the stories have strong appeal and gain credibility from naming specific people or local places; and they are "modern morality stories," with each teaching a moral lesson about life.

IV.   Social Movements

    A.   Social movements consist of large numbers of people, who, through deliberate and sustained efforts, organize to promote or resist social change. At the heart of social movements lie grievances and dissatisfactions.

    B.   Proactive social movements promote social change because a current condition of society is intolerable. In contrast, reactive social movements resist changing conditions in society which they perceive as threatening. To further their goals, people develop social movement organizations.

    C.   The National Action Committee on the Status of Women, The Council of Canadians, and the National Indian Brotherhood are all examples of social movement organizations in Canada whose goal is to promote social change.

V.   Types and Tactics of Social Movements

    A.   David Aberle classified social movements into four broad categories according to the type and amount of social change they seek.

        1.   Two types seek to change people but differ in terms of the amount of change desired: alternative social movements seek to alter only particular aspects of people

(e.g., Mothers Against Drunk Driving); while redemptive social movements seek to change people totally (e.g., a religious social movement such as fundamental Christianity that stresses conversion).

2. Two types seek to change society but also differ in terms of the amount of change desired: reformative social movements seek to reform only one part of society (e.g., the environment); transformative social movements seek to change the social order itself and to replace it with their own version of the ideal society (e.g., revolutions in the American colonies, France, Russia, and Cuba).

3. Today some social movements, called new social movements, have a global orientation, committed to changing a specific condition throughout the world. The women's, environmental, and animal rights movements are examples.

B. Tactics of social movements are best understood by examining levels of membership, publics they address, and their relationship to authorities.

1. Three levels of membership are the inner core (the leadership that sets goals. timetables, etc.); people committed to the goals of the movement, but not to the same degree as members of the inner core; and people who are neither as committed nor as dependable.

2. Publics can be described as sympathetic (sympathize with goals of movement but have no commitment to movement), hostile (keenly aware of group's goals and want the movement stopped), and people who are unaware of or indifferent toward the movement. In selecting tactics, the leadership considers these different types of publics.

3. The movement's relationship to the authorities is important in determining tactics: if authorities are hostile to a social movement, aggressive or even violent tactics are likely; if authorities are sympathetic, violence is not likely. If a social movement is institutionalized, accepted by the authorities and given access to resources they control, the likelihood of violence is very low.

4. Other factors that can influence the choice of tactics include the nature of friendships, race, and even the size of towns.

C. In selecting tactics, leaders of social movements are aware of their effects on the mass media. Their goal is to influence public opinion about some issue.

1. Propaganda is a key to understanding social movements. Propaganda simply means the presentation of information in an attempt to influence people.

2. The mass media play a critical role in social movements. They have become, in effect, the gatekeepers to social movements. If those who control and work in the mass media are sympathetic to a "cause," it will receive sympathetic treatment. If the social movement goes against their own biases, it will either be ignored or receive unfavorable treatment.

VI. **Why People Join Social Movements**

A. In the mass society theory, William Kornhauser proposed that social movements offer a sense of belonging to people who have weak social ties.

1. Mass society, characterized as an industrialized, highly bureaucratized, impersonal society, makes many people feel isolated and, as a result, they are attracted to social movements because they offer a sense of belonging.

2. However Doug McAdam (who studied those involved in civil rights movements) found that many who participate in social movements have strong family and community ties, and joined such movements to right wrongs and overcome injustice, not because of isolation. The most isolated (the homeless) generally do not join anything except food lines.

B. According to deprivation theory people who are deprived of things deemed valuable in society—whether money, justice, status, or privilege—join social movements with the hope of redressing their grievances.

1. Absolute deprivation is people's actual negative condition; relative deprivation is what people think they should have relative to what others have, or even compared with their own past or perceived future.

2. While the notion of absolute deprivation provides a beginning point for looking at why people join social movements, it is even more important to look at relative deprivation in trying to understand why people join social movements.

3. Improved conditions fuel human desires for even better conditions, and thus can spark revolutions.

C. James Jasper and Dorothy Nelkin note that people join a particular social movement because of moral issues and an ideological commitment to the movement. It is the moral component, they argue, that is a primary reason for some people's involvement in social movements.

D. An agent provocateur is a special type of social movement participant.

1. An agent of the government or of a social movement, the agent provocateur's job is to spy on the leadership and sabotage their activities. Some are recruited from the membership itself, while others go underground and join the movement.

2. On occasion a police agent is converted to the social movement on which he or she is spying. Sociologist Gary Marx noted that this occurs because the agent, to be credible, must share at least some of the class, age, ethnic, racial, religious, or sexual characteristics of the group. This makes the agent more likely to sympathize with the movement's goals and to become disenchanted with the means being used to destroy the group.

3. Sometimes the agent provocateur will go to great lengths, even breaking the law, to push the social movement into illegal activities.

VII. On the Success and Failure of Social Movements

A. Social movements have a life course; that is, they go through five stages as they grow and mature.

1. Initial unrest and agitation because people are upset about some social condition; at this stage leaders emerge who verbalize people's feelings.

2. Mobilization of resources such as time, money, people's skills, technologies, attention by the mass media, and legitimacy among the public and authorities.

3. An organization emerges with a division of labor, with leadership that makes policy decisions and a rank and file that actively supports the movement.

4. Institutionalization occurs as the movement becomes bureaucratized and leadership passes to career officials who may care more about their position in the organization than about the movement itself.

5. The organization declines, but there may be a possibility of resurgence. Some movements cease to exist; others become reinvigorated.

VIII. An Overview of Social Change

A. Social change is a shift in the characteristics of culture and societies over time.

IX. How Technology Changes Society

A. Technology refers to both the tools used to accomplish tasks and to the skills or procedures to make and use those tools.

1. Technology is an artificial means of extending human abilities.

      2.   Although all human groups use technology, it is the chief characteristic of postindustrial societies because it greatly extends our abilities to analyze information, to communicate, and to travel.

      3.   The way technology alters people's way of life is of great significance.

B.   Modernization (the change from traditional to modern societies) produces sweeping changes in societies.

C.   William Ogburn identified three processes of social change.

      1.   *Inventions* can be either material (computers) or social (capitalism); *discovery* is a new way of seeing things; and *diffusion* is the spread of an invention, discovery, or idea, from one area to another.

      2.   Ogburn coined the term cultural lag to describe the situation in which some elements of a culture adapt to an invention or discovery more rapidly than others. We are constantly trying to catch up with technology by adapting our customs and ways of life to meet its needs.

D.   Ogburn has been criticized because of his view that technology controls almost all social change.

      1.   People also take control over technology, developing the technology they need and selectively using existing technology. Both can happen—technology leads to social change, and social change leads to technology.

E.   New technologies can reshape an entire society. Five ways in which technology can shape an entire society are: (1) Transformation of existing technologies; (2) Changes in social organization; (3) Changes in ideology; (4) Transformation of values; and (5) Transformation of social relationships.

F.   The automobile is an example of technological change. The automobile has pushed aside old technology; it has changed the shape of cities; it has changed architecture; it has changed courtship practices and sexual norms; and it has had a major effect on the lives of women.

G.   The computer is another example, changing medicine, education, and the workplace. On the negative side are increased surveillance of workers and depersonalization.

H.   With the information superhighway, homes and businesses are connected by a rapid flow of information. The implications of this superhighway for national and global stratification are severe.

      1.   On a national level, we may end up with information have-nots, thus perpetuating existing inequalities.

      2.   On a global level, the highly industrialized nations will control the information superhighway, thereby destining the least industrialized nations to a perpetual pauper status.

I.   Today's global divisions began to emerge in the 16th century, as capitalism and industrialization extended the economic and political ties among the world's nations.

      1.   Dependency theory asserts that because those nations that were not industrialized became dependent on those that had industrialized, they were unable to develop their own resources.

      2.   The world's industrial giants (the United States, Canada, Great Britain, France, Germany, Italy, and Japan — the G7) have decided how they will share the world's markets; by regulating global economic and industrial policy they guarantee their own dominance, including continued access to cheap raw materials from the less industrialized nations.

J.   The recent resurgence of ethnic conflicts threatens the global map drawn by the G7/G8.

X.   Other Theories of Social Change

    A.   Alternative theories of social change include: Evolutionary theories (unilinear or multilinear); Marxist conflict theories; Cyclical theories; Feminist theories; and Postmodern theories.

I.   The Difficult Road to Success

    A.   Social movements rarely solve all of society's social problems, as movements must appeal to a broad constituency in order to effectively mobilize resources. However, many have become powerful forces for social change, as they highlight problems and provide direction towards a resolution. Others become powerful forces in resisting undesirable social change.

☞ KEY TERMS

After studying the chapter, review the definition for each of the following terms.

acting crowd: Herbert Blumer's term for an excited group that collectively moves toward a goal

agent provocateur: someone who joins a group in order to spy on it and to sabotage it by provoking its members to commit illegal acts

alienation: Marx's term for workers' lack of connection to the product of their labor, caused by their being assigned repetitive tasks on a small part of a product

alternative social movement: a social movement that seeks to alter only particular aspects of people

circular reaction: Robert Park's term for a back-and-forth communication between the members of a crowd whereby a "collective impulse" is transmitted

collective behavior: extraordinary activities carried out by groups of people; includes lynchings, rumors, panics, urban legends, and fads and fashions

collective mind: Gustave LeBon's term for the tendency of people in a crowd to feel, think, and act in extraordinary ways

cultural lag: Ogburn's term for human behavior lagging behind technological innovation.

diffusion: the spread of invention or discovery from one area to another; identified by William Ogburn as the final of three processes of social change

discovery: a new way of seeing reality; identified by William Ogburn as the second of three processes of social change

emergent norms: Ralph Turner and Lewis Killian's term for the development of new norms to cope with a new situation, especially among crowds

fad: a temporary pattern of behavior that catches people's attention

fashion: a pattern of behavior that catches people's attention, which lasts longer than a fad

invention: the combination of existing elements and materials to form new ones; identified by William Ogburn as the first of three processes of social change

mass society: industrialized, highly bureaucratized, impersonal society

mass society theory: an explanation for participation in social movements based on the assumption that such movements offer a sense of belonging to people who have weak social ties

milling: a crowd standing or walking around as they talk excitedly about some event

minimax strategy: Richard Berk's term for the effort people make to minimize their costs and maximize their rewards

modernization: the process by which a traditional society is transformed into a modern society

moral panic: a fear that grips large numbers of people that some evil group or behavior threatens the well-being of society, followed by intense hostility, sometimes violence, toward those thought responsible

new social movement: social movement with a new emphasis on the world, instead of on a condition in a specific country

panic: the condition of being so fearful that one cannot function normally, and may even flee

postmodern society: another term for postindustrial society; its chief characteristic is the use of tools that extend the human abilities to gather and analyze information, to communicate, and to travel

proactive social movement: a social movement that promotes social change

propaganda: in its broad sense, the presentation of information in the attempt to influence people; in its narrow sense, one-sided information used to try to influence people

public: a dispersed group of people who usually have an interest in the issue on which a social movement focuses; the sympathetic and hostile publics have such an interest, but a third public is either unaware of the issue or indifferent to it

public opinion: how people think about some issue

reactive social movement: a social movement that resists social change

redemptive social movement: a social movement that seeks to change people totally

reformative social movement: a social movement that seeks to change only particular aspects of society

relative deprivation theory: the belief that people join social movements based on their evaluations of what they think they should have compared with what others have

resource mobilization: a theory that social movements succeed or fail based on their ability to mobilize resources such as time, money, and people's skills

riot: violent crowd behavior aimed against people and property

role extension: the incorporation of additional activities into a role

rumor: unfounded information spread among people

social change: the alteration of culture and societies over time

social movement: a large group of people who are organized to promote or resist social change

social movement organization: an organization developed to further the goals of a social movement

technology: often defined as the applications of science, but can be conceptualized as tools, items used to accomplish tasks, along with the skills or procedures necessary to make and use those tools

transformative social movement: a social movement that seeks to change society totally

urban legend: a story with an ironic twist that sounds realistic but is false

☞ KEY PEOPLE

Review the major theoretical contributions or findings of these people.

David Aberle: Aberle classified social movements into four types: alternative, redemptive, reformative and transformative based on the amount of intended change and the target of the change.

Richard Berk: Berk developed the minimax strategy to explain collective behavior; this is that people are more likely to act when costs are low and anticipated rewards high.

Herbert Blumer: Blumer identified five stages that precede the emergence of an active crowd (an excited group that moves towards a goal. These are tension or unrest; an exciting event; milling; a common object of attraction; and common impulses.

Jan Brunvand: This folklorist studied urban legends and suggests that they are modern morality stories.

Hadley Cantril: This psychologist suggests that people panicked after hearing the famous *War of the Worlds* because of widespread anxiety about world conditions.

James Flink: Flink examined the numerous ways in which the automobile has transformed U.S. society and culture, from architecture to women's roles.

James Jasper and Dorothy Nelkin: These sociologists argue that many become involved in social movements because of moral issues and an ideological commitment.

William Kornhauser: Kornhauser proposed mass society theory to explain why people are attracted to social movements. He suggested that these movements fill a void in some people's lives by offering them a sense of belonging.

Gustave LeBon: LeBon argued that a collective mind develops within a crowd and people are swept away by any suggestion that is made.

Alfred and Elizabeth Lee: These sociologists found that propaganda relies on seven basic techniques, which they labeled "tricks of the trade."

John Loftand: Lofiand identified four different types of fads: object fads, activity fads, idea fads, and personality fads.

Charles Mackay: Mackay was the first to study collective behavior; he suggested that a "herd mentality" takes over and explains the disgraceful things people do when in crowds.

Gary Marx: This sociologist investigated the agent provocateur and found that some are converted to the movement because they share the some of the same social characteristics as the movement's members.

Karl Marx: Marx analyzed the emergence of capitalism and saw changes in the factory system as a source of alienation.

Doug McAdam: McAdam challenged the mass society theory on the basis of research findings related to people's decision to become involved in the civil rights struggle. He found they were well integrated into society, rather than isolated from it as mass society theory suggests.

William Ogburn: Ogburn identified three processes of social change: invention, discovery, and diffusion. He also coined the term "cultural lag" to describe a situation in which some elements of culture adapt to an invention or discovery more rapidly than others.

Robert Park: Park suggested that social unrest is the result of the circular reaction of people in crowds.

Victor Rodriguez: This sociologist suggests that minorities in the middle class might participate in riots when they feel frustrated with being treated as second-class citizens even when they are employed and living stable lives.

Ellen Scott: Scott studied the movement to stop rape and found that close friendships, race, and even size of town are important in determining tactics.

Ralph Turner and Lewis Killian: These sociologists use the term "emergent norm" to explain the rules that emerge in collective behavior.

☞ SELF-TEST

After completing this self-test, check your answers against the Answer Key at the back of this Study Guide and against the text on page(s) indicated in parentheses.

MULTIPLE CHOICE QUESTIONS

1.   Which of the following statements about Charles Mackay is *incorrect*? (430-431)
     a.   He noticed that ordinary people did disgraceful things when in a crowd.
     b.   He suggested that people have a "herd mentality" when in a crowd.
     c.   He proposed that a collective mind develops once a group of people congregate.
     d.   His work marked the beginnings of the field of collective behavior.

2.   Gustave LeBon's term for the tendency of people in a crowd to feel, think, and act in extraordinary ways is: (430)
     a.   social unrest.
     b.   the "herd mentality."
     c.   collective behavior.
     d.   collective mind.

3.   According to Park, which is most conducive to the emergence of collective behaviour? (431)
     a.   social alienation.
     b.   social apathy.
     c.   social unrest.
     d.   social cohesion.

4.   A crowd's back-and-forth communication whereby a collective impulse is transmitted is: (431)
     a.   a circular reaction.
     b.   milling.
     c.   an acting crowd.
     d.   a collective mind.

5.   Acting crowd: (431)
     a.   is a term coined by Herbert Blumer.
     b.   is an excited group that collectively moves toward a goal.
     c.   is the end result of the five stages of collective behavior.
     d.   All of the above.

6.   Richard Berk used the term "minimax strategy" to describe the tendency for: (432)
     a.   crowds to operate with a minimum of strategy.
     b.   humans to minimize costs and maximize rewards.
     c.   those in authority to maximize the costs of an action in order to minimize rewards.
     d.   society to respond to even the most minimum of social movements.

7.   The development of new norms to cope with a new situation is: (432)
     a.   emergent norms.
     b.   developmental norms.
     c.   surfacing norms.
     d.   None of the above.

8.   Urban riots are usually caused by: (433)
     a.   extreme poverty.
     b.   social deviants who display antisocial behavior.
     c.   feelings of frustration and anger at being deprived of the same opportunities as others.
     d.   a population that is forced to live within a small space—overcrowded neighborhoods.

9.   Failure to function normally, and even fleeing, is the result of _____ (435)
     a.   disturbance.
     b.   panic.
     c.   fad.
     d.   riot.

10. Sociologists have found that when a disaster such as a fire occurs: (435)
    a. everyone panics.
    b. some people continue to perform their roles.
    c. people leave it to the police and fire fighters to solve the problem.
    d. no one panics.

11. Which statement about moral panics is *incorrect*? (435-436)
    a. Moral panics occur when people are concerned about something viewed as immoral.
    b. Moral panics are generally based on an event that has been verified as true.
    c. Moral panics thrive on uncertainty and anxiety.
    d. Moral panics are fueled by the mass media.

12. Sociologists refer to unfounded information spread among people as: (436)
    a. hearsay.
    b. scuttlebutt.
    c. rumor.
    d. gossip.

13. A temporary pattern of behavior that catches people's attention is a: (436)
    a. panic.
    b. trend.
    c. fashion.
    d. fad.

14. Eating goldfish and bungee jumping are both examples of: (436)
    a. object fads.
    b. urban legends.
    c. activity fads.
    d. rumors.

15. Social movements that seek to change people totally are: (438)
    a. alternative social movements.
    b. redemptive social movements.
    c. reformative social movements.
    d. transformative social movements.

16. A social movement that seeks to change society totally is a(n): (438)
    a. alternative social movement.
    b. redemptive social movement.
    c. reformative social movement.
    d. transformative social movement.

17. Levels of membership in social movements include: (439)
    a. the inner core.
    b. the committed.
    c. a wider circle of members.
    d. All of the above.

18. The public that social movements face can really be divided into: (439-440)
    a. supporters and opponents.
    b. informed supportive public, informed oppositional public, and uninformed mass.
    c. receptive audience, hostile audience, and disinterested mass.
    d. sympathetic public, hostile public, and disinterested people.

19. How people think about some issue is: (440)
    a. irrelevant to most social scientists.
    b. public opinion.
    c. propaganda.
    d. mass-society theory.

20. Which statement about propaganda is *incorrect?* (440-441)
    a. Propaganda plays a key role in social movements.
    b. Propaganda generally involves negative images.
    c. Propaganda has become a regular and routine part of modern life.
    d. Propaganda is the presentation of information in an attempt to influence people.

21. Advertising is: (441)
    a. a type of propaganda.
    b. an organized attempt to manipulate public opinion.
    c. a one-sided presentation of information that distorts reality.
    d. All of the above.

22. The mass media: (441-442)
    a. are the gatekeepers to social movements.
    b. engage in biased reporting, controlled by people who have an agenda to get across.
    c. are sympathetic to some social movements, while ignoring others; it all depends on their individual biases.
    d. All of the above.

23. According to mass society theory, social movements offer people: (442)
    a. a set of rules or guidelines to govern their behavior.
    b. an outlet for leisure activities.
    c. a sense of belonging.
    d. answers to basic questions concerning morality.

24. In order to turn a group of people who are upset about a social condition into a social movement, there must be: (443-444)
    a. agitation.
    b. resource mobilization.
    c. organization.
    d. institutionalization

25. The alteration of culture and society over time is: (445)
    a. social transformation.
    b. social metamorphose.
    c. social alternation.
    d. social change.

26. Technology refers to: (445)
   a. items that people use to accomplish a wide range of tasks.
   b. skills and procedures that are employed in the development and utilization of tools.
   c. tools ranging from combs or hairbrushes to computers and the Internet.
   d. All of the above.

27. Ogburn called the process of change that involves new ways of seeing reality: (446)
   a. invention.
   b. discovery.
   c. diffusion.
   d. exploration.

28. The situation in which some elements of a culture adapt to an invention or discovery more rapidly than others is: (446)
   a. cultural downtime.
   b. cultural lag.
   c. cultural delay.
   d. cultural drag.

29. According to Karl Marx, the change-over to the factory system produced: (446)
   a. rationality.
   b. alienation.
   c. efficiency.
   d. worker satisfaction.

30. The automobile: (447-448)
   a. has changed the shape of cities.
   b. has stimulated mass suburbanization.
   c. has altered dating and courting rituals.
   d. all of the above.

31. A new development that allows doctors in one state or country to check the heart condition of a patient in an entirely different location is: (449)
   a. electronic imaging technology.
   b. remote heart monitoring.
   c. telemedicine.
   d. cardiac computerization.

32. One concern about the expansion of the information superhighway is: (450)
   a. interest in accessing it will outstrip capacity to carry so many users.
   b. social inequalities will become greater, both on a national and global basis.
   c. people will tie up the services with non-essential activities.
   d. people will become even more alienated as they relate more and more through their computers and less and less face to face.

33. The least industrialized nations become dependent on countries that have already industrialized and they are unable to develop their own resources according to: (450)
   a. dependency theory.
   b. capitalist exploitation theory.
   c. evolutionary theory.
   d. multilinear evolution theory.

34. Which of the following does the author of the text identify as a threat to the global map that was drawn up by the G7/G8? (450)
    a. stricter environmental controls in the least industrialized nations
    b. stiffer tariff regulation world-wide
    c. resurgence of ethnic conflicts
    d. ecosabotage

35. _____ theories assume that all societies follow the same path, evolving from simple to complex through uniform sequences. (451)
    a. Cyclical
    b. Uniformity
    c. Unilinear evolution
    d. Multilinear evolution

TRUE-FALSE QUESTIONS

T F   1. Collective behavior is characterized by a group of people becoming emotionally aroused and engaging in extraordinary behavior. (430)

T F   2. Gustave LeBon's central idea was that the individual is transformed by the crowd. (430)

T F   3. The term "circular reaction" refers to the process by which people become swept up in the crowd, reacting to any suggestion that is put forth. (431)

T F   4. Herbert Blumer identified five stages of collective behavior. (431)

T F   5. The term acting crowd is applied only to violent activities such as lynch mobs or people engaged in riots. (431)

T F   6. Emergent norms is the development of new norms to cope with a new situation, especially among crowds. (432)

T F   7. The event that precipitates a riot is less important than the riot's general context. (433)

T F   8. The fears that produce moral panics are generally out of proportion to any supposed danger. (435)

T F   9. People believe rumors because they replace ambiguity with some form of certainty. (436)

T F   10. Urban legends are just another kind of rumor. (436-437)

T F   11. Jan Brunvand considers urban legends to be modern day morality stories. (437)

T F   12. All social movements seek to change society. (437-438)

T F   13. A social movement's relationship to authorities is significant in determining whether the tactics to be used are peaceful or violent. (440)

T F   14. Propaganda and advertising are defined quite differently from one another. (440-441)

T F   15. Deprivation theory and relative deprivation theory are identical perspectives. (442-443)

T F   16. Moral shock is of little importance in motivating people to join a social movement. (443)

T F   17. The role of the agent provocateur as a spy on the leadership of a social movement, and perhaps trying to sabotage their activities, is generally unsuccessful. (443)

T F   18. Before resources can be mobilized, a social movement must become organized, and in some cases even institutionalized. (443-444)

T F   19. In the final stage of a social movement, decline is certain. (444)

T F   20. Technology is not a very powerful force for social change. (445)

T F   21. Invention, discovery, and diffusion are Ogburn's three processes of social change. (446)

T F   22. Technology usually changes first, followed by culture. (446)

T F   23. Marx believed that the change to the factory system was a source of alienation. (446)

T F   24. While technology may produce ideological changes, it has little impact on underlying social values. (446)

T F   25.   Automobiles altered the architecture of North American homes. (447)

T F   26.   The use of computers in education will significantly reduce existing social inequalities between school districts. (449)

T F   27.   Computers create the possibility for increased surveillance of workers and depersonalization. (449)

T F   28.   Today's information revolution will perpetuate global stratification. (450)

T F   29.   The assumption of unilinear evolutionary theories, that all societies progress along the same path from a primitive state to a highly complex state, is still accepted. (451)

T F   30.   Cyclical theories assume that civilizations go through processes of birth, maturity, and death. (451)

FILL-IN QUESTIONS

1.   Gustave LeBon's term for the tendency of people in a crowd to feel, think, and act in extraordinary ways is _____. (430)

2.   A crowd standing or walking around as they talk excitedly about some event is _____. (431)

3.   Ralph Turner and Lewis Killian's term for the development of new norms to cope with a new situation, especially among crowds is _____. (432)

4.   A(n) _____ is violent crowd behavior aimed against people and property. (433)

5.   A fear that grips large numbers of people that some evil group or behavior threatens the well- being of society, followed by intense hostility, and sometimes violence, towards those thought responsible is _____. (435)

6.   _____ are unfounded information spread among people. (436)

7.   A temporary pattern of behavior that catches people's attention is a(n) _____. (436)

8.   A(n) _____ is a story with an ironic twist that sounds realistic but is false. (436)

9.   A religious social movement that stresses conversion, which will produce a change in the entire person, is an example of _____. (438)

10.   Social movements that span the globe, emphasizing changing conditions throughout the world rather than in just one country, are referred to as _____. (438-439)

11.   _____ is how people think about some issue. (440)

12.   _____ is industrialized, highly bureaucratized, impersonal society. (442)

13.   _____ states that people who are deprived of things deemed valuable in society join social movements with the hope of redressing their grievances. (442)

14.   _____ is the alteration of culture and societies over time. (445)

15.   The combination of existing elements and materials to form new ones is _____. (446)

16.   _____ is a new way of seeing reality. (446)

17.   According to Ogburn, because of travel, trade, or conquest, _____ of an invention or discovery occurs. (446)

18.   The situation in which some elements of a culture adapt to an invention or discovery more rapidly than others is _____. (446)

19.   _____ is Marx's term for workers' lack of connection to the product of their labor caused by their being assigned repetitive tasks on a small part of a product. (446)

20.   The assumption that all societies follow the same path, from the same starting point to the same end point, is central to _____. (451)

MATCH THESE SOCIAL SCIENTISTS WITH THEIR CONTRIBUTIONS

__1. Charles Mackay
__2. William Kornhauser
__3. Robert Park
__4. Turner and Killian
__5. Gustave LeBon
__6. David Aberle
__7. Herbert Blumer
__8. Richard Berk
__9. James Flink
__10. William Ogburn
__11. Karl Marx

a. *emergent norm*
b. *herd mentality*
c. *minimax strategy*
d. *social movements classified by type and amount of social change*
e. *mass society theory*
f. *social unrest and circular reaction*
g. *the acting crowd*
h. *collective mind*
i. *changes to factory system produced worker alienation*
j. *studied the impact of the auto on U.S. society*
k. *three processes of social change*

ESSAY QUESTIONS

1. Compare and contrast the early explanations of collective behavior, as advanced by Charles Mackay, Gustave LeBon, Robert Park, and Herbert Blumer, with more contemporary explanations developed by Richard Berk, Ralph Turner and Lewis Killian.

2. Discuss the different theories about why people join social movements and consider how they could all be accurate.

3. Consider why the author combined the topics of collective behavior and social movements in one chapter.

4. Choose a particular technology—you can use the automobile or the computer—and discuss the impact that it has had on Canadian society.

5. Discuss Ogburn's three processes of social change and provide examples to illustrate each.

'DOWN-TO-EARTH SOCIOLOGY"

1. Read "Which Side of the Barricades? The Pros and Cons of Trade Unions in Canada" on page 438. In thinking about this social movement, where would you place yourself in relationship to memberships and/or publics? What kind of tactics does each side use in order to promote its cause without alienating sympathetic publics? How does each side try to influence public opinion by making use of some of the "tricks of the trade"?

2. After reading "Tricks of the Trade: The Fine Art of Propaganda" on page 441, listen carefully to politicians and others advocating a particular idea. Are they using some of the techniques described? If yes, which ones?

3. Before reading the article about the movement against the MAI (p. 444), were you aware of this movement? What stages did this social movement go through? What kinds of tactics did the movement use? Has this movement gone into decline or has it been able to keep itself alive in the years since 1997?

4. Why do you think there is a tendency to view new technologies so negatively ("When Old Technology was New: Misguessing the Future" on p. 447)? Can you think of some new technology today, whose introduction has been met with mostly negative responses?

CHAPTER-BY-CHAPTER ANSWER KEY

☞ **ANSWERS FOR CHAPTER 1**

ANSWERS FOR THE MULTIPLE-CHOICE QUESTIONS

1. b   The sociological perspective is an approach to understanding human behavior by placing it within its broader social context. (4)

2. b   Using systematic methods to study and explain the social and natural worlds is the intent of scientists. (5)

3. c   Sociology is the study of society and human behavior. (5)

4. d   Positivism is the application of the scientific approach to the social world. (9)

5. a   Auguste Comte was interested in the twin problems of social order and social change and was the individual responsible for giving the name "sociology" to the new social science. (9)

6. b   The proletariat is the large group of workers who are exploited by the small group of capitalists who own the means of production, according to Karl Marx. (9)

7. a   Durkheim believed that social factors—patterns of behavior that characterize a social group—explain many types of behavior, including suicide rates. (10)

8. c   Max Weber's research on the rise of capitalism identified religious beliefs as the key. (11)

9. d   All are correct. Replication helps researchers overcome distortions that values can cause, results can be compared when a study is repeated, and replication involves the repetition of a study by other researchers. (12)

10. c   Social facts and *Verstehen* go hand-in-hand. Social facts are patterns of behavior that characterize a social group. By applying *Verstehen*—your understanding of what it means to be human and to face various situations in life—you gain an understanding of people's behavior. (13)

11. b   In the 19th century, it was unlikely that women would study sociology because sex roles were rigidly defined; women were supposed to devote themselves to the four K's—*Kirche, Kuchen, Kinder, und Kleider* (church, cooking, children, and clothes). (13)

12. c   W.E.B. Du Bois was an African American sociologist who wrote extensively on race relations. In both his personal and professional life he experienced prejudice and discrimination. His commitment to racial equality led him to establish the NAACP. (16)

13. b   Symbolic interactionism is the theoretical perspective which views society as composed of symbols that people use to establish meaning, develop their views of the world, and communicate with one another. (17)

14. c   The symbolic interaction perspective focuses on the symbolic meaning attached to social relationships to understand the social world. (17)

15. a   According to Robert Merton, an action intended to help maintain a system's equilibrium is a manifest function. (18)

16. a   Conflict theory was first asserted by Karl Marx. (18)

17. b   Conflict theorists such as Dahrendorf attribute conflict in society to relations of authority in all layers of society. (19)

18. c   Liberal feminist theories attribute gender inequality to legal restraints and customs in a society. (19)

19. b. Postmodernism emphasizes the cultural and sexual diversity of contemporary societies. (20)

20. a   The symbolic interactionist perspective does not focus on macro-level analysis but rather on the micro-level. It emphasizes social interaction and communication. (21)

21. b   In studying the homeless, functionalists would focus on how changes in parts of the society are related to homelessness. Symbolic interactionists would emphasize what the homeless say and what they do. Conflict theorists tend to focus on macro-level inequalities in society—such as how the policies of the wealthy push certain groups into unemployment. (21)

22. d   Since each theoretical perspective provides a different, often sharply contrasting picture of our world, no theory or level of analysis encompasses all of reality. By putting the contributions of each perspective and level of analysis together, we gain a more comprehensive picture of social life. (21)

23. a   The purpose of pure or basic sociological research is to make discoveries about life in human groups, not to make changes in those groups. On the other hand, applied and clinical sociology are more involved in suggesting or bringing about social change. (21)

24. c   Sociologists who conduct research for government commissions or agencies investigating social problems are practicing applied sociology. (21)

25. c   According to the text, in recent years sociologists have emphasized applied sociology. (21)

ANSWERS FOR TRUE-FALSE QUESTIONS

1. *True.* (4)
2. *True.* (4)
3. *False.* Sociologists focus on external influences (people's experiences) instead of internal mechanisms, such as instincts. (4)
4. *True.* (5)
5. *True.* (5-6)
6. *False.* Sociology has many similarities to the other social sciences. What distinguishes sociology from other disciplines is that sociologists do not focus on single social institutions, they study industrialized societies, and they stress factors external to the individual. (6)
7. *True.* (8)
8. *True.* (9-10)
9. *True.* (10)
10. *False.* Weber agreed with much of what Marx wrote, but he strongly disagreed that economics is the central force in social change. Weber saw religion as playing that role. (11)
11. *True.* (13)
12. *True.* (13)
13. *False.* Harriet Martineau's ground-breaking work on social life in Great Britain and the United States was largely ignored; she is remembered for her translations of Auguste Comte's work. (13)
14. *True.* (17)
15. *True.* (17)
16. *False.* Although functionalists do believe the family has lost many of its traditional purposes, they do not believe they have all been lost. Some of the existing functions are presently under assault or are being eroded. (17-18)
17. *False.* Some conflict theorists use this theory in a much broader sense. For example, Ralf Dahrendorf sees conflict as inherent in all relationships that have authority. (19)
18. *False.* The three feminist theories have a number of things in common: they recognize that gender differences are not simply derived from biology; that the gender division of labour is hierarchical; that gender relations are intertwined in many areas of social life; that knowledge is largely derived from men's experiences because of their position of authority within the social order. (19-20)
19. *True.* (20)

20.   *False*. Many sociologists are seeking ways to apply their knowledge, and many departments of sociology now offer courses in applied sociology. (21)

ANSWERS FOR THE FILL-IN QUESTIONS

1.   People's group memberships because of their location in history and society are known as SOCIAL LOCATION. (4)
2.   The NATURAL SCIENCES are the intellectual and academic disciplines designed to comprehend, explain, and predict the events in our natural environment. On the other hand. the SOCIAL SCIENCES examine human relationships. (5)
3.   The use of objective systematic observation to test theories is SCIENTIFIC METHOD. (8)
4.   CLASS CONFLICT was Karl Marx's term for the struggle between the proletariat and the bourgeoisie. (9)
5.   Durkheim used the term SOCIAL INTEGRATION to refer to the degree to which people feel a part of social groups. (10)
6.   VALUE FREE is the view that a sociologist's personal values or biases should not influence social research, while OBJECTIVITY is total neutrality. (12)
7.   The meanings that people attach to their own behavior are called SUBJECTIVE MEANINGS. (13)
8.   Durkheim used the term SOCIAL FACT to refer to patterns of behavior that characterize a social group. (13)
9.   A THEORY is a general statement about how some parts of the world fit together and how they work. (17)
10. The theoretical perspective in which society is viewed as composed of symbols that people use to establish meaning, develop their views of the world, and communicate with one another is SYMBOLIC INTERACTIONISM. (17)
11. FUNCTIONAL analysis is a theoretical framework in which society is viewed as composed of various parts, each with a function that contributes to society's equilibrium. (17)
12. Power that people consider legitimate is known as AUTHORITY. (19)
13. MARXIST FEMINIST THEORIES stress that the exploitation of women includes their objectification into roles that serve men's interests. (19)
14. MACRO-LEVEL analysis examines large-scale patterns of society, while MICRO-LEVEL analysis examines small-scale patterns of society. (21)
15. PURE (OR) BASIC sociology makes discoveries about life in human groups, not to make changes in those groups; APPLIED sociology is the use of sociology to solve problems. (21)

ANSWERS TO MATCH THESE SOCIAL SCIENTISTS WITH THEIR CONTRIBUTIONS

1.   b   Auguste Comte: *proposed the use of positivism*
2.   e   Karl Marx: *believed the key to human history was class struggle*
3.   f   C. Wright Mills: *encouraged the use of the sociological perspective*
4.   c   Emile Durkheim: *stressed social facts*
5.   g   Harriet Martineau: *published Society in America and translated Comte's work into English*
6.   h   Robert K. Merton: *stressed the need for middle-range theories*
7.   a   W.E.B. Du Bois: *was an early African American sociologist*
8.   d   Max Weber: *believed religion was a central force in social change*

GUIDELINES FOR ANSWERING THE ESSAY QUESTIONS

1. *Explain what the sociological perspective encompasses and then, using that perspective, discuss the forces that shaped the discipline of sociology.*

    There are two parts to this question. First, you are asked to define the sociological perspective. As you define this, you would want to mention the idea of social location, perhaps by bringing into your essay C. Wright Mills' observations on the connection between biography and history. Another way to get at what the perspective is would be to contrast sociology with other disciplines, talking about what sociology is and what it isn't. The second part of the essay is to discuss the forces that shaped sociology and its early followers. What you are being asked is to think about what was going on in the social world in the early 19th century that might have led to the birth of this new discipline. Referring back to the book, you would want to identify three: (1) the Industrial Revolution; (2) imperialism; and (3) the emergence of the scientific method. You would conclude by discussing how each of the early sociologists—Auguste Comte, Herbert Spencer, Karl Marx, Emile Durkheim, Max Weber—was influenced by these broader forces in making a contribution to sociology. You could also bring into the discussion some of the material on sexism in early sociology, noting that the ideas about the appropriate role for women in society functioned to exclude women like Harriet Martineau and Jane Addams from the discipline, or you could talk about the emergence of sociology in North America.

2. *The textbook notes that Verstehen and social facts go hand in hand, explain how this is so. Assume that you have been asked to carry out research to find out more about why growing numbers of women and children are homeless and what particular problems they face. Discuss how you could you use both Verstehen and social facts in your study.*

    First, you would want to define what Verstehen and social facts are and how they are compatible in terms of arriving at a complete picture of a social pattern. Then you can argue that social facts would be most appropriate in trying to explain why growing numbers of women and children are homeless—you might suggest that you would look at the changing economic status of women in society, the increase in the number of female-headed households, and the decline in the amount of affordable housing. On the other hand, by applying Verstehen, you would be able to discover what particular problems they face—through face-to-face interviews at shelter sites you would be able to experience firsthand some of what they are experiencing.

3. *Explain each of the theoretical perspectives that is used in sociology and describe how a sociologist affiliated with one or another of the perspectives might undertake a study of gangs. Discuss how all five can be used in research.*

    There are five major perspectives in sociology: symbolic interactionism, functional analysis, conflict theory, feminist theories, and postmodernism. Your first step is to explain the essential nature of each perspective and then to propose a research topic that would be consistent with the perspective. For example, symbolic interactionism focuses on the symbols that people use to establish meaning, develop their views of the world, and communicate with one another; a symbolic interactionist would want to find out what meaning gangs and gang membership have for individuals who belong to them as well as those who live in communities in which gangs operate. Functional analysis, which tries to identify the functions of a particular social pattern, would choose to study what contributions gangs make within the fabric of social life as well as the dysfunctions of gangs. A conflict theorist would study the competition for scarce resources among gangs and between gangs and the larger society because he or she is interested in struggles over power and control within social groups. A feminist theorist would study the gender dynamics of gangs, while a postmodernist would focus on the social and cultural diversity of gangs in contemporary society. You would conclude by noting that each perspective provides an answer to an important question about the social order and by combining perspectives you arrive at a more complete picture.

☞ ANSWERS FOR CHAPTER 2

ANSWERS FOR MULTIPLE CHOICE QUESTIONS

1. b   A researcher interested in doing a macro-level study would choose race relations as a topic. Waiting in public places, interactions between people on street corners, and meat packers at work are all topics that would interest a micro-level researcher. (28)

2. d   "All of the above" is correct. Sociologists believe that research is necessary because common sense ideas may or may not be true; they want to move beyond guesswork; and researchers want to know what really is going on. (28)

3. a   Ethnomethodology is the study of how people use background assumptions to make sense of life and, thus, is a part of symbolic interactionism. Surveys, unobtrusive measures, and secondary analysis are research methods for gathering data. (29-30)

4. c   A sample is defined as the individuals intended to represent the population to be studied. (30)

5. c   A random sample ensures that everyone in the population has an equal chance of being included in the study. (30)

6. b   Given the time and cost factors, you are most likely to choose to use self-administered questionnaires, because this method allows a larger number of people to be sampled at a relatively low cost. (30)

7. b   The advantage of structured interviews is that they are faster to administer and make it easier for answers to be coded. (30)

8. d   Problems which must be dealt with in conducting participant observation include the researcher's personal characteristics; developing rapport with respondents; and generalizability. Therefore, "all of the above" is the correct response. (31-32)

9. b   A researcher might "load the dice" in designing a research project because of a vested interest in the outcome of the research. He or she may be hired by business firms and is thus motivated to find results that are consistent with the interests of the firm. (31)

10. a   Qualitative interviews are very useful at obtaining descriptive information. (32-33)

11. c   The analysis of data already collected by other researchers is secondary analysis. (33)

12. b   Sources such as newspapers, diaries, bank records, police reports, household accounts and immigration files are documents that provide useful information for investigating social life. (33)

13. c   In order to study patterns of alcohol consumption in different neighborhoods, you decide to go through the recycling bins in your town and count the number of beer cans, and wine and hard liquor bottles. This study would be using unobtrusive methods because you are making observations on people without their knowledge that they are being studied. (34)

14. a   A researcher who is trying to identify causal relationships is likely to use an experiment. (34)

15. b   In an experiment, the group not exposed to the independent variable in the study is the control group. (34)

16. c   Eight steps are involved in scientific research. (35)

17. a   The change behavior that occurs when subjects know they are being studied is referred to as the Hawthorne effect. (35)

18. c   Surveys are more likely to be used by researchers trained in quantitative techniques. (35)

19. a   Marketing researchers use a combination of quantitative and qualitative methods. (36)

20. c   Researchers review the literature in order to help them to narrow down the problem by pinpointing particular areas to examine; to get ideas about how to do their own research; and to determine whether or not the problem has been answered already. They are not concerned about whether or not the topic is controversial. (38)
21. a   A relationship between or among variables is predicted by a hypothesis. (38)
22. b   Reliability refers to the extent to which data produce consistent results. (38)
23. c   In analyzing data gathered by participant observation, a researcher is likely to choose qualitative analysis. (38)
24. c   Replication is the repetition of research in order to test its findings. (40)
25. d   All of the above is correct. Research ethics require openness; that a researcher not falsify results or plagiarize someone else's work; and that research subjects should not be harmed by the research. (40)

ANSWERS FOR TRUE-FALSE QUESTIONS

1.   *True.* (28)
2.   *False.* Research often does not confirm common sense. The application of research methods takes us beyond common sense and allows us to penetrate surface realities so we can better understand social life. (29)
3.   *True.* (30)
4.   *False.* In survey research, it is always desirable for respondents to express their own ideas. (30)
5.   *True.* (30)
6.   *True.* (30)
7.   *True.* (31-32)
8.   *False.* Many feminist methodologists reject the impersonal nature of scientific research and are drawn to qualitative techniques, particularly interviewing. (33)
9.   *False.* Secondary analysis and use of documents are not the same thing. The data used in secondary analysis are gathered by other researchers while documents may be anything from diaries to police records. (33)
10. *True.* (34)
11. *False.* It is not always unethical to observe behavior in people when they do not know they are being studied. However, there are circumstances when the issue of ethics should be raised. (34)
12. *False.* In an experiment, the experimental group is exposed to the independent variable in the study. The control group is not exposed to the independent variable. (34)
13. *True.* (35)
14. *True.* (38)
15. *True.* (38)
16. *False.* Sociologists do not place one above the other. Rather, they take great care to assure that both are achieved. (38)
17. *True.* (38)
18. *False.* Computers are valuable to researchers not because they store information efficiently, but because they reduce large amounts of data to basic patterns, they take the drudgery out of analyzing data, they can do different statistical tests easily, and they free the researcher up to do more interpretation of the data. (39)
19. *True.* (39)
20. *False.* Scully and Marolla's research demonstrates that it is possible to do research that contributes to our body of sociological knowledge under less than ideal conditions. (42)

ANSWERS FOR FILL-IN QUESTIONS

1. The seven research methods are: (I) SURVEYS, (2) SECONDARY ANALYSIS, (3) DOCUMENTS, (4) PARTICIPANT OBSERVATION, (5) EXPERIMENTS, (6) UNOBTRUSIVE MEASURES, and (7) QUALITATIVE INTERVIEWS. (29-30)
2. A SELF-ADMINISTERED QUESTIONNAIRE allows a large number of people to be sampled at a relatively low cost. (30)
3. Closed-ended questions are used in STRUCTURED INTERVIEWS. (30)
4. RAPPORT is a feeling of trust between researchers and subjects. (30)
5. PARTICIPANT OBSERVATION is a form of research where the researcher spends a great deal of time with the people he or she is studying. (31)
6. Generalizability is one of the major problems in PARTICIPANT OBSERVATION. (32)
7. Sociologists rarely use EXPERIMENTS, as they do not reveal broader social relationships. (34)
8. To conduct an experiment, the researcher has two groups: (1) EXPERIMENTAL GROUP and (2) CONTROL GROUP. (34)
9. Research in which the emphasis is placed on precise measurement, the use of statistics and numbers is QUANTITATIVE TECHNIQUES. (35)
10. Research in which the emphasis is placed on describing and interpreting people's behavior is QUALITATIVE TECHNIQUES. (35)
11. A factor or concept thought to be significant for human behavior, which varies from one case to another, is a(n) VARIABLE. (38)
12. Hypotheses need OPERATIONAL DEFINITIONS, which are precise ways to measure variables. (38)
13. RELIABILITY is the extent to which data produce consistent results. (38)
14. Research ETHICS require openness, honesty, and truth. (40)
15. Research and THEORY are interdependent, and sociologists combine them in their work. (41-42)

ANSWERS TO THE MATCHING QUESTIONS

1. b   Hawthorne effect: *behavior change due to subject's awareness of being studied*
2. f   Population: *the target group to be studied*
3. h   Sample: *the individuals intended to represent the population to be studied*
4. c   Interview bias: *the effect that interviewers have on respondents that leads to biased answers*
5. g   Secondary analysis: *the analysis of data already collected by other researchers*
6. e   Documents: *written sources of data*
7. i   Independent variable: *a factor that causes a change in another variable*
8. d   Dependent variable: *a factor that is changed by an independent variable*
9   a   Unobtrusive measures: *the observation of people who do not know that they are being studied*

GUIDELINES FOR ANSWERING THE ESSAY QUESTIONS

1. *Choose a topic and explain how you would go through the different steps in the research model.*

    In order to answer this question, you must select a topic and then develop this from the beginning to the end of the research process, identifying all eight steps and explaining what tasks are carried out each step of the way. Your answer should make reference to variables, hypothesis, operational definitions, the different research methods, validity and reliability, different ways of analyzing the data, and replication.

2.   *Discuss some of the things that can go wrong in the process of doing research and provide suggestions on how to overcome such problems.*

There are a number of problems that can arise if the researcher is not careful. Included would be: (1) deriving invalid and unreliable results because of inadequate operational definitions and inaccurate sampling procedures; (2) obtaining biased answers because biased questions were asked; (3) failing to establish rapport with research subjects because of personal qualities or characteristics; and (4) failing to gain access to necessary documents because those who control the documents are unwilling to cooperate. Each of these potential problems can be overcome if the researcher follows the steps in the research process carefully.

3.   *Explain why ethical guidelines are necessary in social science research.*

Ethical guidelines are necessary for several reasons. First and foremost, the researcher is working with human subjects; there must be guidelines to protect these subjects from any undue physical or psychological harm. Second, the research is only valid and reliable if the subjects have honestly and accurately provided information to the researcher. For this reason, they must have confidence in the researcher and the research process; guidelines assure subjects that their identities will remain anonymous and their information will be confidential. Finally, an essential aspect of research is that it be shared with others in the research community as well as members of the wider society. Guidelines regarding falsification and plagiarism guarantee that all research will be carefully scrutinized, thereby assuring its validity and reliability.

☞ **ANSWERS FOR CHAPTER 3**

ANSWERS FOR MULTIPLE CHOICE QUESTIONS

1.   b   Sociologists would use the term "nonmaterial culture" to refer to a group's ways of thinking and doing, including language and other forms of interaction as nonmaterial culture. (48)

2.   d   Material culture includes weapons and machines, eating utensils, jewelry, hairstyles, and clothing: language is part of the nonmaterial, rather than the material, culture. (48)

3.   d   The disorientation that James Henslin experienced when he came into contact with the fundamentally different culture of Morocco is known as cultural shock. (48)

4.   a   The one statement that is not true regarding culture is that "people generally are aware of the effects of their own culture." (49)

5.   c   A Canadian who thinks citizens of another country are barbarians if they like to attend bullfights is demonstrating ethnocentrism. (49)

6.   d   Gestures can lead to misunderstandings and embarrassment when their meanings are not shared. (51-52)

7.   a   It is possible for human experience to be cumulative and for people to share memories because of language. (52)

8.   c   The example of the Inuit children and their perceptions about different types of snow illustrates the Sapir-Whorf hypothesis, which suggests that language not only reflects a culture's way of thinking and perceiving the work, but also helps to shape thought and perception. (54)

9.   d   You have violated folkways, norms related to everyday behavior that are not strictly enforced. (54-55)

10. a   Mores are essential to our core values and require conformity. (55)

11. d   Subcultures are a world within a world; have values and related behaviors that distinguish their members from the dominant culture; and include occupational groups. Therefore, all of the above are correct. (55-56)

12. c   Sociologically speaking, heavy metal adherents who glorify Satanism, cruelty, and sexism are examples of countercultures. (55-56)

13. a   A sociologist would describe Canada as a pluralistic society because it is made up of many different groups. (56)

14. d   The statement that is not correct is that "They [core values] rarely create much conflict as they change." In fact, core values do not change without meeting strong resistance from traditionalists. (56-61)

15. a   Value contradictions occur when a value, such as the one that stresses group superiority, comes into direct conflict with other values, such as democracy and equality. (59-60)

16. b   Ideal culture reflects the values and norms which a people attempt to follow; it is the goals held out for them. (61)

17. d   The perspective that views human behavior as the result of natural selection and considers biological characteristics to be the fundamental cause of human behavior is sociobiology. (62)

18. c   Studies of animal culture, such as those conducted by Goodall, have led to the conclusion that animal culture exists but researchers are still studying to learn more about it. (63-64)

19. d   Continuing to visit physicians and to rely on the judgment about diagnosis and treatment of illness, even when computer tests do a better job, is an example of cultural lag. (66)

20. c   The adoption of bagels, woks and hammocks in Canada illustrates the process of cultural diffusion. (67)

ANSWERS FOR TRUE-FALSE QUESTIONS

1. *True.* (49)
2. *False.* Culture has a great deal to do with our ideas of right and wrong. For example, folkways and mores have sanctions attached to them to encourage people to do the right thing. (50)
3. *True.* (50)
4. *True.* (50)
5. *False.* The gesture of nodding the head up and down to indicate "yes" is not universal. In some societies this gesture means "no." (51-52)
6. *False.* Humans could not plan future events without language to convey meanings of past, present, and future points in time. (54)
7. *True.* (55)
8. *False.* One society's folkways may be another society's mores. (55)
9. *False.* Motorcycle enthusiasts who emphasize personal freedom and speed, while maintaining values of success, form part of a subculture, not a counterculture. Motorcycle gangs who commit crimes and use illegal drugs are an example of a counterculture. (56)
10. *True.* (57)
11. *False.* Seventy-one percent of Canadians believe the gap between the rich and poor is increasing and 50 percent say that the government should more actively intervene to narrow this gap. (59)
12. *False.* The text identifies five core values in Canadian society: leisure, self-fulfillment, physical fitness, youth, and concern for the environment. (60-61)
13. *False.* Porter remarked that Canadians, unlike Americans, lack a unifying national ideology. (61)
14. *False.* Concern for the environment has not always been a core value in Canadian society. It is one of the emergent values that is now increasing in importance. (61)
15. *True.* (61)
16. *True.* (62-63)
17. *True.* (62)
18. *True.* (64)

19. *False.* New technologies not only affect the material culture, but they have a profound impact on the nonmaterial culture, including the way people think and what they value. (64)
20. *False.* According to Ogburn, it is the *material* culture that changes first, with the nonmaterial culture lagging behind. (66)

ANSWERS FOR FILL-IN QUESTIONS

1.   Objects such as art, buildings, weapons, utensils, machines, hairstyles, clothing, and jewelry that distinguish a group of people are known as MATERIAL CULTURE; their ways of thinking and doing are NONMATERIAL CULTURE. (48)
2.   A SYMBOL is something to which people attach meaning and then use to communicate with others. (51)
3.   LANGUAGE is a system of symbols that can be combined in an infinite number of ways and can represent not only objects but also abstract thought. (52)
4.   VALUES are ideas of what is desirable in life. (54)
5.   The expectations or rules of behavior that develop out of values are referred to as NORMS. (55)
6.   A TABOO is a norm so strongly ingrained that even the thought of its violation is greeted with revulsion. (55)
7.   VALUE CLUSTERS are a series of interrelated values that together form a larger whole. (60)
8.   CULTURAL UNIVERSALS may not exist because even though there are universal human activities, there is no universally accepted way of doing any of them. (62)
9.   Studies of chimpanzees indicate that they were able to make and use TOOLS; they actually modified objects and used them for specific purposes. (63)
10. In its broader sense, TECHNOLOGY includes the skills or procedures necessary to make and use tools. (64)
11. Both the printing press and the computer represent NEW TECHNOLOGIES because they had a significant impact on society following their introduction. (64)
12. The idea that technology is the single greatest force in shaping our lives is central to the point of view called TECHNOLOGICAL DETERMINISM. (65)
13. William Ogburn used the term CULTURAL LAG to reflect the condition in which not all parts of a culture change at the same pace. (66)
14. The spread of cultural characteristics from one group to another is CULTURAL DIFFUSION. (67)
15. When Western industrial culture is imported and diffused into developing nations, the process is called CULTURAL LEVELING. (67)

ANSWERS TO MATCH THESE SOCIAL SCIENTISTS WITH THEIR CONTRIBUTIONS

1.   f   Edward Sapir and Benjamin Whorf: *stated that language shapes reality*
2.   i   John Porter: *remarked that Canadians lack a unifying ideology*
3.   c   George Murdock: *looked for cultural universals*
4.   a   Jane Goodall: *studied animal culture*
5.   h   Robert Edgerton: *criticized aspects of cultural relativism*
6.   g   Edward Wilson: *believed that natural selection produced human behavior*
7.   j   William Sumner: *developed the concept of ethnocentrism*
8.   d   Allen and Beatrice Gardner: *taught chimps a gestural language*
9.   b   William Ogburn: *introduced the concept of cultural lag*
10. e   Marshall McLuhan: *coined the term "global village"*

GUIDELINES FOR ANSWERING THE ESSAY QUESTIONS

1. *Explain cultural relativism and discuss both the advantages and disadvantages of practicing it.*

   You would begin your essay by defining cultural relativism and explaining that it developed in reaction to ethnocentrism. The primary advantage of this approach to looking at other cultures is that we are able to appreciate another way of life without making judgments, thereby reducing the possibilities for conflict between cultures. The primary disadvantage is that it can be used to justify any cultural practice and especially those that endanger people's health, happiness, and survival. You could conclude with a reference to Robert Edgerton's proposed "quality of life" scale.

2. *Consider the degree to which the real culture of Canada falls short of the ideal culture. Provide concrete examples to support your essay.*

   Your first step is to define what real and ideal culture mean. Then you would want to refer to the core values that are identified in the text as reflective of the ideal culture and discuss the ways in which Canadians fall far short of upholding these values in their everyday lives. An interesting example of the difference between ideal and real culture would be the increasing value we place on leisure, and yet we are working more hours than ever before, or the value we place on physical fitness and yet we are more obese and less physically fit that ever.

3. *Evaluate what is gained and what is lost as technology advances in society.*

   One way to frame a response to this would be to identify a specific technology that has had a significant impact on our society and then to discuss both the gains and losses. For example, the automobile provided us with new opportunities for mobility, freeing us from the constraints of public transportation. The automobile created economic opportunities as new industries and services opened up—car dealerships, gas stations, fast food restaurants, and malls are just a few examples. At the same time, automobiles have contributed to urban sprawl and the decline of downtown shopping areas. We have become more isolated as we travel around in our cars rather than meeting and travelling with others on public transportation. The use of automobiles has contributed to increased congestion and air pollution. Finally, you could make the argument that the automobile has contributed to cultural leveling within Canada, as regional differences have disappeared under the spread of national businesses in malls and food chains.

☞ ANSWERS FOR CHAPTER 4

ANSWERS FOR MULTIPLE CHOICE QUESTIONS

1. b   Feral children supposedly were abandoned or lost by their parents and raised by animals. (72-73)
2. a   From the case of Isabelle, we can conclude that humans have no natural language. (72-73)
3. c   The study of Genie leads to the conclusion that if bonding and learning to communicate with others do not occur prior to age 13, the biological window of opportunity may close. (73)
4. d   Studies of isolated rhesus monkeys demonstrated that the monkeys were not able to adjust to monkey life, did not instinctively know how to enter into "monkey interaction" with other monkeys or how to engage in sexual intercourse. (73-74)
5. b   This statement "we move beyond the looking-glass self as we mature" is incorrect. All of the other statements about the development of self are correct: the development of self is an ongoing, lifelong process; the process of the looking-glass self applies to old age; and the self is always in process. (74)

6. c   According to Mead's theory, children pretend to take the roles of specific people during the play stage. (75)

7. a   To George Mead, the 'I' is the self as subject. (76)

8. b   According to Jean Piaget, children develop the ability to use symbols during the preoperational stage. (76)

9. d   Researchers have suggested that the stages of cognitive development may be modified by social experiences. (77)

10. c   Freud's term for a balancing force between the inborn drives for self-gratification and the demands of society is the ego. (77)

11. d   Sociologists have been critical of Freud's theories for "all of the above" reasons. (77)

12. b   The significance of the example of smoking is that it illustrates that the pressures from our social environment influence our behavior. (78)

13. c   According to this chapter, the significance of socialization is that it shapes our fundamental sense of self. (78)

14. b   The ways in which society sets children onto different courses for life purely because they are male or female are called gender socialization. (78)

15. d   Psychologists Susan Goldberg and Michael Lewis observed mothers with their six-month-old infants in a laboratory setting and concluded that the mothers unconsciously rewarded daughters for being passive and dependent. (79)

16. a   Research by Melissa Milkie indicates that young males actively used media images to help them understand what was expected of them as males in our society. (81)

17. c   Erving Goffman defines the family as a socialization depot. (81)

18. d   "All of the above" is the correct response. Participation in religious services teaches us beliefs about the hereafter; ideas about dress, and speech and manners appropriate for formal occasions. (82)

19. c   Summarizing the findings of studies on the impact that day care has on preschool children, we can say that children from stable families receive no clear benefits or harm from day care, but children from poor and dysfunctional families benefit from quality day care. (82)

20. b   When schools teach young people to think that social problems such as poverty and homelessness have nothing to do with economic power, conflict theorists refer to this as the hidden curriculum. (82-83)

21. d   In terms of children's peer groups and academic achievement, research by Patricia Adler, Steven Kless, and Peter Adler suggests that for boys, to do well academically is to lose popularity, while for girls, getting good grades increases social standing. (83)

22. d   Resocialization occurs when a person takes a new job, joins a cult, or goes to boot camp. (85)

23. b   The statement that is *incorrect* is: "They are not very effective in stripping away people's personal freedom." In fact, total institutions are very effective in stripping away individuals' personal freedom because they are isolated from the public, they suppress preexisting statuses. they suppress cultural norms, and they closely supervise the entire lives of their residents. (85)

24. c   Historians have concluded that childhood—as we know it—did not exist in the past: children were considered miniature adults, dressing like adults and treated like adults, expected to work from a very young age. (86-87)

25. d   The "sandwich generation" refers to people in their later middle years who are caught between caring for their own children and their aging parents. (88)

ANSWERS FOR TRUE-FALSE QUESTIONS

1. *True.* (73)
2. *False.* Studies of feral and isolated children demonstrate that some of the characteristics that we take for granted as being "human" traits result not from basic instincts but rather from early close relations with other humans. (72-73)
3. *False.* Because humans are not monkeys, we must always be careful about extrapolating from animal studies to human behavior. (74)
4. *True.* (75)
5. *False.* Piaget concluded that children go through four stages: the sensorimotor stage; the preoperational stage; the concrete operational stage; and the formal operational stage. (76)
6. *True.* (77)
7. *False.* Socialization has a great deal to do with smoking, as it is a learned behavior. Peer groups play a particularly important role. (78)
8. *True.* (78)
9. *False.* Because social groups expect boys and girls to be different, they nurture the "natural" differences they find. (78)
10. *True.* (80)
11. *False.* We do not yet have studies of how these games affect their players' ideas of gender. (80)
12. *True.* (82)
13. *False.* It is a manifest function of education, not a latent function, to transmit skills and values appropriate for a role in the world beyond the family. (82)
14. *True.* (83)
15. *False.* Resocialization does not always require learning a radically different perspective; it usually only modifies existing orientations to life. (85)
16. *True.* (85)
17. *True.* (87)
18. *True.*(88)
19. *True.* (89)
20. *False.* Sociologists study the ways in which historical location and social location create different experiences within the stages of life. (89)

ANSWERS FOR FILL-IN QUESTIONS

1. Sociologists are interested in studying how the SOCIAL ENVIRONMENT influences the development of human characteristics. (72)
2. SOCIALIZATION is the process by which people learn the characteristics of their group—the attitudes, values, and actions thought appropriate for them. (74)
3. Charles H. Cooley coined the term LOOKING-GLASS SELF to describe the process by which a sense of self develops. (74)
4. SIGNIFICANT OTHER is the term used to describe someone, such as a parent and/or a sibling, who plays a major role in our social development. (74)
5. According to George Herbert Mead, the development of the self through role-taking goes through three stages: (1) IMITATION; (2) PLAY; and (3) GAMES. (75)
6. The idea that personality consists of the id, ego, and superego was developed by SIGMUND FREUD. (77)
7. We refer to the behaviors and attitudes which are considered appropriate for females and males as GENDER ROLES. (78)
8. Television, music, and advertising are all types of MASS MEDIA which reinforce society's expectations of gender. (80-81)

9. AGENTS OF SOCIALIZATION include the family, school, religion, peers, mass media, and workplace. (82)
10. Reading, writing, and arithmetic are all part of the MANIFEST FUNCTIONS of education. (82)
11. The HIDDEN CURRICULUM refers to values that may not be taught explicitly, but nevertheless form an inherent part of a school's "message." (82-83)
12. PEER GROUPS are made up of individuals the same age linked by common interests. (83)
13. The mental rehearsal for some future activity, or learning to play a role before actually entering it, is referred to as ANTICIPATORY SOCIALIZATION. (83-84)
14. Resocialization often takes place in TOTAL INSTITUTIONS such as boot camps, prisons, and concentration camps. (85)
15. DEGRADATION CEREMONY refers to the attempt to remake the self by stripping away an individual's self-identity and stamping a new identity in its place. (85)

ANSWERS TO MATCH THESE SOCIAL SCIENTISTS WITH THEIR CONTRIBUTIONS

1. d Erving Goffman: *studied total institutions*
2. c George Herbert Mead: *coined the term "generalized other"*
3. a Charles H. Cooley: *coined the term "looking-glass self"*
4. f Jean Piaget: *discovered that there are four stages in cognitive development*
5. b Harry and Margaret Harlow: *conducted studies of isolated rhesus monkeys*
6. e Sigmund Freud: *asserted that human behavior is based on unconscious drives*
7. g Melissa Milkie: *studied the impact of media messages on adolescent males*

GUIDELINES FOR ANSWERING THE ESSAY QUESTIONS

1. *Explain what is necessary in order for us to develop into full human beings.*

    You might want to begin by stating that in order for us to become full human beings we need language and intimate social connections to others. You could draw on the information presented in the previous chapter as to what language enables us to do—grasp relationships to others, think in terms of a shared past and future, and make shared plans. Our knowledge of language, and our ability to use it, develop out of social interaction, as the evidence of those children raised in isolation demonstrates. Furthermore, we learn how to get along with others only through close personal experiences with others. The experience of Genie and the children raised in institutionalized settings confirms this.

2. *Why do sociologists argue that socialization is a process and not a product?*

    Sociologists would argue that socialization is a process rather than a product because there is no end to socialization. It begins at birth and continues throughout one's life, whenever you take on a new role. Cooley was the first to note that we are continually modifying our sense of self, depending on our reading of others' reactions to us. Researchers have identified a series of stages through which we pass as we age; at each stage we are confronted by new demands and new challenges that need to be mastered.

3. *After reading this chapter, how would you answer the question "What is the sociological significance of the life course?"*

    From reading this chapter and learning more about socialization and the life course you have hopefully learned that the self is dynamic, interacting with the social environment and being affected by it and in turn affecting it. Our experiences throughout the life course are dependent upon our social and historical location, and will vary by such factors as class, gender, and race.

☞ **ANSWERS FOR CHAPTER 5**

ANSWERS FOR MULTIPLE CHOICE QUESTIONS

1. a   Microsociology focuses on social interaction. (94)

2. c   Sociologists who study social class and how groups are related to one another are using macrosociology. (94)

3. b   As a budding sociologist who is interested in homeless women's parenting strategies, you would use a microsociological approach. (94)

4. d   The term social structure refers to "all of the above": the framework of society; the patterns of society; and relationships between individuals or groups within a society. (95-96)

5. c   Religion, politics, education, and the military are examples of social institutions. (96)

6. b   Sociologists would use the term "functional requisites" to describe such activities as replacing members and socializing new members of a society. (98)

7. b   The conflict perspective states that social institutions are controlled by an elite that uses them to its own advantage. (98)

8. d   All of the above is correct. Organic solidarity refers to a society with a highly specialized division of labor; whose members are interdependent on one another: and with a high degree of impersonal relationships. (99)

9. a   *Gemeinschaft* is the type of society in which everyone knows everyone else, people conform because they are very sensitive to the opinions of others and want to avoid being gossiped about, and people draw comfort from being part of an intimate group. (99)

10. b   Social status is the term referring to the position that an individual occupies within a society or social group; social class reflects income, education and occupation, social role refers to the social expectations about the behavior appropriate to a social status, and social location refers to an individual's place in the social structure. (100)

11. d   Being a daughter, a lawyer, a wife, and a mother represents a person's status set. (100)

12. a   A sociologist would use the term "ascribed status" to describe race, sex, and the social class of his or her parents. (101)

13. c   Wedding rings, military uniforms, and clerical collars are all examples of status symbols. (101)

14. c   The incorrect statement is: "Status symbols are always positive signs or people would not wear them." Some social statuses are negative, and therefore, so are their status symbols (e.g., prison clothing issued to inmates). (101-102)

15. b   A master status is one that cuts across the other statuses that a person holds. (102)

16. a   Status inconsistency is most likely to occur when a contradiction or mismatch between statuses exists. (102)

17. d   The behaviors, obligations, and privileges attached to statuses are called roles. (102)

18. b   Sociologically, roles are significant because they are an essential component of culture. (102)

19. d   People who have something in common and who believe that what they have in common is significant make up a(n) group. (103)

20. c   People who have similar characteristics are a category. (104)

21. c   Emile Durkheim believed that small groups help to prevent anomie, because, through their intimate relationships, they provide a sense of meaning and purpose to life. (104)

22. a   Cooley saw that primary groups are essential to an individual's psychological well-being. (104)

23. d   "All of the above" is correct. Secondary groups have members who are likely to interact on the basis of specific roles; are characteristic of industrial societies; and are essential to the functioning of contemporary societies. (104)

24. d   Attacks against immigrants or a national anti-immigration policy is an example of xenophobia, or the fear of strangers. (105)

25. c   Reference groups are important because they provide us with a standard to evaluate ourselves. Your reference group may include family and friends, with whom you engage in face-to-face interaction, or groups to which you belong and feel a sense of loyalty, but they do not have to be. A reference group can provide you with standards even when you are not actually a member of the group. (105-106)

26. a   Sociologically speaking, the social ties radiating outward from the self that link people together are social networks. (106)

27. a   The conscious use or cultivation of networks for some gain is referred to as networking. (106)

28. d   "All of the above" is correct. Dyads are the most intense or intimate of human groups; require continuing active participation and commitment of both members, and are the most unstable of social groups. (109)

29. c   Personal space might be a research topic for a sociologist using symbolic interactionism. (114)

30. b   Goffman suggests that we go to back stages to be ourselves. (116)

31. d   Susan, both a full-time student and a full-time worker, finds herself experiencing role conflict when her boss asks her to work during the same hours that she is expected to be in class. (117)

32. a   If you have ever been in the situation described, of being torn between answering the professor's question or showing up your peers, then you have experienced role strain. (117)

33. b   The social setting, appearance, and manner are all sign-vehicles used by individuals for managing impressions. (118)

34. c   According to ethnomethodologists, people use commonsense understandings to make sense out of their lives. (120)

35. c   The Thomas theorem would fall within symbolic interactionism. (120)

ANSWERS FOR TRUE-FALSE QUESTIONS

1.   *False.* Social structure has a large impact on the typical individual because it gives direction to and establishes limits on a person's behavior. (95-96)

2.   *False.* Sociologists have identified at least nine basic social institutions in contemporary societies. (96)

3.   *False.* Although the author sees the mass media as another social institution, because the media influences our attitudes towards social issues, other people, and even our own self-concepts, not all sociologists would agree. (96)

4.   *False.* According to Emile Durkheim, as a society's division of labor becomes more complex, social cohesion is achieved because people come to depend on one another. (99)

5.   *False.* It is *Gesellschaft* society, not *Gemeinschaft* society, that is characterized by impersonal, short-term relationships. (99)

6.   *True.* (100)

7.   *False.* Social class is a large number of people with similar amounts of income and education who work at jobs that are roughly comparable in prestige. Social status refers to the social position that a person occupies (mother, teacher, daughter, or wife). Thus, sociologists use the two terms quite differently. (100)

8.   *True.* (101)

9.   *True.* (101)

10. *False.* Being male or female is considered a master status. (102)

11. *True.* (102)

12. *False.* The amount and nature of control that a group has over you depends on the group. Some groups, like a stamp collecting club, don't have that much control over many aspects of our behavior, while other groups, like our family or friendship group, exert considerable control over a wide range of our behaviors. (103)

13. *True.* (103)

14. *True.* (104)

15. *False.* Members of secondary, not primary, groups are likely to interact on the basis of specific roles. (104)

16. *True.* (104)

17. *True.* (106)

18. *True.* (106)

19. *True.* (106)

20. *False.* Dyads are more intimate than triads because there are only two members of a dyad, as opposed to three members in a triad, but their smaller size also makes them less stable than a triad, rather than more stable. (109)

21. *True.* (109)

22. *False.* To study conformity the Asch experiment used cards with lines on them. To study obedience to authority the Milgram experiment used fake electrical shocks. (111-112)

23. *True.* (114)

24. *True.* (115)

25. *False.* Researchers have found that higher-status individuals tend to touch more, because they have more social power. (116)

26. *True.* (116)

27. *False.* The same setting will often serve as both a back and a front stage. When you are alone in your car it is back stage, but when you are driving around with friends it becomes a front stage. (117)

28. *False.* Role strain, not role conflict, is defined as a conflict someone feels within a role. Role conflict is when the expectations of one role are incompatible with those of another role. (117)

29. *False.* Studied nonobservance, not impression management, is a face-saving technique in which people give the impression that they are unaware of a flaw in someone's performance. Impression management describes people's efforts to control the impressions that others receive of them. (118)

30. *False.* Symbolic interactionists do not assume that reality has an independent existence, and people must deal with it. They believe that people define their own reality and then live within those definitions. (120)

ANSWERS FOR FILL-IN QUESTIONS

1. MACROSOCIOLOGY investigates such things as social class and how groups are related to one another. (94)

2. The level of sociological analysis used by symbolic interactionists is MICROSOCIOLOGY (94-95)

3. The FUNCTIONALIST perspective states that societies must replace their members, teach new members, produce and distribute goods and services, preserve order, and provide a sense of purpose. (98)

4. A society's basic needs, that are required in order to guarantee survival, are called FUNCTIONAL REQUISITES (98).

5. Durkheim referred to a collective consciousness that people experience due to performing the same or similar tasks as MECHANICAL SOLIDARITY. (99)

6. STATUS SET is all of the statuses or positions that an individual occupies. (100)

7.   A social position that a person assumes voluntarily is ACHIEVED STATUS. (101)
8.   STATUS SYMBOLS are signs used to identify a status. (101)
9.   Groups in which people are assigned membership rather than choose to join are INVOLUNTARY MEMBERSHIPS (OR INVOLUNTARY ASSOCIATIONS). (103)
10. The term AGGREGATE is used to describe individuals who temporarily share the same physical space but do not see themselves as belonging together. (104)
11. A SECONDARY group is characterized by relatively temporary, more anonymous, formal, and impersonal relationships. (104)
12. IN-GROUPS provide a sense of identification or belonging while producing feelings of antagonisms towards OUT-GROUPS. (104)
13. The groups we use as standards to evaluate ourselves are REFERENCE GROUPS. (106)
14. Individuals who interact with one another on the Internet, whether on a regular basis or not, are known as a(n) ELECTRONIC COMMUNITY. (107)
15. The smallest possible group is a(n) DYAD. (109)
16. Someone who influences the behavior of others is a(n) LEADER. (110)
17. An individual who tries to keep the group moving toward its goals is a(n) INSTRUMENTAL leader. An individual who increases harmony and minimizes conflict is a(n) EXPRESSIVE leader. (110)
18. A(n) AUTHORITARIAN leader is one who gives orders; a(n) DEMOCRATIC leader is one who tries to gain consensus among group members; and a(n) LAISSEZ-FAIRE leader is one who is highly permissive. (110)
19. GROUPTHINK is a narrowing of thought by a group of people, which results in overconfidence and tunnel vision. (113)
20. SYMBOLIC INTERACTIONISM focuses on face-to-face social interactions. (114)
21. Erving Goffman believed that in order to communicate information about the self, individuals use three types of SIGN-VEHICLES. (118)
22. Goffman called the sign-vehicle that refers to the attitudes that we demonstrate as we play our roles MANNER. (118)
23. BACKGROUND ASSUMPTIONS are the ideas that we have about the way life is and the way things ought to work. (120)
24. What people define as real because of their background assumptions and life experiences is the SOCIAL CONSTRUCTION OF REALITY. (121)
25. The THOMAS THEOREM states, "If people define situations as real, they are real in their consequences." (122)

ANSWERS TO MATCH THESE SOCIAL SCIENTISTS WITH THEIR CONTRIBUTIONS

1. b   Emile Durkheim: *wrote about mechanical/organic solidarity*
2. a   Ferdinand Tönnies: *described* Gemeinschaft *and* Gesellschaft *societies*
3. d   Edward Hall: *studied the concept of personal space*
4. c   Erving Goffman: *analyzed everyday life in terms of dramaturgy*
5. e   W.I. Thomas: *wrote the theorem about the nature of social reality*
6. k   Irving Janis: *groupthink*
7. h   Georg Simmel: *dyads*
8. j   Emile Durkheim: *small groups and anomie*
9. g   Stanley Milgram: *obedience to authority*
10. l   Solomon Asch: *conformity to peer pressure*
11. f   Charles H. Cooley: *primary group*
12. m   Robert K. Merton: *in-group prejudice leads to a double standard*
13. i   Ronald Lippitt and Ralph White: *classic study on leadership styles*

GUIDELINES FOR ANSWERING THE ESSAY QUESTIONS

1. *Choose a research topic and discuss how you approach this topic using both macrosociological and microsociological approaches.*

    The way to answer this question is to first think of a topic—I've chosen the topic of labor unions. Remember that the macrosociological level focuses on the broad features of society. From this level, I might research the role that unions play within the economy of the political system, what types of workers are organized into unions, the level of union organization among workers, or the level of union activity. Shifting to a microsociological level of analysis, I would want to look at what happens within unions or between unions and management in terms of social interaction. From this perspective, I might want to investigate the behavior of union members and leaders at a union meeting, or the behavior of union and management negotiators at a bargaining session. By combining both perspectives, I have achieved a much broader understanding of the role of unions within society.

2. *Today we can see many examples of people wanting to re-create a simpler way of life. Using Tönnies' framework, analyze this tendency.*

    You would want to begin by describing Tönnies' framework of *Gemeinschaft* and *Gesellschaft*, discussing the characteristics of each. Using these concepts, you would indicate that individuals' search for community reflects a rejection of the ever-increasing impersonality and formality of modern society. In their actions, people are trying to re-create a social world where everyone knows each other within the context of intimate groups. Some sociologists have used the term "pseudo-Gemeinschaft" to describe the attractiveness of the past—people building colonial homes and decorating them with antiques.

3. *Discuss the benefits and drawbacks to in-groups and out-groups.*

    What are the benefits of such an arrangement? You could mention feelings of loyalty and a sense of belonging, and the control that in-groups have over our behavior. Feeling a part of an in-group, set against an out-group, may also build self-esteem and contribute to social solidarity. While this is good, there are also drawbacks. Attachments to an in-group can quickly get out of hand if such feelings develop into ethnocentrism and rivalries between in-groups and out-groups. In the most extreme cases, such ethnocentrism can be the basis for very destructive actions directed against out-groups.

4. *Explain the three different leadership styles and suggest reasons why the democratic leader is the best style of leader for most situations.*

    You would want to begin by identifying the three styles of leadership and listing the characteristics of each. Then you should evaluate how characteristics of a democratic leader—like holding group discussions, outlining the steps necessary to reach the goals, suggesting alternatives, and allowing the group members to work at their own pace—all contributed to the outcomes of greater friendliness, group-mindedness, and mutual respect, and ability to work without supervision. Finally, consider why those qualities and outcomes were thought to be the best.

5. *Assume that you have been asked to give a presentation to your sociology class on Goffman's dramaturgy approach. Describe what information you would want to include in such a presentation.*

    You could begin by explaining how Goffman saw life as a drama that was acted out on a stage. This would lead you to making a distinction between front stage and back stage. You might even want to provide some examples—for instance, you are presenting on a front stage, but you practiced for this presentation in your bedroom without any audience. An important contribution of Goffman's was his insights into impression management, so you would want to explain what that is and how it involves the use of three different types of sign-vehicles—social setting, appearance, and manner. Finally, you could conclude with his concept of teamwork, especially as it relates to face-saving behavior. And remember to include examples of all of these concepts as you proceed.

☞ ANSWERS FOR CHAPTER 6

ANSWERS FOR MULTIPLE CHOICE QUESTIONS

1. b   The division of large numbers of people into layers according to their relative power, property, and prestige is social stratification. (129)
2. b   Slavery is a form of social stratification in which some people own other people. (130)
3. a   A clan system is one in which each individual is linked to a large network of relatives; membership is determined by birth and is lifelong. (131)
4. a   Class systems are characterized by social mobility—either upward or downward. (131)
5. b   Marx concluded that social class depends on the means of production. (131-132)
6. a   According to Max Weber, social class is determined by one's property, prestige, and power. (132-133)
7. c   The subjective method of measuring social class asks people to identify their own social class. (134)
8. b   The vast majority of Canadians identify themselves as middle class. (134)
9. b   The objective method of measuring social class is based on ranking people according to objective criteria such as wealth, power, and prestige. (134)
10. c   According to economist Paul Samuelson, if an income pyramid were made out of a child's blocks,
most people would be near the bottom of the pyramid. (135)
11. c   All of the following are true regarding jobs that have the most prestige—they pay more, require more education, and offer greater autonomy. They do not necessarily require special talent or skills. (137)
12. b   Mills used the term "power elite" to refer to those at the top of society who make the important decisions. (137)
13. d   According to the functionalist view, social stratification is not dysfunctional, but is an inevitable feature of social organization. (139)
14. b   Melvin Tumin's criticisms included the measurement problems (a), the reality that family background matters (b), and the dysfunctional aspects of stratification (c). The one statement that does not reflect his criticisms is "d"—in fact, what Tumin noted was that functionalists place too great an emphasis on income and ignore the fact that some people are motivated to take jobs for reasons of status or power. (139-140)
15. a   A form of social stratification in which all positions are awarded on the basis of merit is called a meritocratic system. (140)
16. b   According to conflict theorists, the basis of social stratification is conflict over limited resources. (140)
17. c   The majority of the world's population lives in the Least Industrialized nations. (142)
18. d   "All of the above" is the correct answer. (143)
19. a   Imperialism is a nation's pursuit of unlimited geographical expansion. (143)
20. d   According to Wallerstein these groups of interconnected nations exist: core nations which are

rich and powerful; nations on the semiperiphery which have become highly dependent on trade with core nations; nations on the periphery which sell cash crops to the core nations: and the external area—including most of Africa and Asia—which has been left out of the development of capitalism and has had few, if any, economic connections with the core nations. (144)

21. c   The culture of poverty theory was used to analyze global stratification by John Kenneth Galbraith. (144)

22. b   Neocolonialism refers to the economic policies of the Most Industrialized Nations that are designed to control the markets of the Least Industrialized nations; they are able to set the prices they will charge for their manufactured goods and control the international markets where they purchase raw materials from the Least Industrialized nations. (145)

23. a   Multinational corporations are companies that operate across many national boundaries. According to the text, they do not always exploit the Least Industrialized Nations directly, but they do not benefit these nations as much as they do the Most Industrialized Nations. (145-146)

24. d   Wright responded to the criticism that Marx's categories were so broad that they did not accurately reflect the realities of people's lives by creating the concept of contradictory class location, which recognizes that some people can be members of more than one class simultaneously. (146)

25. b   All of the following are characteristics of the working class: most are employed in relatively unskilled blue-collar and white-collar jobs; most hope to get ahead by achieving seniority on the job; and about thirty percent of the population belong to this class. However, most have not attended college for one or two years. (148)

26. d   The classes which benefit from technology are the capitalist and upper middle classes. For capitalists, technology enables them to integrate production globally and to increase profits. The upper middle class benefits because they take a leading role in managing this new global economy; they also use the technology to advance in their chosen professions. (149-150)

27. c   According to Melvin Kohn lower-class parents are concerned that their children be conformists; they want them to obey conventional norms and authority figures while middle class parents encourage their children to be creative and independent. (150)

28. a   Members of the capitalist class tend to bypass public schools entirely, in favor of exclusive private schools. (151)

29. c   Members of the lower classes are more likely to be robbed, burglarized, or murdered. (151)

30. d   A homeless person whose father was a physician has experienced downward mobility. (151)

31. a   As compared with their fathers, most Canadian men have a status higher than that of their fathers. (152)

32. c   Higgenbotham and Weber studied women professionals from working class backgrounds and found parental encouragement for postponing marriage and getting an education. (152)

33. c.   The Low-Income Cut-off is based on a percentage of gross income relative to spending on food, clothing, and shelter.   (153)

34. d.   "All of the above." Race/ethnicity, education, and sex of the person who heads the family are all predictors of poverty. (154)

35. b   In trying to explain poverty, sociologists are most likely to stress features of the social structure that contribute to poverty rather than any individual characteristics. (158)

ANSWERS FOR TRUE-FALSE QUESTIONS

1.   *False.* Your text notes that social stratification does not simply refer to individuals but rather to a way of ranking large groups of people into a hierarchy that shows their relative privileges. (129)

2.   *False.* Historically, slavery was based on defeat in battle, a criminal act, or a debt, but not some supposedly inherently inferior status such as race. (130)
3.   *True.* (130)
4.   *True.* (130)
5.   *True.* (131)
6.   *True.* (131)
7.   *True.* (132)
8.   *False.* The reputational method of measuring social class involves asking people who are familiar with the reputations of others to judge those people's social class. (134)
9.   *False.* Wealth and income are not the same. Wealth includes both property and income. (134-135)
10.   *True.* (136)
11.   *False.* Occupational prestige rankings are remarkably stable across countries and over time. (137)
12.   *False.* Functionalists believe that society offers greater rewards for its more responsible, demanding, and accountable positions because society works better if its most qualified people hold its most important positions. From this standpoint, unique abilities would not be more important than the type of position held by the individual. (139)
13.   *True.* (140)
14.   *True.* (141)
15.   *False.* In maintaining stratification, elites find that technology, especially monitoring devices, is useful. (141)
16.   *True.* (143)
17.   *False.* Beginning more than 200 years ago, most industrialized nations pursued policies of imperialism in order to expand their economic markets and gain access to cheap raw materials: as a result of this strategy, many acquired colonies in the Middle East, Africa, Asia, and Central/South America. (143-144)
18.   *True.* (144)
19.   *False.* Most sociologists find imperialism, world systems and dependency theory preferable to an explanation based on the culture of poverty. (144)
20.   *True.* (145)
21.   *True.* (147)
22.   *True.* (148)
23.   *True.* (149)
24.   *True.* (150)
25.   *True.* (150-151)
26.   *True.* (151)
27.   *True.* (151-152)
28.   *True.* (152)
29.   *False.* Research indicates that most people's experiences with poverty is short-term, lasting one year or less. (158)
30.   *True.* (158-159)

ANSWERS FOR FILL-IN QUESTIONS

1.   SOCIAL STRATIFICATION is a system in which people are divided into layers according to their relative power, property, and prestige. (129)
2.   A form of social stratification in which some people own other people is SLAVERY. (130)
3.   A CASTE system is a form of social stratification in which individual status is determined by birth and is lifelong. (130)
4.   Sociologists refer to movement up or down the social class ladder as SOCIAL MOBILITY. (131)

5. According to Marx, the tools, factories, land, and investment capital used to produce wealth is THE MEANS OF PRODUCTION. (131)

6. According to Marx, the awareness of a common identity based on one's position in the means of production is CLASS CONSCIOUSNESS. (132)

7. According to Max Weber, the three dimensions of social class are: (1) WEALTH; (2) POWER; and (3) PRESTIGE. (132)

8. Most sociologists use the OBJECTIVE method of measuring social class in which people are ranked according to objective criteria such as wealth, power, and prestige. (134)

9. Property and income together make up an individual's WEALTH. (134)

10. According to C. Wright Mills, the POWER ELITE makes the big decisions in society. (137)

11. A MERITOCRACY is a form of social stratification in which all positions are awarded on the basis of merit. (140)

12. The DIVINE RIGHT OF KINGS is the idea that the king's authority comes directly from God. (141)

13. COLONIZATION is the process in which one nation takes over another nation, usually for the purpose of exploiting its labor and natural resources. (143)

14. GLOBALIZATION is the extensive interconnections among world nations resulting from the expansion of capitalism. (144)

15. CULTURE OF POVERTY is a way of life that perpetuates poverty from one generation to the next. (144)

16. NEOCOLONIALISM refers to the economic and political dominance of the Least Industrialized Nations by the Most Industrialized Nations. (145)

17. Companies that operate across many national boundaries are MULTINATIONAL CORPORATIONS. (145)

18. Erik Wright referred to a position in the class structure that generates inconsistent interests as CONTRADICTORY CLASS LOCATION. (146)

19. According to Gilbert and Kahl, the capitalist class can be divided into two groups: (1) OLD MONEY and (2) NEW MONEY. (147)

20. UPWARD MOBILITY is movement up the social class ladder. (151)

21. The official measure of poverty is referred to as the LOW-INCOME CUT-OFF. It is a calculation based on a ratio of gross income to family spending on food, clothing, and shelter. (153)

22. THE FEMINIZATION OF POVERTY is a trend whereby most poor families in Canada are headed by women. (155)

23. Sociologists focus on SOCIAL STRUCTURE as the source of poverty. (158)

24. The DESERVING POOR are people who, in the public mind, are poor through no fault of their own, while the UNDESERVING POOR are viewed as having brought on their own poverty. (159)

25. Forgoing something in the present in hope of achieving greater gains in the future is DEFERRED GRATIFICATION. (159)

ANSWERS TO MATCH THESE SOCIAL SCIENTISTS WITH THEIR CONTRIBUTIONS

1. d   Karl Marx: *false consciousness*
2. e   Kingsley Davis and Wilbert Moore: *the functionalist view on stratification*
3. a   Immanuel Wallerstein: *world system theory*
4. f   Michael Harrington: *neocolonialism*
5. c   John Kenneth Galbraith: *stressed the culture of poverty*
6. g   Max Weber: *class based on property, prestige and power*
7. b   Melvin Tumin: *criticism of the functionalist view on stratification*
8. j   Gerhard Lenski: *status inconsistency*

9.   h   C. Wright Mills: *power elite*
10. k   Erik Wright: *updated Marx's model*
11. m   Gilbert and Kahl: *updated Weber's model*
12. l   W. Lloyd Warner: *pioneered the reputational method*
13. i   Melvin Kohn: *social class patterns of child rearing*

GUIDELINES FOR ANSWERING THE ESSAY QUESTIONS

1.   *Compare and contrast Marx's theory of stratification with Weber's theory.*

Your task is to summarize these two perspectives, pointing out the similarities as well as the differences between the two.

2.   *Assume that you carry out a study of social class. Review the different ways that social class can be measured and select the one that would be most appropriate for your study. Explain your selection.*

You would want to begin by describing what kind of study of social class you would like to do and on what scale. Then you would want to review the three different ways of measuring social class—subjective, reputational, and objective—and point out the advantages and/or disadvantages of each. Finally, you would indicate which method you are choosing and why. Your choice might be based on the scale; perhaps you are going to study a small community or a neighborhood within a city and the reputational approach would work well. On the other hand, this would not work in a large city or on a national scale.

3.   *Consider why ideology is a more effective way of maintaining stratification than brute force.*

You should begin by considering why it is even necessary to "maintain stratification." On the surface, the idea that some people get more than other people should produce widespread instability—after all, isn't it natural for those without to want to do whatever they can to take some away from those with? However, this doesn't often happen because the elites have a number of methods for maintaining stratification, ranging from ideology to force. Without question, the most effective is ideology. Once a system of beliefs develops and people accept the idea in their minds that a particular system of stratification is right or just, then they will go along the status quo.

4.   *In the 1960s most former colonies around the globe won their political independence. Since that time the position of these countries has remained largely unchanged within the global system of stratification. Provide some explanation as to why political independence alone was not enough to alter their status.*

In order to answer this question you need to review the different explanations as to what forces led to the initial system of global stratification. Three of the four theories presented in your book focus on economic forces—the only one that does not is the culture of poverty explanation. So the initial system of global stratification was based on economic relationships. Even after these countries won their political independence, they were still intimately linked together in economic terms. Therefore, the explanation as to why so little has changed continues to be economic. To explain this, you would want to refer to neocolonialism, the development of multinational corporations, and the role of technology.

5.   *Describe which groups are at greatest risk of poverty and then suggest ways in which poverty can be reduced by targeting these populations.*

You would want to begin by identifying those groups that are at greater risk—the rural poor, minorities, the undereducated, female heads of household, and children. You would then discuss specific ideas you have for overcoming some of the conditions that place these groups at greater risk: some possible programs would be improvements in education, including more funding for postsecondary and technical training, increases in minimum wage, increased number of jobs that pay a living wage, and more aggressive enforcement of anti-discrimination laws.

☞ **ANSWERS FOR CHAPTER 7**

ANSWERS FOR MULTIPLE CHOICE QUESTIONS

1. d   Gender stratification cuts across all aspects of social life and all social classes and it refers to men's and women's unequal access to power, prestige, and property on the basis of their sex. It is *incorrect* to think that it is not a structured feature of society. (166)
2. b   The term "sex" refers to the biological characteristics that distinguish females and males. (166)
3. c   According to sociologists, if biology were the principal factor in human behavior, around the world we would find women to be one sort of person and men another. (167)
4. d   "All of the above" is correct. Patriarchy is a society in which men dominate women, it has existed throughout history, and it is universal. (168)
5. a   The association of behaviors with one sex or the other is called sex-typing. (169)
6. c   What Murdock found was that there was nothing about biology that required men and women to be assigned different work; rather it was social attitudes. (169)
7. c   In regard to the prestige of work, greater prestige is given to male activities. (170)
8. b   The incorrect statement is the one that claims that Canada leads the world in the number of women who hold public office. In fact, it is Norway, where 40% of the legislators are women. (170)
9. b   Women still do not have the right to vote in Kuwait. (170)
10. d   A minority group is a group that is discriminated against on the basis of its members' physical or cultural characteristics. (170)
11. c   Historically in Canada, women could not serve on juries or hold property in their own names. (172)
12. d   All of the answers are correct. A "second wave" of protest and struggle against gender inequalities began in the 1960s when women began to compare their working conditions with those of men; it had as its goals everything from changing work roles to changing policies on violence against women. (174)
13. c   Gender inequality in education is perpetuated by the use of sex to sort students into different academic disciplines. (174-177)
14. c   Researchers who have studied conversation patterns between men and women conclude that even in everyday conversation, the talk between a man and a woman reflects social inequality. (177-178)
15. c   The pay gap between men and women at all educational levels. (178)
16. c   The glass ceiling refers to the invisible barrier that keeps women from reaching the executive suite. Men who go into fields that are traditionally associated with women often encounter a glass escalator—they advance quickly—rather than a glass ceiling. (179)
17. b   Of the four statements, the one that says "Women do not seek out opportunities for advancement and do not spend enough time networking with powerful executives" is the only one that is not a reason why more women are not found in core corporate positions; all the rest represent valid reasons as to why women are under-represented in top corporate offices. (179)
18. d   Felice Schwartz suggested that corporations create two parallel career paths. These are the "mommy track" and the "fast track." (181)

19. c   Sexual harassment involves a person in authority, usually a male, who uses that position to force unwanted sexual actions on a subordinate, usually a female. (181-182)

20. d   Date rape is not an isolated event; it is more likely to happen after a couple has dated for a period of time rather than on the first few dates; and it is difficult to prosecute because of the preexisting relationship. (183)

21. a   Rather than higher testosterone levels in males, feminists would point to video games in which barely clad women are hunted down and killed, the association of strength and virility with violence, and cultural traditions that are patriarchal as sources for gender violence. (184)

22. c   Women are reluctant to get involved in politics because the demands of political life are in conflict with the demands of their roles as wives and mothers. (184)

23. b   In many parts of Canada today, the primary concern of voters is whether the candidate can win; gender is of less concern than winning. (185)

24. c   Increased female participation in decision-making processes of social institutions is most likely going to result in breaking down the stereotypes that lock both males and females into traditional gender activities. (186)

25. d   "All of the above" is correct. (186)

ANSWERS FOR TRUE-FALSE QUESTIONS

1.   *False.* Sex refers to biological characteristics that distinguish females and males. Gender refers to social characteristics that a society considers proper for its males and females. (166-167)

2.   *False.* The study supports the view that biological factors play a role in structuring behavior, but that social factors are also important. (169)

3.   *False.* Universally, greater prestige is given to male activities, regardless of what the activities are. (170)

4.   *False.* Female circumcision is still quite common in parts of Africa and southeast Asia. (170)

5.   *False.* As China has begun the cautious transition to capitalism, the situation of women within that country has actually deteriorated. (171)

6.   *True.* (172)

7.   *True.* (173)

8.   *True.* (174)

9.   *True.* (174)

10.   *False.* While women have made gains in terms of the proportion of degrees earned, and exceed men in earning bachelor of arts degrees, they still lag behind in post-graduate and professional degrees. (175)

11.   *True.* (175)

12.   *True.* (177)

13.   *False.* Men are more likely to interrupt a conversation and to control changes in topics than are women. (177-178)

14.   *False.* Fuller and Schoenberger found that the 11 percent difference between men and women business majors in starting pay had grown to 14 percent after five years in the workplace. (178)

15.   *True.* (179-181)

16.   *False.* The "glass escalator" refers to the opportunities that men have to advance quickly in traditional female occupations. (179-180)

17.   *True.* (181-182)

18.   *False.* In Canada, women are more likely to be victims of violence than men. (182)

19.   *True.* (184)

20.   *False.* There are several other factors that also contribute to women not holding public office: they are underrepresented in law and business, traditional recruiting grounds for public office, the

demands of running for and holding public office often conflict with a woman's other role responsibilities, they do not see themselves as a class in need of special representation. (185-185)

ANSWERS FOR FILL-IN QUESTIONS

1. Males' and females' unequal access to power, prestige, and property on the basis of sex reflects GENDER STRATIFICATION. (166)
2. SEX refers to biological characteristics that distinguish females and males, consisting of primary and secondary sex characteristics. (166)
3. The social characteristics that a society considers proper for its males and females make up an individual's GENDER. (167)
4. You inherit your SEX, but you learn your GENDER as you are socialized into specific behaviors and attitudes. (167)
5. A society in which women dominate men is called a MATRIARCHY. (168)
6. When activities become associated with one sex or the other they are said to be SEX-TYPED. (169)
7. SUTTEE, the burning of a living widow with her dead husband's body, is an example of violence against women that is embedded in social customs. (170)
8. FEMALE CIRCUMCISION is a particular form of violence directed exclusively against women. (170)
9. A MINORITY is a group that is discriminated against on the basis of its members' physical characteristics. (170)
10. FEMINISM is the philosophy that men and women should be politically, economically, and socially equal. (173)
11. The GLASS CEILING prevents women from advancing to top executive positions. (179)
12. Men who move into traditionally female occupations are likely to climb onto a GLASS ESCALATOR, moving very quickly into more desirable work assignments, higher level positions, and larger salaries. (179-180)
13. The proposed MOMMY TRACK would address the stresses that many working women experience when they attempt to combine careers and families. (181)
14. The abuse of one's position of authority to force unwanted sexual demands on someone is referred to as SEXUAL HARASSMENT. (181)
15. DATE RAPE most commonly occurs between couples who have known each other about a year. (183)

ANSWERS TO MATCH THESE SOCIAL SCIENTISTS WITH THEIR CONTRIBUTIONS

1. l   Janet Chafetz: *studied the second wave of feminism in the 1960s*
2. g   Alice Rossi: *women are better prepared biologically for "mothering" than are men*
3. e   Felice Schwartz: *associated with the notion of the mommy track and the fast track*
4. b   Christine Williams: *men in non-traditional occupations often experience a glass escalator*
5. i   Gerda Lerner: *patriarchy may have had different origins around the globe*
6. h   Catharine McKinnon: *identified sexual harassment as a structural problem in work places*
7. a   George Murdock: *surveyed 324 societies and found evidence of sex-typed activities*
8. k   Samuel Stouffer: *noted the devaluation of things associated with women among soldiers*
9. c   Marvin Harris: *male dominance grew out of the greater strength that men had*
10. f   Steven Goldberg: *differences between males and females are due to inborn differences*
11. j   Frederick Engels: *male dominance developed with the origin of private property*
12. d   Douglas Foley: *study supports the view that things feminine are generally devalued*

GUIDELINES FOR ANSWERING THE ESSAY QUESTIONS

1. *Summarize the sociobiology argument concerning behavioral differences between men and women. Explain which position most closely reflects your own—biological, sociological, or sociobiological.*

   You would want to begin by stating how sociologists and biologists each explain the basis for differences in gendered behavior and then discuss how sociobiology tries to bridge the gulf between these two disciplines' views. In discussing sociobiology you could refer to Alice Rossi's suggestion concerning the biological basis for mothering and the connection between biological predispositions and cultural norms. As further evidence of the relationship between biology and social forces, you could discuss the study cited in the text—the case of the young boy whose sex was changed. Your final task would be to state which view you think is most consistent with what you have learned about gender inequality and explain why.

2. *Compare and contrast the two waves of the feminist movement in Canada by identifying the forces that contributed to both waves.*

   You could begin by noting that both waves of the feminist movement were committed to ending gender stratification and both met with strong opposition from both males and females. The first wave was characterized by rather narrow goals—the movement focused on winning the vote for women—hile the second wave was broader and wanted to address issues ranging from changing work roles to changing policies on violence against women.

3. *Evaluate Felice Schwartz's proposed "mommy track," stating both the strengths and weaknesses of this approach to the problem of gender inequality.*

   You would want to begin by defining what Schwartz's notion of a "mommy track" is. The major strength of this proposal is that it gives working women flexibility in trying to combine work and family roles by recognizing that they often face conflicting demands. This is important for all women, but especially important for women who are single parents and need to work in order to support their families. At the same time, as the author of your text notes, this proposal has been subject to much criticism. First, it tends to confirm men's stereotypes of women executives as not seriously committed to their careers if they opt to go into this track. Second, it is not gender equitable because it assumes child-care is women's job and does not provide for a parallel "daddy track." Finally, if women slow down they will never reach the top, thus maintaining a system in which men hold all the power.

☞ ANSWERS FOR CHAPTER 8

ANSWERS FOR MULTIPLE CHOICE QUESTIONS

1. b   Race is inherited physical characteristics that distinguish one group from another. (192)
2. b   People often confuse race and ethnicity because of the cultural differences people see and the way they define race. (194)
3. a   A minority group is discriminated against because of physical or cultural differences. (194)
4. a   The dominant group in a society almost always considers its position to be due to its own innate superiority. (194)
5. c   Prejudice and discrimination appear to characterize every society. (195)
6. d   "All of the above" is correct. Prejudice is an attitude, it may be positive or negative, and it often is the basis for discrimination. (195)
7. d   Racism is discrimination based on race. (195)

8. a   The negative treatment of one person by another on the basis of that person's characteristics is referred to as individual discrimination. (195)

9. d   Hartley's research confirmed that prejudice does not depend on negative experiences with others.(196)

10. d   "All of the above" is correct. Sociologists encourage researchers to examine how discrimination is woven into the fabric of society; how it is routinized; and how it sometimes becomes a matter of social policy. (196)

11. c   The functionalists see prejudice as functional because it helps to create solidarity within the group by fostering antagonisms directed against other groups; at the same time it can be dysfunctional because it has a negative impact on social relationships. (196)

12. d   "All of the above" is correct. According to conflict theorists, prejudice benefits capitalists by splitting workers along racial or ethnic lines; contributes to the exploitation of workers, thus producing a split-labor market; and is a factor in keeping workers from demanding higher wages and better working conditions. (197)

13. c   Symbolic interactionists stress that prejudiced people learn their prejudices in interaction with others. (197)

14. b   From his research on racist groups, Raphael Ezekiel concluded that the leaders of these groups take advantage of the masses' anxieties concerning *economic insecurity* and of their *tendency to* see the "Establishment" as the cause of economic problems. He discovered that they are likely to see that races represent fundamental categories, with race representing the essence of the person. (198)

15. d   "All of the above" is correct. Genocide occurred when Hitler attempted to destroy all Jews, it is the systematic annihilation of a race or ethnic group, and it often requires the cooperation of ordinary citizens. (198)

16. b   When a minority is expelled from a country or from a particular area of a country, the process is called direct population transfer. (199)

17. c   A society's policy of exploiting a minority group, using social institutions to deny the minority access to the society's full benefits, is referred to as internal colonialism. (199)

18. b   The process of being absorbed into the mainstream culture is assimilation. (199)

19. d   Multiculturalism is another term for pluralism. (199)

20. b   The French and English white settlers are referred to as the "Charter Groups." (200)

21. c   Many Native groups are unsatisfied with the Charter of Rights and Freedoms because some provincial governments do not recognize many rights to Native land claims. (201)

22. d   The unequal distribution of economic power between the two Charter Groups was meant to be balanced by political accommodation at the federal level. (203)

23. a   Porter termed Canadian society as a "vertical mosaic" because it is structured like a pyramid with the English at the top. (204)

24. c   The Canadian economic elite has become more insular, more integrated with the economic interests of the United States, and more exclusive. It has not become more culturally diverse. (204)

25. d   Spencer found that unemployment and discrimination lead some immigrants to return to their native countries. (205)

ANSWERS FOR TRUE-FALSE QUESTIONS

1. *False.* There is not general agreement as to how many races there are—the range is from two to thousands. (193)

2. *False.* Race is physical characteristics; ethnicity is cultural. (194)

3. *True.* (194)

4. *False.* Sociologically speaking, size is not an important defining characteristic of minority group status. Being singled out for unequal treatment and being objects of collective discrimination are. (194)
5. *True.* (195)
6. *True.* (195)
7. *False.* Although discrimination is unfair treatment, it is not based solely on racial characteristics, but can also be based on many other characteristics, including age, sex, height, weight, income, education, marital status, sexual orientation, disease, disability, religion, and politics. (195)
8. *True.* (195)
9. *True.* (195)
10. *False.* In order to understand discrimination it is necessary to explain the patterns of institutional discrimination. (195-196)
11. *True.* (196)
12. *True.* (196)
13. *True.* (197)
14. *False.* Conflict theorists, not functionalists, focus on the role of the capitalist class in exploiting racism and ethnic inequalities. (197)
15. *True.* (197)
16. *True.* (198)
17. *True.* (199)
18. *True.* (201)
19. *True.* (204)
20. *True.* (205)

ANSWERS FOR FILL-IN QUESTIONS

1. RACE is inherited physical characteristics that distinguish one group from another. (192)
2. Membership in a minority group is a(n) ASCRIBED status; that is, it is not voluntary, but comes through birth. (194)
3. RACISM is discrimination on the basis of race. (195)
4. INSTITUTIONAL discrimination is the negative treatment of a minority group that is built into a society's institutions. (195-196)
5. Theodor Adorno's term for people who are prejudiced and rank high on scales of conformity, intolerance, insecurity, respect for authority, and submissiveness to superiors is THE AUTHORITARIAN PERSONALITY. (196)
6. FUNCTIONAL theorists believe that prejudice can be both functional and dysfunctional. (197)
7. Dual-labor market is used by CONFLICT theorists to explain how racial and ethnic strife can be used to pit workers against one another. (197)
8. The term used to describe the unemployed who can be put to work during times of high production and then discarded when no longer needed is THE RESERVE LABOR FORCE. (197)
9. SELECTIVE PERCEPTION is the ability to see certain points but remain blind to others. (197)
10. The systematic annihilation or attempted annihilation of a race or ethnic group is GENOCIDE. (198)
11. The types of population transfer are: (1) DIRECT and (2) INDIRECT. (199)
12. The policy of forced expulsion and genocide is referred to as ETHNIC CLEANSING. (199)
13. ASSIMILATION is the process of being absorbed into the mainstream culture. (199)
14. MULTICULTURALISM is a philosophy or political policy that permits or even encourages ethnic variation. (199)
15. VERTICAL MOSAIC is Porter's term to describe the economic and political dominance of Canada by the English charter group. (204)

ANSWERS TO MATCH THESE SOCIAL SCIENTISTS WITH THEIR CONTRIBUTIONS

1. d   Theodor Adorno: *identified the authoritarian personality type*
2. c   W.I. Thomas: *observed that defining a situation as real makes it real in its consequences*
3. a   John Dollard: *suggested that prejudice is the result of frustration*
4. e   Raphael Ezekiel: *studied racism in neo-Nazis and the KKK organizations*
5. b   Louis Wirth: *offered a sociological definition of minority group*

GUIDELINES FOR ANSWERING THE ESSAY QUESTIONS

1. *Explain what the author means when he says that race is both a myth and a reality.*

   You would begin by defining the concept of race. Then you would move on to talking about the myth of race—how there is no universal agreement as to how many races there are and how a system of racial classification is more a reflection of the society in which one lives than any underlying biological bases. At the same time, race is a reality—in terms of people's subjective feelings about race and the superiority of some, and the inferiority of other, races. You should bring Thomas's observations into the essay—if people believe something is real, then it is real in its consequences.

2. *Using the experiences of different racial and ethnic groups in Canada, identify and discuss the six patterns of intergroup relations.*

   The book identifies six different types of intergroup relations—genocide, population transfer, internal colonialism, segregation, assimilation, and multiculturalism. You could begin by mentioning how these are arranged along a continuum from rejection and inhumanity to acceptance and humanity. Then, as you define each pattern, bring into your discussion an example, or examples, from Canadian history. For example, in discussing population transfer you could mention the treatment of Native peoples by the Canadian government; in discussing assimilation and multiculturalism you could examine the experiences of European and non-European immigrants.

3. *Explore how both psychological and sociological theories can be used together to gain a deeper understanding of prejudice and discrimination.*

   Your essay should discuss how psychological theories provide us with a deeper understanding of individual behavior, while sociological theories provide insights into the societal framework of prejudice and discrimination. You could discuss the work of Theodor Adorno on the authoritarian personality or Dollard's work on individual frustration and the role of scapegoats. But without an understanding of the social environment, this work is incomplete. Bridging the two perspectives is symbolic interactionism and the analysis of the role of labels, selective perception, and the self-fulfilling prophecy in maintaining prejudice. But you should also include in your essay some reference to the functionalist analysis and the work of Muzafer and Carolyn Sherif as well as the conflict theorists and how the capitalist class exploits racial and ethnic strife to retain power and control in society.

☞ **ANSWERS FOR CHAPTER 9**

ANSWERS FOR MULTIPLE CHOICE QUESTIONS

1. b   The Abkhasians are an interesting example regarding age because they live such long lives. (210)

2. d   It is the process of industrialization that contributes to an increase in the number of people who reach older ages. (212)

3. b   The process by which older persons make up an increasing proportion of the Canadian population is referred to as the graying of Canada. (213)

4. d   Native Canadians have a lower life expectancy due to higher rates of unemployment, economic marginalization, homelessness, and inadequate housing. (213)

5. c   Gender age refers to the relative value that a culture places on men's and women's ages. (215)

6. d   "All of the above" is correct. Factors that may spur people to apply the label of old to themselves include personal history or biography, cultural signals about when a person is old, and biological factors. (215-216)

7. b   This policy reflects ageism, prejudice and discrimination based on age. (217)

8. b   It has been suggested that the Baby Boom generation will have a positive effect on Canadian social images of the elderly in the years to come, given their numbers and economic clout. (217)

9. d   "All of the above" is correct. The mass media communicate messages that reflect the currently devalued status of the elderly. They also tell us what people over sixty-five should be like and often treat the elderly in discourteous and unflattering terms. (217-218)

10. b   Some researchers believe that the process of disengagement begins during middle age. (219)

11. a   The belief that satisfaction during old age is related to a person's level and quality of activity is called activity theory. (219)

12. b   Conflict theorists believe that pension legislation is the result of a struggle between competing interest groups. (221)

13. b   As the population of Canada grays, there is concern that the ratio of working people to retired people will become smaller, making it more difficult to support programs like pension benefits. This ratio is referred to as the dependency ratio. (221)

14. a   Isolation is a problem for many people over 65, especially for women. This is because of differences in patterns of mortality between men and women. Because elderly women are more likely to live longer than their husbands, most elderly men are still living with their wives, while most elderly women are not. (224)

15. d   "All of the above" is correct. Drawbacks include: a disproportionate responsibility is placed on women; few men and women have the time and energy to provide informal care; and the responsibility for an ailing senior may be too emotionally and physically exhausting. (226)

16. b   Researchers have found that elder abuse is fairly extensive. (226)

17. a   Because of different government programs, the percentage of Canadians 65 and over who live below the poverty line has declined since the 1980s. (227)

18. b   Karen Cerulo and Janet Ruane use the term technological lifespace to describe a form of existence that is neither life nor death—the brain is dead but the body lives on. (227)

19. a   In preindustrial societies, the sick were taken care of at home. (227)

20. d   All of the answers are correct. In trying to explain the pattern of a sharp rise in suicide of seniors, sociologists point towards: feelings of lack of meaning in life; feelings of isolation and loneliness; and ill health. (229)

ANSWERS FOR TRUE-FALSE QUESTIONS

1. *True.* (210)

2. *False.* Industrialization is critical for the increase in the number of elderly within a society. Industrialization produces a higher standard of living, a more plentiful food supply, better public health measures, and success in fighting diseases that kill people at younger ages. (212)

3. *False.* Life expectancy refers to the number of years an individual can expect to live, while life span refers to the maximum length of life. (213)
4. *True.* (214-215)
5. *True.* (215)
6. *False.* A gerontocracy is a society (or other group) run by the old. (216)
7. *True.* (218)
8. *True.* (219)
9. *True.* (219)
10. *True.* (221)
11. *True.* (221)
12. *False.* Most researchers have found that the elderly are less isolated than stereotypes would lead us to believe. (224)
13. *True.* (226)
14. *False.* The income level of Canada's seniors has increased since 1980, largely due to government income support. (227)
15. *True.*(227)

ANSWERS FOR FILL-IN QUESTIONS

1. The process by which older persons make up an increasing proportion of Canada's population is called THE GRAYING OF CANADA. (213)
2. The LIFE EXPECTANCY of an average newborn is the number of years he or she can expect to live. (213)
3. While experts may disagree on the actual number, LIFE SPAN refers to the maximum length of life of a species. (213)
4. The relative value that a culture places on men's and women's ages is referred to as GENDER AGE. (215)
5. GERONTOCRACY is a society (or other group) run by the old. (216)
6. AGEISM is the discrimination against the elderly because of their age. (217)
7. The MASS MEDIA not only communicate messages about the devalued status of the elderly in Canadian society but also contribute to the ideas. (217-218)
8. An AGE COHORT is people born at roughly the same time who pass through the life course together. (219)
9. The belief that society prevents disruption by having the elderly vacate their positions of responsibility is DISENGAGEMENT THEORY. (219)
10. ACTIVITY theory asserts that satisfaction during old age is related to a person's level and quality of activity. (219)
11. The number of workers required to support the portion of the population aged 64 and older and 15 and under is the DEPENDENCY RATIO. (221)
12. Founded in the 1960s by Margaret Kuhn, the GRAY PANTHERS encourages people of all ages to work for the welfare of both the old and the young. (222)
13. Resistance to government efforts to DE-INDEX PENSIONS provides a telling example of the ability of seniors to mobilize effectively. (223)
14. Sociologists Cerulo and Ruane use the term TECHNOLOGICAL LIFESPACE to describe a form of existence in which, due to technology, the body lives on even after brain function is gone. (227)
15. HOSPICE is a place, or services brought into someone's home. for the purpose of bringing comfort and dignity to a dying person. (228)

ANSWERS TO MATCH THESE SOCIAL SCIENTISTS WITH THEIR CONTRIBUTIONS

1. c   Robert Butler: *coined "ageism" to refer to prejudice or discrimination based on age*
2. d   Dorothy Jerrome: *criticized disengagement theory for its implicit bias against the old*
3. e   E. Kübler-Ross: *suggested that facing death sets in motion a five-stage process*
4. a   Cerulo and Ruane: *use the term "technological lifespace "for life sustained by technology*
5. b   Cumming and Henry: *developed disengagement theory*

GUIDELINES FOR ANSWERING THE ESSAY QUESTIONS

1. *Choose one of the three different perspectives and discuss how that perspective approaches the subject of aging. Consider both the strengths as well as the weaknesses of the perspective you chose.*

   In this question you have the option of writing about symbolic interactionism, functionalism, or conflict theory. If you choose symbolic interactionism, you would want to talk about the process of labeling—both the cultural labels and factors that affect the individual's adoption of those labels. You would also want to bring up the concept of "ageism," the role of the media in defining images, and how the labels change over time. In particular, you could discuss how these labels changed with industrialization and how they are once again changing with the advent of a postindustrial society. The strength of this perspective is that it provides us with insights into the social nature of a biological process; a weakness would be that it does not consider the conflict that may surround the labeling process.

   If you choose to write about functionalism, remember that this perspective focuses on how the different parts of society work together. The two theories associated with this perspective are disengagement theory and activity theory. Strengths might be the focus on adjustment and the smooth transitioning from one generation to the next. Weaknesses are tied to the theories; disengagement theory overlooks the possibility that the elderly disengage from one set of roles (work-related) but may engage in another set of roles (friendship), while activity theory does not identify the key variables that underlie people's activities.

   Finally, if you choose conflict theory, you would want to focus on the conflict that is generated between different age groups in society as they compete for scarce resources. As an example you would want to discuss the controversy over social security—from its birth to the present time. A strength of this perspective is that it provides us with an understanding of why the elderly have reduced the level of poverty over time; a weakness might be that it tends to emphasize conflict to the extent that cooperation between generations is overlooked.

2. *Discuss the impact that industrialization and technology has had on aging as well as dying.*

   You could begin the essay by talking about how technology and industrialization has brought improvements as well as new developments. You might want to refer to some of the discussion in this chapter on the cross-cultural variations in aging—the Abkhasians, the Tiwi, Inuit, and Chinese. These were all pre-industrial societies with various views on the elderly. To talk about the impact of industrialization, you should refer to the improvements in the quality of life as well as the changes in cultural views on aging. Finally, you would want to talk about how technology enables us to sustain life for longer periods of time, but that the quality of that life is often compromised.

☞ **ANSWERS FOR CHAPTER 10**

ANSWERS FOR MULTIPLE CHOICE QUESTIONS

1. c   Rationality is the acceptance of rules, efficiency, and practical results as the right way to approach human affairs. (234)

2. a   The idea that the past is the best guide for the present is the traditional orientation. (235)

3. b   One of the major obstacles to industrialization was a traditional orientation to life that led people to resist change. (235)

4. d   "All of the above" is correct. According to Max Weber, capitalism is the investment of capital in the hopes of producing profits. It became an outlet for the excess money of Calvinists, as well as producing success for many that was then interpreted as a sign of God's approval. (235-236)

5. d   Because sociologists have not been able to determine whose views are most accurate, the two views still remain side by side. (236)

6. b   A secondary group designed to achieve explicit objectives is the sociological definition of a formal organization. (236)

7. b   In a bureaucracy assignments flow downward—not upward—and accountability flows upward—not downward. (237)

8. a   Ideal types are composites of characteristics based on many specific examples. (239)

9. c   George Ritzer used the term "the McDonaldization of society" to refer to the increasing rationalization of daily living. (239)

10. b   The force behind "the McDonaldization of society" is the increased efficiency which contributes to lower prices. (239)

11. d   "All of the above" is correct because alienation, goal displacement, and red tape are dysfunctions of bureaucracies. (240-242)

12. b   What Linda is feeling is referred to as alienation by sociologists. (241)

13. d   "All of the above" is correct because workers resist alienation by forming primary groups, praising each other and expressing sympathy when something goes wrong, and putting pictures and personal items in their work areas. (241)

14. c   According to your text, the alienated bureaucrat is not likely to do anything for the organization beyond what he or she is required to do. (241-242)

15. c   Goal displacement occurs when an organization adopts new goals. (242)

16. b   The Peter Principle states that each employee of a bureaucracy is promoted to his or her level of incompetence. (242)

17. d   "All of the above" is correct. Voluntary associations are groups made up of volunteers who organize on the basis of some mutual interest. They include political parties, unions, professional associations, and churches, and they have been an important part of American life. (243)

18. a   Voluntary associations exist in Canada because they meet people's basic needs. (243)

19. c   The tendency for organizations to be dominated by a small, self-perpetuating elite is called the iron law of oligarchy. (244)

20. a   According to Rosabeth Moss Kanter, in a large corporation the corporate culture determines an individual's corporate fate. (245)

21. d   Humanizing a work setting refers to organizing a workplace in such a way that human potential is developed rather than impeded. Among the characteristics of more humane bureaucracies are the availability of opportunities on the basis of ability and contributions, a more equal distribution of power, and less rigid rules and more open decision making. (247)

22. d   Research on the costs and benefits of employer-financed day care demonstrates that such a benefit can save the employer money in terms of reducing employee turnover and absenteeism. (248)

23. b   The cooperative is the type of organization that attempts to provide a high level of personal satisfaction for members at the same time that they are working towards their goals. (249)

24. c   According to conflict theorists the interests of workers and owners are fundamentally opposed and, in the final analysis, workers are always exploited. (249)

25. d   "All of the above" is correct. Computers in the workplace have the potential of improving the quality of work life, could lead to more surveillance of workers by managers, may be the first step towards a society in which every move a citizen makes is recorded. (249-250)

ANSWERS FOR TRUE-FALSE QUESTIONS

1.   *True.* (234)
2.   *False.* Traditional orientation is not based on the idea that the present is the best guide for the future. It is based on the idea that the past is the best guide for the present. (235)
3.   *False.* Max Weber did not believe that the growth of capitalism contributed to the rise of the Protestant ethic but, rather, that the rise of the Protestant ethic as a result of Calvinism contributed to the growth of capitalism. (235-236)
4.   *True.* (235-236)
5.   *True.* (236)
6.   *False.* By definition, only secondary groups can be formal organizations. The text defines a formal organization as "a secondary group designed to achieve explicit objectives." (236)
7   *True.* (237)
8.   *False.* Most colleges and universities do have written systems of accountability for faculty members. (237)
9.   *True.* (237)
10. *True.* (239)
11. *True.* (241)
12. *False.* It is difficult for workers to resist becoming alienated because of the nature of the organizational environment in which they work. According to Marx, alienation occurs because workers are cut off from the product of their own labor, which results in estrangement not only from the products but from their whole work environment. (241-242)
13. *False.* The Peter Principle has not been proven to be true. If it were generally true, bureaucracies would be staffed entirely be incompetents, and none of these organizations could succeed. In reality, bureaucracies are remarkably successful. (242)
14. *True.* (243)
15. *True.* (243-244)
16. *True.* (244)
17. *False.* Bureaucracies are not likely to disappear as our dominant form of social organization in the near future because they generally are effective in getting the job done. Most people spend their working lives in such organizational environments. (246)
18. *True.* (246-248)
19. *True.* (249)
20. *True.* (251)

ANSWERS FOR FILL-IN QUESTIONS

1.   RATIONALITY is the acceptance of rules, efficiency, and practical results as the right way to approach human affairs. (234)

2. The idea that the past is the best guide for the present is known as TRADITIONAL ORIENTATION. (235)

3. THE PROTESTANT ETHIC AND THE SPIRIT OF CAPITALISM was written by Max Weber and emphasizes that religion holds the key to understanding the development of certain types of economic systems. (235)

4. The investment of capital in the hope of producing profits is called CAPITALISM. (236)

5. A secondary group designed to achieve explicit objectives is referred to as a(n) FORMAL ORGANIZATION. (236)

6. George Ritzer has coined the term "McDONALDIZATION OF SOCIETY" to refer to the increasing rationalization of life's routine tasks. (239)

7. ALIENATION is a feeling of powerlessness and normlessness; the experience of being cut off from the product of one's labor. (241)

8. GOAL DISPLACEMENT occurs when new goals are adopted by an organization to replace previous goals which may have been fulfilled. (242)

9. A group made up of volunteers who have organized on the basis of some mutual interest is called a(n) VOLUNTARY ASSOCIATION. (243)

10. THE IRON LAW OF OLIGARCHY refers to the tendency of formal organizations to be dominated by a small, self-perpetuating elite. (244)

11. The orientation that characterizes corporate work settings is referred to as CORPORATE CULTURE. (245)

12. Women and minorities are often SHOWCASED, which means that they are placed in highly visible positions with little power in order to demonstrate to the public and affirmative action officials how progressive the company is. (246)

13. QUALITY CIRCLES consist of perhaps a dozen workers and a manager or two who meet regularly to try to improve the quality of the work setting and of the company's products. (248)

14. Humanizing a work setting is just another attempt to manipulate workers into active cooperation in their own exploitation, according to CONFLICT theorists. (249)

15. Lean production, almost total involvement, broad training, and collective decision making are characteristics of the JAPANESE CORPORATE model. (250-251)

ANSWERS TO MATCH THESE SOCIAL SCIENTISTS WITH THEIR CONTRIBUTIONS

1. e   Max Weber: *the rationalization of society*
2. a   Robert Michels: *the iron law of oligarchy*
3. f   William Ouchi: *the Japanese corporate model*
4. d   Karl Marx: *the exploitation of workers by capitalists*
5. c   Rosabeth Moss Kanter: *the hidden values in the corporate culture*
6. b   George Ritzer: *the McDonaldization of society*

GUIDELINES FOR ANSWERING THE ESSAY QUESTIONS

1. *Explain what an ideal type is and why such constructs are useful.*

    You would begin by explaining how Weber studied several different bureaucracies and used these real entities to construct composite characteristics that he thought were typical of bureaucratic structures. The result was a list of characteristics that a bureaucratic organization would ideally have. This constructed list of characteristics can then be used to measure the degree to which any organization is bureaucratized.

2.   *Define the iron law of oligarchy and discuss why this problem occurs in voluntary associations.*

You would begin by explaining that the iron law of oligarchy is the tendency within organizations for the leadership to become self-perpetuating. Although this problem occurs in all types of organizations, it is particularly evident in voluntary associations. A major reason for this is because the membership varies in its degree of commitment to and involvement in the organization. Turnover is high, so that members come and go, but the leadership stays on.

3.   *Evaluate whether or not the use of computer technology to control workers is an inevitable aspect of bureaucracy.*

You would want to begin by identifying the defining characteristics of bureaucracy—the presence of a hierarchy, a division of labor, written rules, written communications and records, and impersonality. You should then consider the ways in which computers are tied to these various characteristics. Zuboff's research noted how computers enable supervisors to monitor subordinates without ever having face-to-face contact (hierarchy); the computer's capacity to be accessed from remote sites means that managers can communicate with workers at any time and from any place; the workers input on computers enable the managers to maintain records of their productivity (written communication and records); and computers promote impersonality. Your conclusion is to evaluate the degree to which such steps are inevitable.

☞ **ANSWERS FOR CHAPTER 11**

ANSWERS FOR MULTIPLE CHOICE QUESTIONS

1.   d   "All of the above" is correct. Market is any process of buying and selling. It is the mechanism that establishes values for the exchange of goods and services. It also means the movement of vast amounts of goods across international borders. (258)
2.   c   Hunting and gathering societies are characterized by a subsistence economy. (258)
3.   b   In pastoral and horticultural economies a more dependable food supply led to the development of a surplus. This surplus was one of the most significant events in human history because it fundamentally altered people's basic relationships. (258)
4.   d   Industrial economies are based on machines powered by fuels. Industrial economies also created a surplus unlike anything the world had seen, and these economies were based on the invention of the steam engine. Therefore, the incorrect answer is "A service sector developed and employed the majority of workers"; this is actually a characteristic of a *postindustrial society*. (259)
5.   d   Thorstein Veblen used the term conspicuous consumption to describe the lavishly wasteful spending of goods in order to enhance social prestige. (259)
6.   c   Postindustrial economies are characterized by a large surplus of goods; extensive trade among nations; and a "global village." While machines may still be powered by fuel, this is *not* a defining characteristic of this type of economy. (259-260)
7.   a   Money was first used extensively in agricultural societies. (261)
8.   a   The gross national product is total goods and services produced by a nation. (261)
9.   c   The debit card came into existence in the postindustrial economy. (261)
10. d   Private ownership of the means of production is an essential feature of capitalism. (261)
11. c   "Pure" capitalism is a system where market forces operate without interference from government. (262)
12. b   An economic system characterized by the public ownership of the means of production, central planning, and the distribution of goods without a profit motive is socialism. (264)

13. b   Some Western nations have developed systems of democratic socialism as a response to dissatisfaction with both capitalism and socialism. (264-265)

14. b   Some critics believe that underemployment is a problem caused by capitalism. (265)

15. c   The joint ownership of a business enterprise, whose liabilities and obligations are separate from those of its owners, is a corporation. (267)

16. a   Oligopoly is the control of an entire industry by several large companies. (267)

17. c   When stockholders are satisfied with the profits and their stock dividends, they generally just rubber-stamp whatever recommendations are made by management; a stockholders' revolt occurs when dissatisfaction with the overall level of performance leads to their refusal to approve management's recommendations. (267)

18. c   The elite who sit on the boards of directors of not just one but several companies are referred to as interlocking directorates. (268)

19. d   Rigorous educational training, authority over clients based on the specialized training, and service to society rather than to the self are all characteristics that describe a profession. (271)

20. a   Work binds us together, according to the functionalist perspective. (272)

21. b   As societies industrialize, they become based on organic solidarity. (272)

22. c   According to conflict theory, low-level workers bear the brunt of technological change. (272)

23. b   Workers who package fish, process copper into electrical wire, and turn trees into lumber and paper are in the secondary sector. (273)

24. c   The fundamental changes in society that follow the movement of vast numbers of women from the home to the work force is referred to as the quiet revolution. (274)

25. d   "All of the above" is correct. The underground economy is an exchange of goods and services that is not reported to the government; it helps many Canadians avoid what they consider exorbitant taxes; and it includes illegal activities such as drug dealing. (275)

ANSWERS FOR TRUE-FALSE QUESTIONS

1.   *False.* Pastoral and horticultural societies, not hunting and gathering societies, were the first economies to have a surplus. (258)

2.   *True.* (258)

3.   *True.* (259)

4.   *False.* Postindustrial economies, not industrial economies, are based on information processing and providing services. (259)

5.   *True.* (260)

6.   *True.* (261)

7.   *False.* Credit cards and debit cards are not the same thing. A credit card allows its owner to purchase goods but to be billed later. A debit card allows its owner to purchase against his or her bank account. (261)

8.   *True.* (262)

9.   *True.* (264)

10. *True.* (264)

11. *False.* According to convergence theory, socialist nations will gradually adopt features of capitalism and capitalist nations will adopt features of socialism to the point where a new, hybrid form will emerge. (266)

12. *False.* Oligopolies are formed when a small number of large companies operate within a single industry, dictating prices, setting the quality of their products, and protecting their markets. (267)

13. *True.* (269)

14. *True.* (271)

15. *False.* Durkheim's concept of organic solidarity is no longer an adequate concept for understanding the interdependency that exists among the nations of the world today; the author suggests a new term, "superorganic solidarity," to describe the emerging global division of work. (272)

16. *True.* (272)

17. *False.* Researchers have found that women workers are more likely than male workers to be concerned with maintaining a balance between their work and family lives. (274)

18. *True.* (274)

19. *True.* (275)

20. *False.* In recent decades, workers in Canada have actually experienced an increase in work hours and a decrease in leisure, which is contrary to the pattern found in other western industrialized nations. (276)

ANSWERS FOR FILL-IN QUESTIONS

1. ECONOMY is the term for a system of distribution of goods and services. (258)

2. The means (for example, currency, gold, and silver) by which people value goods and services in order to make an exchange is the MEDIUM OF EXCHANGE. (260)

3. A CREDIT CARD allows its owners to purchase goods but to be billed later. A DEBIT CARD allows its owners to charge purchases against his or her bank account. (261)

4. The economic system where market forces operate without interference from government is called LAISSEZ-FAIRE CAPITALISM. (262)

5. The law of supply and demand is referred to as MARKET FORCES. (264)

6. UNDEREMPLOYMENT is the condition of having to work at a job beneath one's level of training and abilities, or of being able to find only part-time work. (265)

7. The view that as capitalist and socialist economic systems each adopt features of the other, a hybrid (or mixed) economic system may emerge is CONVERGENCE THEORY. (266)

8. One way in which the wealthy use corporations to wield power is by means of INTERLOCKING DIRECTORSHIPS, or serving as directors of several companies simultaneously. (268)

9. Durkheim's term for the unity that comes from being involved in similar occupations or activities is MECHANICAL SOLIDARITY. (272)

10. Members of the INNER CIRCLE may compete with one another, but they are united by a mutual interest in preserving capitalism. (272)

11. That part of the economy in which raw materials are turned into manufactured goods is the SECONDARY SECTOR. (273)

12. In the TERTIARY sector, workers are primarily involved in providing services. (273)

13. The QUIET REVOLUTION has contributed to a transformation of consumer patterns, relations at work, self-concepts, and relationships with family and friends. (274-275)

14. The UNDERGROUND ECONOMY consists of economic activities, whether legal or illegal, that people don't report to the government. (275)

15. LEISURE is time not taken up by work or required activities such as eating and sleeping. (276)

ANSWERS TO MATCH THESE SOCIAL SCIENTISTS WITH THEIR CONTRIBUTIONS

1. c   Daniel Bell: *identified six characteristics of postindustrial society*

2. e   Emile Durkheim: *contributed the concepts of mechanical and organic solidarity*

3. a   Michael Useem: *studied the activities of the "inner circle"*

4. b   Wallace Clement: *studied the concentration of corporate power in Canada*

5. d   Thorstein Veblen: *created the term "conspicuous consumption"*

GUIDELINES FOR ANSWERING THE ESSAY QUESTIONS

1. *Discuss the advantages and disadvantages of both capitalism and socialism as ideologies and as economic systems.*

    This is a difficult question to answer because it is laden with social values. In this country we have been taught that capitalism is good and socialism is bad. Nevertheless, you should try to approach this from as objective a position as possible. You would want to begin by discussing the advantages and disadvantages of capitalism. For advantages you could mention the idea of private ownership and the pursuit of profits, the motivation among workers to work hard, and the vast array of goods that are available in the marketplace. Among the disadvantages you could note the possibility for monopoly, the creation of constant discontent through advertising, and the violation of certain basic human right like freedom from poverty. Turning to socialism, you could note that advantages include production for the general welfare rather than individual enrichment and the distribution of goods and services according to need rather than ability to pay. Critics point out that socialism violates basic human rights such as individual freedom of decision and opportunity.

2. *Identify the defining characteristics of professions and discuss the usefulness of this framework for understanding work.*

    Your first task is to discuss the five characteristics that symbolic interactionists have identified as the defining characteristics of professions. You would then want to discuss how these create a kind of "ideal type" of professions against which real professions can be measured. Rather than seeing this as an "either/or" situation—work is either a profession or a job—these characteristics should be used to measure the degree to which specific work reflects one or more of them.

3. *The chapter discusses several different economic trends that have been occurring in the second half of this century. Discuss the role of technology in each of the following: the global corporation, the movement of women into the economy, unemployment and the shrinking paychecks, and patterns of work and leisure.*

    This question asks you to draw information from throughout this and other chapters in order to think about what impact technology has had on our lives, our society, and our economy. The first development is the global corporation; you could refer back to Chapter 6, and the discussion of the growth of multinational corporations and their use of technology to create a globally integrated system of production. Women's opportunities to work have been linked to the growth of the service sector—which was fueled by technology and the "information explosion" brought about by the microchip. The shrinking of workers' paychecks is also connected to technology—as employers introduce new technologies to increase productivity and profits, workers are working harder but not necessarily being paid more, and many are laid off because technology has reduced the number of jobs in the workforce. Finally, technology has contributed to increased leisure for workers because machines can take over much of the work that was previously done by humans, and because in an industrial economy, workers have organized and demanded greater leisure.

☞ ANSWERS FOR CHAPTER 12

ANSWERS FOR MULTIPLE CHOICE QUESTIONS

1. d   "All of the above" is correct. Power was defined by Max Weber; is the ability to carry out one's will in spite of resistance from others; is an inevitable part of everyday life. (284)

2. b   Governments, whether dictatorships or the elected forms, are examples of macropolitics. (284)
3. c   Peter Berger considered violence to be the ultimate foundation of any political order. (285)
4. d   "All of the above" is correct. Traditional authority is the hallmark of preliterate groups; is based on custom; and was identified by Max Weber. (285)
5. d   "All of the above" is correct. Pierre Elliott Trudeau was a rational-legal leader; was also a charismatic leader; and is an example of a leader who is difficult to classify in terms of ideal types. (287)
6. c   The least stable type of authority is the charismatic. (287)
7. b   An individual who seizes power and imposes his will onto the people is a dictator. (288)
8. c   A form of government that exerts almost total control is a totalitarian regime. (288)
9. a   Canada's political system is a parliamentary democracy. (288)
10. b   The history of the political party system in Canada demonstrates that a multi-party system developed during the 20th century. (291-292)
11. c   The Quiet Revolution and the rise of the sovereignty movement (both in Quebec) have transformed Canadian politics. (292-293)
12. d   Most European countries base their elections on a system of proportional representation. (293-294)
13. b   Functionalists believe that pluralism prevents any one group from gaining control of the government. (294)
14. a   Functionalists suggest that political conflict is minimized as special-interest groups negotiate with one another and reach compromise. (294)
15. d   Members of the power elite are drawn from all three arenas: the largest corporations, the armed services, and political office. (295)
16. c   According to conflict theorists, the ruling class is made up of people whose backgrounds and orientations to life are so similar that they automatically share the same goals. (295)
17. a   War is armed conflict between nations or politically distinct groups. It is not necessarily universal nor is it chosen for dealing with disagreements by all societies at one time or another. (296)
18. a   A cultural tradition of war, an antagonistic situation in which two or more states confront incompatible objectives, and the presence of a "fuel" that heats the antagonistic situation to a boiling point are the three essential conditions of war identified by Nicholas Timasheff. The existence of a strong, well-armed military force was not one of the factors he identified as essential. (296)
19. b   The act or process of reducing people to objects that do not deserve the treatment accorded humans is dehumanization. (297)
20. d   "All of the above" is correct. Today, national boundaries are becoming less meaningful because of the embrace of capitalism by more and more nations, the worldwide flow of information, capital and goods, and the formation of large economic and political units like the European Union. (298)

ANSWERS FOR TRUE-FALSE QUESTIONS

1. *True.* (284)
2. *False.* Authority, not coercion, refers to legitimate power. (284)
3. *True.* (285)
4. *True.* As societies industrialize, traditional authority is undermined; however, it never totally dies out. Parental authority provides an excellent example. (285-286)
5. *True.* (286)

6. *False.* It is because the authority of charismatic leaders is based on their personal ability to attract followers that they pose a threat to the established political system. They work outside the political structure and owe allegiance to nothing. (286-287)
7. *True.* (287)
8. *True.* (287)
9. *False.* City-states, each with their own monarchies, were the first types of government. (287-288)
10. *True.* (288)
11. *True.* (288)
12. *False.* The idea of universal citizenship caught on very slowly in Canada. (288)
13. *False.* Public sector employees constitute over 40% of the Canadian labour force. (292)
14. *False.* While employment equity policies have addressed discrimination in federal public service hiring to some degree, women and people of colour only have made limited advances. (292)
15. *False.* The European system is based on proportional representation which encourages minority parties and the formation of noncentrist parties. (293-294)
16. *True.* (294)
17. *False.* According to C. Wright Mills, the three groups that make up the power elite do not share power equally; the leaders of the top corporations have a greater share of the power than either of the other two groups. (295)
18. *False.* War is not universal; it is simply one option that groups may choose for dealing with disagreements. (296)
19. *False.* Sociologists attribute the causes of war to social causes—conditions in a society that encourage or discourage combat between nations. (296)
20. *True.* (297)

ANSWERS FOR FILL-IN QUESTIONS

1. The exercise of power in everyday life, such as deciding who is going to do the housework is referred to as MICROPOLITICS. (284)
2. STATE is synonymous with government; the source of legitimate violence in society. (285)
3. A REVOLUTION is armed resistance designed to overthrow a government. (285)
4. TRADITIONAL AUTHORITY is authority based on custom. (285)
5. Bureaucratic authority is also called RATIONAL-LEGAL AUTHORITY. (286)
6. An independent city whose power radiates outward, bringing the adjacent area under its rule, is a CITY-STATE. (287)
7. DIRECT DEMOCRACY is a form of democracy in which the eligible voters meet together to discuss issues and make their decisions. (288)
8. The concept that birth and residence in a country impart basic rights is known as CITIZENSHIP. (288)
9. A form of government that exerts almost total control over the people is TOTALITARIANISM. (288)
10. An electoral system in which seats in a legislature are divided according to the proportion of votes each political party receives is called PROPORTIONAL REPRESENTATION. (294)
11. A COALITION GOVERNMENT is a government where the party with the most seats aligns itself with one or more of the smaller parties to maintain power. (294)
12. A state of lawlessness or political disorder caused by the absence or collapse of governmental authority is ANARCHY. (294)
13. POWER ELITE is C. Wright Mills's term for the top people in leading corporations, the most powerful generals and admirals of the armed forces, and certain elite politicians. (295)

14. The act or process of reducing people to objects that do not deserve the treatment accorded humans is DEHUMANIZATION. (297)

15. Today NATIONALISM, a strong identity with a nation, accompanied by the desire for that nation to be dominant, challenges efforts to forge a new world order. (299)

ANSWERS TO MATCH THESE SOCIAL SCIENTISTS WITH THEIR CONTRIBUTIONS

1. b   Peter Berger: *violence is the foundation of the political order*
2. d   John Porter: *identified Canadian elite*
3. g   C. Wright Mills: *power elite*
4. c   Max Weber: *three types of authority*
5. f   Nicholas Timasheff: *essential conditions of war*
6. e   Tamotsu Shibutani: *the process of dehumanization*
7. a   Pitirim Sorokin: *war as a fairly routine experience*

GUIDELINES FOR ANSWERING THE ESSAY QUESTIONS

1. *Distinguish between macropolitics and micropolitics, explaining what each is and which perspectives are associated with each, and provide your own examples to illustrate each.*

   You would begin by defining what each of these is—micropolitics is the exercise of power in everyday life, while macropolitics is the exercise of large-scale power over a large group. In general, symbolic interactionists focus more on micropolitics, because it is rooted in the social interactions that take place within social groups, although some conflict theorists could also take a micropolitical approach by focusing on the conflict that is generated by power inequalities. On the other hand, functionalists and conflict theorists are concerned with macropolitics, because they are concerned with the large-scale structures and patterns of a society. (Note: You could refer to the differences between macro and micro sociology.) Finally, you would include some of your own examples of micropolitics (struggles between husbands and wives, parents and children) and macropolitics (struggles between political parties, between unions and elected officials, between nations).

2. *Compare and contrast the systems of democracy found in Canada and Europe.*

   For this essay you would want to point out that both systems are democratic, which means that the ultimate power resides in the people. Both are representative rather than direct democracies, which means that citizens vote for representatives who actually make the decisions rather than the citizens themselves voting on each decision. Despite these similarities, the two systems have differences. You would want to mention the proportional representation of the European system vs. the parliamentary democratic system in Canada; the encouragement of minority parties in the European system vs. the multi-party system in Canada; and the implications of systems of coalition governments in Europe vs. single-party governments in Canada.

3. *Discuss what you see as the future of the new world order.*

   The author poses alternatives—the development of a world order that transcends national boundaries or the fracturing of globe into warring factions based on national identities. You have your choice as to which alternative you want to support, but whichever you choose must be grounded in solid arguments. On the one hand, you could discuss how the globalization of capital, as well as recent attempts at multinational associations like NAFTA or the EU, would support the first alternative. On the other hand, the continuing tensions between national groups — Arabs and Israelis, Indians and Pakistanis, Serbs, Croatians, and Muslims in the former Yugoslavia to name a few—suggest that national identities continue to be an extremely important source of conflict and division rather than peace and unity.

☞ ANSWERS FOR CHAPTER 13

ANSWERS FOR MULTIPLE CHOICE QUESTIONS

1. a   Polyandry is a marriage in which a woman has more than one husband. (305)
2. b   Endogamy is the practice of marrying within one's own group. (306)
3. a   In a matrilineal system descent is figured only on the mother's side. (306)
4. d   "None of the above" is correct; family of orientation is the one in which a person grows up. (307)
5. b   According to functionalists, the family serves certain essential functions in all societies. (308)
6. d   "All of the above" is correct. The incest taboo is rules specifying the degrees of kinship that prohibit sex or marriage; helps families avoid role confusion; and facilitates the socialization of children. (308)
7. c   According to research findings, men who earn less money than their wives feel most threatened by doing housework and consequently do the least. (309)
8. b   In Luxton's study, hiring someone else to do the work was not a strategy married men engaged in to avoid doing housework. (310-312)
9. b   Researchers conclude that the reason men and women give different answers to the same question is because they have different perspectives on the motivation for love-making. Jessie Bernard has concluded that in general husbands and wives see their marriage differently, resulting in two marriages within one union. (313)
10. c   The tendency of people with similar characteristics to marry one another is homogamy. (314)
11. b   According to Lillian Rubin, social class is the key to how couples adjust to the arrival of children. Among working-class couples, the first baby arrives 9 months after the marriage and the couple have hardly had time to adjust to being a husband and wife before they must take on the roles of mother and father. In the middle class, the couples postponed having children until they had time to adjust to one another. (315)
12. d   "None of the above" is correct. In regard to child rearing, researchers have concluded that parents of different social classes socialize their children differently. Working-class parents are more likely to use physical punishment than middle-class parents, who are more likely to withdraw privileges or affection. (315)
13. a   The empty nest syndrome is not a reality for most parents. (315)
14. d   "All of the above" is correct. According to your text, language, cultural beliefs, and cultural values all contribute to family diversity in Canada. (316-317)
15. d   Family formation in First Nations communities has been undermined by missionary-led residential schools and non-Native child welfare agencies. (318)
16. b   Since 1961, the number of one-parent families in Canada has increased by 316%. (318)
17. d   "All of the above" is correct. Children from single-parent families are more likely to drop out of school; become delinquent; and be poor as adults. (318)
18. c   Sociologist Kathleen Gerson found that couples choose not to have children because of unstable relationships, lost career opportunities, and financial considerations, NOT because they had selfish and immature attitudes. (319)
19. c   A family whose members were once part of other families is known as a blended family. (319)
20. d   Common law marriage is two people living together without a formal married union. (322)

21. d   The "sandwich generation" refers to people who find themselves caught between two generations, simultaneously responsible for the care of their children and their aging parents. (323)

22. d   The first three statements are all correct. The last one is incorrect; in fact, the presence of children in a second marriage significantly increases the chances of that marriage also ending in divorce. (323-324)

23. d   "All of the above" is correct. When confronted with tensions of divorce, children of divorce may cling to the idea that their parents may be reunited; side with one parent and reject the other; and become confused and insecure. (324)

24. d   According to research by Diana Russell, uncles are most likely to be the offender in instances of incest; they are followed by first cousins, fathers/stepfathers, and then brothers. (326)

25. d   According to the author of the text, all of the trends—increase in cohabitation, increase in age at first marriage, and more equality in the husband-wife relationship—are likely to continue into the next century. Other trends likely to continue are more married women working for wages and more families struggling with the demands of raising children and caring for aging parents. (326)

ANSWERS FOR TRUE-FALSE QUESTIONS

1.   *True*. (305)
2.   *False*. Canada does not have laws that prohibit interracial marriages. (306)
3.   *False*. Households are people who live together in the same housing unit; families consist of two or more people who consider themselves related by blood, marriage or adoption. (307)
4.   *True*. (307)
5.   *True*. (308)
6.   *True*. (309)
7.   *False*. Luxton found that the majority of women with children under 12 were working in the paid labour force. (310)
8.   *False*. Hochschild, like Luxton, found considerable evidence of resistance to household duties. (311)
9.   *False*. Symbolic interactionists have found that husbands and wives have vastly different perceptions about their marriages. For instance, when asked how much housework each does, wives and husbands give very different answers; they even disagree about whether or not they fight over doing housework! Jessie Bernard has suggested that their experiences are in such contrast that every marriage actually contains two separate marriages—his and hers. (312-313)
10. *True*. (313-314)
11. *False*. Social class does significantly influence the way in which couples adjust to the arrival of children. (315)
12. *True*. (315)
13. *False*. Researchers have found that most husbands and wives do not experience the empty nest when their last child leaves home. Often just the opposite occurs because the couple now have more time and money to use at their own discretion. (315)
14. *False*. Women are more likely than men to face the problem of widowhood, not only because they live longer, but also because they are likely to have married older men. (316)
15. *False*. Recent research has found that 4% of women and 6% of men aged 20-29 intend to remain childless. Between the ages of 30-39, 8% of men and women intend to remain child-free. (319)
16. *True*. (319)

17. *False.* Marriage between same-sex couples is not legal in any province; however, in 1998, British Columbia became the first jurisdiction in North America to give same-sex couples rights such as child support, child custody, and child access. (321)
18. *False.* Today, one family in eight is common-law. (322)
19. *True.* (323)
20. *True.* (326)

ANSWERS FOR FILL-IN QUESTIONS

1. A marriage in which a man has more than one wife is POLYGYNY. (305)
2. EXOGAMY is the practice of marrying outside one's group. (306)
3. Female control of a society or group is a(n) MATRIARCHY. (306)
4. A FAMILY is a group who consider themselves related by blood, marriage, or adoption. (307)
5. A(n) NUCLEAR FAMILY is a family consisting of a husband, wife, and child(ren). (307)
6. Rules specifying the degrees of kinship that prohibit sex or marriage are INCEST TABOOS. (308)
7. HOMOGAMY is the tendency of people with similar characteristics to get married. (314)
8. A married couple's domestic situation after the last child has left home is sometimes referred to as the EMPTY NEST. (315)
9. A household with grandparents, children, and grandchildren all living together is a THREE-GENERATION HOUSEHOLD. (317)
10. Historically, IMMIGRATION POLICIES have intentionally blocked family formation among working-class Chinese, South Asian, and Japanese men and women, and more recently black Caribbean women. (318)
11. In 1998, British Columbia became the first jurisdiction in North America to grant custody, access and child support rights to SAME-SEX COUPLES. (321)
12. In Canada, COMMON-LAW MARRIAGE, couples living together without a formal marriage, increased 300% between 1981-1996. (322)
13. The term SANDWICH GENERATION refers to people who find themselves caught between two generations and responsible for the care of both. (323)
14. A situation in which a husband forces his wife to have sex through the use of threats or physical force is MARITAL RAPE. (326)
15. Sexual relations between specified relatives, such as brothers and sisters or parents and children, is INCEST. (326)

ANSWERS TO MATCH THESE SOCIAL SCIENTISTS WITH THEIR CONTRIBUTIONS

1. a   Jessie Bernard: *noted the existence of two marriages within one union*
2. e   Andrew Cherlin: *noted lack of norms regarding remarriage*
3. d   Kathleen Gerson: *identified reasons why couples choose to be child-free*
4. g   Margrit Eichler: *suggested that the definition of the nuclear family supports a very limited view of family life*
5. b   Lillian Rubin: *found that women's satisfaction increased after last child moved out*
6. c   Diana Russell: *studied incest victims*
7. f   Meg Luxton: *studied the gendered division of household labour*

GUIDELINES FOR ANSWERING THE ESSAY QUESTIONS

1. *Identify the stages in the family life cycle, discussing what tasks are accomplished in each stage and what event marks the transition from one stage to the next.*

    You will want to discuss each of the several stages in sequence: love and courtship, marriage, childbirth, child rearing, the empty nest, and widowhood. For each stage, you should include the work that takes place as well as the events that mark the beginning and end of that stage. For example, the first stage is love and courtship. In our culture, this involves romantic love— individuals being sexually attracted to one another and idealizing the other. There are two components—one is emotion, related to feelings of sexual attraction, and the other is cognitive, attaching labels to our feelings. The stage begins with our meeting and being attracted to another person, and ends when we decide to get engaged to be married.

2. *Explain the social forces that have contributed to the emergence of intentional families.*

    For this answer you will need to use some of the knowledge you gained in previous chapters. Specifically, you would want to refer to the shift from Gemeinschaft to Gesellschaft societies and the transformation of relationships. In a Gemeinschaft society, relationships are based on personal relationships; family is a vital social institution. As societies are transformed to Gesellschaft societies because of industrialization, personal ties, family connections, and lifelong friendships are less important. The consequence is that we feel disconnected from others. To overcome this problem, some people have turned to intentional families and consciously created relationships that mirror those of families.

3. *Discuss the impact that divorce has on family members — men, women and children.*

    You would want to discuss each family role separately—children, wives and husbands. In your response, be sure to talk about the research on the impact on children, both short-term and long-term. In the short-term, this includes hostility, anxiety, nightmares, and poor school performance. In the long-term, it includes a loss of connection to parents, and difficulties forming intimate relations. For spouses, there is anger, depression and anxiety following a divorce, but each also experiences unique problems related to gender. For women, there is often a decrease in the standard of living, although the impact varies by social class. For men, there is a loss of connection to their children and the possible development of a series of families.

☞ ANSWERS FOR CHAPTER 14

ANSWERS FOR MULTIPLE CHOICE QUESTIONS

1. a   The use of diplomas and degrees to determine who is eligible for jobs, even though the diploma or degree may be irrelevant to the actual work, is known as a credential society. (332)
2. d   "All of the above" is correct. In earlier societies there was no separate social institution called education; education was synonymous with acculturation; and persons who already possessed certain skills taught them to others. (333)
3. a   Education is a formal system of teaching knowledge, values, and skills. (334)
4. a   All of the following are manifest functions of education: transmitting cultural values; helping to mold students into a more or less cohesive unit; and teaching patriotism. Helping to maintain social inequality is *not* one of the functions, according to the functionalists. (335-339)

5. b   The function of education that sorts people into a society's various positions is social placement. (338)

6. c   The hidden curriculum refers to the unwritten rules of behavior and attitudes that are taught in school. (339)

7. c   Public schools are largely supported by local property taxes. (341)

8. b   The correspondence principle is the ways in which schools correspond to, or reflect, the social structure of society. (342)

9. a   From a conflict perspective, the real purpose of education is to perpetuate existing social inequalities. (342)

10. c   Teacher expectations and the self-fulfilling prophecy are of interest to symbolic interaction theorists. (342)

11. c   Ray Rist found that social class was the underlying basis for assigning children to different tables in a kindergarten classroom. (342-343)

12. a   A self-fulfilling prophecy is an originally false assertion that becomes true simply because it was predicted. (343)

13. b   When compared to grades forty years ago, today's grades are higher. (344)

14. c   High school graduates who have difficulty with basic reading and math are known as functional illiterates. (344)

15. d   Durkheim wrote *The Elementary Forms of the Religious Life* in order to identify elements common to all religions. (347)

16. c   Durkheim used the word church in an unusual way to refer to a group of believers organized around a set of beliefs and practices regarding the sacred. (347)

17. a   All of the following are functions of religion: support for the government, social change, and social control. Encouraging wars for holy causes is a dysfunction of religion. (348)

18. c   War and religious persecution are dysfunctions of religion. (348)

19. c   Religion is the opium of the people according to some conflict theorists. (350)

20. d   "All of the above" is correct. These are all examples of the use of religion to legitimize social inequalities: the divine right of kings; a declaration that the Pharaoh or Emperor is god or divine: and the defense of slavery as being God's will. (351)

21. a   Weber believed that religion held the key to modernization. (351)

22. d   None of the above is correct. The spirit of capitalism is the desire to accumulate capital as a duty—not to spend it, but as an end in itself. It is not the desire to accumulate capital in order to spend it and show others how one "has it made." Nor is it Marx's term for the driving force in the exploitation of workers or the ideal of a highly moral life, hard work, industriousness, and frugality (which is the Protestant ethic). (351)

23. c   Polytheism is the belief that there are many gods. (352)

24. a   An unanticipated outcome of the Reformation was the splintering of Christianity into separate branches. (352)

25. b   The religion with no specific founder is Hinduism. (353)

26. c   Reincarnation is the return of the soul after death in a different form. (353)

27. d   "All of the above" is correct. A cult is a new religion with few followers; has teachings and practices which put it at odds with the dominant culture; and often is at odds with other religions. (354)

28. c   Although larger than a cult, a sect still feels substantial hostility from society. (355)

29. d   "All of the above" is correct. Churches are highly bureaucratized; have more sedate worship services; and gain new members from within, from children born to existing members. (356)

30. a   Eastern non-Christian religions, such as Islam, Hinduism, and Buddhism, were the only religious groups that grew in any significant degree between 1986 and 1996 in Canada. (357)

ANSWERS FOR TRUE-FALSE QUESTIONS

1. *True.* (332-333)
2. *False.* In earlier societies there was no separate social institution called education. (334)
3. *True.* (334)
4. *False.* Rates of high school are not evenly distributed across the provinces. (335)
5. *True.* (335)
6. *False.* Canadian schools encourage, rather than discourage, individualism and although teamwork is encouraged, individuals are singled out for praise when the team does well. (336)
7. *True.* (336)
8. *False.* Parental influence is generally not strong enough to challenge the influence of peer culture when it comes to molding students' appearance, ideas, speech patterns, and interactions with the opposite sex. (336)
9. *False.* Functional theorists believe that social placement is helpful, not harmful, to society because the process helps insure that the "best" people will acquire a good education and subsequently perform the most needed tasks of society. (338)
10. *True.* (339)
11. *False.* Conflict theorists, not functionalists, emphasize the hidden curriculum in their analysis of Canadian education. (339)
12. *True.* (341)
13. *True.* (342)
14. *False.* Research by Ray Rist concluded that the child's journey through school was preordained by the eighth day, not the end of the first year, of kindergarten. (342-343)
15. *False.* Teacher expectations are shaped by their class background. For example, teachers with a middle-class background have been observed to encourage middle-class students and react negatively to working-class students. (343)
16. *False.* The goal of the sociological study of religion is to analyze the relationship between society and religion and to gain insight into the role that religion plays in people's lives. It is not to determine which religions are most effective in people's lives. (347)
17. *True..* (347)
18. *True.* (348)
19. *True.* (348)
20. *True.* (350)
21. *False.* Conflict theorists believe that religion mirrors and legitimates existing social inequalities. (350-351)
22. *False.* Max Weber wrote *The Protestant Ethic and the Spirit of Capitalism.* (351)
23. *False.* Contemporary Judaism comprises three main branches: Orthodox, Reform, and Conservative. (352)
24. *True.* (352)
25. *True.* (353)
26. *True.* (354)
27. *False.* Both cults and sects stress evangelism, or the active recruitment of new members. (355)
28. *True.* (356)
29. *False.* Survey research indicates that the incidence of those in Canada reporting "no religion" has grown significantly over the past four decades. (357)
30. *False.* Feminist approaches to spirituality have attempted to challenge sexist practices and create more space for women within different religious traditions. (358)

ANSWERS FQR FILL-IN QUESTIONS

1. Using diplomas and degrees to determine eligibility for jobs occurs in a CREDENTIAL SOCIETY. (332)
2. ACCULTURATION is the transmission of culture from one generation to the next. (333)
3. A formal system of teaching knowledge, values, and skills is the definition for EDUCATION. (334)
4. Tracking and social placement both contribute to the GATEKEEPING function of education. (337-338)
5. A new function of education today is MAINSTREAMING, incorporating people with disabilities into regular social activities. (338)
6. The unwritten rules of behavior and attitude, such as obedience to authority and conformity to cultural norms, is referred to as the HIDDEN CURRICULUM. (339)
7. CONFLICT theorists believe that culturally biased IQ tests favor the middle classes and discriminate against minorities and students from lower-class backgrounds. (341)
8. The idea that schools reflect the social structure of society is the CORRESPONDENCE PRINCIPLE. (342)
9. SYMBOLIC INTERACTION theorists found that the expectations of teachers are especially significant for determining what students learn. (342)
10. GRADE INFLATION refers to the trend of giving higher grades for the same work, so that there is a general rise in student grades despite the fact that neither learning nor test scores have increased. (344)
11. It is not uncommon today for schools to practice SOCIAL PROMOTION, which involves passing students to the next grade even though they have not mastered basic material. (344)
12. Someone who has graduated from high school but still has difficulties with reading and writing is considered FUNCTIONAL ILLITERATE. (344)
13. Durkheim's term for common elements of everyday life was PROFANE.   (347)
14. Answering questions about ultimate meaning, providing emotional comfort, and uniting believers into a community are FUNCTIONS of religion. (348)
15. Ceremonies or repetitive practices that help unite people into a moral community are RITUALS. (349)
16. COSMOLOGY is teachings or ideas that provide a unified picture of the world. (350)
17. According to conflict theorists, religion is the OPIUM OF THE PEOPLE. (350)
18. THE PROTESTANT ETHIC is Weber's term to describe the ideal of a highly moral life, hard work, industriousness, and frugality. (351)
19. The belief that there is only one God is MONOTHEISM. (352)
20. The belief that all objects in the world have spirits, many of which are dangerous and must be outwitted is. ANIMISM (352)
21. FUNDAMENTALISM is the belief that true religion is threatened by modernism and that the faith as it originally was practiced should be restored. (352)
22. A(n) CHARISMATIC LEADER is someone who exerts extraordinary appeal to a group of followers. (354-355)
23. A group larger than a cult that still feels substantial hostility from and toward society is a(n) SECT. (355)
24. A(n) ECCLESIA is a religious group so integrated into the dominant culture that it is difficult to tell where the one begins and the other leaves off. (356)
25. Within the categories of feminist spirituality, REVOLUTIONARIES seek to change the established orthodoxy by importing language, images, and rituals from other traditions. (358)

ANSWERS TO MATCH THESE SOCIAL SCIENTISTS WITH THEIR CONTRIBUTIONS

1. b   Randall Collins: *credential society*
2. c   Bowles and Gintis: *correspondence principle*
3. d   Ray Rist: *tracking and expectations of kindergarten teachers*
4. f   Coleman and Hoffer: *student performance linked to setting higher standards*
5. e   Harry Gracey: *kindergarten as boot camp*
6. a   Davis and Moore: *gatekeeping sorts people on the basis of merit*
7. g   George Farkas: *students are rewarded for the signals they send teachers*
8. j   Emile Durkheim: The Elementary Forms of the Religious Life
9. k   Johanna Stuckey: *outlined four categories of feminist spirituality*
10. h   Max Weber: The Protestant Ethic and the Spirit of Capitalism
11. l   John Hostetler: *studied "shunning"*
12. m   Ernst Troeltsch: *cult-sect-church-ecclesia typology*
13. i   Karl Marx: *"religion is the opium of the people"*

GUIDELINES FOR ANSWERING THE ESSAY QUESTIONS

1. *Explain the link between democracy, industrialization and universal education.*

   For this question there are two strains of thought that need to be developed. The first is the link between democracy and universal education. Here you will want to talk about the need for voters who are knowledgeable about the issues and are capable of making sound decisions; it is necessary that they read and understand news that is published in newspapers. In addition, the political culture is maintained through the educational system, as children learn patriotism and the facts of the political process. The second strain is to connect industrialization and universal education. Here you would want to talk about the need for an educated work force that is able to read instructions and learn how to use increasingly complex machines. The work force must also be able to move from job to job, learning new skills as the work requires. The most efficient way in which to train workers, both to have the specific skills needed for a particular job and the general skills needed to survive in a constantly changing workplace, is through universal education. For these two reasons, universal education developed in Canada, as well as other industrialized nations.

2. *Select one of the three perspectives and design a research project to test the claims of that perspective about the nature of education.*

   In order to answer this question you must first choose one of the three perspectives. For example, you might choose the conflict perspective and decide to do a research project on the relationship between ethnicity and individual educational achievement and goals. Your research will involve an analysis of student choices of curricula, their grades, retention rates, and graduation from a large racially/ethnically diverse high school. You have access to student records and you collect data on students in one class as this class moves through the high school. You will compare students' records in order to test whether the conflict theorists are correct in their assertion that the educational system reproduces the students' class background.

3. *Assume that you have been asked to make a presentation about religion to a group of people who have absolutely no idea what religion is. Prepare a speech in which you define religion and explain why it exists.*

   For this question, your first task is to explain what religion is. To do this you might want to refer to Durkheim's work on the elementary forms of religious life, talking about the differences between the sacred and profane, the presence of beliefs, practices, and a moral community. Once you've done this you next task is to discuss why religion exists. Here you could talk about either the functionalist perspective or the conflict perspective or both. If you choose to focus only on the functionalist view, you would want to talk about how religion meets basic human needs; you might also want to refer to the symbolic interactionist views on community. If you want to focus only on conflict theory, or add that to your discussion of functionalism, you would want to talk about how, for Marx, religion is like a drug that helps the oppressed forget about their exploitation at the hands of the capitalists. Furthermore, conflict theorists point out that capitalists use religion legitimate social inequalities and maintain the status quo.

4. *Discuss the process by which a religion matures from a cult into a church.*

This is a pretty straight-forward question. All you are asked to do is to discuss the process by which a religion moves from cult to sect to church. You would want to talk about what each is, how they range along a continuum, and what events mark the shift from one type to the next.

☞ ANSWERS FOR CHAPTER 15

ANSWERS FOR MULTIPLE CHOICE QUESTIONS

1. d   Sociologists focus on medicine as a profession, a bureaucracy, and a business; therefore, "all of the above" would be the correct answer. (366)

2. c   The healing specialist of a preliterate tribe who attempts to control the spirits thought to cause a disease or injury is a shaman. (366-367)

3. d   The components include the physical, social, and spiritual, so the one that is not a component is hereditary. (367)

4. b   When a person is unable to fulfill her or his normal obligations because sick or injured, the person is said to be in the sick role. (367)

5. b   The individual's claim to the sick role is legitimized primarily by a doctor's excuse. (368)

6. d   "All of the above" is correct.   Life expectancy in the Least Developed Nations is lower than in the Developed Industrial Nations in part because of lack of access to affordable medical technology; malnutrition; and higher risk of catching life-threatening diseases. (368-369)

7. c   The field of epidemiology is the study of how medical disorders are distributed throughout a population. (369)

8. a   The top causes of death for Canadians are cancer, heart diseases, and cerebrovascular diseases. (369)

9. d   The criteria of the Canada Health Act are comprehensive scope, universal coverage and public administration, portability, and accessibility. (371)

10. c   The most significant findings of the National Population Health Survey point to the fact that social factors such as class, gender, age, and ethnicity influence health. (372)

11. a   Depersonalization is the practice of dealing with people as though they were objects; means treating patients as though they were merely cases and diseases; and occurs when an individual is treated as if he or she was not a person. The one statement that is incorrect is that "It is less common today because of all the development of the Canada Health Act." (372-373)

12. a   Doctor recommendations for total hysterectomies even when no cancer is present is are an example of sexism in medicine. (373)

13. c   The pressures of the "double day," which lead to increased stress and excessive demands on women's time and energy, illustrate that there are gender differences in experiences of health and illness. (374)

14. c   The term medicalization refers to the process of turning something that was not previously medical into a medical matter. (375)
15. b   AIDS is known to be transmitted by exchange of blood and/or semen. (375)
16. c   A cure for AIDS has not been found. (377)
17. d   Diseases today have the potential of becoming truly global threats because contact between people of different countries has increased due to global travel. (377-378)
18. b   Rather than the rate of cigarette smoking increasing, it has in fact declined. (378-379)
19. a   An environment that is harmful to health is referred to as a disabling environment. (379)
20. d   In order to implement a national policy of "prevention, not intervention" it would be necessary for the medical establishment and the general public to eliminate disabling environments and reduce the use of harmful drugs. (379-380)

ANSWERS FOR TRUE-FALSE QUESTIONS

1. *True.* (367)
2. *False.* People who don't seek competent help when they are sick are not behaving according to the expectations of the sick role; in the sick role an individual is expected to seek help in order to get better and return to his/her normal routine. Someone who doesn't do this is denied the right to claim sympathy from others; they get the cold shoulder for wrongfully claiming the sick role. (367-368)
3. *False.* There is often ambiguity between the well role and the sick role because the decision to claim the sick role is often more a social than a physical matter. (368)
4. *True.* (369)
5. *False.* Epidemiology is the study of the distribution of medical disorders throughout a population. (369)
6. *True.* (369)
7. *True.* (370)
8. *True.* (370)
9. *False.* Universal, government-funded health care has only been available since 1971. (371)
10. *True.* (371)
11. *False.* The Canada Health Act sets out national standards for health care that must be complied with by the provinces. (371)
12. *True.* (372)
13. *True.* (373)
14. *True.* (374)
15. *True.* (375)
16. *False.* The globalization of AIDS has had the greatest impact on Africa. (377)
17. *False.* The number of deaths due to AIDS in Canada began to decline in 1996. (377)
18. *False.* While alcohol consumption (in moderation) has some positive effects, it increases the risk of a variety of diseases, from cancer to stroke. It also increases possibilities of birth defects. (378)
19. *False.* While the health risks of some occupations is evident, in many occupations people do not become aware of the risks until years after they were exposed. (379)
20. *True.* (379)

ANSWERS FOR FILL-IN QUESTIONS

1. The healing specialist of a preliterate tribe who attempts to control the spirits thought to cause a disease or injury is a SHAMAN. (366-367)

2. HEALTH is a human condition measured by four components: physical, mental, social, and spiritual. (367)
3. The SICK ROLE is a social role that excuses people from normal obligations because they are sick or injured. (367)
4. Parents and physicians are the primary GATEKEEPERS to the sick role.   (368)
5. One consequence of the inequitable distribution of economic and military power between nations is the GLOBAL STRATIFICATION of medical care.   (368)
6. The study of disease and disability patterns in a population is EPIDEMIOLOGY. (369)
7. In 1984, the CANADA HEALTH ACT was enacted to ensure that health services would be available to all Canadians. (371)
8. The practice of dealing with people as though they are cases, not individuals, is termed DEPERSONALIZATION. (372)
9. The fact that women are less likely than men to be given heart surgery, except in the more advanced stages of heart disease, is an example of SEXISM in medicine. (373)
10. The theory of SOCIAL ACCEPTABILITY suggests that due to socialization women are more likely to accept help in dealing with their health problems. (374)
11. The term MEDICALIZATION refers to the process whereby what was not previously considered medical is transformed into a medical matter.   (375)
12. A(n) LIVING WILL is a statement people in good health sign that clearly expresses their feelings about being kept alive on artificial life-support systems. (375)
13. One of the most significant sociological aspects of AIDS is its STIGMA. (375)
14. Of all drugs, NICOTINE is the most harmful to health.   (378)
15. Lumberjacking, mining, and the construction industry are all examples of DISABLING ENVIRONMENTS. (379)

ANSWERS TO MATCH THESE SOCIAL SCIENTISTS WITH THEIR CONTRIBUTIONS

1. b   Talcott Parsons: *sick role*
2. a   Erich Goode: *compared health of smokers and nonsmokers*
3. c   Haas and Shaffir: *transformation of medical students*
4. d   Diana Scully: *sexism in medicine*
5. e   Leonard Stein: *interaction games played by doctors and nurses*

GUIDELINES FOR ANSWERING THE ESSAY QUESTIONS

1. *Describe the elements of the sick role and identify variations in the pattern of claiming this role.*

    In order to answer this question you should acknowledge Talcott Parsons' contribution to our understanding of the sick role and his work in identifying the elements in that role. In terms of variations in claiming that role, the text talks about gender differences, but you could expand beyond this to talk about other variations within our society. For instance, children and old people have an easier time claiming this role because they are seen as more vulnerable and more dependent than are adults.

2. *Explain the pattern of the worldwide AIDS epidemic and suggest reasons why this threat to the health of the world's population has not be addressed more aggressively.*

    You could immediately point out that the distribution of AIDS cases is not evenly balanced around the globe, but heavily concentrated in Sub-Saharan Africa and South and Southeast Asia. What is even more interesting is the percentage change in cases between 1992 and 1996; among the Most Industrialized Nations the percentage change has been relatively small—and in some cases in the negative column—while the change among the Least Industrialized Nations has been great. Looking at AIDS globally, you would want to point out this maldistribution and note that those countries most directly affected have the least amount of money to spend. Looking at AIDS within Canada, you would want to point out that the number of deaths due to AIDS began to decline in 1996. Furthermore, the most common way in which to contract the disease is through behaviors that are stigmatized in our society—homosexual sex, promiscuous heterosexual sex, and I.V. drug use. You could point out that policy makers may have been slow to respond because of the character of those most directly affected by the epidemic.

3.   *Discuss the obstacles to developing preventive medicine and suggest ways in which these obstacles can be overcome.*

To answer this question you should note the obstacles—resistance from the medical community, the public, businesses, and other nations. In your essay remember to outline the nature of each of these obstacles. Then you should suggest ways around each of these. For example, overcome public resistance could be accomplished through educational programs or through initiatives like lower health insurance costs for people who can demonstrate they have adopted preventive measures, e.g., regular exercise programs, altered diet, and no drug use. You would need to do this for each of the obstacles listed.

☞ ANSWERS FOR CHAPTER 16

ANSWERS FOR MULTIPLE CHOICE QUESTIONS

1. b   In sociology, the term deviance refers to all violations of social rules. (384)
2. c   The function of the stigma is to define or identify the person who violates the norm as deviant. (384)
3. d   The pluralistic theory of social control takes the view that different groups mediate and balance their competing interests with the result that social stability is achieved. (386)
4. b   According to conflict theory, social control represents the interests of the wealthy and powerful. (386)
5. c   Differential association theory is based on the symbolic interactionist perspective. (388)
6. c   The idea that two control systems—inner controls and outer controls—work against our pushes and pulls toward deviance is called control theory. (389)
7. c   All of the following are ways of neutralizing deviance: appeal to higher loyalties, denial of responsibility, and denial of injury and of a victim. Denial of deviant labels is not one of the ways of neutralizing such behavior. (390)
8. a   The term for acts of deviance that have little effect on the self-concept is primary deviance. (390-391)
9. c   Tertiary deviance is deviant behavior that is normalized by relabeling it as nondeviant; primary deviance is the initial acts of deviance that do not become part of the individual's self-concept; secondary deviance involves self-labeling, when deviance becomes part of the self-concept. (391)
10. b   William Chambliss's study of the Saints and the Roughnecks suggests that people often live up to the labels that a community gives them. (391-392)
11. d   "All of the above" is correct. William Chambliss states that all of these are factors which influence whether or not people will be seen as deviant: social class, the visibility of offenders, and their styles of interaction. (392)
12. a   According to the functionalist perspective, deviance promotes social unity and social change. (392)

13. d   Recidivism is not one of the responses to anomie identified by Merton. (393)

14. b   According to Merton's strain theory, people who drop out of the pursuit of success by abusing alcohol or drugs are retreatists. (393)

15. d   The illegitimate opportunity structures theory is based on the functionalist perspective. (393)

16. c   Crimes committed by people of respectable and high social status in the course of their occupations are called white-collar crime. (394)

17. b   Conflict theorists see the law as an instrument of oppression because it is used by the powerful to maintain their privileged position. (395)

18. b   According to official statistics working-class boys are more delinquent than middle-class boys. (395-396)

19. c   Feminist theorists relate male violence against women to patriarchal ideologies which promote male superiority. (396)

20. d   "All of the above" is correct. Job creation programs, expanded social services, and anti-sexist self-help groups for men are all examples of public policy strategies to address male violence against women. (396-397)

21. c   Frowns, gossip, and crossing people off guest lists are examples of negative sanctions. (397)

22. a   A court martial in which the insignia of rank are publicly ripped off the uniforms of the officers found guilty is an example of degradation ceremonies. (397)

23. b   Imprisonment follows a public pronouncement that a person is "unfit to live among decent, law-abiding people." (397)

24. c   The medicalization of deviance refers to viewing deviance as a medical matter. (399)

25. d   "All of the above" is correct. A more humane approach to dealing with social deviance is needed because social deviance is inevitable; it is often the result of systems of inequality; and a measure of a society is how it treats deviant behavior. (400-401)

ANSWERS FOR TRUE-FALSE QUESTIONS

1.   *False.* What is deviant to some is not deviant to others. This principle holds true within a society as well as across cultures. Thus, acts perfectly acceptable in one culture may be considered deviant in another culture. (384)

2.   *False.* According to your text, a college student cheating on an exam and a mugger lurking on a dark street do have something in common: they are both engaged in deviant behavior, thus making them "deviants." (384)

3.   *True.* (386)

4.   *True.* (386)

5.   *True.* (386)

6.   *True.* (387)

7.   *True.* (388)

8.   *False.* It is in the third stage (tertiary deviance), when the deviant behavior is normalized by relabeling it as nondeviant. (390)

9.   *False.* Some people and groups do embrace deviance and want to be labeled with a deviant identity. Examples include: teenagers who make certain that their clothing, music, and hairstyles are outside adult norms; and outlaw bikers. (391)

10. *True.* (391)

11. *True.* (392)

12. *True.* (392)

13. *False.* According to strain theory, everyone does not have an equal chance to get ahead in society because of structural factors in the society (e.g., racism, sexism, and social class) which may deny them access to the approved ways of achieving cultural goals. (392-393)

14. *True.* (392-393)
15. *True.* (394)
16. *False.* White-collar crime often is more costly than street crime. (394)
17. *False.* Conflict theorists believe that the criminal justice system functions for the well-being of the capitalist class. (395)
18. *False.* Official statistics are not always accurate counts of the crimes committed in our society. Both conflict theorists and symbolic interactionists believe that these statistics have bias built into them because of police discretion in arresting people, as well as many other factors. (395-396)
19. *True.* (396)
20. *False.* The purpose of positive sanctions is to reward people for conforming to social norms. (397)

ANSWERS FOR FILL-IN QUESTIONS

1. DEVIANCE is the violation of rules or norms. (384)
2. Erving Goffman used the term STIGMA to refer to attributes that discredit people. (384)
3. Formal and informal means of enforcing norms constitute a system of SOCIAL CONTROL. (386)
4. According to the CONFLICT perspective, society is made up of competing groups, and the group that holds power uses social control to maintain its position of privilege. (386)
5. NORMS make social life possible by making behavior predictable. (386)
6. SOCIAL ORDER is a group's usual and customary social arrangements, on which its members depend and on which they base their lives. (387)
7. CONTROL theory is the idea that two control systems—inner controls and outer controls—work against our pushes and pulls toward deviance. (389)
8. Labeling theory is based on the SYMBOLIC INTERACTIONIST perspective. (390)
9. SECONDARY DEVIANCE occurs at the point when individuals incorporate a deviant identity into their self-concept. (390)
10. Strain theory is based on the idea that large numbers of people are socialized into desiring CULTURAL GOALS (the legitimate objects held out to everyone) but many do not have access to INSTITUTIONALIZED MEANS in order to achieve those goals. (392-393)
11. Robert Merton used the term ANOMIE to describe the sense of normlessness that some people are frustrated in their efforts to achieve success. (393)
12. Edwin Sutherland used the term WHITE-COLLAR CRIME to refer to crimes that people of respectable and high social status commit in the course of their occupations. (394)
13. In combination the policy, courts, and prisons that deal with people who are accused of having committed crimes make up the CRIMINAL JUSTICE SYSTEM. (395)
14. Steps to strip an individual of his or her identity as a group member occur during DEGRADATION CEREMONIES. (397)
15. The view that deviance, including crime, is the product of mental illness is referred to as MEDICALIZATION OF DEVIANCE. (399)

ANSWERS TO MATCH THESE SOCIAL SCIENTISTS WITH THEIR CONTRIBUTIONS

1. d   Edwin Sutherland: *white-collar crime*
2. a   Robert Merton: *strain theory*
3. g   Erving Goffman: *importance of stigma*
4. i   Thomas Szasz: *myth of mental illness*
5. e   Emile Durkheim: *functions of deviance*
6. f   William Chambliss: *effects of labeling*
7. h   Gresham Sykes and David Matza: *techniques of neutralization*

8. b   Walter Reckless: *control theory*
9. c   Harold Garfinkel: *degradation ceremonies*

GUIDELINES FOR ANSWERING THE ESSAY QUESTIONS

1. *Discuss how the different sociological perspectives could be combined in order to provide a more complete picture of deviance.*

    You would begin by identifying the strengths of each perspective—symbolic interactionism focuses on group membership and interaction within and between groups, functionalism focuses on how deviance is a part of the social order, and conflict theory focuses on how social inequality impacts on definitions of and reactions to acts of deviance. An example of combining perspectives is reflected in the work of William Chambliss on the Saints and the Roughnecks; he looked at patterns of inequality and different interaction styles to explain the different treatment the two groups received. Another example would be Cloward and Ohlin's work on illegitimate opportunity structures; they added the concept of social class inequality to the notion of the strain between institutionalized means and cultural goals to explain patterns of lower class deviance.

2. *Explain how forms of deviance such as street gangs can be both functional and dysfunctional at the same time.*

    Jankowski studied street gangs and discovered that gangs functioned within low-income neighborhoods as sources of employment (often the only source), recreation, and protection. In a few cases the gangs were involved in legitimate activities such as running small groceries and renovating and renting abandoned apartment buildings. All of these demonstrate the functional nature of gangs. At the same time, gangs generate most of their income through illegal activities—a dysfunctional aspect. Another dysfunctional aspect is the violence that accompanies gangs—violence that is not confined to gangs but often spills over into the neighborhood as a whole.

3. *In light of the different explanations for deviance, evaluate the effectiveness of the various reactions to deviance.*

    In answering this question, you would want to think about what the purpose or goal of each of the reactions is— sanctions, degradation ceremonies, and imprisonment. Then you would want to consider whether or not the goal will effectively address the deviance, given what different sociologists have said about deviance. Consider this question: Would imprisonment be effective against someone who has reached the tertiary stage of deviance and has actively embraced the deviant label?

☞ ANSWERS FOR CHAPTER 17

ANSWERS FOR MULTIPLE CHOICE QUESTIONS

1. c   The specialists who study the size, composition, growth, and distribution of human population are referred to as demographers. (406)
2. b   The proposition that the population grows geometrically while food supply increases arithmetically is known as the Malthus theorem. (406)
3. d   Anti-Malthusians believe that the demographic transition, an explanation of the shift from high birth and death rates to low ones that occurred previously in Europe, is an accurate picture of what will happen in the future in the Least Industrialized Nations of the world. (407-409)

4. b   The three-stage historical process of population growth is the demographic transition. (408)
5. c   The process by which a country's population becomes smaller because its birth rate and immigration are too low to replace those who die and emigrate is population shrinkage. (408-409)
6. b   Starvation occurs not because there is not enough fertile land, or there are too many people, or there are natural disasters. Rather, experts argue that it occurs because some parts of the world lack food while other parts of the world produce more than they can consume. (409-410)
7. d   "All of the above" is correct. People in the Least Industrialized Nations have so many children because parenthood provides status, children are considered to be an economic asset, and the community encourages people to have children. (410-411)
8. a   Factors that influence population growth (fertility, mortality, and net migration) are demographic variables. (411)
9. b   Fecundity refers to the number of children that women are capable of bearing. (412)
10. a   The annual number of deaths per 1,000 population is the crude death rate. (412)
11. d   The factors pushing someone to emigrate include poverty, lack of religious and political freedoms, and political persecution. (412)
12. a   According to your text, it is difficult to forecast population growth because of government programs that impact on fertility. (412)
13. d   Urbanization is when an increasing proportion of a population lives in cities. (415)
14. d   "All of the above" is correct. Today's urbanization means that more people live in cities, today's cities are larger, and about 200 of the world's cities contain at least one million people. (416)
15. b   The concentric-zone model was proposed by Ernest Burgess. (416)
16. d   The pattern of a growing number of immigrants sealing an area, with the consequence that those already living in the area move out because they are threatened by their presence is referred to invasion-succession cycle. (417)
17. c   The model which is based on the idea that land use in cities is based on several centers, such as a clustering of restaurants or automobile dealerships, is the multiple-nuclei model. (417)
18. c   While a sense of community is natural to *Gemeinschaft*, because everyone knows everyone else, alienation can result as a society industrializes and *Gesellschaft*, based on secondary, impersonal relationships, emerges. (419)
19. d   "All of the above" is correct. According to Gans' typology, the trapped includes downwardly mobile persons, elderly persons, and alcoholics and drug addicts. (420)
20. b   Suburbanization is the movement from the city to the suburbs. (420)
21. d   Acid rain, the greenhouse effect, and global warming are all consequences of the burning fossil fuels. (421)
22. c   Conflict theorists note that there is no energy shortage. Rather, they argue that multinational corporations are unwilling to develop alternative energy sources, because it would threaten their monopoly over existing fossil fuels and cut into their profits. (421-422)
23. c   The disappearance of the world's rain forests presents the greatest threat to the survival of numerous plant and animal species. (422)
24. d   "All of the above" is correct. Environmental sociology examines how the physical environment affects human activities; how human activities affect the physical environment; and the unintended consequences of human actions. (424)
25. b   The goal of environmental sociologists is to do research on the mutual impact that individuals and environments have on one another. (424)

ANSWERS FOR TRUE-FALSE QUESTIONS

1. *False*. Thomas Malthus was not a sociologist at the University of Chicago in the 1920s. He was an English economist who lived from 1766 to 1834. (406)
2. *True*. (406)
3. *False*. It is the New Malthusians, not the Anti-Malthusians, who believe that people breed like germs in a bucket. (408)
4. *False*. There are three stages, not four, in the process of demographic transition. (408)
5. *False*. The main reason why there is starvation is because those countries that produce food surpluses have stable populations, while those with rapidly growing populations have food shortages. (409-410)
6. *False*. The major reason why people in poor countries have so many children is not necessarily because they do not know how to prevent conception. The reason is more sociological in nature, including the status which is conferred on women for producing children, as well as the need for children to take care of a person when she or he is old. (410-411)
7. *True*. (412)
8. *True*. (412)
9. *True*. (412)
10. *True*. (412)
11. *True*. (415)
12. *True*. (416)
13. *False*. No one model is considered to be the most accurate because different cities develop and grow in different ways, especially if there are certain kinds of natural barriers such as rivers or mountains. (417)
14. *True*. (420)
15. *True*. (420)
16. *False*. There is evidence that past civilizations—Mesopotamia, the Anasazi, the Mayans—were destroyed because of environmental abuse. (421)
17. *False*. Rain containing sulfuric and nitric acid, released into the air with the burning of fossil fuels, is acid rain. While the burning of fossil fuels contributes to the greenhouse effect, acid rain itself does not. (421)
18. *False*. Scientists are not in agreement that the problems of acid rain and the greenhouse effect must be solved quickly. Some even doubt that the greenhouse effect exists. (421)
19. *True*. (424)
20. *False*. The goal of environmental sociology is to study the relationships between humans and the physical environment. (424)

ANSWERS FOR FILL-IN QUESTIONS

1. DEMOGRAPHY is the study of the size, composition, growth, and distribution of human populations. (406)
2. A pattern of growth in which numbers double during approximately equal intervals, thus accelerating in the latter stages, is the EXPONENTIAL GROWTH CURVE. (406)
3. The Anti-Malthusians believe that Europe's DEMOGRAPHIC TRANSITION, a three-stage historical process of population growth, provides an accurate picture of the future. (408)
4. When the people in a society do not produce enough children to replace the people who die, there is concern about POPULATION SHRINKAGE. (409)
5. The FERTILITY RATE refers to the number of children that the average woman bears. (412)
6. The basic demographic equation is growth = BIRTHS − DEATHS + MIGRATION. (412)

7. When women bear only enough children to replace the population, ZERO POPULATION GROWTH has been achieved. (412)

8. CITY is a place in which a large number of people are permanently based and do not produce their own food. (415)

9. URBANIZATION is the process by which an increasing number of people live in cities. (416)

10. A central city, surrounding smaller cities and their suburbs, forming an interconnected urban area, is a METROPOLIS. (416)

11. HUMAN ECOLOGY is the relationship between people and their environment. (416)

12. The displacement of the poor by the relatively affluent, who renovate the former's homes, is GENTRIFICATION. (417)

13. COMMUNITY exists when people identify with an area and with one another. (419)

14. The greenhouse effect is believed to produce GLOBAL WARMING. (421)

15. A world system that takes into account the limits of the environment, produces enough material goods for everyone's needs, and leaves a heritage of a sound environment for the next generation is the definition of SUSTAINABLE ENVIRONMENT. (423)

ANSWERS TO MATCH THESE SOCIAL SCIENTISTS WITH THEIR CONTRIBUTIONS

1. a   Thomas Malthus: *theorem on population growth*
2. c   Ernest Burgess: *concentric-zone model*
3. d   Herbert Gans: *urban villagers*
4. e   Homer Hoyt: *sector model*
5. b   Robert Park: *human ecology*

GUIDELINES FOR ANSWERING THE ESSAY QUESTIONS

1. *State the positions of the New Malthusians and the Anti-Malthusians and discuss which view you think is more accurate, based on the information provided about each position.*

   You should begin this essay by summarizing each side's arguments. For the New Malthusians you would want to include the idea of the exponential growth curve, while for the Anti-Malthusians you would want to refer to the concepts of the demographic transition and population shrinkage. For both you would want to include some of the facts—that world population growth does seem to reflect the exponential growth curve (New Malthusians), while the Least Industrialized Nations reflect the second stage of the demographic transition and the population of European countries is shrinking (Anti-Malthusians). Finally, you need to draw conclusions about which view you think is more accurate.

2. *Identify the problems that are associated with forecasting population growth.*

   Your first step is to define the basic demographic equation, that calculation which is used to project population growth. Then you need to identify problems that make the demographer's job more difficult. These would include natural phenomena (famines and plagues), economic factors (short-term booms and busts as well as longer-term industrialization), political factors (wars and government policy), and social factors (educational levels). In your essay you need to not only identify these, but discuss the ways in which they make forecasting a challenge.

3. *Discuss whether or not cities are impersonal* Gesellschafts *or communal* Gemeinschafts.

   For this essay you would want to refer to the work of Louis Wirth and Herbert Gans. Wirth talked about the breakup of kinship and neighborhoods with the growth of cities; the result was alienation. On the other hand, Gans found evidence of villages embedded within urban landscapes, which provided people with a sense of community. In particular, he discusses the "ethnic villagers." If you decide to argue for the impersonality of urban life, you should also include some discussion of the norm of noninvolvement and the diffusion of responsibility. If you choose to talk about communities within cities, then you should refer to how people create intimacy by personalizing their environment, developing attachments to sports teams, objects, and even city locations.

4.   *Discuss the role that global stratification plays in the worldwide environmental problems.*

For this essay you would want to first divide the world into three camps—the Most Industrialized Nations, the Industrializing Nations, and the Least Industrialized Nations—and then discuss the type of environmental problems, and the source of those problems, within each of the worlds of industrialization. You would also want to talk about how these three worlds are inter-connected when it comes to environmental problems; pollution and environmental degradation does not stop at national boundaries. It is important to bring into your discussion how the global inequalities that were first discussed in Chapter 6 play a critical role in global pollution.

☞ ANSWERS FOR CHAPTER 18

ANSWERS FOR MULTIPLE CHOICE QUESTIONS

1.   c   It was Gustave LeBon, not Charles Mackay, who suggested that the crowd develops a collective mind. (430-431)

2.   d   Gustave LeBon's term for the tendency of people in a crowd to feel, think, and act in extraordinary ways is collective mind. (430)

3.   c   Social unrest is the condition most conductive to the emergence of collective behavior. (431)

4.   a   A back-and-forth communication between the members of a crowd whereby a collective impulse is transmitted is a circular reaction. (431)

5.   d   "All of the above" is correct. Acting crowd is a term coined by Herbert Blumer; is an excited group that collectively moves toward a goal; and is the end result of the five stages of collective behavior. (431)

6.   b   Richard Berk used the term "minimax strategy" to describe the tendency for humans to minimize costs and maximize rewards. This is true whether an individual is deciding what card(s) to discard in a poker game or what store to loot in an urban riot. (432)

7.   a   The development of new norms to cope with a new situation is emergent norms. (432)

8.   c   Urban riots are usually caused by feelings of frustration and anger at being deprived of the same opportunities as others. (433)

9.   b   A behavior that results when people become so fearful that they cannot function normally and may even flee is a panic. (435)

10. b   Sociologists have found that when a disaster such as a fire occurs some people continue to perform their roles. (435)

11. b   Moral panics are generally fed by rumor, information for which there is no discernible source and which is usually unfounded. (435-436)

12. c   Sociologists refer to unfounded information spread among people as rumor. (436)

13. d   A temporary pattern of behavior that catches people's attention is a fad. (436)

14. c   Eating goldfish and bungee jumping are both examples of activity fads. Fads are novel forms of behavior that briefly catch people's attention. (436)

15. b   Social movements that seek to change people totally are redemptive social movements. (438)

16. d   A social movement that seeks to change society totally is a transformative social movement. (438)

17. d "All of the above" is correct. Levels of membership in social movements include the inner core, the committed, and a wider circle of members. (439)

18. d The public that social movements face can really be divided into sympathetic public, hostile public, and disinterested people. (439-440)

19. b How people think about some issue is public opinion. (440)

20. b Although the term is often used to refer to a one-sided presentation of information that distorts reality, it is actually a neutral word. (440-441).

21. d "All of the above" is correct. Advertising is a type of propaganda, an organized attempt to manipulate public opinion, and a one-sided presentation of information that distorts reality. (441)

22. d All of the answers are correct. The mass media are the gatekeepers to social movements; they engage in biased reporting, controlled and influenced by people who have an agenda to get across; and they are sympathetic to some social movements, while ignoring others; it all depends on their individual biases. (441-442)

23. c According to mass society theory, as societies become more industrialized, bureaucratized, and impersonal, members of such mass societies experience feelings of isolation. For them, social movements fill a void, because they offer them a sense of belonging. (442)

24. b In order to turn a group of people who are upset about a social condition into a social movement, there must be resource mobilization. The resources that must be mobilized include time, money, people's skills, technologies such as direct mailings and fax machines, attention by the mass media, and even legitimacy among the public and authorities. (443-444)

25. d The shift in the characteristics of culture and society over time is social change. (445)

26. d All of the choices refer to technology; it includes items that people use to accomplish a wide range of tasks; the skills and procedures that are employed in the development and utilization of tools; and tools ranging from combs or hairbrushes to computers and the Internet. (445)

27. b Ogburn called the process of change that involves new ways of seeing reality discovery. The other two processes he identified were invention and diffusion. (446)

28. b The situation in which some elements of a culture adapt to an invention or discovery more rapidly than others is cultural lag. (446)

29. b According to Karl Marx, the change-over to the factory system produced alienation. (446)

30. d "All of the above" is correct. The automobile has changed the shape of cities; has stimulated mass suburbanization; and changed dating and courtship rituals. (447-448)

31. c With the latest developments in medical technology, it is now possible for a doctor at one site to check the heart condition of a patient at another site; this new arrangement is referred to as telemedicine. (449)

32. b One concern about the expansion of the information superhighway is social inequalities will become greater, both on a national and global basis. (450)

33. a Dependency theory argues that the least industrialized nations became dependent on countries that have already industrialized. (450)

34. c The resurgence of ethnic conflicts are identified as a threat to the global map drawn up by the G7/G8. (450)

35. c Unilinear evolution theories assume that all societies follow the same path, evolving from simple to complex through uniform sequences. (451)

ANSWERS FOR TRUE-FALSE QUESTIONS

1. *True.* (430)
2. *True.* (430)
3. *False.* The term "circular reaction" refers to the back-and-forth communication that goes on; it can create a "collective" impulse" that comes to dominate people in the crowd. This collective

impulse, similar to the collective mind described by Gustave LeBon, leads people in the crowd to act on any suggestion that is put forth. (431)

4. *True.* (431)
5. *False.* The term acting crowd is not applied just to violent activities such as lynch mobs or people engaged in riots. It includes such diverse activities as food fights! (431)
6. *True.* (432)
7. *True.* (433)
8. *True.* (435)
9. *True.* (436)
10. *False.* Urban legends are not just another kind of rumor. According to Jan Brunvand, they are passed on by people who think that the event happened to "a friend of a friend"; he sees them as modern morality stories, teaching us moral lessons about life. (436-437)
11. *True.* (437)
12. False. Not all social movements seek to change society; some seek to change people. (437-438)
13. *True.* (440)
14. *False.* Propaganda and advertising are not quite different from one another. In essence, advertising is a type of propaganda because it fits both the broad and the narrow definition of propaganda perfectly. (440-441)
15. *False.* Deprivation theory and relative deprivation theory are not identical perspectives. Deprivation theory is based on the idea that people who are deprived of things deemed valuable in society join social movements with the hope of redressing their grievances. Relative deprivation theory asserts that it is not people's actual negative conditions that matter but, rather, it is what people think they should have relative to what others have, or even compared with their own past or perceived future. (442-443)
16. *False.* For some, moral shock, a sense of outrage at finding out what is really going on, is the motivating factor in deciding to join a social movement. (443)
17. *False.* There is evidence that at times the agent provocateur has been able to push the social movement into illegal activity. (443)
18. *False.* Resources mobilization precedes the organization and institutionalization of a social movement. (443-444)
19. *False.* In the final stage of a social movement, decline is not always certain. Sometimes an emerging group with the same goals and new leadership will take over the "cause." (444)
20. *False.* Technology is a very powerful force for social change because it alters the ways in which those tools are used. (445)
21. *True.* (446)
22. *True.* (446)
23. *True.* (446)
24. *False.* Technology not only produces ideological changes, it can also transform social values. For example, today's emphasis on materialism depends on a certain state of technology. (446)
25. *True.* (447)
26. *False.* The use of computers in education is likely to increase, rather than decrease, the social inequality between school districts, because poor districts will not be able to afford the hardware. (449)
27. *True.* (449)
28. *True.* (450)
29. *False.* The assumption of evolutionary theories that all societies progress from a primitive state to a highly complex state has not been proven. With Western culture in crisis, it is no longer assumed that society holds the answers to human happiness; consequently, the assumption of progress has been cast aside and evolutionary theories have been rejected. (451)
30. *True.* (451)

ANSWERS FOR FILL-IN QUESTIONS

1. Gustave LeBon's term for the tendency of people in a crowd to feel, think, and act in extraordinary ways is COLLECTIVE MIND. (430)
2. A crowd standing or walking around as they talk excitedly about some event is MILLING. (431)
3. Ralph Turner and Lewis Killian's term for the development of new norms to cope with a new situation, especially among crowds, is EMERGENT NORMS. (432)
4. A(n) RIOT is violent crowd behavior aimed against people and property. (433)
5. A fear that grips large numbers of people that some evil group or behavior threatens the well- being of society, followed by intense hostility, and sometimes violence, towards those thought responsible is MORAL PANIC. (435)
6. RUMORS are unfounded information spread among people. (436)
7. A temporary pattern of behavior that catches people's attention is a(n) FAD. (436)
8. A(n) URBAN LEGEND is a story with an ironic twist that sounds realistic but is false. (436)
9. A religious social movement that stresses conversion, which will produce a change in the entire person, is an example of REDEMPTIVE SOCIAL MOVEMENTS. (438)
10. Social movements that span the globe, emphasizing changing conditions throughout the world rather than in just one country, are referred to as NEW SOCIAL MOVEMENTS. (438-439)
11. PUBLIC OPINION is how people think about some issue. (440)
12. MASS SOCIETY is industrialized, highly bureaucratized, impersonal society. (442)
13. DEPRIVATION THEORY states that people who are deprived of things deemed valuable in society join social movements with the hope of redressing their grievances. (442)
14. SOCIAL CHANGE is the alteration of culture and societies over time. (445)
15. The combination of existing elements and materials to form new ones is INVENTION. (446)
16. DISCOVERY is a new way of seeing reality. (446)
17. According to Ogburn, because of travel, trade, or conquest, DIFFUSION of an invention or discovery occurs. (446)
18. The situation in which some elements of a culture adapt to an invention or discovery more rapidly than others is CULTURAL LAG. (446)
19. ALIENATION is Marx's term for workers' lack of connection to the product of their labor caused by their being assigned repetitive tasks on a small part of a product. (446)
20. The assumption that all societies follow the same path, evolving from the simple to complex, is central to UNILINEAR EVOLUTIONARY THEORY. (451)

ANSWERS TO MATCH THESE SOCIAL SCIENTISTS WITH THEIR CONTRIBUTIONS

1. b   Charles Mackay: *herd mentality*
2. e   William Kornhauser: *mass society theory*
3. f   Robert Park: *social unrest and circular reaction*
4. a   Ralph Turner and Lewis Killian: *emergent norms*
5. h   Gustave LeBon: *collective mind*
6. d   David Aberle: *classified social movements by type and amount of social change*
7. g   Herbert Blumer: *the acting crowd*
8. c   Richard Berk: *minimax strategy*
9. j   James Flink: *studied the impact of the auto on U.S. society*
10. k   William Ogburn: *three processes of social change*
11. i   Karl Marx: *changes to factory system produced worker alienation*

GUIDELINES FOR ANSWERING THE ESSAY QUESTIONS

1. *Compare and contrast the early explanations of collective behavior, as advanced by Charles Mackay, Gustave LeBon, Robert Park and Herbert Blumer, with more contemporary explanations developed by Richard Berk, Ralph Turner and Lewis Killian.*

    You must first discuss the elements that these different theories have in common and then move on to the elements that separate them. First, they are all trying to explain why people act differently when they are swept up into a crowd of people. That is probably the single point on which there is agreement. The early explanations focused on the individual and how he or she was affected by forces outside the self. Mackay talked about the herd, LeBon the collective mind, and Park the collective impulse. While Blumer developed a more systematic explanation, his also focused on events outside of the individual that impacted on his or her behavior. In contrast, the more contemporary explanations focus on the individual as a rational actor. Berk depicts humans as calculating, weighing the costs against the benefits before taking any action. Turner and Killian also see humans as rational; in their work they argue that people develop new norms when confronted with new and unfamiliar situations. They also suggest that there are different kinds of participants, with different motives for being involved.

2. *Discuss the different theories about why people join social movements and consider how they could all be accurate.*

    The text presents three different theories about why people get involved in social movements— mass society theory, deprivation theory, and ideological commitment theory. Each provides us with an understanding of why some people get involved, but no one theory explains why all people get involved in social movements. One theory may be more appropriate at explaining why some people get involved in some social movements but not others. By using all three, we come away with a better understanding of the process by which individuals are drawn into social movements. You might also want to tie this discussion to that of the different types of members. For example, those people at the core of the movement may be connected for moral or ideological reasons, while those further out—the committed or less committed—may be involved because they feel isolated or alienated by modern society.

3. *Consider why the author combined the topics of collective behavior and social movements in one chapter.*

    Different types of collective behavior—riots, panics, rumors, fads, and urban legends—that are largely unorganized and temporary seem to be incompatible with social movements, which are generally well-organized and more long-lasting. So why did the author include these two within the same chapter? One point you might want to make is that both involve large numbers of people. Both emerge out of circumstances of situations of uncertainty, change, or ambiguity. And although one is fleeting while the other hangs around for a while, neither is institutionalized and lasts across generations.

4. *Choose a particular technology—you can use the automobile or the computer—and discuss the impact that it has had on Canadian society.*

    The author presents five different ways in which technology can transform society— transformation of existing technologies; changes in social organization; changes in ideology; transformation of values; and transformation of social relationships. The first part of your essay should include some discussion of these five. Then you would want to discuss how one particular technology impacts these five different aspects of social life. The book provides information on automobiles and computers, but you could choose another one—television, airplanes, the telephone but to name a few significant ones. Remember to provide examples to illustrate each aspect.

5.   *Discuss Ogburn's three processes of social change and provide examples to illustrate each.*

This is a fairly straightforward essay question. What you need to do is to discuss each of Ogburn's processes—invention, discovery, and diffusion—and provide examples for each.

GLOSSARY

acculturation: the transmission of culture from one generation to the next

achieved statuses: positions that are earned, accomplished, or that involved at least some effort or activity on the individual's part

acid rain: rain containing sulfuric and nitric acids

acting crowd: Herbert Blumer's term for an excited group that collectively moves toward a goal

activity theory: the view that satisfaction during old age is related to a person's level and quality of activity

age cohort: a group of people born at roughly the same time who pass through the life course together

ageism: prejudice, discrimination, and hostility directed against people because of their age; can be directed against any age group, including youth

agent provocateur: someone who joins a group in order to spy on it and to sabotage it by provoking its members to commit illegal acts

agents of socialization: people or groups that affect our self-concept, attitudes, or other orientations toward life

aggregate: individuals who temporarily share the same physical space but do not see themselves as belonging together

alienation: Marx's term for workers' lack of connection to the product of their labour; caused by their being assigned repetitive tasks on a small part of a product

alternative social movement: a social movement that seeks to alter only particular aspects of people

anarchy: a condition of lawlessness or political disorder caused by the absence or collapse of governmental authority

animal culture: learned, shared behaviour among animals

animism: the belief that all objects in the world have spirits, some of which are dangerous and must be outwitted

anomie: Durkheim's term for a condition of society in which people become detached, cut loose from the norms that usually guide their behaviour

anticipatory socialization: learning part of a future role because one anticipates it

anti-Semitism: prejudice, discrimination, and persecution directed against Jews

appearance: how an individual looks when playing a role

applied sociology: the use of sociology to solve problems—from the micro level of family relationships to the macro level of crime and pollution

ascribed statuses: positions an individual either inherits at birth or receives involuntarily later in life

assimilation: the process by which the dominant group absorbs a minority group

authoritarian leader: a leader who leads by giving orders

authoritarian personality: Theodor Adorno's term for people who are prejudiced and rank high on scales of conformity, intolerance, insecurity, respect for authority, and submissiveness to superiors

authority: power that people accept as rightly exercised over them; also called legitimate power

back stage: where people rest from their performances, discuss their presentations, and plan future performances

background assumptions: deeply embedded common understandings, or basic roles, concerning our view of the world and of how people ought to act

barter: the direct exchange of one item for another

basic demographic equation: growth rate = births − deaths + net migration

bilateral (system of descent): a system of reckoning descent that counts both the mother's and the father's side

blended family: a family whose members were once part of other families

bourgeoisie: Karl Marx's term for capitalists, those who own the means to produce wealth

bureaucracy: a formal organization with a hierarchy of authority; a clear division of labour; emphasis on written rules, communications, and records; and impersonality of positions

capitalism: an economic system characterized by the private ownership of the means of production, the pursuit of profit, and market competition; the investment of capital with the goal of producing profits

capitalist class: the wealthy who own the means of production and buy the labour of the working class

capitalist world economy: the dominance of capitalism in the world along with the international interdependence that capitalism has created

caste system: a form of social stratification in which one's status is determined by birth and is lifelong

category: people who have similar characteristics

causation: if a change in one variable leads to a change in another variable, causation is said to exist

centrist party: a political party that represents the centre of political opinion

charismatic authority: authority based on an individual's outstanding traits, which attract followers

charismatic leader: an individual who inspires people because he or she seems to have extraordinary qualities

church: according to Durkheim, one of the three essential elements of religion—a moral community of believers or a large, highly organized group with formal, sedate worship services and little emphasis on personal conversion

circular reaction: Robert Park's term for a back-and-forth communication between the members of a crowd whereby a "collective impulse" is transmitted

citizenship: the concept that birth (and residence) in a country impart basic rights

city: a place in which a large number of people are permanently based and do not produce their own food

city-state: an independent city whose power radiates outward, bringing the adjacent area under its rule

clan: an extended network of relatives

clan system: a form of social stratification in which individuals receive their social standing through belonging to an extended network of relatives

class conflict: Marx's term for the struggle between the proletariat and the bourgeoisie

class consciousness: Karl Marx's term for awareness of a common identity based on one's position in the means of production

class system: a form of social stratification based primarily on the possession of money or material possessions

clinical sociology: the direct involvement of sociologists in bringing about social change

clique: a cluster of people within a larger group who choose to interact with one another; an internal faction

closed-ended questions: questions followed by a list of possible answers to be selected by the respondent

coalition: the alignment of some members of a group against others

coalition government: a government in which a country's largest party aligns itself with one or more smaller parties

coercion: power that people do not accept as rightly exercised over them; also called illegitimate power

collective behaviour: extraordinary activities carried out by groups of people; includes lynchings, rumours, panics, urban legends, and fads and fashions

collective mind: Gustave LeBon's term for the tendency of people in a crowd to feel, think, and act in extraordinary ways

colonization: the process by which one nation takes over another nation, usually for the purpose of exploiting its labour and natural resources

common sense: those things that "everyone knows" are true

community: a place people identify with, where they sense that they belong and that others care what happens to them

compartmentalize: to separate acts from feelings or attitudes

conflict theory: a theoretical framework in which society is viewed as composed of groups competing for scarce resources

conspicuous consumption: Thorstein Veblen's term for a change from the Protestant ethic to an eagerness to show off wealth by the elaborate consumption of goods

contradictory class location: Erik Wright's term for a position in the class structure that generates contradictory interests

control theory: the idea that two control systems—inner controls and outer controls—work against our tendencies to deviate

convergence theory: the view that as capitalist and socialist economic systems each adopt features of the other, a hybrid (or mixed) economic system will emerge

corporate capitalism: the domination of the economic system by giant corporations

corporate culture: the orientation that characterizes a corporate work setting

corporation: the joint ownership of a business enterprise, whose liabilities and obligations are separate from those of its owners

correlation: **the simultaneous occurrence of two or more variables**

correspondence principle: the sociological principle that schools correspond to (or reflect) the social structure of society

cosmology: teachings or ideas that provide a unified picture of the world

counterculture: a group whose values, beliefs, and related behaviours place its members in opposition to the broader culture

credential society: the use of diplomas and degrees to determine who is eligible for jobs, even though the diploma or degree may be irrelevant to the actual work

credit card: a device that allows its owner to purchase goods but to be billed later

crime: the violation of norms that are written into law

criminal justice system: the system of police, courts, and prisons set up to deal with people accused of having committed a crime

crude birth rate: the annual number of births per 1000 population

crude death rate: the annual number of deaths per 1000 population

cult: a new or different religion, with few followers, whose teachings and practices put it at odds with the dominant culture and religion

cultural diffusion: the spread of cultural characteristics from one group to another

cultural goals: the legitimate objectives held out to the members of a society

cultural lag: William Ogburn's term for human behaviour lagging behind technological innovations

cultural levelling: the process by which cultures become similar to one another, and especially by which Western industrial culture is imported and diffused into developing nations

cultural relativism: understanding a people from the framework of its own culture

cultural transmission: in reference to education, the ways schools transmit a society's culture, especially its core values

cultural universal: a value, norm, or other cultural trait that is found in every group

culture: the language, beliefs, values, norms, behaviours, and even material objects passed from one generation to the next

culture contact: contact between people from different cultures, or with some parts of a different culture

culture of poverty: the assumption that the values and behaviours of the poor make them fundamentally different from other people, that these factors are largely responsible for their poverty, and that parents perpetuate poverty across generations by passing these characteristics on to their children

culture shock: the disorientation that people experience when they come in contact with a fundamentally different culture and can no longer depend on their taken-for-granted assumptions about life

currency: paper money

debit card: a device that allows its owner to charge purchases against his or her bank account

deferred gratification: forgoing something in the present in the hope of achieving greater gains in the future

definition of the situation: the way we look at matters in life; the way we define reality or some particular situation

degradation ceremony: a term coined by Harold Garfinkel to describe an attempt to remake the self by stripping away an individual's self-identity and stamping a new one in its place; a ritual designed to strip an individual of his or her identity as a group member—for example, a court martial or the defrocking of a priest

dehumanization: the act or process of reducing people to objects that do not deserve the treatment accorded humans

democracy: a system of government in which authority derives from the people; derived from two Greek words that translate literally as "power to the people"

democratic leader: a leader who leads by trying to reach a consensus

democratic socialism: a hybrid economic system in which capitalism is mixed with state ownership

demographic transition: a three-stage historical process of population growth: first, high birth rates and high death rates; second, high birth rates and low death rates; and third, low birth rates and low death rates

demographic variables: the three factors that influence population growth: fertility, mortality, and net migration

demography: the study of the size, composition, growth, and distribution of human populations

denomination: a "brand name" within a major religion, for example, Methodist or Baptist

dependency ratio: the number of paid workers required so that dependent individuals, usually seniors and children, can be adequately supported

dependency theory: the view that the Least Industrialized Nations have been unable to develop their economies because they have grown dependent on the Most Industrialized Nations

depersonalization: dealing with people as though they were objects—in the case of medical care, as though patients were merely cases and diseases, not persons

deposit receipts: a receipt stating that a certain amount of goods is on deposit in a warehouse or bank; the receipt is used as a form of money

dictatorship: a form of government in which power is seized by an individual

differential association: Edwin Sutherland's term to indicate that associating with some groups results in learning an "excess of definitions" of social deviance, and, by extension, in a greater likelihood that one will become socially deviant

diffusion: the spread of invention or discovery from one area to another; identified by William Ogburn as the final of three processes of social change

direct democracy: a form of democracy in which the eligible voters meet together to discuss issues and make their decisions

disabling environment: an environment harmful to health

discovery: a new way of seeing reality; identified by William Ogburn as the second of three processes of social change

discrimination: an act of unfair treatment directed against an individual or a group

disengagement theory: the view that society prevents disruption by having the elderly vacate (or disengage from) their positions of responsibility so the younger generation can step into their shoes

divine right of kings: the idea that the king's authority comes directly from God

division of labour: the splitting of a group's or a society's tasks into specialties

documents: In its narrow sense, written sources that provide data; in its extended sense, archival material of any sort, including photographs, movies, and so on

dominant group: the group with the most power, greatest privileges, and highest social status

downward social mobility: movement down the social-class ladder

dramaturgy: an approach, pioneered by Erving Goffman, analyzing social life in terms of drama or the stage; also called dramaturgical analysis

dual labour market: workers split along racial, ethnic, gender, age, or any other lines; this split is exploited by owners to weaken the bargaining power of workers

dyad: the smallest possible group, consisting of two people

ecclesia (plural *ecclesiae*): a religious group so integrated into the dominant culture that it is difficult to tell where the one begins and the other leaves off; also referred to as *state religion*

economy: a system of distribution of goods and services

education: a formal system of teaching knowledge, values, and skills

egalitarian: authority more or less equally divided between people or groups, for example, between husband and wife in a family

ego: Freud's term for a balancing force between the id and the demands of society

electronic community: individuals who more or less regularly interact with one another on the Internet

electronic primary group: individuals who regularly interact with one another on the Internet, who see themselves as a group, and who develop close ties with one another

emergent norms: Ralph Turner and Lewis Killian's term for the development of new norms to cope with a new situation, especially among crowds

endogamy: the practice of marrying within one's own group

environmental sociology: a subdiscipline of sociology that examines how human activities affect the physical environment and how the physical environment affects human activities

epidemiology: the study of disease and disability patterns in a population

ethnic (and ethnicity): having distinctive cultural characteristics

ethnic cleansing: a euphemism for the slaughter, during the Bosnian war, of Muslims and some Croatians who lived in areas the Serbs captured, forcing survivors to flee their homeland

ethnic work: activities designed to discover, enhance, or maintain ethnic and racial identification

ethnocentrism: the use of one's own culture as a yardstick for judging the ways of other individuals or societies, generally leading to a negative evaluation of their values, norms, and behaviours

ethnomethodology: the study of how people use background assumptions to make sense out of life

euthanasia: mercy killing

evangelism: an attempt to win converts

exchange mobility: about the same numbers of people moving up and down the social-class ladder, such that, on balance, the social-class system shows little change

exogamy: the practice of marrying outside one's group

experiment: the use of control groups and experimental groups and dependent and independent variables to test causation

exponential growth curve: a pattern of growth in which numbers double during approximately equal intervals, thus accelerating in the latter stages

expressive leader: an individual who increases harmony and minimizes conflict in a group; also known as a socioemotional leader

extended family: a nuclear family plus other relatives, such as grandparents, uncles, and aunts, who live together

face-saving behaviour: techniques used to salvage a performance that is going sour

fad: a temporary pattern of behaviour that catches people's attention

false consciousness: Karl Marx's term to refer to workers identifying with the interests of capitalists

family: two or more people who consider themselves related by blood, marriage, or adoption

family of orientation: the family in which a person grows up

family of procreation: the family formed when a couple's first child is born

fashion: a pattern of behaviour that catches people's attention and lasts longer than a fad

fecundity: the number of children women are theoretically *capable* of bearing

fee for service: payment to a physician to diagnose and treat a patient's medical problems

feminism: (1) the philosophy that men and women should be politically, economically, and socially equal; (2) organized activity on behalf of this principle

feral children: children assumed to have been raised by animals, in the wilderness isolated from other humans

fertility rate: the number of children the average woman bears

fiat money: currency issued by a government that is not backed by stored value

folkways: norms that are not strictly enforced

formal organization: a secondary group designed to achieve explicit objectives

front stage: where performances are given

functional analysis: a theoretical framework in which society is viewed as composed of various parts, each with a function that, when fulfilled, contributes to society's equilibrium; also known as functionalism and structural functionalism

functional requisites: the major tasks a society must fulfill if it is to survive

fundamentalism: the belief that true religion is threatened by modernism and that the faith as it was originally practised should be restored

gatekeeping: the process by which education opens and closes doors of opportunity; another term for the social placement function of education

Gemeinschaft: a type of society dominated by intimate relationships; a community in which everyone knows everyone else and people share a sense of togetherness

gender: the social characteristics that a society considers proper for its males and females; masculinity or femininity

gender age: the relative values of men's and women's ages in a particular culture

gender role: the behaviours and attitudes considered appropriate because one is a female or a male

gender socialization: the ways society sets children on different courses in life because they are male or female

gender stratification: males' and females' unequal access to power, prestige, and property on the basis of their sex

generalizability: the extent to which the findings from one group (or sample) can be generalized or applied to other groups (or populations)

generalization: a statement that goes beyond the individual case and is applied to a broader group or situation

generalized other: the norms, values, attitudes, and expectations of "people in general"; the child's ability to take the role of the generalized other is a significant step in the development of a self

genetic predispositions: inborn tendencies, in this context, to commit socially deviant acts

genocide: the systematic annihilation or attempted annihilation of a people based on their presumed race or ethnicity

gentrification: the displacement of the poor by the relatively affluent, who renovate the former's homes

gerontocracy: a society (or some other group) run by the elderly

Gesellschaft: a type of society dominated by impersonal relationships, individual accomplishments, and self-interest

gestures: the ways in which people use their bodies to communicate with one another

global warming: an increase in the earth's temperature due to the *greenhouse effect*

globalization: the extensive movement of capital and ideas between nations due to the expansion of capitalism

goal displacement: replacement of one goal by another; in this context, the adoption of new goals by an organization; also known as *goal replacement*

gold standard: paper money backed by gold

graying of Canada: a term that refers to the rising proportion of older people as a percentage of the Canadian population

greenhouse effect: the buildup of carbon dioxide in the earth's atmosphere that allows light to enter but inhibits the release of heat; believed to cause global warming

gross national product (GNP): the amount of goods and services produced by a nation

group: defined differently by various sociologists, but in a general sense, people who have something in common and who believe that what they have in common is significant; also called a *social group*

group dynamics: the ways individuals affect groups and the ways groups influence individuals

groupthink: Irving Janis' term for a narrowing of thought by a group of people, leading to the perception that there is only one correct answer, and a situation in which to even suggest alternatives becomes a sign of disloyalty

growth rate: the net change in a population after adding births, subtracting deaths, and either adding or subtracting net migration

health: a human condition measured by four components: physical, mental, social, and spiritual

hidden curriculum: the unwritten goals of schools, such as obedience to authority and conformity to cultural norms

homogamy: the tendency of people with similar characteristics to marry one another

hospice: a place, or services brought into someone's home, for the purpose of bringing comfort and dignity to a dying person

household: all people who occupy the same housing unit

human ecology: Robert Park's term for the relationship between people and their environment (natural resources such as land)

humanizing a work setting: organizing a workplace in such a way that it develops rather than impedes human potential

hypothesis: a statement of the expected relationship between variables according to predictions from a theory

id: Freud's term for our inborn basic drives

ideal culture: the ideal values and norms of a people, and the goals held out for them

ideal type: a composite of characteristics based on many specific examples ("ideal" in this case means a description of the abstracted characteristics, not what one desires to exist)

ideology: beliefs about the way things ought to be that justify social arrangements

illegitimate opportunity structures: opportunities for crime that are woven into the texture of life

imperialism: a nation's attempt to create an empire; its pursuit of unlimited geographical expansion

impression management: the term used by Erving Goffman to describe people's efforts to control the impressions others receive of them

incest: sexual relations between specified relatives, such as brothers and sisters or parents and children

indentured service: a contractual system in which someone sells his or her body (services) for a specified period of time in an arrangement very close to slavery, except that it is voluntarily entered into

individual discrimination: the negative treatment of one person by another on the basis of that person's perceived characteristics

inflation: an increase in prices

in-groups: groups toward which one feels loyalty

institutional discrimination: negative treatment of a minority group that is built into a society's institutions; also called systemic discrimination

institutionalized means: approved ways of reaching cultural goals

instrumental leader: an individual who tries to keep the group moving toward its goals; also known as a task-oriented leader

intentional family: people who declare themselves a family and treat one another as members of the same family; originated in the late twentieth century in response to the need for intimacy not met due to distance, divorce, and death

intergenerational mobility: the change that family members make in social class from one generation to the next

interlocking directorates: the same people serving on the board of directors of several companies

internal colonialism: the policy of economically exploiting minority groups

interview: direct questioning of respondents

invasion-succession cycle: the process of one group of people displacing a group whose racial-ethnic or social-class characteristics differ from their own

invention: the combination of existing elements and materials to form new ones; identified by William Ogburn as the first of three processes of social change

iron law of oligarchy: Robert Michels' phrase for the tendency of formal organizations to be dominated by a small, self-perpetuating elite

labelling theory: the view, developed by symbolic interactionists, that the labels people are given affect their own and others' perceptions of them, thus channelling their behaviour into either social deviance or conformity

laissez-faire capitalism: unrestrained manufacture and trade (loosely, "leave alone" capitalism)

laissez-faire leader: an individual who leads by being highly permissive

language: a system of symbols that can be combined in an infinite number of ways and can represent not only objects but also abstract thought

latent functions: the unintended consequences of people's actions that help to keep a social system in equilibrium

leader: someone who influences other people

leadership styles: ways people express their leadership

leisure: time not taken up by work or required activities such as eating, sleeping, commuting, child care, and housework

life course: the sequence of events that we experience as we journey from birth to death

life expectancy: the number of years an average newborn can expect to live

living will: a statement people in good health sign that clearly expresses their feelings about being kept alive on artificial life support systems

looking-glass self: a term coined by Charles Horton Cooley to refer to the process by which our self develops through internalizing others' reactions to us

macro-level analysis: an examination of large-scale patterns of society

macropolitics: the exercise of large-scale power, the government being the most common example

macrosociology: analysis of social life focusing on broad features of social structure, such as social class and the relationships of groups to one another; an approach usually used by functionalist and conflict theorists

mainstreaming: helping people become part of the mainstream of society

Malthus theorem: an observation by Thomas Malthus that although the food supply increases only arithmetically (from 1 to 2 to 3 to 4 and so on), population grows geometrically (from 2 to 4 to 8 to 16 and so forth)

manifest function: the intended consequences of people's actions designed to help some part of a social system

manner: the attitudes people show as they play their roles

marginal working class: the most desperate members of the working class, who have few skills, little job security, and are often unemployed

market: any process of buying and selling; on a more formal level, the mechanism that establishes values for the exchange of goods and services

market competition: the exchange of items between willing buyers and sellers

market force: the law of supply and demand

market restraints: laws and regulations that limit the capacity to manufacture and sell products

marriage: a group's approved mating arrangements, usually marked by a ritual of some sort

mass media: forms of communication, such as radio, newspapers, and television, directed to mass audiences

mass society: industrialized, highly bureaucratized, impersonal society

mass society theory: an explanation for participation in social movements based on the assumption that such movements offer a sense of belonging to people who have weak social ties

master status: a status that cuts across the other statuses an individual occupies

material culture: the material objects that distinguish a group of people, such as their art, buildings, weapons, utensils, machines, hairstyles, clothing, and jewellery

matriarchy: authority vested in females; female control of a society or group; a society in which women dominate men

matrilineal (system of descent): a system of reckoning descent that counts only the mother's side

means of production: the tools, factories, land, and investment capital used to produce wealth

mechanical solidarity: Durkheim's term for the unity that comes from being involved in similar occupations or activities

medicalization: the transformation of something into a matter to be treated by physicians

medicalization of social deviance: to make social deviance a medical matter, a symptom of some underlying illness that needs to be treated by physicians

medicine: one of the major social institutions that sociologists study; a society's organized ways of dealing with sickness and injury

medium of exchange: the means by which people value goods and services in order to make an exchange, for example, currency, gold, and silver

megalopolis: an urban area consisting of at least two metropolises and their many suburbs

meritocracy: a form of social stratification in which all positions are awarded on the basis of merit

metropolis: a central city surrounded by smaller cities and their suburbs

micro-level analysis: an examination of small-scale patterns of society

micropolitics: the exercise of power in everyday life, such as deciding who is going to do the housework

microsociology: analysis of social life focusing on social interaction; an approach usually used by symbolic interactionists

middle-range theories: explanations of human behaviour that go beyond a particular observation or research but avoid sweeping generalizations that attempt to account for everything

milling: a crowd standing or walking around as they talk excitedly about some event

minimax strategy: Richard Berk's term for the effort people make to minimize their costs and maximize their rewards

minority group: a group discriminated against on the basis of its members' physical or cultural characteristics

modernization: the process by which a *Gemeinschaft* society is transformed into a *Gesellschaft* society; the transformation of traditional societies into industrial societies

monarchy: a form of government headed by a king or queen

money: any item (from seashells to gold) that serves as a medium of exchange; today, currency is the most common form

monotheism: the belief that there is only one God

moral panic: a fear that grips large numbers of people that some evil group or behaviour threatens the well-being of society, followed by intense hostility, sometimes violence, toward those thought responsible

mores: norms that are strictly enforced because they are thought essential to core values

multiculturalism (also called pluralism): a philosophy or political policy that permits or encourages ethnic variation

multinational corporations: companies that operate across many national boundaries; also called *transnational corporations*

nationalism: a strong identity with a nation, accompanied by the desire for that nation to be dominant

natural sciences: the intellectual and academic disciplines designed to comprehend, explain, and predict events in our natural environment

negative sanction: an expression of disapproval for breaking a norm, ranging from a mild, informal reaction such as a frown to a formal prison sentence or an execution

neocolonialism: the economic and political dominance of the Least Industrialized Nations by the Most Industrialized Nations

net migration rate: the difference between the number of immigrants and emigrants per 1000 population

networking: the process of consciously using or cultivating networks for some gain

new social movements: social movements with a new emphasis on the world, instead of on a condition in a specific country

new technology: the emerging technologies of an era that have a significant impact on social life

noncentrist party: a political party that represents less popular ideas

nonmaterial culture: a group's ways of thinking (including its beliefs, values, and other assumptions about the world) and doing (its common patterns of behaviour, including language and other forms of interaction)

nonverbal interaction: communication without words through gestures, space, silence, and so on

norms: the expectations or rules of behaviour that develop out of values

nuclear family: a family consisting of a husband, wife, and child(ren)

objective method (of measuring social class): a system in which people are ranked according to objective criteria such as their wealth, power, and prestige

objectivity: total neutrality

official deviance: a society's statistics on lawbreaking; its measures of crimes, victims, lawbreakers, and the outcomes of criminal investigations and sentencing

oligarchy: a form of government in which power is held by a small group of individuals; the rule of the many by the few

oligopoly: the control of an entire industry by several large companies

open-ended questions: questions that respondents are able to answer in their own words

operational definitions: the way in which a variable in a hypothesis is measured

organic solidarity: Durkheim's term for the interdependence that results from people needing others to fulfill their jobs; solidarity based on the interdependence brought about by the division of labour

out-groups: groups toward which one feels antagonism

panic: the condition of being so fearful that one cannot function normally, and may even flee

participant observation (or fieldwork): research in which the researcher participates in a research setting while observing what is happening in that setting

patriarchy: authority vested in males; male control of a society or group; a society in which men dominate women

patrilineal (system of descent): a system of reckoning descent that counts only the father's side

patterns: recurring characteristics or events

peer group: a group of individuals roughly the same age linked by common interests

personal identity kit: items people use to decorate their bodies

personality disorders: the view that a personality disturbance of some sort causes an individual to violate social norms

Peter principle: a bureaucratic "law" according to which the members of an organization are promoted for good work until they reach their level of incompetence, the level at which they can no longer do good work

pluralism: the diffusion of power among many interest groups, preventing any single group from gaining control of the government

pluralistic society: a society made up of many different groups

pluralistic theory of social control: the view that society is made up of many competing groups, whose interests manage to become balanced

polyandry: a marriage in which a woman has more than one husband

polygyny: a marriage in which a man has more than one wife

polytheism: the belief that there are many gods

population: a target group to be studied

population shrinkage: the process by which a country's population becomes smaller because its birth rate and immigration are too low to replace those who die and emigrate

population transfer: involuntary movement of a minority group

positive sanction: a reward or positive reaction for approved behaviour, for conformity

positivism: the application of the scientific approach to the social world

postmodern society: another term for postindustrial society; its chief characteristic is the use of tools that extend the human abilities to gather and analyze information, communicate, and travel

postmodernism: analysis of contemporary social life where the use of images to convey meaning replaces social reality

power: the ability to carry out one's will, even over the resistance of others

power elite: C. Wright Mills' term for those who rule the United States: the top people in the leading corporations, the most powerful generals and admirals of the armed forces, and certain elite politicians, who make the nation's major decisions

prejudice: an *attitude* of prejudging, usually in a negative way

prestige: respect or regard

primary group: a group characterized by intimate, long-term, face-to-face association and cooperation

primary sector: that part of the economy which extracts raw materials from the environment

primary social deviance: Edwin Lemert's term for acts of social deviance that have little effect on the self-concept

private ownership of the means of production: the ownership of machines and factories by individuals who decide what shall be produced

proactive social movement: a social movement that promotes some social change

profane: Durkheim's term for common elements of everyday life

profession: (as opposed to a job) an occupation characterized by rigorous education, a theoretical perspective, self-regulation, authority over clients, and a professional culture that stresses service to society

professionalization of medicine: the development of medicine into a field in which education becomes rigorous, and in which physicians claim a theoretical understanding of illness, regulate themselves, claim to be doing a service to society (rather than just following self-interest), and take authority over clients

proletariat: Karl Marx's term for the exploited class, the mass of workers who do not own the means of production

propaganda: in its broad sense, the presentation of information in the attempt to influence people; in its narrow sense, one-sided information used to try to influence people

proportional representation: an electoral system in which seats in a legislature are divided according to the proportion of votes each political party receives

Protestant ethic: Weber's term to describe the ideal of a self-denying, highly moral life, accompanied by hard work and frugality

public: a dispersed group of people who usually have an interest in the issue on which a social movement focuses; the sympathetic and hostile publics have such an interest, but a third public is either unaware of the issue or indifferent to it

public opinion: how people think about some issue

pure or basic sociology: sociological research whose only purpose is to make discoveries about life in human groups, not to make changes in those groups

qualitative research methods: research in which emphasis is placed on observing, describing, and interpreting people's behaviour

quantitative research methods: research in which emphasis is placed on precise measurement, numbers, and statistics

questionnaire: a list of questions to be asked

quiet revolution: the fundamental changes in society that occur as a result of vast numbers of women entering the work force

race: inherited physical characteristics that distinguish one group from another

racism: prejudice and discrimination on the basis of race

random sample: a sample in which everyone in the target population has the same chance of being included in the study

rapport: a feeling of trust between researchers and subjects

rationality: the acceptance of rules, efficiency, and practical results as the right way to approach human affairs

rationalization of society: a widespread acceptance of rationality and a social organization largely built around this idea

rational-legal authority: authority based on law or written rules and regulations; also called *bureaucratic authority*

reactive social movement: a social movement that resists some social change

real culture: the norms and values that people actually follow

redemptive social movement: a social movement that seeks to change people totally

reference groups: the groups we use as standards to evaluate ourselves

reformative social movement: a social movement that seeks to change only particular aspects of society

reformists: a category of study of feminist spirituality represented by those who advocate revealing the "liberating core" of religious teachings with female imagery and exposing and refusing to accept rituals that are clearly sexist

reincarnation: in Hinduism and Buddhism, the return of the soul after death in a different form

rejectionists: a category of study of feminist spirituality represented by those who judge the traditional teachings to be hopelessly sexist and have left it to establish a new spiritual tradition

relative deprivation theory: in this context, the belief that people join social movements on the basis of their evaluations of what they think they should have compared with what others have

reliability: the extent to which data produce consistent results

religion: according to Durkheim, beliefs and practices that separate the profane from the sacred and unite its adherents into a moral community

replication: repeating a study in order to test its findings

representative democracy: a form of democracy in which voters elect representatives to govern and make decisions on their behalf

reputational method (of measuring social class): a system in which people who are familiar with the reputations of others are asked to identify their social class

research method (or research design): one of seven procedures sociologists use to collect data: surveys, participant observation, qualitative interviews, secondary analysis, documents, unobtrusive measures, and experiments

reserve labour force: the unemployed; unemployed workers are thought of as being "in reserve"— capitalists take them "out of reserve" (put them back to work) during times of high production and then lay them off (put them back in reserve) when they are no longer needed

resocialization: the process of learning new norms, values, attitudes, and behaviours

resource mobilization: a theory that social movements succeed or fail on the basis of their ability to mobilize resources such as time, money, and people's skills

respondents: people who respond to a survey, either in interviews or by self-administered questionnaires

revisionists: a category of study of feminist spirituality represented by those who believe that the basic message of the major religions is liberating

revolution: armed resistance designed to overthrow a government

revolutionaries: a category of study of feminist spirituality represented by those who seek to change the established orthodoxy by importing language, images, and rituals from other traditions

riot: violent crowd behaviour aimed against people and property

rituals: ceremonies or repetitive practices; in this context, religious observances or rites, often intended to evoke awe for the sacred

role: the behaviours, obligations, and privileges attached to a status

role conflict: conflicts that someone feels *between* roles because the expectations attached to one role are incompatible with the expectations of another role

role extension: the incorporation of additional activities into a role

role performance: the ways in which someone performs a role within the limits that the role provides; showing a particular "style" or "personality"

role strain: conflicts that someone feels *within* a role

romantic love: feelings of erotic attraction accompanied by an idealization of the other

routinization of charisma: the transfer of authority from a charismatic figure to either a traditional or a rational-legal form of authority

ruling class: another term for the power elite

rumour: unfounded information spread among people

sacred: Durkheim's term for things set apart or forbidden that inspire fear, awe, reverence, or deep respect

sample: the individuals intended to represent the population to be studied

sanctions: expressions of approval or disapproval given to people for upholding or violating norms

Sapir-Whorf hypothesis: Edward Sapir and Benjamin Whorf's hypothesis that language creates ways of thinking and perceiving

scapegoat: an individual or group unfairly blamed for someone else's troubles

science: the application of systematic methods to obtain knowledge and the knowledge obtained by those methods

scientific method: the use of objective, systematic observations to test theories

secondary analysis: the analysis of data already collected by other researchers

secondary group: compared with a primary group, a larger, relatively temporary, more anonymous, formal, and impersonal group based on some interest or activity, whose members are likely to interact on the basis of specific roles

secondary sector: that part of the economy which turns raw materials into manufactured goods

secondary social deviance: Edwin Lemert's term for acts of social deviance incorporated into the self-concept, around which an individual orients his or her behaviour

sect: a group larger than a cult that still feels substantial hostility from and toward society

segregation: the policy of keeping racial or ethnic groups apart

selective perception: seeing certain features of an object or situation, but remaining blind to others

self: the unique human capacity of being able to see ourselves "from the outside"; the picture we gain of how others see us

self-administered questionnaires: questionnaires filled out by respondents

self-fulfilling prophecy: Robert Merton's term for an originally false assertion that becomes true simply because it was predicted

sex typing: the association of behaviours with one sex or the other

sexual harassment: the abuse of one's position of authority to force unwanted sexual demands on someone

shaman: the healing specialist of a preliterate tribe who attempts to control the spirits thought to cause a disease or injury; commonly called a *witch doctor*

sick role: a social role that excuses people from normal obligations because they are sick or injured, while at the same time expecting them to seek competent help and cooperate in getting well

significant other: an individual who significantly influences someone else's life

sign-vehicles: the term used by Erving Goffman to refer to how people use social setting, appearance, and manner to communicate information about the self

slavery: a form of social stratification in which some people own other people

small group: a group small enough for everyone to interact directly with all the other members

social class: a large number of people with similar amounts of income and education who work at jobs roughly comparable in prestige; according to Weber, a large group of people who rank closely to one another in wealth, power, and prestige; according to Marx, one of two groups: capitalists who own the means of production or workers who sell their labour

social cohesion: the degree to which members of a group or a society feel united by shared values and other social bonds

social construction of reality: the process by which people use their background assumptions and life experiences to define what is real for them

social construction of technology: the view (opposed to technological determinism) that culture (people's values and special interests) shapes the use and development of technology

social control: a group's formal and informal means of enforcing its norms

social deviance: the violation of rules or norms

social environment: the entire human environment, including direct contact with others

social facts: Durkheim's term for the patterns of behaviour that characterize a social group

social inequality: a social condition in which privileges and obligations are given to some but denied to others

social integration: the degree to which people feel a part of social groups

social interaction: what people do when they are in one another's presence

social institutions: the organized, usual, or standard ways by which society meets its basic needs

social location: the group memberships that people have because of their location in history and society

social mobility: movement up or down the social-class ladder

social movement: a large group of people who are organized to promote or resist social change

social movement organization: an organization developed to further the goals of a social movement

social network: the social ties radiating outward from the self that link people together

social order: a group's usual and customary social arrangements, on which its members depend and on which they base their lives

social placement: a function of education that funnels people into a society's various positions

social sciences: the intellectual and academic disciplines designed to understand the social world objectively by means of controlled and repeated observations

social setting: the place where the action of everyday life unfolds

social stratification: the division of large numbers of people into layers according to their relative power, property, and prestige; applies both to nations and to people within a nation, society, or other group

social structure: the framework that surrounds us, consisting of the relationship of people and groups to one another, which gives direction to and sets limits on behaviour

socialism: an economic system characterized by the public ownership of the means of production, central planning, and the distribution of goods without a profit motive

socialization: the process by which people learn the characteristics of their group: the attitudes, values, and actions thought appropriate for them

society: a term used by sociologists to refer to a group of people who share a culture and a territory

sociobiology: a framework of thought that views human behaviour as the result of natural selection and considers biological characteristics to be the fundamental cause of human behaviour

sociological perspective: an approach to understanding human behaviour that entails placing it within its broader social context

sociology: the scientific study of society and human behaviour

spirit of capitalism: Weber's term for the desire to accumulate capital as a duty—not to spend it, but as an end in itself—and to constantly reinvest it

spurious correlation: the correlation of two variables actually caused by a third variable; there is no cause-effect relationship

state: a political entity that claims monopoly on the use of violence in some particular territory; commonly known as a *country*

status: social ranking; the position someone occupies in society or a social group

status consistency: ranking high or low on all three dimensions of social class

status inconsistency (or discrepancy): ranking high on some dimensions of social class and low on others; a contradiction or mismatch between statuses

status set: all the statuses or positions an individual occupies

status symbols: items used to identify a status

stereotype: assumptions of what people are like, based on previous associations with them or with people who have similar characteristics,or based on information, whether true or false

stigma: "blemishes" that discredit a person's claim to a "normal" identity

stockholders' revolt: the refusal of a corporation's stockholders to rubber-stamp decisions made by its managers

stored value: the backing of a currency by goods that are stored and held in reserve

strain theory: Robert Merton's term for the strain engendered when a society socializes large numbers of people to desire a cultural goal (such as success) but withholds from many the approved means to reach that goal; one adaptation to the strain is crime, the choice of an innovative means (one outside the approved system) to attain the cultural goal

stratified random sample: a sample of specific subgroups of the target population in which everyone in the subgroups has an equal chance of being included in the study

street crime: crimes such as mugging, rape, and burglary

structural mobility: movement up or down the social-class ladder that is attributable to changes in the structure of society, not to individual efforts

structured interviews: interviews that use closed-ended questions

subculture: the values and related behaviours of a group that distinguish its members from the larger culture; a world within a world

subjective meanings: the meanings that people give their own behaviour

subjective method (of measuring social class): a system in which people are asked to state the social class to which they belong

subsistence economy: a type of economy in which human groups live off the land with little or no surplus

suburbanization: the movement from the city to the suburbs

suburbs: the communities adjacent to the political boundaries of a city

superego: Freud's term for the conscience, the internalized norms and values of our social groups

survey: the collection of data by having people answer a series of questions

sustainable environment: a world system that takes into account the limits of the environment, produces enough material goods for everyone's needs, and leaves a heritage of a sound environment for the next generation

symbol: something to which people attach meanings and then use to communicate with others

symbolic culture: another term for nonmaterial culture

symbolic interactionism: a theoretical perspective in which society is viewed as composed of symbols that people use to establish meaning, develop their views of the world, and communicate with one another

system of descent: how kinship is traced over the generations

taboo: a norm so strong that it brings revulsion if violated

taking the role of the other: putting oneself in someone else's shoes; understanding how someone else feels and thinks and thus anticipating how that person will act

teamwork: the collaboration of two or more persons interested in the success of a performance to manage impressions jointly

techniques of neutralization: ways of thinking or rationalizing that help people deflect society's norms

technological determinism: the view that technology determines culture, that technology takes on a life of its own and forces human behaviour to follow

technology: often defined as the applications of science, but can be conceptualized as tools (items used to accomplish tasks) and the skills or procedures necessary to make and use those tools

tertiary sector: that part of the economy which consists of service-oriented occupations

tertiary social deviance: the normalizing of behaviour considered socially deviant by mainstream society; relabelling the behaviour as nondeviant

theory: a general statement about how some parts of the world fit together and how they work; an explanation of how two or more facts are related to one another

Thomas theorem: William I. Thomas's classic formulation of the definition of the situation: "If people define situations as real, they are real in their consequences."

timetables: the signals societies use to inform their members that they are old; these timetables vary around the world

tool: an object created or modified for a specific purpose

total institution: a place in which people are cut off from the rest of society and are almost totally controlled by the officials who run the place

totalitarianism: a form of government that exerts almost total control over the people

tracking: the sorting of students into different educational programs on the basis of real or perceived abilities

traditional authority: authority based on custom

traditional orientation: the idea—characteristic of tribal, peasant, and feudal societies—that the past is the best guide for the present

transformative social movement: a social movement that seeks to change society totally

triad: a group of three people

underclass: a small group of people for whom poverty persists year after year and across generations

underemployment: the condition of having to work at a job beneath one's level of training and abilities, or of being able to find only part-time work

underground economy: exchanges of goods and services that are not reported to the government and thereby escape taxation

universal citizenship: the idea that everyone has the same basic rights by virtue of being born in a country (or by immigrating and becoming a naturalized citizen)

unobtrusive measures: various ways of observing people who do not know they are being studied

unstructured interviews: interviews that use open-ended questions

upward social mobility: movement up the social-class ladder

urban legend: a story with an ironic twist that sounds realistic but is false

urbanization: the process by which an increasing proportion of a population lives in cities

validity: the extent to which an operational definition measures what was intended

value cluster: a series of interrelated values that together form a larger whole

value contradictions: values that contradict one another; to follow the one means to come into conflict with the other

value-free: an ideal condition in which a sociologist's personal values or biases do not influence social research

values: the standards by which people define what is desirable or undesirable, good or bad, beautiful or ugly; attitudes about the way the world ought to be

variable: a factor or concept thought to be significant for human behaviour, which varies from one case to another

Verstehen: a German word used by Weber that is perhaps best understood as "to have insight into someone's situation"

voluntary association: a group made up of volunteers who have organized on the basis of some mutual interest

war: armed conflict between nations or politically distinct groups

wealth: property and income

welfare (state) capitalism: an economic system in which individuals own the means of production, but the state regulates many economic activities for the welfare of the population

white-collar crime: Edwin Sutherland's term for crimes committed by people of respectable and high social status in the course of their occupations; for example, bribery of public officials, securities violations, embezzlement, false advertising, and price-fixing

working class: those who sell their labour to the capitalist class

world system: economic and political connections that tie the world's countries together

zero population growth: a demographic condition in which women bear only enough children to reproduce the population